Computer Science, Technology and Applications

IoT

Platforms, Connectivity, Applications and Services

COMPUTER SCIENCE, TECHNOLOGY AND APPLICATIONS

Additional books in this series can be found on Nova's website under the Series tab.

Additional e-books in this series can be found on Nova's website under the eBooks tab.

COMPUTER SCIENCE, TECHNOLOGY AND APPLICATIONS

IoT

PLATFORMS, CONNECTIVITY, APPLICATIONS AND SERVICES

ABDULRAHMAN YARALI, PHD
Murray State University, KY, US

Copyright © 2018 by Nova Science Publishers, Inc.

All rights reserved. No part of this book may be reproduced, stored in a retrieval system or transmitted in any form or by any means: electronic, electrostatic, magnetic, tape, mechanical photocopying, recording or otherwise without the written permission of the Publisher.

We have partnered with Copyright Clearance Center to make it easy for you to obtain permissions to reuse content from this publication. Simply navigate to this publication's page on Nova's website and locate the "Get Permission" button below the title description. This button is linked directly to the title's permission page on copyright.com. Alternatively, you can visit copyright.com and search by title, ISBN, or ISSN.

For further questions about using the service on copyright.com, please contact:
Copyright Clearance Center
Phone: +1-(978) 750-8400   Fax: +1-(978) 750-4470   E-mail: info@copyright.com.

NOTICE TO THE READER

The Publisher has taken reasonable care in the preparation of this book, but makes no expressed or implied warranty of any kind and assumes no responsibility for any errors or omissions. No liability is assumed for incidental or consequential damages in connection with or arising out of information contained in this book. The Publisher shall not be liable for any special, consequential, or exemplary damages resulting, in whole or in part, from the readers' use of, or reliance upon, this material. Any parts of this book based on government reports are so indicated and copyright is claimed for those parts to the extent applicable to compilations of such works.

Independent verification should be sought for any data, advice or recommendations contained in this book. In addition, no responsibility is assumed by the publisher for any injury and/or damage to persons or property arising from any methods, products, instructions, ideas or otherwise contained in this publication.

This publication is designed to provide accurate and authoritative information with regard to the subject matter covered herein. It is sold with the clear understanding that the Publisher is not engaged in rendering legal or any other professional services. If legal or any other expert assistance is required, the services of a competent person should be sought. FROM A DECLARATION OF PARTICIPANTS JOINTLY ADOPTED BY A COMMITTEE OF THE AMERICAN BAR ASSOCIATION AND A COMMITTEE OF PUBLISHERS.

Additional color graphics may be available in the e-book version of this book.

Library of Congress Cataloging-in-Publication Data

ISBN: 978-1-53613-400-1

Published by Nova Science Publishers, Inc. † New York

*This book is dedicated to my kids,
Fatemeh and Sadrodin Ali*

Contents

Preface		ix
Acknowledgment		xv
Chapter 1	The Internet of Things (IoT): An Introduction	1
Chapter 2	Technical and Physical Aspects of IoT	17
Chapter 3	The Internet of Things (IoT) and Its Important Roles in Reshaping the Environment	35
Chapter 4	The Internet of Things: Technological, Physical, Business and Socio-Economic Environments	65
Chapter 5	The Internet of Things and 5G Wireless Networks	93
Chapter 6	Critical Issues Facing the Internet of Things (IoT)	103
Chapter 7	Security and Privacy Issues on the Internet of Things	125
Chapter 8	Application and Services in IoT	143
Chapter 9	Industrial Internet of Things (IIoT)	157
Chapter 10	IoT: A New Trends in Enterprise	171
Chapter 11	IoT: Smart Cities and Smarter Citizens	183
Chapter 12	IoT: Architecture and Virtualization	199
Chapter 13	The Internet of Things: A More Connected World	205
Chapter 14	Integration of IoT and AI	235
Chapter 15	The Internet of Things: Machine Learning, Artificial Intelligence, and Automation	253

Chapter 16	The Internet of Things and IT: A Platform Transformation	**291**
About the Author		**317**
Index		**319**

PREFACE

Technology has been defined to have a significant reputation that has been highly emulated in the world of production. The global production landscape has been greatly improved by technology-based, value-added activity providing flexibility and transparency within the technology measures put in place. This means the technology can cut across the end to end activities. Different companies and countries have positioned themselves to implement and emulate new technologies so that recognition of production to their industries can be improved. Shaping the future of production is defined by three steps that are put in place, involving landscape, priority technology, having a technology insight and converging impact foresight of different values.

Across the globe, adoption has varied in different countries depending on the applicability of the chosen technique. This means that values and opportunities tend to be well implemented based on the geographic adoption of technology within advanced robotics, 3D printing, and wearables. With the pace of adoption, affordability will be achieved. Better techniques will be created; mass customization and better service replacing products will be facilitated. Technology and innovation for the future of production have led to an increased value to society.

Implementation of the chosen adoption technique is based on the converging technology that is designed to create new opportunities reflecting the new values put in place. From this value, dimensions will be obtained since the system will empower different aspects. This involves individuals by making sure that self-transcendence and basic needs are achieved based on self-actualizations and convenience. The society will be enhanced by self-sustainability, inclusivity in economic growth and job creation. This industry will be defined by progressive improvements in access and integration of activities will be facilitated. Most importantly, the value will be created in the way that factories approach health, safety, and environment perception. The factory may have an advantageous outlook in regard to the smart innovation approach given both economic skills and collaboration.

Technology drives values across industries in all dimensions, with leadership characteristics playing a significant role in defining the level of success and the path to that success. This means that availability of skills and availability of underlying infrastructure plays a significant role even if technology exacerbates current inequalities. A successful implementation can be obtained when inclusivity of activities is embedded. This may be based on a collaborative network of partners, effective communication and understanding the chemistry that will lead to a transformation journey. More so the underlying factor that will determine the success of the implemented technology will be the level of integration, adoption speed and organization alignment. Any company that stands a chance of emulating the stipulated success factors stands a better position to benefit from technologies in production. This will be based on the impact on technology will be reflected in economic growth, employment and wealth distribution.

However, with all the stipulated expressed advantages that come with technology creation in both internal and external approaches, there tend to be some challenges that can impact potential success; technology readiness, security, standards, interoperability, data management, change management, capability development, and culture in place. This means that companies should focus on better research, effective innovation, and proper technology readiness. More so, democratic production should be accompanied by the appropriate knowledge that will meet the increased standards. Having stated this, technology and innovation can accelerate value creation when a better approach is facilitated.

There has been a tremendous change in technologies and businesses. These changes force companies to develop new business models and compelling new ways to attract customers and reach new markets. Telecommunications is currently one of the fastest changing industries with broadband networks and service providers aggressively competing in their mature subscription points for churn and value-added services to provide consumer experience for a sustainable return on their extensive investments. The technological changes which took place in last few years brought a new revolution namely "The Cloud" and "The Internet of Things." Cloud computing guarantees enhanced expense efficiencies, quickened development, quicker time-to-market, and the capacity to scale applications of interest. There is a significant movement towards the cloud computing model with large revenue potential for those companies embracing the cloud. On the other hand as cloud adoption among organizations is rising, quickly creating concerns and issues, both reasonably and in all actuality, in legitimate/contractual, monetary, administration quality, interoperability, security, and protection, posing noteworthy difficulties.

The confluence of standards/technologies and ability to connect massive smaller devices, objects, and sensors, inexpensively and easily created a hyper-connected world bridging virtual and physical things to generate, process, exchange and consume data for the Internet of Things (IoT). The Internet of Things with the main elements of people, things, data, process and the meaningful format is predicted to have nearly 30 billion devices connected and communicating by the end of the year 2020 making up to two-thirds of the GDP globally per a study performed by Gartner Inc.

In the developing nations around the world, the considerations for deploying IoT infrastructure are slightly different in comparison with developed nations. Regardless of the infrastructure requirements, there are other core concerns that need to be addressed on a global level such as privacy, environmental impact, and the human element. These challenges present a barrier to entry for the Internet of Things, not only in the developing countries but for the entire globe.

In developing nations, the issues are far ranging from political and educational issues to environmental and economic issues. It's an understatement to say that developing nations have many more preconditions when it comes to the Internet of Things. Before it is physically deployed, the first Internet of things related challenge that must be addressed is data regulations and frameworks. Ensuring that users of a completely interconnected network can have privacy, security and trust the integrity of their data is perhaps the most important underlying issue. With world politics increasing in complexity and turmoil, protecting people's privacy and security is the only way to prevent governments from turning such powerful networks into weapons of mass surveillance and infringement. These security concerns should be addressed with standards and be consistent across all nations in order to be effective.

The communications network infrastructure comprised of IoT devices could prove to be challenging for developing nations that either have very little existing infrastructure or inefficient infrastructure. Ideally, future networks would be backward compatible with existing infrastructure, but it may not always be possible. The infrastructure must be power efficient, scalable, intelligent, standardized and heterogeneous. The sheer number of devices that are possible with the Internet of Things is staggering; according to Cisco over 20 billion new devices are expected to be online by 2019. In both developing nations and developed nations, it is important to take into consideration the energy requirements for this amount of equipment to run. It will have to be more efficient than today's infrastructure to handle not only the increase of devices on the internet but also the increase of data centers that will be needed in the future. Self-healing, heterogeneous networks will ensure the networks infrastructure is always on, connected and scalable. The physical infrastructure in developing nations may require some changes to existing regulations to make possible the new large communication networks. In order to handle the magnitude of devices, the new spectrum may need to be allocated, agreements with other government entities and open data policies.

Aside from the standardization, infrastructure and policy concerns, there is also the human element to consider. In developing nations, the technical resources may not be available to deploy the next generation networks or to use the devices connected to them. An example is smart electric meters that are available to customers today. Just because they are available doesn't mean the majority of the end users see it as beneficial or use it to change their behavior. In order for the Internet of Things to truly be beneficial, the end user must be able to understand the possibilities from the devices they have access to and embrace the technological change by integrating them into their life.

Developing nations and developed nations alike share many of the same problems when it comes to the Internet of Things and together a solution must be globally implemented to fix these overlapping issues and concerns. The elements of the network as a whole could be summarized as having layers composed of the human element, the political or instructional element, the data element and the technological element. In regards to the human element, there should be investment and opportunities for developing nations to participate in educational opportunities to see how technology can improve the overall quality of life. Developed nations must realize that in order for a truly global economy and interconnected world to be realized, educational sharing must take place to help developing nations. Globally, the political element could be the biggest challenge, setting aside politics and creating a global standard could be a huge barrier to the deployment of the Internet of Things. New spectrum allocations and licensing could prove to be a roadblock since many different standards in wireless communications exist globally. The standardization of Internet of Things is difficult to obtain from a connectivity standpoint, but having standardization in regards to data privacy and security is of paramount concern, especially when dealing with connectivity on a global level. Regulations and requirements for security, privacy and data storage must be strictly and perfectly implemented. Technologically, our networks must all be able to become flexible and adaptable to be able to efficiently handle the changes Internet of Things will bring. Spectrum efficiency, intelligent protocols, and new security changes will need to evolve to meet the needs of next generation networks.

Solutions to the global and local issues will likely take an extended amount of time to implement. Policy frameworks must be developed to ensure governments, industry, and others fully understand the challenges that need to be addressed and work together to solve the complex problems that are ahead. For example, development groups for frameworks could utilize their influence and knowledge to work together to open up unused radio frequency to promote the growth of IoT networks and Machine to Machine (M2M). Promoting innovation to assist the knowledge sharing needed for next generation networks will foster innovations and create an IoT ecosystem that promotes the economic growth potential IoT can bring. Revolutionizing energy efficient data centers is necessary to keep costs low and to reduce environmental impact, without this effect the costs of IoT networks could scale to unreasonable levels. Standards across the entire IoT infrastructure are necessary to ensure interoperability, security, privacy, integrity, and reliability.

Many companies have a different classification of IoT platform based on their applications and services. Firms with the production of goods and services categorize their IoT applications as "Industrial IoT' while others define their IoT applications based on devices like wearables or locations such as "Smart Home" and "Smart City." Devices are not only replacing people, but they are overcoming the limits of people. Drone usage with cameras and sensors will be able to travel in places where humans cannot reach to gather, store and send data to a smart device instantly. As device companies are manufacturing IoT devices for remote and conditioned–based monitoring and asset tracking, there are inherent challenges such as time to market, interoperability, authentication, security, digital data protection and overcoming technical issues like power consumption, and limited computing process.

With its many implications and massive proliferation of devices, the Internet of Things is widely considered to be one of the largest revolutions in the age of Information. Its effect has the potential to be felt on a global scale in all current fields and occupations. Once we have effectively resolved the current issues of addressing, regulation, and standardization, we can see the development and growth of more complex applications that utilize information from this network. There are unique challenges in developing nations but they are all interconnected in some way to the rest of the world. IoT will need to be a global effort in order to be fully realized.

ACKNOWLEDGMENT

I would like to express my gratitude to all those who provided support and discussions, talked things over, read, wrote, offered comments, allowed me to quote their remarks and assisted in the editing, proofreading. I would like to give special thanks to CTSM, all my graduate and undergraduate students in TSM321, 322, 323,610, 397,571 and TSM695 classes of our distinction program of Telecommunication Systems Management at Murray State University, Kentucky. This book would never find its way to the publisher without these students.

Chapter 1

THE INTERNET OF THINGS (IOT): AN INTRODUCTION

INTRODUCTION

The Internet of Things (IoT) is a trending topic in the world of telecommunications but it is not a new concept. Going back to the early 2000s, Kevin Ashton embarked on a project at MIT AutoID lab that would later become the Internet of Things. According to Xia et al., (2012) state that Ashton became one of the renowned pioneers of IoT as he looked for ways that Proctor and Gamble would use to enhance its business by connecting the RFID information to the internet. It seemed like a simple concept but powerful in reality. Assuming all the objects had identifiers and wireless connectivity, it means that they would be able to communicate with each other and be managed by computers. Currently, the IoT has reached many players and gained massive recognition. Out of the potential IoT application areas such as smart utilities, smart health, smart building, smart public services, and smart transportation, areas such as smart cities, energy and environmental protection, smart industries, and public safety have gained popularity. As a result of this development, a majority of governments in Europe, Asia, and America consider the IoT to be an area of growth and innovation. Even though some larger players in particular application areas have not recognized the full potential of IoT, a majority of them pay attention and increase the pace of adoption through integrating new terms for IoT and adding new information or components to them.

Nevertheless, end-users in the private and business domain have gained significance competence in working with smart devices and networked applications. As the Internet of Things continues to develop, further potential is estimated by an integration of related technology approaches and concepts such as Cloud computing, Big Data, Future Internet, robotics, and Semantic technologies.

Basics Concept of IoT

The Internet of Things (IoT) usually refers to a networked interconnection of computers, devices, and sensors that are capable of processing their data without depending entirely on people for input. The term internet considers the TCP/IP protocol and non-TCP/IP protocol suite simultaneously. On the other hand, the term "things" include various items such as sensors, people, and computers. These "things" are often classified under machine, information, and people. The inter-connected systems often collect data and communicate with external processes through onboard sensors, thus transforming the business world in almost every aspect. According to Cisco/Gatner (2016), the number of "connected things" will increase to 25 billion by 2020 (AT&T, 2015).

In the current world, IoT consists of a loose collection of disparate, function-built networks. Take an example of the latest models of cars, they comprise of multiple networks to control engine functions, communication systems, safety measures, and so forth. Moreover, as stated by Weber and Weber (2010), commercial and residential buildings have several control systems for ventilation and heating (HVAC), telephone services, security, and particular natural disasters. As the nature of IoT progresses, these kinds of networks and much more will be interconnected with increased security, analytics, and management capabilities (Figure 1). As a result, IoT will be able to achieve various powerful potential thereby making people achieve great things.

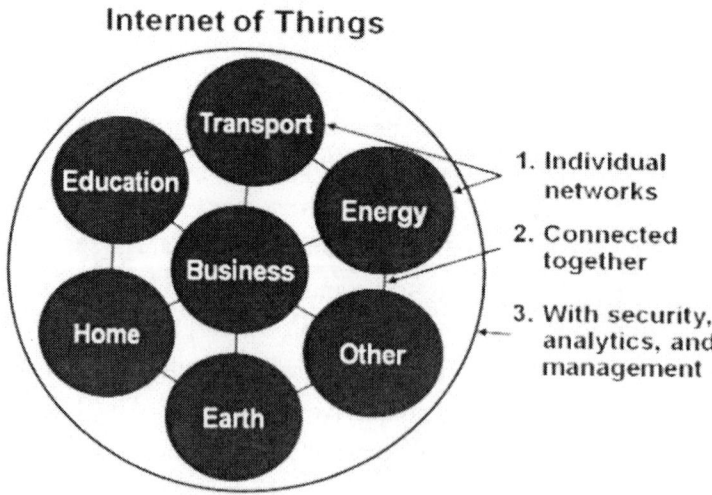

Figure 1. IoT disparate functions, Source: Cisco IBSG, April 2011.

FEATURES OF IoT

The features of IoT cover different aspects of network and applications. The overall aspects of IoT include orders of magnitude larger than the internet. Secondly, the application and services aspects can comprise of machines or devices with multiple application characteristics. The third feature is the networking aspect which is crucial in the providence of common communication technologies that support all applications and the heterogeneous network interfaces. The link or physical feature comprises of many types of network interfaces with varying coverage and data rates. These types of the environment have the features like low power networks such as Bluetooth, IEEE 802.15.4 (6LoWPAN, ZigBee) and so forth. The fifth feature is the smart and connected objects, which are heterogeneous with varying sizes, mobility, power, interconnections, and protocols. A physical object often has the ability to communicate with many entities, perform many functions, and generate data. Lastly, the smart environment of IoT comprises of networks of federated sensors and actuators. These networks are able to cover large areas such as cities. Currently, IoT smart environments are large-scaled thereby increasing its potential.

TECHNICAL CONSIDERATIONS OF IoT

The technical considerations are often perceived to be the general issues affecting IoT. According to a research done Duan, Chen, and Xing (2011) these considerations include scalability, interoperability, discovery, data volume, power supply, fault-tolerance, security and personal privacy, intelligence, and device adaptation.

Scalability

Scalability is the ability of a device to adapt to the changing environment to meet various needs. The Internet of Things usually covers a wide area as compared to other communication hosts. The coverage can either be small scale or large scale area. Objects and things will often communicate with each other seamlessly. According to Anisha, Rivana, and Manjula (2017), scalability of IoT can be vertical or horizontal. When it comes to IoT and scalability, the two concepts are interrelated. It is estimated that by 2020, the IoT network will support approximately 24 billion devices (Gubbi et al., 2013). Moreover, scalability extends to different applications of network and security, management, big data, and so forth, which greatly contribute to the anomaly of scalability. The main areas that are directly connected to scalability include business, marketing, software, hardware, and networks.

Interoperability

Interoperability means having effective communication between devices, which is very crucial for IoT (Uckelmann, Harrison, & Michahelles, 2011). Various objects in IoT often have different communication and processing capabilities. Every object involved in IoT usually use different resources such as power and communication bandwidth requirements. Major IoT solutions often have varying degrees of interoperation and integration. Even though it might not be available currently, companies can strive to build a particular degree of interoperability and integration between products. This means that the technologies at the upper levels are integrated with those at the lower ranks. IoT should have networked devices that harmoniously work together to achieve a great user experience as well as business advancement. It will be frustrating for users to purchase a device with a particular network only to discover they are incompatible with a previous network they are using. Hence, achieving a full potential in IoT and harnessing the benefits greatly depends on this technical consideration.

Data Volume

The Internet of Things/Objects often involves *big data*. In networking, handling big data can be challenging. Each "thing" in IoT has its own memory, storage, and processing capabilities. For instance, if many objects on a peer network are communicating, they may face memory, storage, or processing difficulties. It is often a challenge for networks to maintain big bytes of data all the time. In dealing with this, IoT has been able to utilize periodic communication between "things," data compression, and optimization solutions.

Power Supply

A power supply is a major consideration in IoT because objects/things may often move around making accessibility to power supply difficult. All devices of IoT should have sufficient power supply to operate effectively and efficiently. It should be noted that not all things/objects can retain continuous power supply, and battery availability for any small object may not be practicable. Therefore, it is important to have energy-efficient mechanisms for IoT.

Fault-Tolerance

IoT requires redundancy and ability to adapt to the changing IT environment depending on the quality of service (QoE).

Security and Personal Privacy

IoT should maintain the security as well as provide privacy for their customers. This factor is broadly discussed as the main objective in 2.5.

Device Adaptation

The device used in IoT are of different applications, formats, networks, and so forth. Therefore, every connected device of IoT should be able to adapt to any situation they are subjected to. Moreover, adaptations should be maintained.

IoT products can be classified into five categories based on their areas of operation:

1. Smart home
2. Smart environment
3. Smart wearable
4. Smart city
5. Smart enterprise

Discovery

Discovery refers to the ability to identify suitable objects for IoT in the existing dynamic environment. Customers are always interested in product information, thereby ensuring the availability is crucial. Hence, in discovery, IoT service providers should understand the semantics and explain their functionality.

ARCHITECTURE PATTERNS

Although the internet of thing is still on its verge of development many architectural patterns have been discovered and adopted with a large-scale of acceptance and implementation consideration. To gain further insights requirements, and opportunities for smart IoT platform, exploring the different architectural patters is of importance. Duan, Chen, and Xing (2011) came up with a research exploring the QoS structure for IoT, which are discussed below.

Three-Tier Architecture

In the three-tier architecture, there exist the edge, platform, and enterprise tiers connected by nearness, access, and service networks. Typically, networks in these architectures and those that follow utilize wired and or wireless technologies such as RFID, Z-Wave, ZigBee, Cellular, Ethernet, and Bluetooth. Figure 2 indicates that the edge tier uses the near network to source data from the edge nodes, at the "thing" level. After it is received, the data is forwarded to over the access network to the platform tier. The latter is responsible for processing data from the edge tier for forwarding to the enterprise tier. Moreover, it is also responsible for processing and relaying control commands from the enterprise tier to the edge tier over the access network. As stated by the Industrial Internet Consortium (2015) work of the platform tier is to utilize the service network to interact with the enterprise tier, which is responsible for giving end users interfaces, control protocols, and core-specific applications.

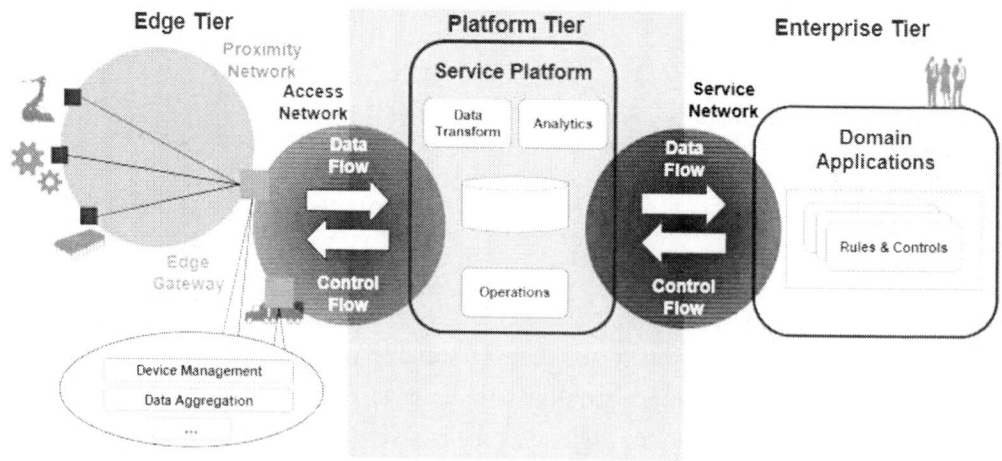

Figure 2. Three-tier architecture pattern.

Gateway-Mediated Edge Connectivity and Management

This is an architecture pattern where the gateway acts as the mediator between a local area network (LAN) of a one-sided edge node and a wide area network (WAN) on the other. It is usually the endpoint for a WAN network and it has the potential if a management entity for the edge devices on the LAN, thereby isolating them from WAN. On the other hand, the sensors and actuators can connect directly to the edge gateway or more routers. The LAN can either have a hub-and-spoke topology or peer-to-peer topology. Other paths are also available for the nodes that are unable to go through the edge gateway.

Edge-to-Cloud

According to a publication by Industrial Internet Consortium (2015), this architecture varies from the gateway-mediated edge pattern as it involves wide-area connectivity for the devices and assets in play, instead of having the edge assets isolated.

Multi-Tier Data Storage

The multi-tier data storage architecture is responsible for optimizing performances and limiting storage constraints by separating storage tiers as per their functionality. For instance, many IoT frameworks now have multi-tier data storage in separate tiers of capacity and performance.

Distributed Analytics

This type of architecture works closely with the proximity analytics and the intensive analytics to establish more centralized parts within the IoT architecture. Having a centralized pattern is important especially when latency or any other network limitation processes a suboptimal solution.

Lambda Architecture

Even though this architecture was not originally designed for the Internet of Things, it is important in understanding IoT because it has the ability to handle the tremendous amounts of data received by the sensors. The Lambda architecture explores the need for real-time processing of the huge data flows linked with IoT big data by separating them into two views, the batch, and the stream view. However, Lambda architecture itself is organized into three layers, which include the batch, serving, and the layer. The batch layers oversee the master, immutable, and append-only data set. The serving layer helps in data retrieval whereas the speed layer offers low-latency functionality and access the latest data for stream view. The Lambda is relevant for the frameworks of IoT because it offers complete processing in spite of the volumes of data involved.

DISCOVERING THE POTENTIAL AND JUSTIFYING GOING IOT

The Internet of Things is not often regarded as a single technology. According to Ruoklainen and Kutvonen (2005), the concept of IoT entails many new interconnected things like embedded sensors, image recognition functionality, integrated communication support, asset management and other services. The two authors argue that a variety of business opportunities arise and additional complexity is added to the concept of IT. Areas such as distribution, transportation, logistics and so forth are the example of areas where new business opportunities that are efficient and profitable can exist.

Moreover, an existing potential of IoT is that it offers the solution regarding the integration of information technology. These include different kinds of software and hardware used to acquire, store, retrieve, and process information (Holler et al., 2014). Usually, the fast integration of communication and information technology takes place at three layers of technology innovation, that is, the cloud, data, and communication channels or networks and devices (Figure 3). For example, having cloud technology is crucial for IoT because of its innate flexibility, affordable costs, and inherent scalability. All these factors boost the IoT projects.

The cooperation of the access and potential data interchange creates a wider opportunity for the development of IoT applications. According to a research done by Jo et al., (2015), currently, over 50% of internet connections are between or with things. The beginning of early 2011 registered over 15 billion things on the Web, with over 50 billion intermittent connections. The convergence of different IoT applications will create opportunities for new industries to emerge and deliver quality and new experiences into the market.

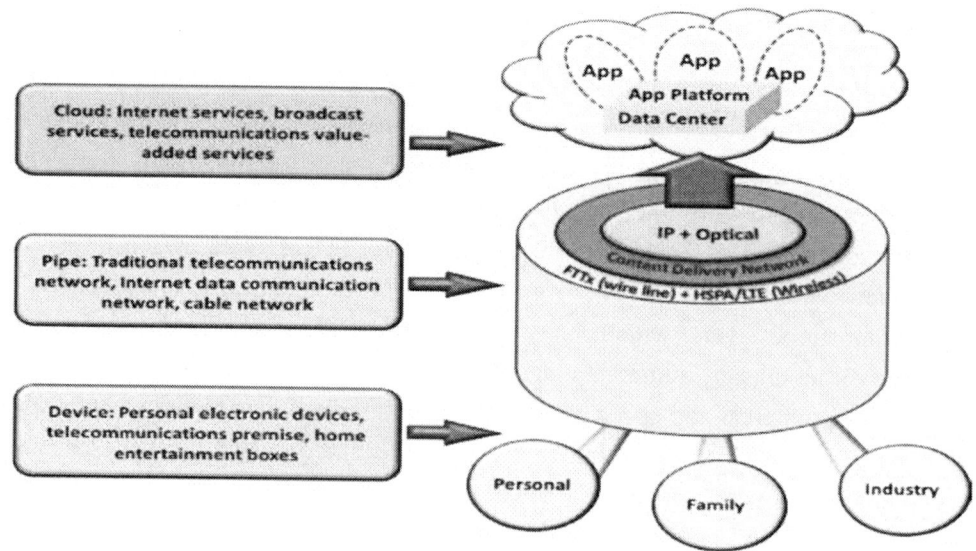

Source: Huawei Technologies.

Figure 3. Factors driving the convergence and contributing to the integration and transformation of cloud, pipe, and device technologies.

The Internet of Things often utilizes things to provide services to all types of applications through the exploitation of identification, data retrieval, processing, and communication capabilities. In doing so, they also ensure that security and privacy protocols are followed. Looking at it from a broader perspective, IoT can be considered as a vision with technological and societal involvement. According to the IERC definition, "IoT potentials lie in a dynamic global network infrastructure with self-configuring abilities based on standard and interoperable communication protocols where physical and virtual "things" have identities, physical attributes, and virtual personalities. They utilize intelligent interfaces, and are seamlessly integrated into the information network."

JOINING FORCES

Joining forces entails collaboration between IT-related companies, which will lead to positive outcomes, solutions, and deeper insights into the world of technology. Partnerships between companies often provide integrated solutions such as the utilization of powerful design tools, worldwide connectivity, enhanced analytics, and other crucial services that make IoT successful. A majority of internet companies have strived to form partnerships amongst themselves to increase the efficiency of IoT. For instance, AT&T and IBM recently joined forces towards improving the service of IoT (AT&T, 2015). Exploring these features has the ability to boost business opportunities in many industries across the world. Joining forces is a key step in attaining Industrial Internet of Things (IoT). For example, two companies that have joined forces include IBM and AT&T. They are widely known in the world of IT to unite powerful platforms, products, and services to engage developers in an active ecosystem to allow them to invent new ideas for IoT (Cooper, 2016).

INTEROPERABILITY

Interoperability means having effective communication between devices, which is very crucial for IoT. Various objects in IoT often have different communication and processing capabilities. Every object involved in IoT usually use different resources such as power and communication bandwidth requirements. Major IoT solutions often have varying degrees of interoperation and integration. Even though it might not be available currently, companies can strive to build a particular degree of interoperability and integration between products. This means that the technologies at the upper levels are integrated with those at the lower ranks. IoT should have networked devices that harmoniously work together to achieve a great user experience as well as business advancement. It will be frustrating to users to purchase a device with a particular network only to discover they are incompatible with a previous network they are using. Hence, achieving a full potential in IoT and harnessing the benefits greatly depends on this.

REGULATIONS AND SECURITY IN IOT

In his research, Weber (2010) stated that the Internet of Things will not achieve success or realize future prospects if there is no security or privacy governance. Security often involves issues of confidentiality, originality, and trustworthiness of communication. To enjoy the potential of IoT, the governments and various businesses need to overcome the challenges of security. In 2010, the IERC strategic research and innovation roadmap identified security-related challenges of IoT. A majority of existing networks have often concentrated on cyber-security and achieving limited end-points. The current potential and future prospects of IoT foresees the strategy to be ineffective or inadequate for the physical and virtual worlds to integrate into the large scale. Businesses will be forced to update or have new security models that cover the whole cyber-physical stack and create system-wide assurance to enhance resiliency and strengthen response frameworks.

MAJOR ADVANCEMENTS AND FUTURE PROSPECTS IN IOT

The Industrial Internet of Things is an upcoming and developing concept in the world of the Internet, where the latest technological change is set to create limitless opportunities as well as risks to businesses and the society. As discussed by Industrial Internet initiative launch meeting (2014) by the World Economic Forum's IT Governors, the IoT revolution has the ability to enhance manufacturing, energy, agriculture, transportation and other industrial departments that directly affect the economies of countries. The IIoT is perceived to be able to control the physical world. However, since it is in its early stages of development, various questions have been raised regarding its impact on the current industries, value chains, business frameworks and workforces, and action to be taken to ensure its success in future.

The various recommendations for seizing the opportunities for IIoT include establishing global security commons, re-orientation of the overall business strategy, and re-evaluation and updating data protection and liability policies to enhance data flow. It was discovered that in future, the four phases of IIoT will include operational efficiency (phase 1) and new products and services (phase 2), which are of near term. The long-term include outcome economy (phase 3) and autonomous pull economy. In conclusion, the IIoT will be transformative as it will change the course of competition because of its various potentials (Industrial Internet Consortium, Industrial Internet reference architecture, 2015).

The main business opportunities of IoT as per the convention of the governors included greatly enhanced operational efficiency through predictive maintenance and remote management. Secondly, there would be the development of an outcome economy through various software and hardware innovation and improved visibility into products and services. Thirdly, there will be emerging interconnected ecosystems and smart cities (Khare & Khare, 2017). Fourthly, close collaboration with people and machines will lead to high productivity and engage many workforces. Conversely, a majority of businesses are more likely to shift from product to outcome-based services. Governments and businesses will have to deal effectively with risks such as security and privacy, and interoperability to realize the full potential of the concept.

ADVANTAGES OF IoT

Safety and Sustainability

IoT products and services have undergone development over time and as at now have a significant influence on how the human population is approaching sustainability. There are various means by which IoT has created sustainability in the modern world:

- Arising from a Circular Economy- Ellen MacArthur is one of the proprietors of the circular economy. According to him, the circular economy is based on its design which is characterized by regeneration and restoration. It is also based on keeping products in their most valuable form. IoT comes in by facilitating communication between manufacturers and industrial plants to increase the lifespan of the manufacturing industry. Aside from that, the use of energy can be monitored and regulated to promote sustainability.
- A Smarter World- This smarter world entails all aspects of transport, households, and work. From household lighting and thermostats, traffic control, rubbish collection to efficient energy supplies, we are assured of reduced carbon footprint. This, in turn, contributes to a more sustainable urban life.

The two above aspects need to be managed in a secure way to ensure that sustainability is achieved. The process of manufacturing and using IoT products exposes most of them to hacking and theft vulnerabilities in form of cyber-attacks. Investments need to be made both by network providers as well as end-users to ensure that IoT products realize their full potential at an affordable cost.

Urban Efficiency

To demonstrate urban efficiency, it is inevitable to discuss how the Internet of Things has led to the emergence of "smart cities." The term has been used to describe an urban strategy for the purpose of increasing a city's efficiency (Peiro & Corradino, 2017). To attain this, urban efficiency can be grouped into:

- Improved mobility through efficient data management, evolution of electronics and communication systems
- Sustainability on the management of resources by enabling smart public street lighting, monitoring of traffic flow among many others.
- Quality delivering of city services.
- Improved energy efficiency through forecasting of energy needs and modify systems to adapt the same.

IMPORTANT FACTOR IN IoT

Ethics, Security, and Privacy

IoT companies need to collect large amounts of data and store it in their cloud networks in order to process the data further. This process leaves the system vulnerable to security and privacy concerns. There are three concerns about the same:

- Data consent: IoT companies can access most of the data by their clients. The issue comes in as to what amount of data should be shared with the company and if any of it should be exposed. Clients should be informed of the amount of data to be shared and if any of it would be exposed.
- Data security: When IoT companies are designing their structure, it is important that they create a defense system that encrypts data to offer security straight from the collection, storage to processing.
- Data minimization: IoT companies are needed to collect only the needed amount of data from their clients. Apart from that, IoT companies should also regulate the amount of time that they retain the acquired data.

Return on Investment

ROI affects two partakers: the network providers and the clients. ROI serves as a barrier to the full embracement and realization of full potential of IoT. It has been argued (Farley, 2017) that some IoT products are too complex while some lack a clear definition of how they are supposed to benefit the consumers.

It is important that network providers are able to offer IoT products that solve everyday life as simply as possible and at the same time get value for their investment. A network providing company needs to identify a point where the optimal value of IoT lies and then focus their resources on the same (Ericsson, 2017). On the other hand, consumers should not feel like they are spending so much on products that are too complex to use and do not meet their needs.

Policies and Regulations

Back in January 2015, the Federal Trade Commission made three recommendations on data minimization, data security, and data consent. A part of the recommendations, the FTC has other measures put in places like the Fair Credit Reporting Act, Children's Online Privacy Protection Act, and the FTC Act.

In the USA, a resolution was passed in March 2015 (Lawson, 2016) by the Congress in order to formulate a national policy on IoT for the sake of spectrum, privacy, and security. Aside from that, four senators in March 2016 proposed a bill in order to assess the need for more spectrum in the connectivity of IoT products (Lawson, 2016); The Developing Innovation and Growing the Internet of Things Act.

Recommendations

1. Investment: Governments should invest in IoT and ensure that emerging economies are efficient and cost-effective
2. There should be increased participation in the technical and industrial development of IoT in intensive research to come u with long-lasting solutions to issues of security and interoperability.
3. There should be different policies and regulations to enhance internet growth and tackle the emerging issues.

4. When it comes to the Industrial Internet of Things (IIoT), The various recommendations for seizing the opportunities for it include establishing global security commons, re-orientation of the overall business strategy, and re-evaluation and updating data protection and liability policies to enhance data flow

Areas of Future Research

One area for future research is exploring the future internet by looking into the internet of things architecture, possible applications, and key challenges.

CONCLUSION

IoT stands out as an upcoming concept of technical, social, and commercial significance. Consumer products, services, industrial components, and other objects are connected to the internet as well as powerful data analytics to improve how humans work and live. The leading characteristic of IoT lies in commercial opportunity and its scalability. Other characteristics include efficiency, security and privacy, intelligence, connectivity, and heterogeneity, IoT has also been detrimental in transportation/supply chain management, healthcare provision, education, work, public service, building, and agriculture. For instance, the increased use of sensors to track goods and livestock has improved delivery and health respectively. Moreover, having partnerships between different companies is beneficial for IoT improvement and innovation. The development of smart cities has led to intelligent solutions that act as a bridge into the future. The main issues facing IoT devices, services, and systems include interoperability and security. With increasing innovation, different networks face the challenge of "connectedness" and security risks. As complex as it still is, interoperability has been dealt with via proliferation of standard efforts, configuration, and so forth. On the other hand, security threats are mainly dealt with through regulations by different certified bodies and constant monitoring of network and device systems. Based on the research, it is highly likely that the future will bring more intelligent non-human futures such as robotics and AR/VR to assist the humans. IoT is a huge phenomenon that will fully take over the world in less than twenty years to come. Based on the definition that the universe is the totality of existence, achieving a full status of IoT universe might just connect everything. Widely known as the industrial IoT, this technology is capable of bringing a variety of opportunities, new risks, businesses and societies. In future, IoT potential will be able to combine the global reach of the internet based on its abilities to fully control the physical world, which comprises of machines, industries, machines, and other infrastructure of the modern world. Based on the outcome of the research, first, the future of IoT will be greatly enhanced by operational efficiency through predictive maintenance and remote management. Secondly, there would be the development of an outcome economy through various software and hardware innovation and improved visibility into products and services. Thirdly, there will be emerging interconnected ecosystems and smart cities. Fourthly, close collaboration with people and machines will lead to high productivity and engage many workforces. A time will come when machines will take over the work of humans. Conversely, a majority of businesses are more likely to shift from product to outcome-based services. Governments and businesses will have to deal effectively with risks such as security and privacy, and interoperability to realize the full potential of the concept.

REFERENCES

Agyapong P., Iwamura M., Staehle D., Kiess W., & Benjebbour, A., "Design considerations for a 5G network architecture." *IEEE Communications Magazine*, 52(11), 65-75.

Anisha Gupta, Rivana Christie, Prof. R. Manjula. (2017). Scalability in the Internet of Things: Features, Techniques and Research Challenges. *International Journal of Computational Intelligence Research* ISSN 0973-1873 Volume 13, Number 7 (2017), pp. 1617-1627© Research India Publications.

Association, C. (2011, February 16). *The evolution of the Internet of Things*. Retrieved September 21, 2017.

AT&T in the Transport and Telematics Space, *M2M Now Magazine*, April-May 2015. http://www.m2mnow.biz/2015/04/27/32498-m2m-nowmagazine-april-may-2015/.

Bandyopadhyay D., & Sen J. (2011). *Internet of things: Applications and challenges in technology and standardization. Wireless Personal Communications,* 58(1), 49-69.

Brown, E. (2016, September 13). *Who needs the internet of things?* Retrieved September 21, 2017.

Communities, C. O. (2009). *Internet of Things- An action plan for Europe*. COM.

Cooper, L. (2016). *IBM and AT&T join forces in the IoT*. Retrieved from https://www.ibm.com/blogs/internet-of-things/ibm-att-join-forces-iot/.

Duan R., Chen X., & Xing T., (2011, October),"A QoS Architecture for IoT," (iThings/CPSCom), 2011. *International Conference on and 4th International Conference on Cyber, Physical and Social Computing* (pp. 717-720). IEEE.

Ericsson. (2017). *Every. Thing. Connected. A study of the adoption of Internet of Things among Danish companies*. Ericsson.

Farley, M. (2017). *Why the consumer Internet of Things is stalling*. Forbes.

Gubbi J., Buyya R., Marusic S., & Palaniswami, M., (2013). Internet of Things (IoT): A vision, architectural elements, and future directions, *Future generation computer systems*, 29(7), 1645-1660.

Holle, J., Tsiatsis V., Mulligan C., Aves & S., Karnouskos S., & Boyle D. (2014). *From Machine-to-machine to the Internet of Things: Introduction to a New Age of Intelligence,* Academic Press.

Industrial Internet Consortium, *Industrial Internet Reference Architecture (Version 1.7),* Object Management Group, Needham, MA, US, 2015.

Jo M., Maksymyuk T., Strykhalyuk B., & Cho, C. H. (2015). Device-to-device-based heterogeneous radio access network architecture for mobile cloud computing. *IEEE Wireless Communications*, 22(3), 50-58.

Khan R., Khan, S. U., Zaheer, R., & Khan, S. (2012, December). Future internet: the internet of things architecture, possible applications, and key challenges. *In Frontiers of Information Technology* (FIT), 2012 10th International Conference on (pp. 257-260), IEEE.

Khare P., & Khare, A., (2017). "The Internet of Things for Smart Cities: *Exploring the Convergence of Big Data and the Internet of Things,"* 96.

Lawson, S. (2016, March 2). *IoT users could win with a new bill in the US Senate.* Retrieved September 25, 2017.

Magrassi, P. (2002). *Why a Universal RFID Infrastructure Would be a Good Thing.* Gartner Research Report.

Mugenda O. M. AG (1999*), Research methods: quantitative and qualitative approaches*, 46-48.

Uckelmann D., Harrison M., & Michahelles F., (2011). *"An architectural approach towards the future internet of things," Architecting the internet of things* (pp. 1-24), Springer Berlin Heidelberg.

Weber, R. H. (2010). Internet of Things–New security and privacy challenges. *Computer law & security review*, 26(1), 23-30.

Weber R. H., Weber R. (2010), *"Internet of things,"* (Vol. 12), New York, NY, USA::Springer.

Xia F., Yang L. T., Wang L., Vinel A., (2012): "Internet of things," *International Journal of Communication Systems,* 25(9), 1101.

Chapter 2

TECHNICAL AND PHYSICAL ASPECTS OF IoT

INTRODUCTION

The infrastructures of the Internet of Things (IoT) are evolving and play a vital role in providing secure, manageable and intelligent networks that can support data consumptions for a broad range of connected devices with diversified applications. Application ranging from homes and works, cars, wearables, light poles, smart meters and industrial automation devices requiring seamless connectivity and convergence among them. As device players are manufacturing IoT devices, there are inherent challenges such as time to market, interoperability, authentication, security, digital data protection and overcoming technical issues like power consumption, and limited computing process.

Based on a guideline released by the Internet Architectural Board (IAB) there are four communication models for IoT device connectivity to enable the end-users to benefit from better access to aggregated data and also to add values to the IoT user devices by accessing data analytics and data visualization. The key requirements for three of these models are device interoperability and open standards.

Device-to-Device (D2D)

In this scenario, devices are linked to one another through detection using protocols like ZigBee, and Bluetooth without connection to any intermediary server over the internet or any IP network. The best example of D2D communication model is smart (automated) home where there is no need for large bulk of data and high data rate transmission among the smart devices. Though there is a challenge in device-to-device protocol compatibility, for example, ZigBee enabled devices are not able to communicate with Z-Wave protocols at the same house.

Device-to-Cloud (D2C)

In this communication models the IoT devices connect to a cloud for remote access from any application through any existing technology legacy like WiFi or Ethernet network. The challenge, in this case, is what we call "vendor lock-in" where a user might be locked to limited services for a specific cloud preventing other alternative cloud connections and usage.

Device-to-Gateway (D2G)

In this case, a gateway node with a provision of data translation and security acts as a middle node between IoT devices using a smartphone app to connect to cloud services.

Back-End Data- Sharing (BEDS)

In this hybrid model, there is a silo data uploading between IoT devices (front-end users) and the cloud with an interoperable architectural model of data sharing to the back-end users of the cloud. It is a stand-alone data connection to a cloud, but with the desire to access and analyze the data in the cloud aggregated from all the variant users of the cloud.

IOT: CHALLENGES AND ISSUES

Internet of Things (IoT) would bring a huge change to the environment around us. There are notable benefits for the community to enjoy and conclude that IoT is indeed the next big thing. However, there are also particular challenges that would be facing IoT both now and in the near future. Some of these Related IoT challenges are:

- Interoperability and how device talks to each other.
- Tracking and mentoring
- the Privacy, and security of personal data while devices connected
- performance metrics and optimized methodology
- Devices identification and labeling

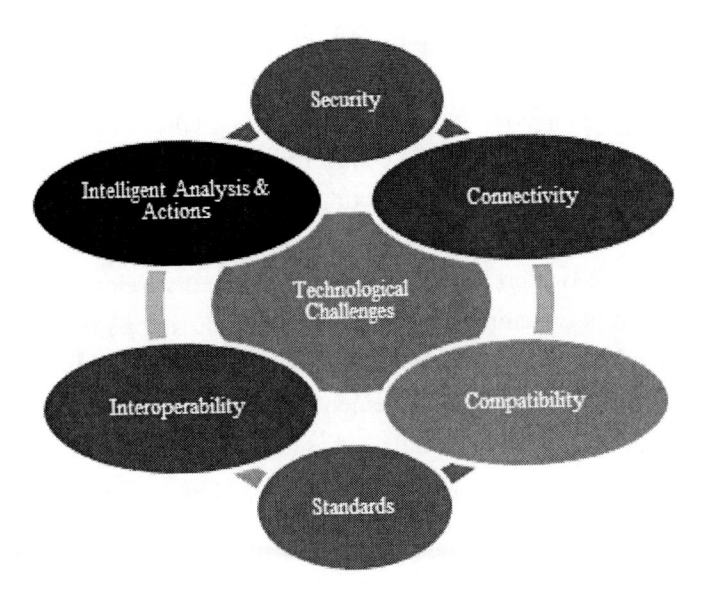

Figure 1. Challenges and issue of IoT.

INTEROPERABILITY

The Internet of Things (IoT) is a ubiquitous system of physical and virtual articles and assets that are outfitted with detecting, registering, activating, and correspondence abilities. However, albeit billions of these articles have been sent as of now, something is abating IoT arrangement selection: gadget incongruence.

The first IoT vision includes a hyper-associated worldwide biological community in which "things" speak with other "things" at whatever point expected to convey profoundly expanded administrations to the client. Such correspondence must be autonomous of the maker of a given section of the framework. Every seller has its own IoT mechanism that is contradictory with different methods, in this way making nearby IoT storehouses. That is the reason, today, numerous IoT scientists and industry pioneers are concentrating on interoperability.

The fundamental core of the internet is that the connected devices must be able to talk to each other through the same language of protocols (interoperable) for sharing, speaking and innovations in an open manner and not only with a subset of networks and services. Interoperability among IoT systems and devices can happen at different layers and levels. Integration flexibility not only has technical effects but also influences the potentials economic impact of IoT from user's point of view and organizational perspectives. Platform interoperability is a major challenge with highly segmented IoT infrastructures. More than 100 IoT platforms with different usage have been identified making it very difficult, if not impossible, to have a single interoperable standard across all devices to provide a collection of compatible elements (hardware & software) for implementing a foundation for applications and services. The Intel IoT platform, the IBM ARM embed IoT device platform, ThingWox, and Axeda cloud service are examples of the various offerings of platforms based on technical or application orientations where there is none or limited regards of device connectivity to a specific industry sector. With a need to transmit and receive data in the cloud, companies must look ahead and select a platform for applications which can create real value for them. Cisco and other companies are leading advocators of connectivity via variant wireless and wired systems.

Greater user benefits, economic opportunity, and innovations can be achieved with open, generic and widely used protocols. The main elements of any IoT platform are connectivity management, device management, and application management. These elements provide and ensure data transmission, security, billing, efficiency, design, and scalability to name a few of the end users connected to the networks.

Device Management profit from the Internet of Things (IoT), it requires an effective IoT gadget administration arrangement that can limit the unpredictability of maintaining an associated business. Building IoT design offers substantial business benefits. It can make new income streams, quicken item development, grow your plan of action and draw in clients in new and energizing ways. In any case, to receive every one of these benefits, it requires an approach to deal with user's associated gadgets effortlessly- and that is the place IoT gadget administration comes in. Safely associating thousands or a large number of gadgets is no simple errand; however, the privilege IoT gadget administration programming will give users a chance to finish it rapidly and efficiently. The IoT gadget administration innovation should likewise make it simple to deal with and to incorporate the expansive volumes of information gadgets will deliver. What's more, a prevalent IoT gadget administration arrangement will help to transform that information into the understanding that you have to grow new items and benefits and to charm your clients with development.

With the incorporation of sensors and control gadgets, whole foundations can be coordinated with data and correspondence advances, bringing about arranged and implanted gadgets that empower smart observing and administration. With the simple arrangement and adaptability of sensor gadgets, remote sensor systems (WSN) can include various sensor hubs that collect data. The collected data then gives a database to further examination; the aftereffects of which can be utilized to enhance the dependability and effectiveness of existing framework frameworks. Considering the quick advancement of sensor innovation, WSNs are relied upon to wind up noticeably a key IoT technology.

SECURITY AND PRIVACY

Security is necessary to any system, and the primary line of barrier against information defilement is cryptography. There can be numerous ways any network infrastructure could be assaulted - handicapping the system accessibility, spoofing, accessing to individual data, and so on. The three physical parts of IoT namely RFID, wireless sensor network, and cloud are defenseless against such assaults. RFID (unusually detached) is by all accounts the most powerless as it permits individual following and also the articles and no abnormal state knowledge can be empowered on these gadgets. These perplexing issues, however, have arrangements that can be given utilizing cryptographic strategies, embedded design and requires more research before they are widely accepted.

A productive and secure information conglomeration technique is required for developing the lifetime of the system, besides, guaranteeing reliable information gathered from sensors. As hub disappointments are a typical normal for WSNs, the system topology ought to have the capacity to recuperate itself. Ensuring security is basic as the framework is naturally connected to actuators and shielding the frameworks from interloper moves toward becoming very important.

Manufactures of devices are under pressure to minimize the cost of the devices designed to be used for short term and long term lifecycle while they need to consider technical risks in the design process. A fundamental priority in IoT products and services must be security. Security and privacy have been a concern in wireless computing IoT solutions as these solutions have multiple layers of the endpoint (users), network, and stored data/applications. The IoT digital data security requirements must be considered for three states, data at rest, data in use and data in motion to avoid the potential damages that could be occurred by accessing and controlling them. Users need assurance that the IoT devices and services are protected from any vulnerabilities because of automatic connection of devices in large-scale connectivity. Data privacy concerns and potential harms can be an impediment to massive adoption of IoT across a broad range of expectations.

TECHNOLOGIES AND PERFORMANCES

The critical metrics for coverage, QoS, mobility, cost, throughput, interoperability, and security and battery life for choosing a right network to meet potential applications are different and hence finding a platform with a one-size-fits-all for all scenarios can be a difficult task, if not impossible. Wireless networks connectivity options have been the focus of many scientific researchers and vendors for IoT. There are many low and wide range technologies which need a careful consideration of network performance vs implementation cost before choosing the right network. Currently, there are several broadband cellular technologies such as 3G and LTE for low and high bandwidth services. 3G mobile technologies have been very efficient for infrequent data usage applications while for delivering improved performance such as video streaming with high bandwidth requirements 4G-LTE technology with significant features such as scalability, diversity has been dominating the large IoT connectivity landscape. The next generation of wireless network called 5G with gigabits per second speed is a platform of platforms, and it is not just about data rate and coverage, but about the connectivity of billions of IoT devices from smartphones, tablets, wearables and any other objects with an on and off modes.

From a general perspective variety of technologies and market trends have brought many players in the sector to agree on a non-standalone approach to bring all devices and connectivity together easily and cheaply. The telecom industry pundits and experts of 3rd Generation Partnership Project (3GPP) behind standardization of wireless cellular communications systems introduced three new standards operating on carrier LTE networks in response to bidirectional Low Power Wide Area Networks (LPWAN) with mesh and star configuration such as LoRa, LoRaWAN, and SigFox; where star topology recommended for its long-range coverage footprint. 3GPP has proposed the standards Long Term Evolution Machine Type Communication (LTE-MTC), Enhanced MTC (eMTC), Narrowband (NB) IoT and Extended Coverage GSM (EC-GSM-IoT) which is based on Enhance GPRS for LPWAN are different from one another and competing against LoRa, LoRaWAN, and SigFox for domination. Low power consumptions for efficiency, complexity reduction for economical devices, coverage extension and penetration to undergrounds and in buildings for ubiquitous coverage, long-life battery usage for UE complexity and cost reduction, support for low throughput devices, voice service support, multicast and low-cost implementation are the main 3GPP required features for these licensed and unlicensed (Industrial, Scientific, and Medical –ISM) LPWAN IoT. LTE-MTC and NB-IoT have licensed spectrum technologies defined under 3GPP. Several LPWAN solutions which exist in the unlicensed portion of spectrums have lower security and coverage compared to the licensed ones. A significant factor to consider when using unlicensed spectrum is the interference from other potential users since ISM frequency band is available to everyone. Majority of protocols use collision detection or avoidance to overcome broadcasting failure. A group of mobile operators - the GSMA (Group Special Mobile Association), has announced their consensus on standardizing LPWAN on a licensed spectrum. This idea was pushed by operators like AT&T, Bell Canada, China Mobile, Deutsche Telecom, Telecom Italia and much more companies worldwide. LPWAN technologies suffer from localization capabilities since they are operating in a narrow bandwidth and low power (weak RF Signal). Most of these techniques are not detected on direct ray, but multipath which is good for data receptions but not for localization capabilities. For comparison of the advertised protocols, standards-in-progress, and proprietary standards the following tables show characteristics of each of these technologies.

Table 1. A Comparison of Low-Power Wide-Area Network Technologies

	LTE-M	NM-IoT	LoRa	Sigfox
Low Power	▢	■	▢	■
Bandwidth	■	■	■	▢
Open Standards	▢	▢		▢
Supplier Breadth	■	■	▢	■
Security	■	▢	▢	▢
Deployments		▢	■	■

Table 2. Current IoT solutions comparison

Solution	Model	Frequency	Range	Data Transfer Rate
Sigfox	Proprietary	868/902 MHz	Rural: 30-50 km Urban: 3~10 km	Upload: <300 bps Download: 8 bits per day
LoRaWAN	Alliance	433/868/780/915MHz	Rural: 15 km Urban: 2~5 km	Upload: 300 bps~50 kbps Download: 300 bps~50 kbps
Ingenu	Proprietary	2.4 GHz	Rural: 5~10 km Urban: 1~3 km	Upload: 624 kbps Download: 156 kbps
Weightless-W	Alliance	400-800 MHz	5 km	Upload: 1 kbps~10 Mbps Download: 1 kbps~10 Mbps
Weightless-N	Alliance	<1 GHz	3 km	Upload: 100 bps Download: 100 bps
Weightless-P	Alliance	<1 GHz	2 km	Upload: 200 bps~100 kbps Download: 200 bps~100 kbps
Dash7	Alliance	433/868/915 MHz	<5 km	Upload: 10, 56, or 167 kbps Download: 10, 56, or 167 kbps

Protocols Comparison

LoRa is not open source, and its PHY is by the originator company Semtech and used with the silicon furnished by the company. It has three types of end node with unscheduled and scheduled downlink and the third one that performs downlink by listening. It has wider bandwidth compare to Sigfox and use spread spectrum with the benefits of detecting signals below the noise floor.

LoRaWAN fabricated by IBM, Semtech, Microchip, and Activity alliance and it the open portion of the protocol; deployable internationally for IoT devices and M2M. LPWAN technologies are ideal for application with low power requirements, IoT, M2M, smart city, precision agriculture, metering, industrial automation and street light.

NB-LTE-M

NB-LTE-M is a technology by 3GPP to reside on current LTE system with using a block of spectrum for IoT services. It is refarming unused 200 KHz of GSM spectrum with a user throughput of about 144Kbps.

LTE-M

LTE-Machine Type Communication (MTC) is a 3GPP overlay of current LTE solution, and it is abbreviated to LTE-M. With extended Discontinues Repetition Cycle (Rx) LTE-M is more energy efficient depending on how often the end user communicate (sleep mode). With higher data rate compared to NB-IoT and NBLTE- M, LTE-M transmit more packet of data suitable for the smart meter, energy management, and wearable to name a few.

NB-IoT

NB-IoT is newer than NB-LTE-M it's introduced by Ericsson and Huawei. It is also called LTE-M2. It is based on direct sequence spread spectrum (DSSS) modulation scheme and can exist independently, in unused single GSM refarming spectrum of 200 KHz, and on eNodeB of LTE guard band resources. With low power consumption during operation and low-cost components, NB-IoT can handle longer coverage compare to LTE-M1 because they have better link budget due to low bitrates. Since NB-IoT is not on LTE construct and it requires guard band which is expensive for operators to roll out.

Also, when 200 KHz of GSM is not ubiquitous and available everywhere that could add more complexity (frontend and antennas) to the system deployment. Although Both NB-IoT and NB-LTE-M are different from in terms of technology, they can be used for similar applications. When approved, there will be some divergence among the carries deciding which standard to select.

802.15

IEEE has assigned seven task force groups for wireless standards for personal area networks (WPAN). These technologies are WPAN/Bluetooth, Mesh networking, high and low rate WPAN, VLC (Visible Light Communication) and BAN (Body Area Networks).

802.15.1

This is technology for short distance transmission both Bluetooth and Bluetooth Low Energy (BLE) also known as Bluetooth4. These are wireless standards used for devices attached to smartphones, and tablet. BLE also referred Bluetooth Smart, its a lower power than legacy Bluetooth and supported by variant operating systems, computer and smartphone makers.

802.15.4

One of the most gaining short ranges and low data rates for sensing and control technology in wireless low power vast area network is ZigBee. With its 128-bit AES encryption, ZigBee has multiple/ self-healing mesh configuration which is an ideal technology for the smart home. For function successfully, ZigBee needs more hardware nodes.

Firmware Over-the-Air (FOTA)

FOTA is a wireless mobile standard for uploading new software, services, and repair of any kind of bugs after distribution of products.

Physical Environment

The confluence of standards/technologies and ability to connect massive smaller devices, objects, and sensors, inexpensively and easily created a hyper-connected world with bridging the virtual and physical things to generate, process, exchange and consume data for the Internet of Things (IoT). Many companies have a different classification of IoT platform based on their applications and services. Firms with the production of goods and services categorized their IoT applications as "Industrial IoT' while others define their IoT applications based on devices like wearables or locations such as "Smart Home " and " Smart City." There are three IoT segments which empower consistent ubiquitous computing:

1. *Hardware* - made up of sensors, actuators, and installed correspondence equipment.
2. *Middleware* - on request stockpiling and processing devices for information examination and
3. *Presentation* - novel straightforward representation and understanding instruments which can generally be gotten to various stages and which can be intended for multiple applications.

The Internet of Things (IoT) with the main elements of people, things, data, process and a meaningful format is predicted to have nearly 20 billion devices connected and communicating by the end of the year 2020 per study performed by Gartner Inc.; displayed in Table 3. These numbers of devices actively or passively connecting to the internet and sharing information in a timely fashion is one of the key steps that remain to be resolved. Therefore, the IoT can be used to its true potential. Many technology experts envision a future that is interconnected to the point where someone's smart car can wirelessly communicate information to apartment or home, and even to medical equipment that might be in the home. This level of interconnectivity lends itself nicely to the concepts of network convergence which is a growing movement to have all types of data contained and monitored on a single type of network. Having wearables, and smart technology that can accurately, and quickly read this information and make meaningful decisions from the information serves to make everyday life more convenient for all members of modern society.

Table 3. Internet of Things (IoT) Units Installed Base by Category (Millions of Units)

Category	2014	2015	2016	2017
Consumer	2,277	3,023	4,024	13,509
Business: cross-industry	632	815	1,092	4,408
Business: vertical-Specific	898	1,065	1,276	2,880
Grand Total	3,8097	4,902	6,392	20,797

Source: Gartner (November 2015).

Network devices have applications in nearly every modern job field. These systems can range from collecting information about ecosystems to monitor a factory floors output or a home's utility usage. This realm of applications is commonly referred as environmental sensors or urban planning applications. Another common source is media related, providers can collect information about their target consumers and effectively provide personalized advertisement and product recommendations based on current products they use, and other products users in similar demographics have purchased and rated highly as well. This creates opportunities for advertisers to measure and analyses a constantly increasing amount of behavioral statistics. This amount of data analysis can revolutionize how certain people are presented and targeted by advertisements. Environmental monitoring lies in a similar vein to environmental sensors; they monitor conditions such as air quality, water purity, soil conditions, atmospheric pressure, some can even track the movement of wildlife. The continued development of these types of monitoring applications allow for early warning systems such as tornado or tsunami alert systems to have access to more accurate information, and can also be implemented commercially by farmers, soil producers, geographers, and even environmentalists to collect more information about wide geographic areas.

The Internet of Things (IoT) can also play a key role in the infrastructure and management of urban and rural cities. Modern infrastructure such as bridges, rail tracks, wind farms, and roadways can be equipped with sensors to report activity, and usage levels, warn of any functionality or integrity issues, and allow engineer and maintenance crews dynamic access to information about the systems without requiring them to leave their office and go out to the field. This reporting technology is also being implemented in the manufacturing fields leading to automated assembly lines, and process control tools that make the packaging, storage, and shipping of bulk and individual items more efficient than ever imaginable.

Overall, the Internet of Things (IoT) is widely considered to be one of the largest revolutions in the age of Information. Its effect has the potential to be felt on a global scale in all current fields and occupations. Once we have resolved the current issues of addressing, regulation, and standardization effectively, we can see the development and growth of more complex applications that utilize information from this network.

POSSIBLE FUTURE IOT INNOVATIONS

Smart home networks could have their privacy compromised by analyzing their network traffic patterns (Yoshigoe, Dai, and Abramson). However, issues like this could be resolved by introducing a synthetic packet injection scheme. Concerning security, IoT devices accessible directly over the internet is supposed to be segmented into their own network whose access should be restricted (Rouse). This independent segmented network then needs to be monitored in case of any traffic that is out of the norm. When constructing new IoT technology, it is important for manufacturers to put into consideration these key elements.

Drones

A drone is also known as an Unmanned Aerial Vehicle. A drone consists of the UAV itself and a controller based on the ground as well as a system of communication linking the two. In the past drones were mostly used for official government or military tasks but as at now, civilian UAVs are more in number. This means that consumption is high and customer assurance and continued use of this technology depends on safeguarding public privacy. Drones with sensors can get real-time data about the health of crops in the field or raw material stockpiles. This will be enabled by advancements in network connectivity through Verizon's Airborne LTE Operations (ALO) initiative, allowing drones to stream video and transmit data to a computer or smartphone.

Pacific Gas & Electric (PG&E) is testing drones to enhance the safety and reliability of its electric and gas service. It's also exploring the use of drones to monitor hard-to-reach infrastructure and to detect methane leaks.

There have been cases where the security of UAVs has been compromised. It is possible to hack into UAV systems and control them. This, however, can be avoided by encrypting the Wi-Fi signal and reinforcing the password protection (Madrigal).

Robotics

Robotics deals with the designing, construction and the use of robots and computer systems to process information and exercise control (Nocks). Like drones, robots are also used to complete tasks that are considered too dangerous or extreme for humans.

When designing robots, cycle lifetime, weight and most importantly safety are key elements that need to be accounted for. Robots can also have their control systems hacked and the actuators and command systems should be safeguarded.

Artificial Intelligence

AI can be defined as the study of devices able to perceive their environment to act in a way to maximize their chances of attaining a goal. In some cases, AI is considered as a threat to overshadow humanity if allowed to progress as steadily as it is (Kolata). Devices falling under AI are charged with transmitting large amounts of data and if compromised can lead to a security breach.

Augmented Reality/Virtual Reality

Virtual Reality has been in the limelight for a long time but one of the world's leading technological companies (Google) made a step to replace it with Augmented Reality (Lee). The ARCore makes it easier for developers to create and test AR applications using a normal phone with no need of a specialized hardware.

Google is keen on ARCores that enable consumers to plan home renovations as well as travel the globe among other things. AR is a brilliant way to link the digital world to the physical world.

Recommendations

- Wi-Fi signal encryption and password strengthening should be adopted by technological companies when developing IoT devices.
- Instead of trying to phase out VR with AR, technological companies like Google should try to make it more compatible with the ever-changing digital world.

DISCUSSIONS

Given the history of the internet, the IoT will most likely not have a strict standard of architectures and protocols. Costs, prices, resources will most likely dictate which protocol will be used. The most likely scenario will be that the lower transport protocols will be diverse and the upper protocol will become standardized and is the opposite of how the internet works now. A minimum viable product (MVP) is a product that is deployed to customers, with the minimum amount of features that are needed to gather information on how it is used so that you can fix any problems. This would be deployed to a few people for testing and would gradually increase as you perfected the product. This style of the rollout is popular with software but not so popular with hardware. Demo products for hardware are typically used to show a looks like and works like a model of the products. Mixing of the "looks like" and works "like the model" can be problematic and can delay the final product.

With all of the new progress in the IoT there is a problem in standardizing the network stack and including connections with ZigBee, Bluetooth, TCP/IP, HTTP, XML, or JSON. Hardware is also difficult to standardize because of data, power, range, and battery life that could really differentiate between products. There are three big connection types that are most familiar to consumers and developers that would work for the IoT, Bluetooth, WiFi, and cellular. Wifi is the most common and versatile for easy connection to the internet but device uses a lot of power. Bluetooth is lower energy; lower data rates and has lower ranges. It does have limited support for IPv6 connections but is usually used for local and small networks that are 30-50 feet. Cellular is vastly different because of its already large consumption, greater physical coverage, and data rates usually are between wifi and Bluetooth. Cellular can use a lot of power and be expensive.

Mesh networks that have been considered are ZigBee and Z-Wave because they can connect to devices 30-300 feet away, use low power, low data rates, and are only limited by the number of devices that are deployed. A newer consideration is Thread because it is based on 6LowPAN and capable of connecting to TCP/IP via IPv6 protocols. In Wide Area, Networks considerations are GSM, UMTS, and SigFox. GSM and UMTS are the most popular but SigFox is the newest consideration because of its long range of 30 miles in rural areas and 6 miles in urban areas. It uses lower data rates and very low amounts of power. Another technology is Neul which uses the frequencies as TV bands and can range around 6 miles. LoRaWan is another WAN technology that has a range of 3 miles in urban areas and 10 miles in suburban, can range between 0.3 – 50 kbps, uses a low amount of power and uses numerous frequencies.

I think that using WiFi or Bluetooth connection types would offer the most versatile types of connections because they are both widely adopted standards that are already in use in today's world. When those devices that are on the IoT the data will need to go somewhere for storage and analysis which will require it to be sent over the internet. If the systems are already in place for this type of data transportation it would make sense to use what we already have rather than to rebuild the infrastructure that we have.

The old hard way of developing hardware products changed with the introduction of the Arduino. The Arduino is an inexpensive microcontroller board that is used in prototyping. It is what started the new 3D printing revolution that a lot of newer companies have begun to produce and develop. Another board that hit the market is the Raspberry Pi which came with a bare OS and new tools to help hit the ground running in building these products. The Arduino allows for you to talk to basic electronics but if you want an OS and the power of an ARM-based board then the Raspberry Pi would work better. It is very popular to add new components to these boards that could support numerous new connections but can be limited by power consumption. The Arduino and Raspberry Pi are great for small project and ideas but there is a specialized board that is built as a base for IoT prototyping such as the LinkIt One. The board that is affordable and each to develop for IoT is the ESP8266, costing only $2 a board and is considered a use anywhere board. They have lower power consumption, small form factors, power management capabilities, and coding interrupts and are usually used for experimentation.

The Arduino is expanding to support ARM, x86, and other board and is gaining support from companies such as Texas Instruments. If you develop for the Arduino you could also port your code over to be used on ESP8266 and LinkIt One. This is helpful because a developer can prototype on any of these boards and move between them or to their own devices. This is because any code running on an Arduino is still C++ running with the help of macros and libraries and with a Raspberry Pi it is using the same Linux tools that are on a desktop or server. Either of these starting points will allow you to port your code over to your final product. It is common for most IoT devices to connect to the internet. The three models of cloud computing are public, private, and hybrid. The public is where services and infrastructure are provided by a specialized company. A private cloud is where it runs on your company servers. A hybrid is a mix of private and public.

When prototyping any device, it will work a lot differently in the laboratory or staged environments rather than when out in the field and therefore it is a good idea to test the system in the intended environment. It would be a good practice to envision what environments the device will be used in and what type of weather, temperatures, moisture, or other elements that the device will be exposed too. It is also wise to consider the enclosure that the device will be housed in and how it will be produced. The case could take a lot of time to develop and product from a manufacturer because of its intricacies. If you are still prototyping the enclosure small batches of can be produced to find the desired model using 3D printers or CNC milling. Once you need to scale to a larger operation, there are companies that can use molds to develop the enclosure and produce hundreds or thousands of the product.

Electronics and computers always generate heat due to the electrical load and processing are done on the devices. This can lead to overheating which can cause errors, device degradation, and performance issues when there are an inefficient heat reduction methods used in the device design. These issues can be combated with the use of heat sinks, fans, water cooling systems, or other cooling systems. Fan cooling is probably the most common method of cooling a device but can also be the noisiest. There are higher grade fans that combat the noise but there is always the consideration of the accumulation of dust that can clog up the computer and cause heat issues if the dust is not cleared out regularly. An alternative to fans is the use of a Peltier cooler that will also cool the electronics to stay within optimal operating temperatures. Considering the look and design of the enclosure can be very important because it can affect how the device operates. There are already many prebuilt enclosures that you can choose from as well as many online designs and ideas that can help in the design.

Depending on the environment of the device and what type of exposure it will be visible to can affect how many sensors or additional hardware will be used on the device. The enclosure could change with any additional hardware that could come into play during the design of the device. It is also beneficial to consider the power requirements of the device and how it will obtain its energy either from a power grid or from another sustainable source, such as solar power. Another consideration for the power would be to not waste power and use it efficiently. This will help to save overall energy and resources because with any over the use of energy will generate more heat which in turn can cause more energy used in the cooling system to keep temperatures down near the device. If the device is off the grid then greater care for energy conservation would need to be implemented so that energy is used efficiently within the system. This can include the use of batteries, the bill of materials costs, costs of the overall device, design of the enclosure, and how the energy will be gathered. Radio and the wireless connections will probably cause the largest energy drain on the device and the proper decision on what device is used to service the radio will greatly determine the energy efficiency of the device.

Devices can also be built to use deep sleep and duty cycle modes to conserve energy. These modes can eliminate unnecessary components such a LED lights or certain sensors that are not necessary throughout the use of the device. Solar power can also be used to help charge the device and batteries so that it can power the device throughout the day. In the sleep modes, certain chips can be used so that the device can "sleep" when it is not in use and then wake up when it is needed for use. Using the best radio standards such as WiFi, ZigBee, or Bluetooth, power conservation and better data throughput can be yield. When the location is too congested with overlapping wireless channel interference can occur and can also slow down communications between devices. A new standard created by NASA is disruption tolerant networking (DTN) that combat data loss and disruption. Connectivity can also be affected by the motion of the device if it is attached to a vehicle in motion. When mobile sometime the only reliable connectivity can be from cellular networks. Storage may also be a problem because in these small devices there is not much room for storage space, except for flash memory and RAM. How and where the data is processed is also very important because the data could be sensitive and in need of protection from unauthorized parties. Moving the large amounts of data can be cumbersome hard to transport back and forth from the cloud.

All of these points are great when considering the building and design of the device. There always seems to be a pro and con for every choice in the design process and figuring out what is best for your needs is what is important. As a product provider you want to make the best product for your customer and that is why you would need to test and develop the many different solutions to fit your customer's needs.

Security plays a major role in the development of the device handling of the data generated will be a great concern for customers. It should be considered throughout the design and development of the device. A big concern is a physical security with the IoT because there are so many devices that are physically accessible. The devices can be spread throughout an organization and can lead to being a single point of failure in security is one device is poorly protected. Authorization is key in verifying the identity of the person who is trying to gain access and then giving them access. Authentication using the username and password may not always work especially if your device does not have a screen on it. The IoT was developed during the dot-com boom and may suffer for not following the same security principle that has been the framework for so many other systems. It is also problematic to try and add older devices that were not meant to gain

Technical and Physical Aspects of IoT

access to the internet, that do not have the same security principles in those devices. This can cause a large number of open vulnerabilities on those systems.

A big problem that happened due to connected devices was the Stuxnet code that nearly took out a nuclear power plant in Iran. The virus attacked Microsoft computers, Siemens software, and PLC controllers that were part of those boxes. The intent was to cause fast-spinning centrifuges to spin out of control by feed the responders some manipulated "data" from the sensors. Luckily this was caught in time and a meltdown was prevented from occurring. Another security issue is the failure to update and protect firmware in a timely manner. There have been cases where people have not updated or the device vendor has not released any updates to firmware and large vulnerabilities have been exposed that would allow hackers to access their systems. For example, the Fitbit WiFi weight scale and Ring smart doorbell both had a problem where the device could be reset to factory setting and the new initialization of network setup could provide hacker the network name and passcode for WPA networks.

Even though these vulnerabilities where patched many users did not know of the firmware update and are still open to this vulnerability. A big problem in patching the firmware is notifying the customer that the update is needed and getting the customer to complete the update. It was proven that there was a big issue in Bluetooth beaconing can if the iBeacon was reconfigured then any application configured to use that beacon would stop working. It is important that the beacons be configured with the identity to trigger the proper behavior when the application came in contact with the beacon. It was also possible to fake a beacon so that people could fake access promotions given by stores that were tagged with the specific beacon. It took the company responsible for this vulnerability one month to fix the issue and deploy out the solution. Other security concerns include the physical security of the device, what ports are that will be exposed, what type of data transport methods will be used and are they secure. While prototyping you need to be aware of what will make it to the final rounds of the device and what won't; and what that means in terms of security for the final product exposure. If you were to use a raspberry pi in your final product, it might be helpful to setup Linux pushed updates and emergency updates in the case of a large botnet type attack on your devices.

Security is always the most important aspect of any system but is often the most overlooked. A lot of people and administrators do not have the time to practice and audit security policies and that is why it is often overlooked. I think in designing any system, security should be the first thing that anyone considers then work your way from there so that security and protection from people seeking to do harm is always the priority.

Technology always gets cheaper as time goes on. Prototypes are not meant to be the final product because they are usually more expensive, are large, not integrated, and are not custom to the developer. A use anywhere board is usually cheap, run on low power and can run from anywhere. Sometimes it is wise to use off the shelf parts because part of the design and development work is already done. Now it is time to customize the ready to go components and get your product to market. In this scenario, the prototype will look a lot like the final product. Sometimes it is tempting to keep using those ready to go components like the raspberry pi or Particle Photon as a final product because it is easy to prototype and get to market. However, it is not wise to do this and would be better if you built your own device from the ground up.

Another consideration for new product manufacturing is the risk. Hardware product usually includes technical risks that can originate from the designers and engineers. The other risk is product risk that is attributed to what the product does when it is delivered but fails all expectations. Product risk depends on how critical device operation is to the customer. When managing product risk it is important to fail gracefully so that failures occur, mistakes are made, and lessons are learned from and not repeated.

I think that the best solution in device design would to start out with a raspberry pi. From there you can configure many different software developments and connected components to get you started on almost any project. Once the software and components are narrowed down then you can begin working on the final product to deliver your product to the consumers. Following these rules from the article is probably the best way to plan for and design any IoT device.

REFERENCES

Brown, Isaac *"A Detailed Breakdown of LPWAN Technologies and Providers"*
Kolata, G. "How can computers get common sense?" *Science* (1982): 1237-1238. Print.
Lee, Nicole. *"Google's AR ambitions push VR to the back seat."* 2016. Document.
Madrigal, Alexis C. *"Inside Google's Secret Drone-Delivery Program."* 2014. Print.
Mattern, Friedmann, and Christian. Floerkemeier. "From the Internet of Computers to the Internet of Things." *Informatik-Spektrum* (2010): 107-121. Print.
Nocks, Lisa. *The Robot: the life story of a technology*. Westport: Greenwood Publishing Group, 2007. Print.
Noto La Diega, Guido, & Ian. Walden. *"Contracting for the 'Internet of Things': Looking into the Nest."* Research Paper. 2016. Print.
Rouse, Margaret. *"IoT Privacy."* 2015. Print.
—. "IoT security." 2015. Print.
Singh, Jatinder, et al. "Twenty Cloud Security Considerations for Supporting the Internet of Things." *IEEE Internet of Things Journal* (2015): 1. Print.
Yoshigoe, Kenji, et al. "Overcoming Invasion of Privacy in Smart Home Environment with Synthetic Packet Injection." *TRON Symposium*. TRONSHOW, 2015. 1. Print. Gartner (November 2015).

Chapter 3

THE INTERNET OF THINGS (IOT) AND ITS IMPORTANT ROLES IN RESHAPING THE ENVIRONMENT

INTRODUCTION

Internet of Things (IoT) is a unique system to interrelate the mechanical, digital and computing devices, where these objects have a unique identifier, relate to one another to transfer the data without any computer-to-device interaction. This method is not limited only to the device, but it is also used to relate animals, objects, and even humans without any direct human-to-human interaction. A "thing" in IoT can be a naturally occurring object, non-living object or a farm animal or human being. It takes only two things as a requirement. Firstly, it is the ability of the thing to assign an IP address, secondly, the capability of that object to transfer a particular data over a specified network. The IoT is more than just sensors; it's about the data that those sensors collect and store in a central database. IoT is useless if no one collects or uses the data. IoT generates data that is consistently shared back and forth and different users derive different insights and value that suits their needs from the same data. IoT has emerged by the mixture of information technology, the internet, and micro-electro-mechanical systems. These convergences of different technologies have helped to break the barrier between Operational Technology (OT) and Information Technology (IT) (internetofthingsagenda.techtarget, n.d.). Thus, allowing the analysis of unsolved machine-generated data for further improvements. The major factor for the development of IoT is the availability of huge IPv6's space.

IoT and environment are related to each other in a marvelous way. It significantly impacts the sustainability approach towards the environment helping to encounter carbon and other such gases to reduce the pollution, by empowering the modern world with efficient utilization of fewer resources. IoT is making possible to minimize the disastrous effects of weather and climate changes. The data produced from the thousands of interconnected devices, humans, machines, buildings, and the vehicles are recorded every single minute. IoT is enabling improvements in business, supply chain, and production methods by supporting people to create and work in better and safer health environment (Huang, internet-of-things, 2016).

Environmental Impacts of IoT

The increasing capabilities and knowledge of "Internet of Things (IoT)" is making new ways for the organizations and institutions to make the environment safer. The capabilities of the Internet of Things (IoT) have been the day by day dialog among experts in the cutting edge industry consistently. Individuals are excited for the insightfulness conveyed by IoT to various parts of the general public, for example, savvy urban areas, keen power matrices, shrewd wearable's, brilliant store network, and so forth. While everybody is taking a glance at the effect of IoT on social life and assembling, the ecological impact of IoT did not get a similar level of consideration and direness.

For example, IoT could have positive effects on ecological conditions. Take estimated natural sensors can now be conveyed, checking the airborne quality, radiation, water quality, dangerous airborne chemicals and numerous other health pointers. Newborn children, asthma patients and individuals working in dangerous or radiation inclined conditions could profit by such data. Associated with advanced cells through Bluetooth and Wi-Fi permits sensors to send large measures of information to the system allows us to have a superior comprehension of our environment and sets us up to discover appropriate answers for environmental problems.

Technological Environment

Internet of Things (IoT) is the current hit wherever setting a history in IT industry. Distributed computing is entering its route introducing as an efficient handling base for the web of things. Distributed computing and IoT will be more remote than the present-day setting. The question that is forward for the most part asked is for-what is the valid reason in cloud registering for the Internet of things? Indeed, both of the innovations are digging in for the long haul (By stay I mean, there is no chance to get out) and cloud will give IoT new status to investigate. Today IoT is slanting from undertakings to residential to open applications, and it will be more inescapable in looming period. IoT needs savvy sensors; portability, solid register and examination control. Cloud empowers versatility developed with an embedded secure innovation, this prospects a combination of both advancements an immaculate mix to put forward enormous capability of IoT, particularly when open deliberation on the security of IoT has enraptured. IoT in cloud condition will make it fundamentally more secure. Not so distant future, you would discover an IoT is sure to develop together with cloud and this will make another path for cloud specialist co-ops as well. Prepare for a day when you're stopping sensors will detect your auto and will trigger your stopping lights and anteroom lights. With Mobile, you could deal with your home gadgets like warm your sustenance in broiler before you achieve home, control your home temperature before you enter, further, every one of these things will get so shrewd that they will work commonly without your mediation abandoning you joyful and agreeable life. IoT in a cloud environment will change society and the ways of our life.

Physical Environment

Primary things that are interconnected contains savvy condition gadgets, sensor devices inserted into the physical condition, e.g., floats coasting in a cove region to identify Tsunamis, and so forth and (portable) gadgets in the move by a versatile host. For example, a Santa in a vehicle or a smartphone that goes with somebody. Some of these condition sensors have a tendency to be associated utilizing a wide-region remote system to a get to the hub. They don't frame a neighborhood Wireless Sensor Network (WSN). The information from the sensors gained in a system database. Applications and clients by implication get the information from the database not specifically from the sensors. Utilizing the haphazardness given by the physical condition to fabricate security arrangements has gotten much consideration as of late. Specifically, the mutual entropy provided by measuring encompassing sound, glow modalities or electromagnetic transmissions been utilized to construct area based, nearness based, or setting based security components. The dominant part of those conventions depends on a standard model comprising channel testing, quantization, data compromise, security intensification, and vital check. The principal issue for all methodologies is the constrained comprehension of the security. For instance, security investigations frequently just address single segments and not the whole framework or depend on extensive deliberations of the real wellspring of arbitrariness. Advance, a major open question is the practicality of such structures for low-asset stages. Our first commitment is a point by point, enhanced acknowledgment of a fundamental foundation framework. We show the plausibility of getting a mutual mystery from associated amounts on asset compelled gadgets with strong power spending plan. Our framework acknowledged on the popular ARM Cortex-M3 processor that reports point by point asset prerequisites. The second real commitment is a rundown and reflection of past cooperates with a thorough security investigation. We substantiate our examination by presenting practical attack results.

Socio-Economic Environment

The dynamic, rapidly changing technology-rich digital environment enables the provision of added value applications that abused a huge number of gadgets contributing administration and data. With the beginning of the Internet of Things (IoT) from the web as a web benefit, huge quantities of devices and conditions are likewise getting to be noticeably more quick-witted and are in the position to cooperate with each other at any other time. IoT has significant development over its first decades, with the goals of connecting billions of sensors to the web, keeping in mind the end goal to utilize sensors proficiently is to viable and proficiently use them ingenious for smart urban areas.

Design layers and application spaces of IoT the unlimited scenes that are offered by IoT will make likely outcomes of the advancement of different quantities of keen Applications, in which a next to no part it is by and by accessible and available our worldwide group. Different zones and savvy condition at which these applications created will likely progress and affect the efficiency of the tone of global lives, from the part of home living, well-being concern, environmental awareness to the work.

Business Environment

The industrial internet is a new and forthcoming innovation that is changing the acts of associations and organizations all over. Through research and application, openings can emerge from executing these new frameworks and gadgets. The Internet of Things (IoT) in the Modern Business Environment (MBE) is a primary reference hotspot for the most recent academic research on shifting parts of the interworking of brilliant gadgets inside a business setting and investigates the effect of these devices on organization operations and models. Highlighting broad scope on a wide scope of subjects, for example, inventory network administration, data sharing, and information investigation, this distribution is in a perfect world intended for specialists, chiefs, and understudies looking for flow inquire about on the development of innovation in business.

The modern web is another and forthcoming innovation that is changing the acts of associations and companies all over the place. Through research and application, openings can emerge from executing these new frameworks and gadgets. IoT in the Modern Business Environment (MBE) is a first reference hotspot for the most recent academic research on differing parts of the interworking of keen gadgets inside a business setting and investigates the effect of these devices on organization operations and models. Including broad scope on wide subjects, for example, inventory network administration, data sharing, and information investigation, this distribution is in a perfect world intended for analysts, supervisors, and understudies looking for ebb and flow inquire about on the extension of technology in commerce.

Animal Tracking

IoT used to protect endangered those species of the animals which are near to extinction. The habits and health of such animals are noted continuously by attaching a GPS device to them for continuous inspection. For instance, Cisco keeps an eye on the movements and actions of the visitors, staff and any other individual who enters the Rhino reserved ground, it is using local area networks, Wi-Fi and Lora based networks. These animals kept under high surveillance and protection. Individual alarms and indicators start to work if any illegal and odd movement or things spotted in the vicinity of that area. So, that certain protective steps and approaches may be adopted to solve the matter.

Energy Management

The main achievement of the Internet of Things (IoT) in this field is the fabrication and introduction of smart grids. These networks enable two-way communication between the customers or consumers and the utility provider, makes possible to consumers to keep an eye on their energy consumption units. IoT technology has made it possible to make smart homes and buildings to minimize the power consumption by the installation of the smart lights, smart heating and cooling systems and ventilation system. It makes it possible to start large-scale changes and up gradations to enhance the ability of energy reuse.

Waste Management

Internet of Things (IoT) helps in reducing the water wastage. Such devices and sensors are invented which can help to reduce the waste. This innovation has helped a lot, especially in the industrial sector to manage the waste. There are two main processes or benefits of this technology in the industrial sector. It indicates the exact time for the collection and deposition of the waste material and secondly, it tells an appropriate route for the trucks in order to reduce the time and protect residential areas from that pollution.

Water Management

IoT is playing a very significant role in water management and perfect agriculture. Agriculture should always be nominated when talking about the water management methods as it is the biggest customer of water around the globe. The farm uses almost

70% of the world's water and out of which 60% is reported to be the waste. According to the "World Wildlife Fund," this wastage of water is due to leakages in the irrigation canals and non-effective ways and methods used by the application of water in agriculture. Similarly, the farmer does not know about the thirst capacity of the crops which they are growing. The cultivation of thirsty crops is also contributing a lot to increase the water waste. IoT is helping the farmers in this regard.

- Different types of actuators and sensor developed by this technique which is helping them to reduce the water waste and increase the capacity of the production. These sensors assist them to keep an eye on the process continuously.
- The optimum level of water required for different crops is defined, and sensors are present to indicate the requirement. These devices designed by considering various factors like temperature, humidity, drought, moisture, light, water pressure and the quality of the water. Soil pH indicated by different actuators which help farmers to select the crops for cultivation accordingly.
- IoT is not confined only to the agriculture. But, it has developed such sensors which are helping at the consumer level in homes, offices, parks, and buildings. These sensors provide a clear analysis sheet to the consumers to identify the amount of water they consumed it helps to save water which is a natural resource (Tracy, 2016).

Device Management

Four fundamental device management prerequisites exist for any Internet of Things (IoT) gadget organization: provisioning and verification, arrangement and control, checking and diagnostics, and programming updates and upkeep.

Once an Internet of Things (IoT) gadget introduced, it is not a "fire and overlooks" situation. There will be bug fixes and programming refreshes required; a few devices will come up short and should be repaired or supplanted; and each time this happens your organization is on the snare to limit downtime – to keep your clients upbeat, as well as to guarantee that you ensure your income stream. Any IoT framework must address four important classifications of gadget administration, which are:

- Provisioning and authentication
- Configuration and control
- Monitoring and diagnostics
- Software updates and maintenance

INDUSTRIAL APPLICATIONS BASED ON IoT

While Intel might seem like an odd place for a biotech researcher, but its biological system help organizations utilize the IoT to tackle long-standing industry-particular difficulties. Rapidly create IoT arrangements that interface things, gather information, and infer bits of knowledge with Intel's method of open and versatile methods so you can decrease costs, enhance efficiency, and increment income.

Automotive

When tied to the IoT, the car transforms information into important knowledge, both inside the auto and in its general surroundings. According to World Health Organization (2010), 1.24 million persons globally died due to a motor vehicle accident. Annually, nearly 30,000 persons die as a result of motor-vehicle accidents. The case is similar to the U.S. whereas in Asia it is worse. In both India and China alone, at least 400,000 persons die in a motor-vehicle accident annually. IoT technology, specifically the emergence of safety-focused sensors on automobiles, is anticipated to lessen the global rate of death from motor-vehicle accidents. Since the greater part of motor-vehicle accidents are due to human error, replacement of human decision-making features in driving is the aim of the self-directed vehicle.

In May 2015 Daimler Trucks North America, owned by the German, made an announcement it was ready to test the Freightliner Inspiration Truck without the driver on Nevada road. Teslax and Google are developing driverless cars which are slowly emerging. A majority of the cars come in the kind of safety sensors that provide motorists a 360 degrees view of their vehicle, whereas others function autonomously, safeguarding the vehicle in the absence of the driver's action. Auto firms as well adopt the data the sensors get to assist them to offer safer and more effective cars. Even though the data-gathering devices pose some privacy issues, they are the subsequent steps in the evolution of the automobile.

Energy

Through the IoT, the energy framework's incalculable gadgets can share data progressively to disseminate and better oversee vitality all the more productively.

Healthcare

There are several innovation changes that are already taking place in the world of healthcare and medicine. For example, medical experts are now making use of electronic health records (EHRs). Similarly, they are also taking advantage of radio frequency identification (RFID) tags (himss.org). With the aid of these technologies, provision of health care services has been made easier. Medical practitioners are now in a better position to keep track of their patient records with ease. Access to patient information is made convenient as these systems rely on cloud computing. To hospitals, they are in a position of stocking their inventories to guarantee that they do not run out of stock. Truly, with these kinds of benefits working in favor of the health industry, there is a good chance of high adoption rate both from the government and businesses as pointed out in the statistics above. There is no jurisdiction over a healthcare that will not adopt IoT technology. At the level of the patient, IoT-aided wearable enables doctors to capture information on health. Annual physicals may become out of date since doctors already have plenty of patient information that allows them to identify if an in-person check-up is guaranteed. Similarly, patients with upsetting health indications that cannot cause symptoms would be identified by a physician prior to leading to more serious problems. Thus, clinicians can utilize the information to help them both in understanding the health of the patient and create information sets of the patient subgroups, with emphasis on treating and preventing the most ancient diseases of humanity.

At the same time, hospitals that have mostly produced as well as stored large amounts of information can adopt IoT technology to establish actionable intelligence in the information they gather. For instance, several hospitals intentionally collect many inventories to eliminate shortages of dire supplies. IoT aided scanners to provide hospital administrators visibility into their collections and identify the moment the shortages arise. IoT devices have the capacity to enhance treatment in hospitals, specifically in situations of emergencies. A paramedic can adopt IoT device to take the patient's vibrant signs including other statistics and are instantly relayed to ER. Thus, the doctors will understand the patient's condition without wasting time, as they will have already identified the situation.

Decreased Costs

Still, on the healthcare field, patients would also be benefiting from the use of internet of things technology. This would come around in the sense of decreased health care costs that they would be incurring. Since data would be stored on cloud servers, they could be attended to without having to visit the doctors. This, in turn, means that they would be reducing health care expenses that they would have incurred in paying regular visit to the medical experts. It is also predicted that there would be advanced home care facilities capable of taking care of patients at home. This also reduces hospital expenses that would have been faced.

From clinical wearables power network's endless gadgets which can share data continuously to distribute to the person on call tablets and modern surgical suite hardware, the IoT is changing and better oversee vitality, all the more healthcare productively.

Smart Manufacturing

IoT technology enables today's factories to unlock operational efficiency, optimize production, and increase worker safety. IoT assures to highly reduce the workplace rate associated injuries and deaths. According to the International Labor Organization, 2.3 million persons die annually from work-associated accidents as well as diseases worldwide. Each year, at least 3 million employees are falling victims of grievous accidents while performing their jobs and 4,000 persons die in workplace accidents as highlighted by European Commission. IoT has the capacity to safeguard workers more so those working in dangerous sites including those of constructions. For instance, wearable technologies should be equipped with fixed sensors to establish when an employee can be dangerous performing a dangerous maneuver. The sensors may as well monitor dangerous conditions of the environment including the availability of toxic substances. Behavioral information gathered from the wearable sensors can assist safety managers to understand an employee is at risk of an accident. The predictive feature of IoT can be one of the most and possibly exploitative aspects, though a majority are yet in form of theories.

Further, data-driven decision-making firms can adopt IoT products to make sure the integrity, safety, quality as well as security of features in their complex chains of supply. It is approximated that by 2020, a 30-times increase on internet-connected physical devices will highly change the supply chain leader data access alongside cyber-risk exposure. IoT devices fixed across the supply chain will offer managers an understanding of their processes compared to before. The IoT technologies feature to transform how firms design, maintain and secure their sensitive chains of supply from in-transit visibility through depot security.

Integration of Data from Multiple Sources

The Internet of Things (IoT) has made the jump to end up noticeably a standard theme. This developing acknowledgment is because of the effect the IoT has had on the business investigation and the potential that still stays undiscovered. Every day, new machines, sensors, and gadgets come on the web and sustain data into information frameworks. As associations leave on new IoT activities and work to concentrate more understanding from swelling data volumes, called for another information administration approach. Conventional databases and examination models will dependably be indispensable, yet the IoT calls for particular abilities to deal with different information always gushing from untold quantities of sources. IoT information is mind-boggling, unlimited, and quick moving. This section looks at the present condition of information administration and subtle elements the abilities expected to oversee IoT information and boost esteem.

Aberdeen servers and storage service provider inspected associations with the capacity to gather, incorporate, and break down information produced by the Internet of Things (IoT). These "IoT associations" try to use the overabundance of data created by unique gadgets, frameworks, and different sources to better comprehend operations and general execution. Investigate has called for organizations to put resources into enhancing framework and information administration capacities to deal with the difficulties and openings exhibited by the IoT. The review of 68 IoT associations uncovered the territories where organizations battle and hope to improve.

Device Diversity and Interoperability

The Internet of Things (IoT) is an unimaginably differing space, including an expansive assortment of equipment frame variables and programming biological systems dissimilar to anything we have found in innovation. Smart watches, associated cameras, rambles, indoor regulators, voice-empowered speakers, brilliant apparatuses and the sky is the limit from there they all live respectively inside the IoT.

In any case, the different qualities and advancements that energize many IoT fans is a major test for producers and engineers, as well as (and above all) buyers. Which innovation alternatives ought to be utilized when planning or conveying IoT gadgets? How would they stay aware of refreshed or new working frameworks? Shouldn't something be said about new programming and availability advancements coming up? Those are recently some of the today's difficulties.

Having a solitary, bound together correspondence and programming structure for the IoT appears like a perfect arrangement. However, the different and quick-paced nature of the IoT makes this ideal world a major test. A different quality in the IoT is not something to be illuminated, but rather a viewpoint that must be embraced and managed.

Flexibility and Evolution of Applications

Internet of Things (IoT) is anticipated that it would incorporate in each part of our lives to produce an outlook change towards a hyper-associated society. As more things associated with the Internet, the bigger measure of information produced and handled into practical activities that can make our lives more secure and less demanding. Since IoT provide overwhelming traffics, it invites a few difficulties to organize cutting edge technology. In this way, IoT framework ought to outline regarding adaptability and versatility. Also, distributed computing has to coordinate with enormous information examination. They permit system to change itself substantially speedier to administration necessities with better operational effectiveness and insight. IoT ought to likewise be vertically enhanced from gadget to application to give ultra-low power operation, post-viability, and consistent quality with guaranteeing full security over the whole flag way. In this chapter, we address IoT challenges and innovative necessities from the specialist organization viewpoint.

There are numerous approaches to characterize the IoT, in spite of the fact that its underlying use has credited to Kevin Ashton, a specialist in advanced development. Regularly IoT alludes to the interconnection of extraordinarily identifiable installed figuring gadgets inside existing web foundation. The term firmly identified with keen protests that associate and speak with different machines, real situations, and structures.

Scale, Data Volume, and Performance

Examined associations with the capacity to gather, coordinate and investigate information created by the Internet of Things (IoT). These "IoT connections" look to use the overabundance of data produced by different gadgets, frameworks, and various sources to better comprehend operations and general execution. Past examine has called for organizations to put resources into enhancing framework and information administration abilities to deal with the difficulties and openings introduced by the IoT. The review of 68 IoT associations uncovered the zones where organizations battle and would like to enhance:

- The traditional IoT Association's aggregate volume of information developed by 30% over the previous year.
- 54% of IoT associations detailed that their present data examination capacities are lacking.
- Half of IoT associations neglected to enhance time-to decision over the last year.

Database construction formally characterizes the structure of a database framework. In the social model, a development characterized in advancing tables and connecting those tables all information additions/refreshes must cling to that diagram. In late information, administration arrangements strengthen vast and various data volumes, it has been standard to go for non-mapping answers for taking into consideration a more flexible structure of the database. There is different exchange offs between upholding a mapping and having a non-construction arrangement. The absence of construction prompts records analyzed at the runtime, rather than load-time parsing that is normal in shared database frameworks, causes corruption in execution for non-pattern frameworks, as pressure turns out to be less potent. The absence of pattern will start prompt clients likewise composing their particular parsers, which bargains the interoperability, which is attractive for IoT applications. Inquiry advancement is trying in non-composition frameworks, on account of the absence of learning about lists, table parcels and cardinalities, and insights about data values.

Mobile

Smart transportation and smart co-ordination's put in a different area because of the way of information sharing and spine execution required. Urban movement is the main supporter of activity commotion contamination and a noteworthy supporter of urban air quality corruption and ozone-harming substance emanations. Movement blockage explicitly forces huge expenses on monetary and social exercises in many cities. Inventory network efficiencies and profitability, incorporating in the nick of time operations, are extremely affected by this blockage bringing about cargo deferrals and conveyance plan disappointments. Dynamic activity data will influence cargo development, permit better arranging and enhanced planning. The vehicle IoT will empower the utilization of vast scale WSNs for web-based checking of travel times, starting point goal (O-D) course decision conduct, line lengths and air contamination and clamor outflows. The IoT is probably going to supplant the data movement gave by the current sensor systems of inductive circle vehicle identifiers utilized at the crossing points of existing activity control frameworks. They will likewise support the advancement of situation based models for arranging, and outline of moderation and mitigation arranges, and additionally enhanced calculations for public activity control, including multi-target control frameworks. Consolidated with data accumulated from the urban activity control structure, substantial and significant data on movement conditions can be displayed to travelers.

Cloud Centric Internet of Things

Internet of Things (IoT) can be seen from two points of view Internet-driven and Thing-driven. The internet-driven engineering will include web administrations being the primary concentration while the items contribute information. In driven design, the shrewd items take the inside stage. A reasonable structure coordinating the omnipresent detecting gadgets and the applications is appeared in keeping in mind the end goal to understand the maximum capacity of distributed computing, and also pervasive sensing, a joined structure with a cloud at the inside by all practical accounts. IoT technology not only gives the adaptability of isolating related expenses most intelligently but at the same time exceptionally versatile in giving the cloud solutions. Detecting specialist co-ops can join the system and offer their information utilizing a capacity cloud; systematic device engineers can provide their product apparatuses; computerized reasoning experts can give their information mining and machine learning instruments valuable in changing over data to learn PC illustrations architect can offer an assortment of perception devices. The distributed computing can provide these administrations with infrastructures, platforms or software where the maximum capacity of human inventiveness can be tapped utilizing them as administrations. This in a way concurs with the ubicomp vision of Weiser and also Rogers's human-driven approach. The information produced, instruments utilized and the representation made vanishes out of the spotlight, tapping the maximum capacity of the Internet of Things (IoT) in different application spaces. As can be seen from Figure 1, the Cloud coordinates all closures of Ubicomp by giving adaptable stockpiling, calculation time and various devices to assemble new organizations. In this area, we portray the cloud stage utilizing Manjra delicate Aneka, and Microsoft Azure steps to exhibit how cloud coordinates stockpiling, calculation and representation ideal models. Besides, we present a critical domain of collaboration between cloud which is valuable for consolidating open and private mists utilizing Aneka. This collaboration is fundamental for application designers keeping in mind the end goal to bring detected data, investigation calculations and representation under one single seamless framework.

IoT architecture has a lot of different definitions described based on the domain technology that has been identified and abstracted. Combining and considering definitions we have a reference model defined for those IoT architecture showing relationships among various components. Big data component present gives a model for abstraction of data. Moreover, a reference design is provided to build upon the IoT model described. There are several IoT architectures present that give a relationship among various components.

For instance, there is defined architecture that has cloud computing at the center that stores data and that is connected to other components present in the architecture. This cloud-centric design is a good comparison with our proposed model. The model defined from the real-time sensing/seamless sensing, big data analytics and presentation of IoT data makes this model as unifying architecture. The cloud-centric architecture present is mostly concerned about the data retrieval from IoT not on analytics and presentation part. So this proposed model will integrate big data analytics in IoT architecture. The Figure1 below shows the proposed architecture. At the bottom of this architecture, we can find IoT components like sensors that generate data. This is connected to the network using wireless networks like RFID, Wi-Fi, ZigBee and Bluetooth technologies. IoT gateway shows a connection of IoT network to analytics section.

The upper layers connected are dealing with the big data analytics, where the data is stored in the cloud and that stored data is accessed through analytics applications. These cloud-based storage and analytics application will have API management and a dashboard to show results working on big data. The main aim of developing this architecture is to give an adequate decision support for business problems, easy architecture maintenance and real-time development of systems and IT environment. Thus, further decisions on IoT architecture are related to code implementation to allow users for understanding integration.

However, developing IoT applications utilizing low-level Cloud programming models and interfaces, for example, Thread and Map Reduce models is unpredictable. To beat this restriction, we require an IoT application particular structure for the fast making of utilization and their arrangement on Cloud foundations, accomplished by mapping proposed structure to Cloud APIs offered by stages, for example, Aneka.

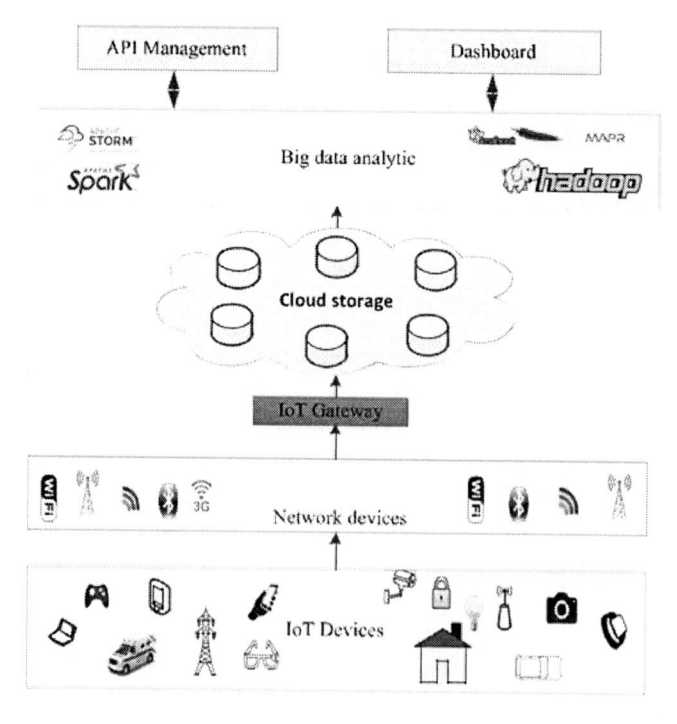

Figure 1. Coordination of Cloud Computing in IoT applications.

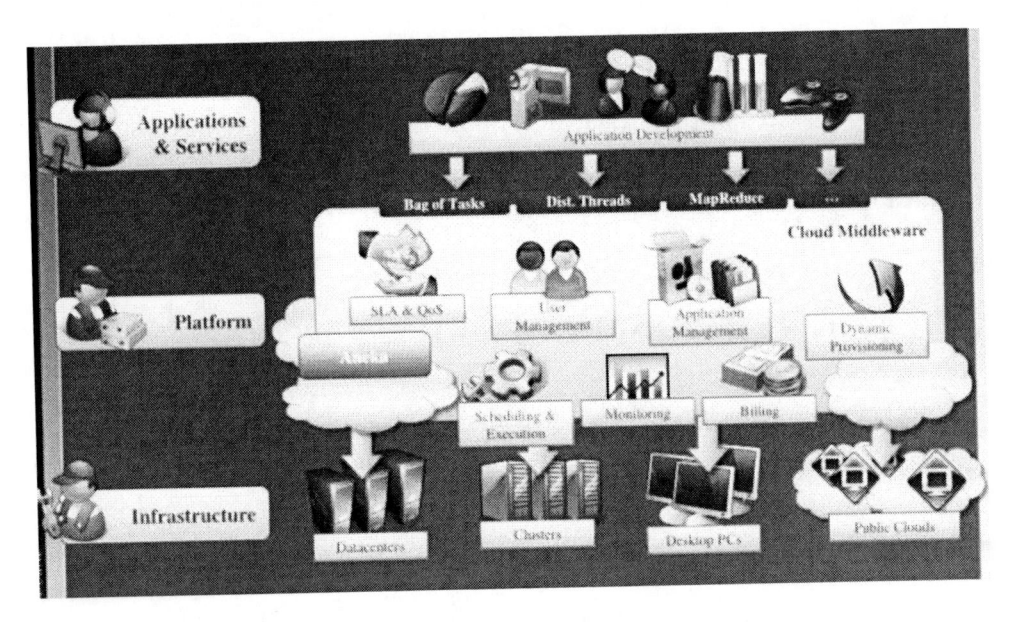

Figure 2. Application scheduler and Dynamic Resource Provisioning in Aneka.

Accordingly, the new IoT application-particular system ought to have the capacity to offer help for:

1. Perusing information streams either from seniors straightforwardly or gets the information from databases.
2. Simple articulation of information investigation rationale as capacities/ administrators that procedure information streams in a straightforward and adaptable way on Cloud infract cutpurse, and if any occasions of premium are distinguished, results ought to be passed to yield steams, which are associated with perception programs.

Utilizing such system, the engineer of IoT applications will ready to outfit the energy of Cloud processing without knowing subtle low-level elements of making sure and scale applications.

The scheduler is responsible for doling out every asset to an assignment in an application for execution given client Quos parameters and the general cost of the specialist co-op. Contingent upon the calculation and information necessities of every sensor application, it guides the dynamic asset provisioning part to instantiate or ends a predetermined number of functions, stockpiling, and system assets while keeping up a line of undertakings to be booked. This rationale installed multi-target application booking calculations. The scheduler can manage asset disappointments by reallocating those undertakings to other appropriate cloud assets. The Dynamic Resource Provisioning (DRP) part actualizes the rationale for provisioning and overseeing virtualized assets in the private and open distributed computing situations given the asset prerequisites as coordinated by the application scheduler. It is accomplished by progressively consulting with the Cloud Infrastructure as a Service (IASI) suppliers for the correct sort of asset for a particular time and cost by considering the past execution history of uses and spending accessibility. This choice is set aside a few minutes when SaaS applications ceaselessly send solicitations to the Aneka cloud platform.

OPEN CHALLENGES AND FUTURE DIRECTIONS

The proposed cloud-centric vision contains an adaptable and open design that is client driven and empowers diverse players to associate in the IoT structure. It permits cooperation in a way appropriate for their particular necessities, as opposed to the IoT pushed onto them. Along these lines, the structure incorporates arrangements to meet diverse needs for information possession, security, protection, and sharing of data.

Some open difficulties are described in IoT components displayed earlier. The challenges incorporate IoT specific, for example, protection, participatory detecting, information investigation, GIS-based representation and Cloud registering separated from the standard WSN challenges including design, vitality proficiency, security, conventions, and Quality of Service (QoS). The real objective is to have Plug n' Play keen articles conveyed in any condition with an interoperable spine permitting them to mix with other brilliant protests around them. Institutionalization of recurrence groups and conventions assumes an essential part of achieving this objective. A guide to the main improvements in IoT looks into inescapable applications. Which incorporates the innovation drivers and key application results expected in the following decade? The segment closes with a couple of worldwide activities in the area which could assume an important part in the success of this rapidly emerging technology.

Energy Efficient Sensing

Efficient heterogeneous detecting of the urban condition needs to at the same time meet contending requests of numerous detecting modalities. This has suggestions on system activity, information stockpiling, and vitality usage. Imperatively, this includes both settled and portable detecting foundation and nonstop and arbitrary inspecting. A summed up structure is required for information gathering and displaying that viable abuses spatial and worldly attributes of the information, both in the detecting space and also the related change areas. For instance, urban clamor mapping needs a continuous gathering of commotion levels utilizing battery fueled hubs using the settled framework and participatory detecting as a key segment for well-being and personal satisfaction administrations for its tenants.

Compressive detecting empowers decreased flag estimations without affecting precise remaking of the flag. A flag scanty in one premise might recoup from few projections onto a moment premise that is garbled with the first. The issue decreases to finding meager arrangements through a littlest 11-standard coefficient vector that concurs with the estimations. In the pervasive detecting setting, suggestions for information pressure; arrange movement and the dissemination of sensors. Compressive remote detecting uses synchronous correspondence to lessen the transmission energy of every sensor transmitting loud projections of information tests to a focal area for aggregation.

Secure Reprogrammable Networks and Privacy

Security will be a major concern for the systems that transmit the data everywhere in the network. There can be numerous ways the framework could be assaulted - handicapping the system accessibility; pushing inaccurate information into the system; getting to individual data; and so on. The three physical parts of IoT are RFID, WSN, and the cloud is defenseless against such assaults. Security is essential to any system, and the primary line of barrier against information defilement is cryptography.

Of the three, RFID (especially detached) is by all accounts the most powerless as it permits individual following and also the articles and no abnormal state knowledge empowered on these gadgets. These difficult issues, however, have arrangements that can be given utilizing cryptographic strategies and requires more research before they are widely accepted.

Quality of Service

Heterogeneous networks are multi-benefit; giving more than one unmistakable application or administration, suggests various activity sorts inside the system, as well as the capacity of a separate system to support all applications without QoS trade-off. There are two application classes: 1) Throughput and postpone tolerantly, flexible movement (e.g., checking climate parameters at low testing rates). 2) Transfer speed and defer delicate inelastic (ongoing) activity (e.g., commotion or activity checking), which can be additionally segregated by information related applications (e.g., high-versus. - low determination recordings) with various QoS prerequisites. Along these lines, a controlled, ideal way to deal with unique server system traffics, each requires particular application QoS. It's hard to give QoS ensures in remote systems, as sections frequently constitute holes' in asset provider because of asset portion and administration capacity requirements in shared remote media. Nature of service in cloud figuring another significant research region which will require increasingly considered as the information and instruments end up plainly accessible on mists. Dynamic booking and asset distribution calculations are given molecule swarm improvement. For high limit applications and as IoT develops, this could become a bottleneck.

New Protocols

The protocols at the sensing end of IoT will assume a key part in entire acknowledgment. They frame the spine for the information burrow amongst sensors and the external world. For the framework to work proficiently, effective MAC convention and fitting steering convention are necessary. A few MAC conventions have been proposed for different spaces with TDMA (crash free), CSMA (low activity effectiveness) and FDMA (impact free yet requires extra hardware in hubs) plans. None of them acknowledged as a standard, and with more things' accessible this situation will get more jumbled, which requires additionally explore.

An individual sensor can drop out for various reasons, so the system must act naturally adjusting and take into consideration multi-way directing. Multi-bounce directing conventions utilized as a part of portable specially appointed systems and earthbound WSNs. They separated into three classifications - information is driven, area-based and progressive, again given various application spaces. Vitality is the important thought for the current steering conventions. On account of IoT, it ought to notice that a spine will be accessible and quantity of bounces in the multi-jump situation will be restricted. In such a case, the current directing conventions ought to suffice in down to earth implementation with minor modifications.

Participatory Sensing

Some projects have started to address the improvement of individual's driven (or participatory) detecting stages. As noted before, people driven detecting offers the likelihood of minimal effort detecting of the earth restricted to the client. It can accordingly give the nearest sign of ecological parameters experienced by the client. It has noticed that environmental information gathered by client frames social cash. These outcomes produce useful information contrasted with the information accessible through a settled foundation sensor organize. Above all, it is the open door for the client to give criticism on their experience of a given fundamental parameter that offers valuable data as setting related to a given occasion.

The impediments of individuals driven detecting place new centrality on the reference information part gave a settled framework IoT as a spine. The issue of missing specimens is a basic confinement of individuals driven detecting. Depending on clients volunteering information and on the conflicting get-together of tests acquired crosswise over different times and changing areas (in light of a client's coveted cooperation and given area or travel way), confines the capacity to deliver significant information for any applications and strategy choices. Just intending to issues and ramifications of data possession, security, and suitable investment impetuses, can such a stage accomplish honestly to goodness end-client engagement. Additionally detecting modalities can be acquired through the option of sensor modules joined to the telephone for particular application detecting. For example, air quality sensors or biometric sensors. In such situations, PDAs wind up plainly basic IoT hubs associated with the cloud toward one side and several sensors at the other end.

Data Mining

Extracting useful information from a mind-boggling detecting condition at various spatial and fleeting resolutions is a testing research issue in automated reasoning. Current cutting-edge strategies utilize shallow learning techniques where pre-characterized occasions and information oddities are removed using managed and unsupervised learning. The following level of knowledge includes gathering nearby exercises by using short data events removed from shallow learning. A definite vision will identify complex occasions in light of bigger spatial and longer transient scales given the two levels sometime recently. The essential research issue that emerges in complex detecting conditions of this nature is the means by which learn portrayals of occasions and exercises at numerous levels of many-sided quality simultaneously (i.e., events, neighborhood exercises and complex exercises). A rising concentration in machine learning research has been the field of profound realizing, which plans to take in various layers of deliberation that can be utilized to decipher given information. The asset limitations in sensor systems lead to new difficulties for profound learning as far as to the requirement for versatile, conveyed and incremental learning techniques.

GIS-Based Visualization

As new display technologies emerge, the innovative perception will be empowered. The advancement from CRT to Plasma, LCD, LED, and AMOLED shows have offered ascend to exceedingly proficient information portrayal utilizing touch interface with the client having the capacity to explore the information over and above anyone's expectations sometime recently. With rising 3D shows, this region is sure to have more innovative work openings. Be that as it may, the information that leaves pervasive registering is not prepared for direct utilization utilizing representation stages and requires additional handling. The situation turns out to be extremely perplexing for heterogeneous porch fleeting information. New perception plans for the portrayal of different sensors in the 3D scene produce the shifts transiently. Another test of envisioning information gathered inside IoT is that they are geo-related and meagerly appropriated. To adapt, a structure in light of Internet GIS is required.

Cloud Computing

An integrated IoT and cloud computing applications empower the formation of keen situations. For instance, Smart Cities should have the capacity to (a) consolidate administrations offered by different partners and scale to bolster countless in a dependable and decentralized way. They should be capable to work in both wired and remote system situations and manage limitations, for example, gadgets or information sources with restricted power and temperamental availability. The cloud application stages should be upgraded to strength:

1. The quick formation of utilization by giving space particular programming apparatuses and conditions and
2. Consistent execution of uses bridling abilities of various dynamic and heterogeneous assets to meet nature of administration prerequisites of different clients.

The Cloud asset administration and booking framework ought to have the capacity to powerfully organize demands and arrangement assets with the end goal that basic solicitations served continuously. The scheduler should increase with assignment duplication calculations for disappointment administration. In particular, the Cloud application booking calculations need to display the accompanying ability:

1. Multi-target improvement: The booking calculations ought to have the capacity to manage QoS parameters. For example, reaction time, cost of administration use, most extreme number of assets accessible per unit cost, and punishments for administration corruption.
2. Errand duplication based adaptation to non-critical failure: Critical assignments of an application will be straightforwardly repeated and executed on various assets so that if one asset neglects to finish the undertaking, by utilizing the recreated rendition. This rationale is vital progressively assignments that should be handled to convey benefits promptly.

International Activities

Internet of Things (IoT) activities with various activities in progress crosswise over the industry, the scholarly world and different levels of government, as key partners try to outline a path forward for the organized acknowledgment of this innovative development. In Europe, significant exertion is in progress to unite the cross-area exercises of research gatherings and associations, traversing M2M, WSN and RFID into a brought together IoT system. Upheld by the European Commission 7th Framework program (EU-FP7), this incorporates the Internet of Things European Research Cluster (IERC). Including various EU FP7 ventures, its destinations are: to set up participation stage and research vision for IoT exercises in Europe and turn into a contact point for IoT investigate on the planet. It incorporates ventures, for instance, CASAGRAS2, a consortium of global accomplices from Europe, the USA, China, Japan, and Korea investigating issues encompassing RFID and its part in understanding the Internet of Things (IoT). Too, IERC incorporates the Internet of Things Architecture (IoT-An) extend built up to decide an engineering reference display for the interoperability of IoT frameworks and key building squares to accomplish this. In the meantime, the IoT Initiative (IoT-I) is a planned activity built up to bolster the advancement of the European IoT people group. The IoT-I anticipate unites a consortium of accomplices to make a joint core and specialized vision for the IoT in Europe that envelops the as of now divided segments of the IoT space comprehensively. At the same time, the Smart Santander venture is building up a city scale IoT tried for research and administration arrangement sent over the city of Santander, Spain, and additionally locales situated in the UK, Germany, Serbia, and Australia.

At the same time, large-scale activities are progressing in countries like Japan, Korea, the USA and Australia, where industry, related associations, and government offices are teaming up on different projects, and similar capacities towards an IoT by incorporating smart city activities, savvy lattice programs consolidating shrewd metering advancements and take off of rapid broadband framework. With the advancement of RFID in industry and consortiums, for example, the Auto-ID lab (established at MIT and now with satellite labs at driving colleges in South Korea, China, Japan, United Kingdom, Australia and Switzerland) committed to making the IoT utilizing RFID and seeking Wireless Sensor Networks (WSN). Essentially, the requirement for IoT specialized issues has seen the foundation of the Internet Protocol for Smart Objects (IPSO) alliance. Now more than 60 organizations from driving innovation, interchanges and vitality organizations working with principles bodies, for example, IETF, IEEE and ITU to indicate new IP-based advances to upgrade industry agreement for gathering the parts for the IoT. Additionally, IoT movement is progressing in China, with its Twelfth Five Year Plan indicating IoT venture and advancement to centered around: an intelligent network; wise transportation; savvy coordination's; keen home; condition and well-being testing; mechanical control and robotic nation; medicinal services; fine farming; back and benefit; military protection with support of foundation of an Internet of Things focusing in Shanghai (with an aggregate venture over US$ 100million) to study innovations and mechanical norms. An industry finance for IoT and an Internet of Things Union Sensing China' has been established in Wuxi, started by more than 60 telecom administrators, foundations and organizations who are the essential drivers of the industry.

Drones for Deforestation

IoT is playing an important role in fabricating drones that are used to fight the fire when burning starts abruptly in the hot season. These drones are also successfully working in Bio carbon engineering for replanting those plants uprooted during deforesting; estimating that more than 6.5 billion trees are lost every year due to deforesting and natural disasters. These drones can replant 1 billion trees in one year.

According to senior bio-medical engineers, the lost plants can be recovered using three techniques simultaneously. Manpower requirement will reduce by using automated technology. It would not only reduce the cost of the process, but it would also increase the speed up the process. Land-scope designs and soil properties required to be done by using drones and other such instruments.

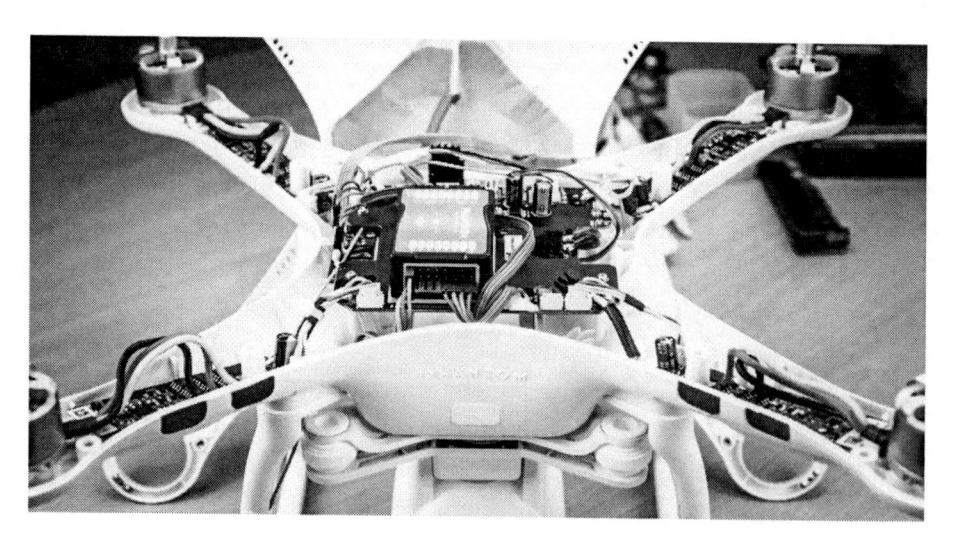

Figure 3. Linking Drone Implementation with IoT.

Natural Disaster Detection

IoT is playing a vital role in the detection of natural disasters. These devices equipped with sensing and connecting devices at the same time. These devices can detect the natural disasters before time, and they help to save humanity and wildlife accordingly. There is a different kind of specially designed tools and instruments for this purpose. Gizmos are a device that is used to detect as well as for forecasting the earthquake. This device placed on the earth surface near the epicenter. It obtains the signals from beneath the surface and transmits it to the surface. Figure 4 shows an Advantech device used to forecast and prevent the damages.

Figure 4. Device Advantech used on Snow Surface.

This device is used to find the resistance level of a snowy surface. A liquid crystal display screen is attached to the device to interpret the result (Tracy, 2016).

BENEFITS OF IoT

There are several benefits of IoT along with its impacts on the environment. Few of them are described below.

Reduce Pollution and Increase Sustainability

According to United Nations Environment Program (UNEP), the 40% of the global energy is absorbed by the buildings. They also consume 25% water of the world and the 60% global electricity. Building emits the greatest amount of greenhouses gases. According to the survey, an average building emits 1/3 percent of greenhouse gases. The environment is significantly affected when there is a reduction in energy consumption of the buildings. Watson IoT technologies are a popular tool of IoT in this regard. There are specific sensors that in this regard which indicates the amount of energy being consumed by the building. It also detects the AC activities, and the movements made by the objects in the building to make safe and secure. This tool helps owners to make better decisions regarding management, development, and maintenance.

Improve Food Security

The population of the world is growing exponentially. According to a survey, 2.3 billion people would increase on the planet by 2050. This increased population would require an increase in 70% present food capacity. IoT is helping the world in this regard. The yield of the crops will be increased using these methods. These tools accurately predict the real-time to plant the crops. They also help farmers by proper forecasting of weather conditions. Better supply chain management is also helping to keep an eye on the field during sowing and harvesting times. Such systems designed which are giving an accurate mixture of fertilizer and water at a perfect time, this is not only reducing extra cost, but it is also reducing the time. The best tool in this regard is Watson IoT platform. It tells the farmers about the water level situation of the certain field, and it also increases the production (Huang, IBM, 2016).

Delivery firms are already providing their customers with the capacity to track their packed orders at every processing point; however, the technology is an essential when adopted for businesses. IoT sensors fixed at the right place at the right time assist firms to track their assets immediately. The gathered information assist firms to find out inadequacies and jams in their chains of supply.

Understanding the Environmental Impacts on Health and Safety

According to the Global Burden of Disease Project, in 2015 about 95 million people around the globe were severely affected by the air pollution. And air pollution is causing 5.5 million deaths per year. Many big cities of the world are now moving towards this technique to provide a better atmosphere for their citizens. Different kind of sensors and mobile technologies are engaged in IoT to help the governments to overcome this problem. IBM and Beijing Environment Protection Bureau have successfully developed such devices to handle the air pollution problems in the major cities of the world. Watson IoT is helping these countries to fight against the air pollution. And according to survey almost 25% air pollution is reduced in Beijing in 2017.

Helping Ways of IoT in Environment

IoT is using several different techniques to help the environment. Some of the techniques are listed below:

Environmental Sensors

The sensor can perform difficult tasks which are not possible by human beings. The sensor is playing a vital role to find the evolution of the environment. There are different types of sensors used for various purposes.

- Different types of elements measured by these sensors like air, water, radiations, and various dangerous chemicals.
- Places which are highly polluted and hazardous to the health of humans can be easily reached and analyzed without risking any lives.
- People having infants and those who are suffering from the asthma problem are pre-informed of such places to take certain safety precautions.

IoT technology greatly is beneficial to medical field especially in transplanting human organs as well as wildlife.

Smart Farming

There is the tremendous impact of active farming on the environment, different kind of sensors and technologies incorporated for the betterment of this field. These sensors have created automatic irrigation which is playing a vital role to cultivate those areas which are water deficient, and they are stricken by the droughts.

- Different kinds of drones are used for the purpose to fly over the entire field and inspect various parameters without crushing and damaging the fields. They have particular spectral sensors on the board which is used to analyze the condition of fertilizers and water in the field.
- Drones are used to spray insecticides and pesticides by the airborne data obtained by the sensors (Telefónica IoT Team, 2016).

Global-Scaled Internet of Things

Global-scale Internet of Things (IoT) utilized in the worldwide scaled region represented with Unmanned Aerial Vehicle (UAV) and satellite systems. Both UAVs and satellites have an extensive scope and can associate with different gadgets on the ground. For example, sensors concentrate on information recovery from a sensor held by using a UAV. By utilizing a UAV to gather information frame sensors, a huge region can be secured, and the data accumulation can be more exile because of the versatility of UAV. Then again, sensors on the ground can gather different sorts of ecological data, for example, temperature, weight, dampness, and forth. Moreover, remote sensor systems are relied upon to assume a noteworthy part in a fiasco location. Especially, after East-Japan Catastrophic Disaster in March 2011, early and precise calamity discovery framework is required. In this manner, the reconciliation of UAV and remote sensor systems is one of the conceivable answers for subjective perception and fiasco identification frameworks. Also, the UAV can add to empowering communication in the disaster area. Inthedisas terrarium where ground-based stations utilized by existing specialized techniques were annihilated, and exchange-specific strategies can be given by handing-off the information from clients on the ground to surviving ground-based station using the UAV. Besides, building a system comprising of numerous UAVs for social affair data on the ground has been considered.

Practical System in Collaboration with IoT

In this section, we introduce two progressive common sense frameworks as cases of even minded IoT frameworks, one is worldwide scale, and another is a neighborhood. In cases, we represent the tidal wave identification structure and movement observing framework for constant concurrent use. In this presentation, the idea of these frameworks and a few examinations which led to these frameworks portrayed in the accompanying.

Energy Efficiency

According to the Boston Consulting Group, the IoT help to reduce the climate change by 17.8%. There is no such kind of technology which could reduce the environment changes till 2020 other than IoT. There are certain different parameters used by this technique right now. It includes the building of smart homes and buildings, smart grid services, using those home appliance which is energy saving and less costly. This technology has also reduced the usage of natural resources and especially in the field of auto- industry by introducing smart vehicles.

Energy Requirements

Internet of Things (IoT) has worked a lot to reduce the power requirements. According to its mega project LPWA, the main aim of the project is to use such sensors which use less power and extended battery life for years and they would be able to operate at long distance using the small antenna to reduce the energy consumption in the field itself (advanced, n.d.).

Future Perspective of IoT

In the future, things might be controlled not just inside the system that they are the parts of additionally with the state of other system scales. In such circumstances, it is important to consider the best approach to use the new kind of IoT frameworks evidently. In this area, we examine the future viewpoint of IoT with a few challenging issues.

Integrated Future IoT Systems

All existing exploration works consider the IoT framework in limited range or utilizing a constrained specialized strategy. In the prior segment, we classify these inquiries about into four gatherings, including the Web of Nana things, Web of Wi-Fi-empowered Devices, Web of Things (WoT) for Smart Society," and "Worldwide scaled Internet of things." As found in these works in each gathering, they endeavored to take care of the issue which happens inside the system that they are concentrating on. Furthermore, they don't utilize a wide assortment of specialized techniques. Also, from a deferent perspective, a significant portion of the prior research works meant to broaden the current examines on Wireless Sensor Networks (WSNs) to construct IoT-based networks.

Data Processing

Finally, we focus on the technology for controlling enormous information as the prerequisites for the future IoT framework. In the coordinated IoT framework, since different sorts of information gathered from numerous structures, massive amounts of information have been controlled. Existing chips away from massive data, there have been a few answers to manage a large measure of information now. Notwithstanding, the sum as well as the quantity of different information is very huge, which causes the difficulty of the elective vast data management in the coordinated IoT framework, administration plans for huge information in each size of the system, and a novel structure to control the abridged information is necessary for each system. As illustrated simply, it is demonstrated that there are many remaining issues to understand the future IoT framework. Since framework, coordinating different frameworks is required to control these old frameworks. Along these lines, to know the future organized IoT

Conclusion

Internet of Things (IoT) is playing an important role in reshaping the environment. It has great influence on the animal and human lives. This technology is much faster and better than any other technology present in the world right now. It is making the lives of people easy and luxurious. There are numerous benefits of IoT technology and highly influence the environment. Internet of things (IoT) is playing its role in every aspect of life. It is protecting and helping in various sectors to neutralize the harmful effects of natural and synthetic disasters. In short, there is no alternative to this technology up till 2020.

References

advancedmp. (n.d.). Retrieved from www..advancedmp.com: http://www.advancedmp.com/environmental-impact-of-IoT/.

Akyildiz I. F., Su W., Sankarasubramaniam Y., Cayirci E., Wireless Sensor Networks: A Survey, *Computer Networks* 38 (2002) 393–422.

Ashton K., That —Internet of Things ‖ Thing, *RFiD Journal*. (2009).

Atzori L., Iera A., Morabito G., The Internet of Things: A survey, *Computer Networks* 54 (2010) 2787–2805.

Belissent J., *Getting Clever About Smart Cities: New Opportunities Require New Business Models*, Forrester Research, 2010.

Buckley J., ed., *The Internet of Things: From RFID to the Next-Generation Pervasive Networked Systems,* Auerbach Publications, New York, 2006.

Caceres R., A. Friday, Ubicomp Systems at 20: Progress, Opportunities, and Challenges, *IEEE Pervasive Computing* 11 (2012) 14–21.

Gartner's Hype Cycle Special Report for 2011, *Gartner Inc.* http://www.gartner.com/technology/research/hype-cycles/ (2012).

Huang, A. (2016, August 31). *IBM*. Retrieved from www.ibm.com: https://www.ibm.com/blogs/internet-of-things/connected-world-sustainable-planet/.

Huang, A. (2016, August 31). *internet-of-things*. Retrieved from www.ibm.com/blogs/internet-of-things/connected-world-sustainable-planet/.

https://www.ibm.com/blogs/internet-of-things/connected-world-sustainable-planet/.

internetofthingsagenda.techtarget. (n.d.). Retrieved from:

www.internetofthingsagenda.techtarget.com: http://internetofthingsagenda.techtarget.com/definition/Internet-of-Things-IoT.

Johnstone R., Caputo D., Cella U., Gandelli A., Alippi C., Grimaccia F. et al., *Smart Environmental Measurement & Analysis Technologies (SEMAT): Wireless sensor networks in the marine environment*, in Stockholm, 2008.

Lin H., Zito R., Taylor M., A review of travel-time prediction in transport and logistics, *Proceedings of the Eastern Asia Society for Transportation Studies*. 5 (2005) 1433–1448.

Poslad, S. *Ubiquitous Computing: Smart Devices, Environments, and Interactions*. Wiley, ISBN: 978-0-470-03560-3, 2009, pp. 26.

Rogers Y., Moving on from weiser's vision of calm computing: Engaging ubicomp experiences, UbiComp 2006: *Ubiquitous Computing*. (2006).

Sundmaeker H., P. Guillemin, P. Friess, S. Woelfflé, Vision and challenges for realizing the Internet of Things, *Cluster of European Research Projects on the Internet of Things - CERP IoT*, 2010.

Telefónica IoT Team. (2016, July 1). *IoT.telefonic*. Retrieved from www.IoT.telefonica.com: https://IoT.telefonica.com/blog/5-ways-the-IoT-is-helping-the-environment.

Tracy, P. (2016, November 18). *rcrwireless.com*. Retrieved from www.rcrwireless.com: http://www.rcrwireless.com/20161118/telco-cloud/IoT-impact-environment-tag31-tag9

Vecchiloa C., University of Menlbourne, https://www.slideserve.com/sela/aneka-a-cloud-computing-platform.

Weiser M., Gold R., The origins of ubiquitous computing research at PARC in the late 1980s, *IBM Systems Journal*. (1999).

Yun M., B. Yuxin, Research on the architecture and key technology of Internet of Things (IoT) applied on smart grid, *Advances in Energy Engineering (ICAEE)*. (2010) 69–72.

Zhang M., Yu T., Zhai G. F., *Smart Transport System Based on ―The Internet of Things,‖Amm*. 48-49 (2011) 1073–1076.

Chapter 4

THE INTERNET OF THINGS: TECHNOLOGICAL, PHYSICAL, BUSINESS AND SOCIO-ECONOMIC ENVIRONMENTS

INTRODUCTION

The Internet of Things (IoT) is a technical revolution that is revitalizing a ubiquitous interconnection of new devices. IoT enables cutting-edge technology to leverage the tools necessary to improve, analyze, track, and respond to operational data at an infinite scale. The limitations of IoT have not been clearly defined because of the complexity and interconnectivity of devices. The possibilities and immersive scaling techniques that IoT bring to infrastructure models like cloud computing, data analytics, machine learning are redefining what is possible and what is the next step in the tech industry. But to clearly and ultimately embrace what IoT can do, one must demonstrate the value in business and social impact that IoT has. IoT embraces all forms of business personnel from engineers, developers, designers, technologists, and analysts and roots itself in the core principals of their roles in technology and business.

The Internet of Things has created a general-purpose solution pattern around the content and devices it controls. Common characteristics exist between each pattern similarly to internet protocols like IPv4, IPv6, IPsec, etc. There are five elements that produce an IoT pattern and provide analytics for real-world scenarios. They are: Solution Creator – Who designs, engineers, and build the IoT solution? Audience – Who buys the solution, and who will use it? Position in the product/service lifecycle – Is the solution positioned as a product or service that is an end-to-itself or does it enhance or augment an existing, mature product or service? Connection – How does the solution connect to the internet? Integration – Does the solution require integration with other business or enterprise systems? These elements are the key to understanding the immersive technical connection IoT can bring to the workplace. The most important part of IoT is the groundbreaking technology that is embedding itself into our daily life. Using these elements consumers and producers alike can diversify and accurately predict models based on live data around goods and services.

The Internet of Things is considered to be an "edge" technology. This means that the sensors, controllers, agents, things etc. that makeup IoT live on the outer portions of the network in order to provide faster connections to the internet. Using tools like gateway servers and cloud controllers allow for IoT devices to relay information even faster. Because the IoT devices are small and use relatively low power consumption it is possible to increase the capacity centralized host operators can handle. This funnels the load into one centralized point instead of requiring each individual point to manually speak to the controller itself. This "funnel" allows for IoT to expand and scale rapidly as new devices are provisioned and more data is generated than ever before. Cloud services and computing power expand the capabilities of IoT infinitely by only limiting the amount of data transferred by bandwidth between endpoints.

The "cloud" and IoT go hand in hand. The cloud is still a groundbreaking technology and enhances every day with models and pricing figures from providers. The days of modern equipment requests and service providers are shifting. Infrastructure as a service (IaaS), Platform as a Service (PaaS), and Software as a Service (SaaS) all create business advantages for companies and consumers to take advantage of. As the cloud emerges into a new standard and revolutionizes the way we compute and handle daily tasks, IoT will expand further. The cloud provides the ability to "pay-as-you-go" and only utilizes what you actually need. There is no wasted computing power or resources because it expands based on the inputs and loads currently expressed to the system. IoT can leverage this tech to parse data and provide results in real time.

The interfaces we currently work with today will not be the interfaces we interact with tomorrow. UX teams across the globe are embracing the software and application solutions required to bring IoT to life. Platforms like iOS, Android, Linux, Windows, MacOS, etc. all leverage elements that feed into IoT. The Power that IoT has is to bring an application to multiple platforms and use the interface of the internet to connect all these devices. Efficiency and quality of development and project management in regards to application design and interaction will directly impact the use and adoption of IoT in the modern world.

IoT will be the next internet revolution. The consumption of devices and services has created a demand for more data than ever before. IoT brings that data with definitive characteristics that allow interpretation by regular users. IoT is the next step in revolutionary technological advancement; it will affect all fields of business, and change the world we live in forever.

In this chapter, we will discuss an outline of the key things identified with the improvement of IoT advancements in various environments. Various research challenges have been distinguished, which are relied upon to wind up distinctly real research inclines in the following years. The most significant application fields will be introduced, and various utilize cases are distinguished. The likelihood of consistently consolidating the genuine and the virtual world, through the monstrous arrangement of installed devices, opens up new energizing bearings for both research and business.

TECHNOLOGICAL ENVIRONMENT IN IoT/IoE

Computers, devices, and machines were at that point associated when the term IoT was created. The idea picked up steam for its capacity to interface the detached physical-first objects already unequipped for producing, transmitting and getting information unless expanded or controlled. Inserting sensors, control systems, and processors into these objects empower flat correspondence over a multi-hub, open network of physical-first objects. In spite of the fact that the idea of the Internet of Everything rose as a characteristic improvement of the IoT development and is to a great extent connected with Cisco's strategies to start another showcasing domain, IoE includes the more extensive idea of connectivity from the point of view of present-day connectivity innovation utilize cases. The Internet of Everything (IoE) sets up a conclusion to-end ecosystem of connectivity including innovations, procedures, and ideas utilized overall connectivity utilize cases. By 2017 connected devices will rise around 1.7 billion, as indicated by the Cisco Visual Networking Index. These connections make up the Internet of Things (IoT) which are particularly identifiable objects and their virtual portrayals in an Internet-like structure.

Ubiquitous sensing is empowered by wireless sensor network cuts crosswise over numerous zones of current living. This offers the capacity to quantify, induce and comprehend environmental pointers, from fragile ecologies and regular assets to urban environments. The expansion of these devices in a conveying activating network makes the Internet of Things (IoT), wherein, sensors and actuators mix consistently with the environment around us, and the data is shared crosswise over stages keeping in mind the end goal to build up a typical operating picture (COP). Powered by the current adjustment of an assortment of empowering gadget innovations, for example, RFID tags etc., NFC devices and inserted sensor and actuator hubs, the IoT has ventured out of its earliest stages and is the following progressive technology in changing the Internet into a completely coordinated Future Internet. As we move from static web pages to informal communication web to universal figuring web, the requirement for information on-request utilizing modern natural questions increments fundamentally. This paper introduces a cloud-driven vision for environmental execution of Internet of Things in various settings like a business, financial, environmental and technological.

Distributed Systems Technology

The distributed execution of routing conventions is one of the major algorithmic building obstructs for networked systems. Be that as it may, as observed above, versatility issues debilitate multi-jump interchanges for environmental information recovery, i.e., monstrous and extensive scale sensor networks don't show up a reasonable answer for IoT.

This territory incorporates all angles identified with empowering objects to fabricate a network, making a distributed stage that empowers the simple usage of administrations on top. This expands on a conventional research line in software engineering, where a distributed system is characterized as a system driven by partitioned segments which might be executed either successively or in parallel on various, interconnected, hubs. The plan of designs and conventions for distributed systems is a key issue for general networked systems and for IoT specifically. Specifically, a few issues, required in the outline of IoT as a distributed system, can be recognized. The examination and outline of IoT can't disregard angles identified with networking advances, for example, routing conventions, stream control power, and synchronization.

From the execution viewpoint, a key issue is to facilitate the between working from an application point of view. Practically speaking, what is normally given is a middleware stage ensuring a pre-characterized framework for improvement and execution of distributed applications. Middleware correspondences may include synchronous, non-concurrent, message or demand arranged techniques. The IoT domain traverses any of those models relying upon the particular application focused on.

Synchronization of timekeepers for assignments, which may experience disappointments and restart, has likewise been tended to widely in the writing. In the IoT situation, the predicted substantial scale enhances the difficulties for both for information consistency reasons and conventions working purposes.

Computing, Identification and Communication in IoT Technologies

The situations imagined for IoT require the improvement of cutting-edge strategies ready to implant figuring, correspondence and distinguishing proof abilities into regular objects. The commonplace approach sought after in such works identifies with the match of the RF front-end initiation examples to the movement design. The utilization of such conventions, notwithstanding, at present does not give a last response to the advancement of vitality utilization versus versatility issues. These are of principal significance for IoT situations, as battery substitution is an exorbitant procedure to be maintained a strategic distance from however much as expected, particularly for large-scale arrangements. Moreover, the essential thought of such conventions is to perform dynamic/rest obligation cycles keeping in mind the end goal to spare the power scattered out. The traverse is wide, running from the exploration on ease low-control utilization miniaturized nano-gadgets, to progression in close field correspondences. Low-control interchanges are a settled research field inside the sensor networking group, as demonstrated by the dynamic research performed in the most recent decade on power utilization mindful medium get to conventions.

The expansion in message dormancy thus should be exchanged off keeping in mind the end goal to adjust between network lifetime and correspondence execution. All the more as of late, advances in the field of nano-scale gatherers and in addition vitality reaping systems show up of noticeable enthusiasm to constrain the requirement for battery substitutions. Specifically, it has been demonstrated that it is conceivable to incorporate a few wellsprings of vitality collecting into sensors, including piezoelectric, thermoelectric and radio waves reviving devices.

The push to diminish the speed of disposing of IoT devices has another measurement of specific significance, which identifies with the equal collaboration amongst calculation and correspondence. The thought of dispersing calculation with a specific end goal to lessen the correspondence overhead, which is for the most part named in-network handling or in network figuring, is commonly connected to remote sensor networks that perform nearby estimations, as it would be the situation of field estimations in IoT situations.

Device Management

Device Management profit from the Internet of Things, you'll require an effective IoT gadget administration arrangement that can limit the unpredictability of maintaining an associated business. Building Internet of Things design offers huge business benefits. You can make new income streams, quicken item development, grow your plan of action and draw in clients in new and energizing ways. In any case, to receive every one of these benefits, you'll require an approach to effortlessly deal with your associated gadgets – and that is the place IoT gadget administration comes in.

Safely associating thousands or a large number of gadgets is no simple errand; however, the privilege IoT gadget administration programming will give you a chance to finish it rapidly and effectively. Your IoT gadget administration innovation should likewise make it simple to deal with and to incorporate the expansive volumes of information your gadgets will deliver. What's more, a prevalent IoT gadget administration arrangement will help you transform that information into the understanding you have to grow new items and benefits and to charm your clients with development.

Lively, a division of LogMeIn offers grant winning IoT gadget administration and IoT cloud arrangements that give a speedier way to benefit in the Internet of Things. Lively gives you a chance to show and interface items rapidly and promptly begin tuning in to the information they give. You'll know right away when another item comes on the web or when a current item encounters an issue. Livery's IoT gadget administration arrangement gives you a chance to incorporate information from your items with existing business frameworks, giving your item advancement groups new understanding from a genuine client base to drive more imaginative item improvement. Also, with lively security IoT highlights, you can without much of a stretch validate clients and ensure information while on gadgets, in travel and inside other applications.

Sensor Data Acquisition in Management

Andy Lin, Senior Manager, Advantech Embedded Core Group in this day and age, the foundation gave by brilliant city and mechanical robotization frameworks empower nonstop availability. The shared trait shared by such frameworks is their relationship with the Internet of Things (IoT). With the incorporation of sensors and control gadgets, whole foundations can be coordinated with data and correspondence advances, bringing about arranged and implanted gadgets that empower smart observing and administration. With the simple arrangement and adaptability of sensor gadgets, remote sensor systems (WSN) can include various sensor hubs that gather data. The gathered data then gives a database to further examination; the aftereffects of which can be utilized to enhance the dependability and effectiveness of existing framework frameworks. Considering the quick advancement of sensor innovation, WSNs are relied upon to wind up noticeably a key IoT technology.

Wireless I/O Connectivity Modules and Gateway Solution

For engineers, the greatest test of planning for the IoT is guaranteeing wireless availability. The idea of the IoT includes new gadgets planned with IoT similarity, as well as existing frameworks that work outside the IoT cloud. Be that as it may, to set up a universal billow of interconnected gadgets, none IP-based gadgets must have the capacity to associate with each other without requiring Ethernet or a Wi-Fi interface and going with convention stack. This can be accomplished utilizing wireless I/O interface modules and passages that empower Internet access with regards to genuine applications. Besides, adding shrewd sensor control programming to passages can rearrange the plan of IoT frameworks by giving access to shared preparing test of planning for the IoT is guaranteeing wireless availability. The idea of the IoT includes new gadgets planned with

IoT similarity, as well as existing frameworks that work outside the IoT cloud. Be that as it may, to set up a universal billow of interconnected gadgets, none IP-based gadgets must have the capacity to associate with each other without requiring Ethernet or a Wi-Fi interface and going with convention stack. This can be accomplished utilizing wireless I/O interface modules and passages that empower Internet access with regards to genuine applications. Besides, adding shrewd sensor control programming to passages can rearrange the plan of IoT frameworks by giving access to shared preparing resources.

Industrial Applications Based on IoT

In short, the Internet of Things alludes to the quickly developing system of associated items that can gather and trade information utilizing inserted sensors. Indoor regulators, autos, lights, iceboxes, and more apparatuses can all be associated with the IoT. To help clear up how the Internet of Things functions, we've laid out a few applications for the IoT, alongside some particular gadgets and illustrations.

Smart Home: The smart home is likely the most prominent IoT application right now since the one is most reasonable and promptly accessible to shoppers. From the Amazon Echo to the Nest Thermostat, there are many items available that clients can control with their voices to make their lives more associated than ever.

Wearable: Watches are no longer only to tell time. The Apple Watch and different smartwatches available have transformed our wrists into cell phone holsters by empowering content informing, telephone calls, and that's only the tip of the iceberg. What's more, gadgets, for example, Fitbit and Jawbone have altered the wellness world by giving individuals more information about their workouts?

Connected Car: These vehicles are equipped with Internet functioning much the same as interfacing with a remote system in a home or office. More vehicles are beginning to come outfitted with this usefulness, so plan to see more applications incorporated into future cars.

Data Integration

The Internet of Things (IoT) is a systems administration worldview where interconnected, brilliant questions consistently produce information and transmit it over the Internet. A significant part of the IoT activities is adapted towards assembling ease and vitality effective equipment for these items, and additionally the correspondence advancements that give objects interconnectivity. Notwithstanding, the answers for overseeing and use the monstrous volume of information delivered by these articles are yet to develop. Conventional database administration arrangements miss the mark in fulfilling the advanced application needs of an IoT organize that has a really worldwide scale. Current answers for IoT information administration address incomplete parts of the IoT condition with exceptional concentrate on sensor systems. In this paper, we study the information administration arrangements that are proposed for IoT or subsystems of the IoT. We highlight the particular outline primitives that we accept ought to be tended to in an IoT information administration arrangement, and examine how they are drawn closer by the proposed arrangements. We at long last propose an information administration structure for IoT that mulls over the talked about plan components and goes about as a seed to a complete IoT information administration arrangement. The structure we propose adjusts a unified, information and sources-driven way to deal with a connection the differing Things with their wealth of information to the potential applications and administrations that are imagined for IoT.

Conventional information administration frameworks handle the capacity, recovery, and refresh of rudimentary information things, records and documents. With regards to IoT, information administration frameworks must outline information on the web while giving stockpiling, logging, and evaluating offices for disconnected examination. This grows the idea of information administration from disconnected stockpiling, inquiry handling, and exchange administration operations into online-disconnected correspondence/stockpiling double operations. We first characterize the information lifecycle inside the setting of IoT and after that diagram the vitality utilization profile for each of the stages keeping in mind the end goal to have a superior understanding of IoT data management.

Interoperability and Diversity

The Internet of Things (IoT) is a ubiquitous system of physical and virtual articles and assets that are outfitted with detecting, registering, activating, and correspondence abilities. However, albeit billions of these articles have as of now been sent, something is abating IoT arrangement selection: gadget incongruence.

The first IoT vision includes a hyper-associated worldwide biological community in which "things" speak with other "things" at whatever point expected to convey profoundly expanded administrations to the client. Such correspondence must be autonomous of the maker of a given section of the framework. Actually, notwithstanding, every seller has its own IoT arrangement that is contradictory with different arrangements, in this way making nearby IoT storehouses.

That is the reason, today, numerous IoT scientists and industry pioneers are concentrating on interoperability. The EU's Unify-IoT extends, for instance, as of late broke down more than 300 accessible IoT stages and found that around 20 are "to some degree prominent to famous." Based on this investigation, the EU has chosen to reserve seven research ventures (see the IoT Projects sidebar) that try to address interoperability between and inside IoT biological communities.

This December 2016 Computing Now subject presents six articles in this imperative research region. As a result of the unlimited scope of points identified with IoT interoperability, we likewise incorporate a video from industry agents, interviews with six specialists from IoT-arranged organizations, and three sidebars with connections to extra articles (Further Reading), pertinent sites (IoT Projects), and learning materials.

Applications

The Internet of Things (IoT) is on its approach to turning into the following innovative unrest. As indicated by Gartner, income created from IoT items and administrations will surpass $300 billion in 2020, and that presumably is quite recently the tip of the ice sheet. Given the gigantic measure of income and information that the IoT will produce, its effect will be felt over the whole enormous information universe, constraining organizations to redesign current apparatuses and procedures, and innovation to advance to oblige this extra information volume and exploit the bits of knowledge this new information without a doubt will convey.

When we discuss IoT, one of the primary things that ring a bell is a gigantic, consistent stream of information hitting organizations' information stockpiling. Server farms must be prepared to deal with this extra heap of heterogeneous information. Because of this immediate effect on huge information stockpiling framework, numerous associations are moving toward the Platform as a Service (PaaS) display as opposed to keeping their own stockpiling foundation, which would require a persistent extension to deal with the heap of huge information. PaaS is a cloud-based, oversaw arrangement that gives adaptability, adaptability, consistency, and a modern engineering to store profitable IoT information.

Distributed storage alternatives incorporate private, open, and half-breed models. On the off chance that organizations have touchy information or information that is liable to administrative consistence necessities that require increased security, a private cloud model may be the best fit. Something else, an open or half-breed model can be picked as a capacity for IoT information. While choosing the innovation stack for huge information handling, the enormous flood of information that the IoT will convey must be remembered. Associations should adjust innovations to outline IoT information. System, circle, and register control all will be affected and ought to be wanted to take care of this new type of data.

Performance

In the context of the Internet of Things also, huge scale information created from these gadgets, Intel Internet of Things Analytics Dashboard offers information mining from geologically dispersed gadgets sensors. The temperature remote online sensors sent all through the transportation expressways topographically total the information to a nearby information accumulation point. The Intel IoT Analytics site accumulates the majority of this information by association with a variety of sensor-construct arranges in light of the web and preprocesses the substantial scale web information created from the Internet of Things gadgets for giving dashboard investigation. This huge measure of information goes to the information accumulation point at first through remote, wired, or Bluetooth arrange. The greater part of this information gets gathered into Intel Galileo and Edison Dashboards. One the information is gathered preprocessed through the standards motor, the information gets stored on IoT analytics web servers.

VISION, ARCHITECTURAL ELEMENTS, AND FUTURE DIRECTIONS

Ubiquitous sensing empowered is Wireless Sensor Network (WSN) advancements cut crosswise over numerous regions of current living. This offers the capacity to quantify, surmise and comprehend ecological pointers, from fragile ecologies and normal assets to urban conditions. The multiplication of these gadgets in a conveying inciting system makes the Internet of Things (IoT), wherein, sensors and actuators mix consistently with the earth around us, and the data is shared crosswise over stages keeping in mind the end goal to build up a typical working picture (COP). Fueled by the current adjustment of an assortment of empowering remote innovations, for example, RFID labels and installed sensor and actuator hubs, the IoT has ventured out of its outset and is the following progressive innovation in changing the Internet into a completely incorporated Future Internet. As we move from www (static pages web) to web2 (informal communication web) to web3 (universal registering web), the requirement for information on-request utilizing complex natural questions increments altogether. This paper exhibits a Cloud-driven vision for overall usage of the Internet of Things. The key empowering advances and application areas that are probably going to drive IoT to look into sooner rather than later are examined. A Cloud usage utilizing Aneka, which depends on the connection of private and open Clouds, is exhibited. We close our IoT vision by developing the requirement for the union of WSN, the Internet and appropriated figuring coordinated at innovative research community.

The IoT Connectivity

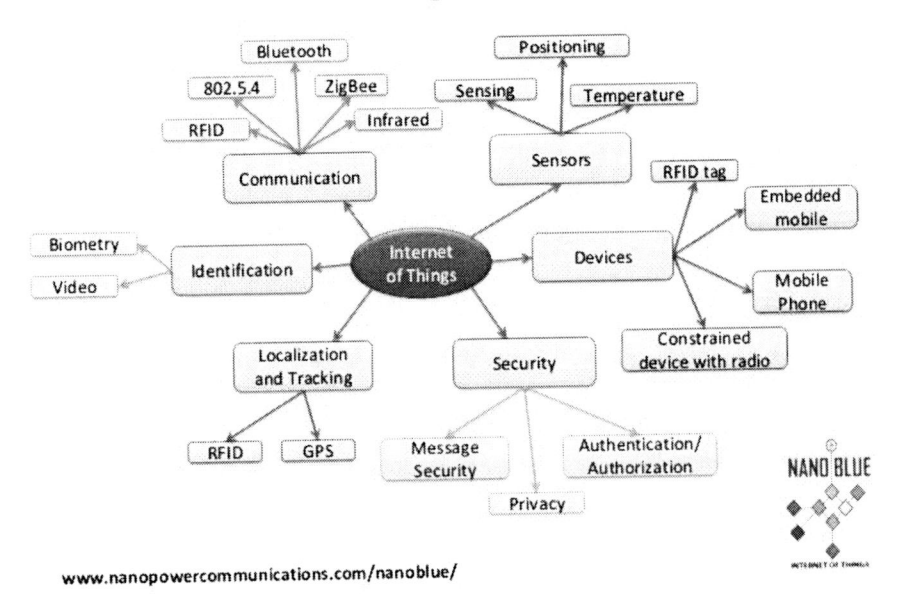

Figure 1. Interconnected gadgets.

The next wave in the era of figuring will be outside the domain of the customary desktop. In the Internet of Things (IoT) worldview, a large portion of the items that encompass us will be on the system in some shape. Radio Frequency Identification (RFID) and sensor organize innovations will ascend to meet this new test, in which data and correspondence frameworks are imperceptibly inserted in the earth around us. These outcomes in the era of huge measures of information which must be put away prepared and displayed in a consistent, productive, and effortlessly interpretable shape. This model will comprise of administrations that are items and conveyed in a way like customary wares. Distributed computing can give the virtual foundation to such utility processing which coordinates checking gadgets, stockpiling gadgets, examination apparatuses, perception stages and customer conveyance. The cost-based model that Cloud registering offers will empower end-to-end benefit provisioning for organizations and clients to get to applications on request from anywhere.

The term Internet of Things was initially instituted by Kevin Ashton in 1999 with regards to production network administration. Be that as it may, in the previous decade, the definition has been more comprehensive covering an extensive variety of utilizations like social insurance, utilities, transport, and so on. Despite the fact that the meaning of 'Things' has changed as innovation developed, the main objective of appearing well and good data without the guide of human intercession continues as before. A radical development of the present Internet into a Network of interconnected items that not just collect data from nature detecting and interfaces with the physical world incitation/summon/control, additionally utilizes existing Internet norms to give administrations to data exchange, examination, applications, and interchanges. Fuelled by the pervasiveness of gadgets empowered by open remote innovation, for example, Bluetooth, radio recurrence recognizable proof (RFID), Wi-Fi, and telephonic information benefits and additionally implanted sensor and actuator hubs, IoT has ventured out of its early stages and is very nearly changing the present static Internet into a completely incorporated future internet. The internet unrest prompted the interconnection between individuals at an exceptional scale and pace. The following unrest will be the interconnection between items to make a keen domain. Just in 2011, the quantity of interconnected gadget on the planet surpassed the real number of individuals. Right now there are 9 billion interconnected gadgets and it is relied upon to achieve 24 billion devices by 2020.

Ubiquitous Computing in the Next Decade

The effort by researchers to create a human-to-human interface through innovation in the late 1980s brought about the production of the universal registering discipline, whose goal is to insert innovation out of the spotlight of regular daily existence. Presently, we are in the post-PC time where advanced mobile phones and other handheld gadgets are changing our condition by making it more intelligent and also useful. Check Weiser, the progenitor of Ubiquitous Computing (ubicomp), characterized a shrewd situation as the physical world that is luxuriously and undetectably entwined with sensors, actuators Internet of Things Schematic demonstrating the end clients and application ranges in view of information and computational components, inserted flawlessly in the ordinary objects of our lives, and associated through a ceaseless system.

The formation of the Internet has denoted a preeminent point of reference towards accomplishing ubicomp vision which empowers singular gadgets to speak with whatever another gadget on the planet. The between systems administration uncovers the capability of an apparently interminable measure of circulated figuring assets and capacity possessed by different proprietors.

As opposed to Weiser's Calm registering approach, Rogers proposes a human-driven ubicomp which makes utilization of human imagination in misusing the earth and amplifying their capacities. He proposes an area particular ubicomp arrangement when he says In terms of who ought to profit, it is valuable to consider how ubicomp innovations can be created not for the Sal's of the world, but rather for specific spaces that can be set up and altered by an individual firm or association, for example, for agribusiness generation, natural restoration or retailing.

IoT Elements

We present a taxonomy that will help in characterizing the parts required for the Internet of Things from an abnormal state point of view. Particular scientific categorizations of every segment can be discovered somewhere else. There are three IoT segments which empower consistent ubicomp: a) Hardware - made up of sensors, actuators and installed correspondence equipment b) Middleware - on request stockpiling and processing devices for information examination and c) Presentation - novel straightforward representation and understanding instruments which can be generally gotten to on various stages and which can be intended for various applications. In this segment, we examine a couple empowering advances in these classifications which will make up the three segments stated above.

Radio Frequency Identification (RFID)

RFID technology is a significant achievement in the implanted correspondence worldview which empowers plan of microchips for remote information correspondence. They help in the programme ID of anything they are appended to going about as an electronic standardized tag. The aloof RFID labels are not battery controlled and they utilize the energy per user's cross-examination flag to convey the ID to the RFID reader. This has brought about numerous applications especially in retail and store network administration. The applications can be found in transportation (substitution of tickets, enlistment stickers and get to control applications too. The inactive labels are as of now being utilized as a part of many bank cards and street toll labels which is among the principal worldwide arrangements. Dynamic RFID peruses have their own battery supply and can instantiate the correspondence. Of the few applications, the fundamental utilization of dynamic RFID labels is in port holders for monitoring cargo.

Wireless Sensor Networks (WSN)

Recent technological advances in low power incorporated circuits and wireless communications have made accessible proficient, ease, low power small-scale gadgets for use in remote detecting applications. The mix of these variables has enhanced the feasibility of using a sensor network comprising of countless sensors, empowering the accumulation, handling, examination, and spread of important data, assembled in an assortment of situations. Dynamic RFID is about the same as the lower end WSN hubs with constrained handling capacity and capacity. The logical difficulties that must be overcome with a specific end goal to understand the gigantic capability of WSNs are generous and multidisciplinary in nature. Sensor information is shared among sensor hubs and sent to an appropriated or brought together a framework for investigation. The segments that make up the WSN monitoring network include.

1. *WSN equipment:* Typically a hub (WSN center equipment) contains sensor interfaces, preparing units, handset units and power supply. Quite often, they contain numerous A/D converters for sensor interfacing and more present-day sensor hubs can convey utilizing one recurrence band making them more adaptable.
2. *WSN correspondence stack*: The hubs are required to be conveyed in an ad way for general applications. Planning a fitting topology, directing and MAC layer is basic for adaptability and lifespan of the sent system. Hubs in a WSN need to impart among themselves to transmit information in single or multi-jump to a base station. The correspondence stack at the sink hub ought to have the capacity to interface with the outside world through the Internet to go about as a door to the WSN subnet and the Internet.
3. *WSN Middleware:* A component to join digital framework with a Service Oriented Architecture (SOA) and sensor systems to give access to heterogeneous sensor assets in an organization freeway. This depends on secluding assets that can be utilized by a few applications. A stage free middleware for creating sensor applications is required, for example, an Open Sensor Web Architecture (OSWA). OSWA is based upon a uniform arrangement of operations and standard information portrayals as characterized in the Sensor Web Enablement Method (SWE) by the Open Geospatial Consortium (OGC).

Secure Data Accumulation

A productive and secure information conglomeration technique is required for developing the lifetime of the system and in addition, guaranteeing solid information gathered from sensors. As hub disappointments are a typical normal for WSNs, the system topology ought to have the capacity to recuperate itself. Guaranteeing security is basic as the framework is naturally connected to actuators and shielding the frameworks from interlopers moves toward becoming very important.

Addressing Schemes

The ability to uniquely identify Things' is basic for the accomplishment of IoT. This won't just permit us to interestingly distinguish billions of gadgets additionally to control remote gadgets through the Internet. A couple of most basic components of making a special address are uniqueness, dependability, determination, and versatility. Each component that is as of now associated and those that will be associated must be recognized by their one of a kind ID, area, and functionalities. The current IPv4 may support a degree where a gathering of living together sensor gadgets can be recognized topographically, however not independently. The Internet Mobility properties in the IPV6 may lighten a portion of the gadget recognizable proof issues; be that as it may, the heterogeneous way of remote hubs, variable information sorts, simultaneous operations and conversion of information from gadgets compounds the issue promote.

Persevering system working to channel the information activity universally and steadily is another part of IoT. Despite the fact is that the TCP/IP deals with this instrument by steering in a more solid and proficient path, from source to goal, the IoT faces a bottleneck at the interface between the portal and remote sensor gadgets. Besides, the adaptability of the gadget address of the current system must be practical. The expansion of systems and gadgets must not hamper the execution of the system, the working of the gadgets, and the unwavering quality of the information over the system or the viable utilization of the gadgets from the UI.

To address these issues, the Uniform Resource Name (URN) framework is viewed as basic for the advancement of IoT. URN makes imitations of the assets that can be gotten to through the URL. With a lot of spatial information being accumulated, it is frequently very essential to exploit the advantages of metadata for exchanging the data from a database to the client by means of the Internet. IPv6 likewise gives a decent alternative to get to the assets remarkably and remotely. Another basic advancement intending to is the improvement of a light-weight IPv6 that will empower tending to home appliances uniquely.

Data Storage and Analytics

One of the most important outcomes of this developing field is the production of an exceptional measure of information. Capacity, possession, and expiry of the information wind up noticeably basic issues. The web expands up to 5% of the aggregate vitality created today and with these sorts of requests, it is certain to go up considerably further. Thus, server farms that keep running on the reaped vitality and are concentrated will guarantee vitality productivity and additionally dependability. The information must be put away and utilized wisely for shrewd observing. It is critical to creating man-made brainpower calculations which could be brought together or dispersed in light of the need. Novel combination calculations should be produced to comprehend the information gathered. Cutting edge non-straight, fleeting machine learning strategies in light of developmental calculations, hereditary calculations, neural systems, and other manmade brainpower methods are important to accomplish mechanized basic leadership. These frameworks demonstrate qualities, for example, interoperability, combination and versatile correspondences. They likewise have a measured engineering both regarding equipment framework configuration and in addition programming advancement and are normally extremely appropriate for IoT applications. All the more important, it brought together a foundation to bolster stockpiling and investigation is required. This structures the IoT middleware layer and there are various difficulties included which are examined in future segments. Starting at 2012, Cloud-based capacity arrangements are winding up plainly progressively prominent and in the years ahead, cloud-based investigation and representation platforms are foreseen.

Visualization

Visualization is critical for an IoT application as this permits association of the client with nature. With late advances in touchscreen innovations, utilization of shrewd tablets and telephones has turned out to be exceptionally instinctive. For a layman to completely profit by the IoT upheaval, appealing and straightforward perception must be made. As we move from 2D to 3D screens, more data can be given in important approaches to shoppers. This will likewise empower strategy producers to change over information into learning, which is basic in quick basic leadership. Extraction of significant data from crude information is non-trifling. This includes both occasion recognition and representation of the related crude and displayed information, with data spoke to as indicated by the necessities of the end-user.

APPLICATIONS

There are several application spaces which will be affected by the rising of the Internet of Things. The applications can be grouped in view of the sort of system accessibility, scope, scale, heterogeneity, repeatability, client association, and effect. We arrange the applications into four application areas: (1) Personal and Home; (2) Enterprise; (3) Utilities; and (4) Mobile. which speaks to Personal and Home IoT at the size of an individual or home, Enterprise IoT at the size of a group, Utility IoT at a national or territorial scale and Mobile IoT which is normally spread crosswise over different areas for the most part because of the way of network and scale. There is an enormous hybrid in applications and the utilization of information between areas. For example, the Personal and Home IoT produces power utilization information in the house and makes it accessible to the power (utility) organization which can thus streamline the free market activity in the Utility IoT. Web empowers sharing of information between various specialist organizations in a consistent way making numerous business openings. A couple of run of the mill applications in each domain are given.

Personal and Home

The sensor information gathered is utilized just by the people who specifically possess the system. Normally Wi-Fi is utilized as the spine empowering higher transmission capacity information (video) exchange and in addition, higher examining rates (Sound). Omnipresent medicinal services have been imagined for as long as two decades. IoT gives an immaculate stage to understand this vision utilizing body territory sensors and IoT backend to transfer the information to servers. For example, a Smartphone can be utilized for correspondence alongside a few interfaces like Bluetooth for interfacing sensors measuring physiological parameters. Up until this point, there are a few applications accessible for Apple iOS, Google Android and Windows Phone working framework that measure different parameters. In any case, it is yet to be brought together in the cloud for general doctors to access the same.

Control of home hardware, for example, aeration and cooling systems, fridges, clothes washers and so forth will permit better home and vitality administration. This will see shoppers wind up plainly required in the IoT insurgency in an indistinguishable way from the Internet transformation itself. Long range interpersonal communication is set to experience another change with billions of interconnected articles. An intriguing improvement will utilize a Twitter-like idea where individual Things 'in the house can occasionally tweet the readings which can be effortlessly taken after from anyplace making a Twee tot. Despite the fact that this gives a typical structure utilizing the cloud for data get to, another security worldview will be required for this to be fully realized.

Utilities

The information from the systems in this application space is for the most part for administration improvement as opposed to customer utilization. It is as of now being utilized by service organizations (brilliant meter by power supply organizations) for asset administration keeping in mind the end goal to improve cost versus benefit. These are comprised of exceptionally broad systems (typically laid out by extensive association on the territorial and national scale) for observing basic utilities and proficient asset administration. The spine organizes utilized can fluctuate between cell, Wi-Fi and satellite correspondence.

Savvy matrix and keen metering is another potential IoT application which is being actualized the world over [38]. Effective vitality utilization can be accomplished by constantly checking each power point inside a house and utilizing this data to adjust the way power is devoured. This data at the city scale is utilized for keeping up the heap adjust inside the matrix guaranteeing the high quality of service.

Distributed AI

A related research field is that of distributed artificial intelligence (AI), which addresses how independent programming elements, more often than not alluded to as 'specialists,' can be made ready to collaborate with the environment and among themselves in such an approach to viably seek after a given worldwide objective. See that in this domain a noteworthy test must be confronted, contrasted with the customary plan of a distributed system. Indeed, consider a basic undertaking that includes the coordination of a few self-governing elements: e.g., voting, selling, or bunch arrangement. The plan of such applications needs to represent the way that piece of the control lives on single specialists. Those are the substances that at last associate and may pick diverse methodologies relying upon a specific utility capacity. In this way, at system configuration time, it is conceivable to use the hypothesis of aggressive/agreeable recreations and let operators contend/shape coalitions upon their requirements. Hypothetical establishments for these themes are established in diversion hypothesis and social welfare. The entrance to the IoT devices is probably not going to be midway booked; on the other hand, it will be likely chosen in light of nearby connection of IoT clients and devices. This thus may animate a diversion hypothetical way to deal with the subsequent issue of asset sharing in the IoT.

TECHNOLOGICAL IMPACT AREAS AND APPLICATIONS

The idea of Internet-of-Things, with its vision of Internet-associated objects of different abilities and shape elements, could support the part of ICT as advancement empowering agent in an assortment of use markets.

The expansion in the utilization of RFID, preparing to make Internet-of-Things the truth, is not just a consequence of technological push; it is likewise determined by the market pull since ventures are progressively understanding the business advantages of uses that can be acknowledged with Internet-of-Things advancements. Presently, envision this connectivity being conveyed to regular objects: coolers, autos, glasses, keys, and so ones it will be empowered by IoT. One of the technological mainstays IS of the Internet-of-Things, to be specific RFID technology, has as of now been fused into a wide exhibit of items. Selection of RFID technology in the industry stopped in 2008 as an outcome of the worldwide monetary downturn, yet this decline got adjusted by the government approvals of RFID.

A gigantic market opportunity exists for Internet-of-Things, identified with the likelihood of networking keen things and of giving applications utilizing said connectivity. Other than improving the aggressiveness of different vertical markets, IoT innovations can open up new business openings by: (I) connecting vertical markets, offering ascend to cross-cutting applications and administrations, in view of the utilization of a typical fundamental ICT stage, (ii) empowering the emerging and development of new market portions and applications, made conceivable by the capacity, gave by IoT advances, to communicate with physical objects through computerized means and (iii) streamlining business forms by utilizing on cutting edge examination procedures connected to IoT information streams.

Right now the electronic apparatuses and the expansive scale retail exchange speak to isolate modern segments. Without an arrangement of regular specialized measures and interfaces joining the exercises of such two divisions, an IoT-empowered gadget like the keen cooler couldn't occur.

Application of IOT Environment

As far as application fields and market parts where IoT arrangements can give upper hands over current arrangements, we recognized six ones which we do accept can assume the main part in the appropriation of IoT advances: environmental observing; savvy urban communities; brilliant business/stock and item administration; keen homes/shrewd building administration; social insurance and security and reconnaissance. In the accompanying, we quickly talk about the significance and potential effect of IoT advances on the intensity of players in such markets.

Smart Homes/Smart Buildings: Building structures with cutting-edge IoT advancements may help in both diminishing the utilization of assets related to structures (power, water) and in addition in enhancing the fulfillment level of people populating it, be it specialists for office structures or inhabitants for private houses. The effect is both in financial terms (decreased operational uses) and societal ones. In this application, a key part is played by sensors, which are utilized to both screen asset utilization and also to proactively recognize current clients' needs. Such a situation coordinates various distinctive subsystems, and subsequently requires an abnormal state of institutionalization to guarantee interoperability. Capacity to reason in a distributed, helpful manner, and to activate is additionally essential to guarantee that choices gone up against the assets under control are in accordance with the clients' needs and desires, which thus are entirely interwoven to the exercises they attempt as well as a plan to take.

Smart Cities: This term is utilized to indicate the digital physical eco-system developing by sending propelled correspondence foundation and novel administrations over far-reaching situations. By the method for cutting-edge administrations, it is, in reality, conceivable to enhance the use of physical city foundations (e.g., street networks, control framework, and so forth.) and personal satisfaction for its natives. IoT advancements can locate various different applications in brilliant urban community's situations. Through IoT, it will be conceivable to screen auto movement in huge urban communities or parkways and convey administrations that offer activity routing exhortation. In this point of view, autos will be comprehended as speaking to 'savvy objects.' What's more, keen stopping devices system, in light of RFID and sensor innovations, may permit to screen accessible parking spots and furnish drivers with computerized stopping exhortation, in this way enhancing versatility in an urban region. Besides, sensors may screen the stream of vehicular activity on expressways and recover total data, for example, normal speed and quantities of autos. Sensors could recognize the contamination level of air, recovering brown haze data, for example, the level of carbon dioxide and so forth and convey such data to wellbeing offices. Besides, sensors could be utilized as a part of a criminology setting, by recognizing infringement and by transmitting the important information to law implementation organizations so as to distinguish the violator, or to store data that will be given if there should arise an occurrence of mischance to resulting mischance scene examination.

Technological Environment

IoT networks require giant data centers to process and bolster their requirements. Subsequently, the vitality utilization by the server farms is huge. The assets expected to deliver that vitality will add an enormous weight to nature. Albeit enormous server farms are attempting to use as meager vitality as could be allowed, it's as yet going to influence the vitality part overall. Moreover, the vitality and assets used to fabricate a large number of new gadgets is another wellspring of vitality utilization brought on by IoT.

For condition, IoT is a twofold sword bringing both advantages and difficulties. Individuals ought to know about both sides so they can measure the advantages and disadvantages altogether to profit the most and give up the minimum. A few specialists propose that for such a goliath organize as IoT, the best way to deal with address the natural effect is an outline for the earth approach. Taking natural effect from the earliest starting point to coordinate it with IoT improvement as a framework will be all the better we can accomplish for who and what is to come. At Advanced MP Technology, we are completely mindful of the natural effect of items we purchase and offer every day. Affirmed with ISO 14001 and agreeing to RoHS and REACH, we ensure that we deal with the item legitimately to limit the environmental impact.

Physical Environment

The Internet of Things term has been utilized from showcasing buzz the distance to research distributions and meeting titles. We thought it would be useful alongside a concise Internet of Things history to investigate the assortment of ways individuals have been characterizing the term in nature. Looking for foundation data? Visit our IoT Historical Timeline page here and the terms creation by Kevin Ashton in 1999. Looking for a realistic diagram of the term and its advances? See our IoT Overview Infographic.

Physical Internet, Ubiquitous Computing, Ambient Intelligence, Machine to Machine (M2M), Industrial Internet, Web of Things, Connected Environments, Smart Cities, Spumes, Every ware, Pervasive Internet, Connected World, Wireless Sensor Networks, Situated Computing, Future Internet and Physical registering. A worldwide system framework is connecting physical and virtual protests through the misuse of information catch and correspondence abilities. This foundation incorporates existing and advancing Internet and system advancements. It will offer particular question recognizable proof, sensor, and association capacity as the reason for the improvement of free agreeable administrations and applications. These will be described by a high level of self-governing information catch, occasion exchange, organize network and interoperability.

The Internet of Things (IoT) portrays the upheaval effectively underway that is seeing a developing number of web-empowered gadgets that can organize and speak with each other and with other web-empowered devices. IoT alludes to a state where Things (e.g., objects, situations, vehicles, and garments) will have increasing data related with them and may be able to detect, convey, system and create new data, getting to be an integral part of the Internet

Socio-Economic Environment

The Internet Society distributed this 50-page whitepaper giving a review of the IoT and investigating related issues and difficulties. You may download the entire report at the connection above. The Executive Summary is incorporated beneath to give a review of the full report. The Internet of Things is a developing point of specialized, social, and financial centrality. Shopper items, strong merchandise, autos and trucks, mechanical and utility parts, sensors, and other ordinary articles are being joined with Internet availability and capable information investigative abilities that guarantee to change the way we work, live, and play. Projections for the effect of IoT on the Internet and economy are great, with some envisioning upwards of 100 billion associated IoT gadgets and a worldwide monetary effect of more than $11 trillion by 2025.

In the meantime, in any case, the Internet of Things raises critical difficulties that could obstruct understanding its potential advantages. Consideration getting features about the hacking of Internet-associated gadgets, reconnaissance concerns, and security fears as of now have caught open consideration. Specialized difficulties remain and the new approach, legitimate and advancement difficulties are rising.

This review archive is intended to help the Internet Society people group explore the discourse encompassing the Internet of Things in light of the contending forecasts about its guarantees and dangers. The Internet of Things draws in an expansive arrangement of thoughts that are mind-boggling and interlaced from various perspectives.

Enabling Technologies: The concept of joining PCs, sensors, and systems to screen and control gadgets has existed for quite a long time. The current juncture of a few innovations advertises patterns, in any case, is conveying the Internet of Things nearer to far-reaching reality. These incorporate Ubiquitous Connectivity, Widespread Adoption of IP-based Networking, Computing Economics, Miniaturization, Advances in Data Analytics, and the Rise of Cloud Computing.

Connectivity Models: IoT implementations utilize distinctive specialized interchanges models, each with its own particular attributes. Four basic interchanges models depicted by the Internet Architecture Board include Device-to-Device, Device-to-Cloud, Device-to-Gateway, and Back-End Data-Sharing. These models highlight the adaptability in the ways that IoT gadgets can interface and offer some benefit to the user.

Transformational Potential: If the projections, what's more, patterns towards IoT progress toward becoming reality, it might constrain a move in deduction about the suggestions and issues in this present reality where the most widely recognized collaboration with the Internet originates from aloof engagement with associated questions as opposed to dynamic engagement with substance. The potential acknowledgment of this result – a hyper-connected world is a demonstration of the broadly useful nature of the Internet design itself, which does not put inalienable constraints on the applications or administrations that can make utilization of the innovation. Five key IoT issue territories are inspected to investigate probably the most squeezing difficulties and inquiries identified with the innovation. These incorporate security; protection; interoperability and guidelines; lawful, administrative, and rights; and rising economies and development.

Business Environment

The Internet of Things in the Modern Business Environment is a basic reference hotspot for the most recent insightful research on differing parts of the interworking of brilliant gadgets inside a business setting and investigates the effect of these gadgets on organization operations and models. Including broad scope on a wide scope of themes, for example, store network administration, data sharing, and information investigation, this distribution is in a perfect world intended for scientists, supervisors, and understudies looking for flow explore on the development of innovation in trade.

The modern web is another and forthcoming innovation that is changing the acts of associations and enterprises all over the place. Through research and application, openings can emerge from executing these new frameworks and gadgets. The Internet of Things in the Modern Business Environment is a fundamental reference hotspot for the most recent insightful research on changing parts of the interworking of keen gadgets inside a business setting and investigates the effect of these gadgets on organization operations and models. Including broad scope on a wide scope of points, for example, production network administration, data sharing, and information investigation, this distribution is in a perfect world intended for analysts, directors, and understudies looking for ebb and flow examine on the development of innovation in business.

In the course of recent years, the across the board utilization of the Internet and quick improvement of Internet-based innovations has come about likewise into shorter life cycles of item and administrations, requiring along these lines quicker changing plans of action. This paper gives a review of plans of action for the Internet of Things, Services, and People applications. The idea of the Internet of Things and Services imagines physical gadgets and machines to be utilized as effortlessly as a web benefit and consistently incorporated into arranged applications with required usefulness. Innovatively this idea is clear, and a few brilliant applications are as of now a work in progress core, Hydra, Confidence or ventures. Notwithstanding the business point of view of data as an advantage in its own correct remains an open issue. To deal with this issue we apply an initially esteem based prerequisite procedure, e3-esteem, to model esteem creation and esteem trade inside an e-business system of numerous business performing artists. Utilizing this approach the business action can be diminished to its center components, which in the least difficult case contain the incentivized offer, circulation channels and the clients of the organization, clarifying how a multi-on-screen character arrange makes, disperses and consumes value by the production of a good or providing a service.

ARCHITECTURAL LAYERS AND APPLICATION DOMAINS OF IoT

The endless scenes that are offered by IoT will make conceivable outcomes of the development of different quantities of shrewd Applications, in which an almost no segment it is by and by accessible and available our worldwide group. Different zones and shrewd condition at which these applications are created will likely progress and the effect of the tone of worldwide native's lives, from the part of Home living, health concern, environmental awareness to the work.

Application Domain: States that various IoT Applications can be grouped into three principle area i.e., An Industrial Domain, the keen city area, and Health welfare space. Despite their Application range, such Application space's aspiration is to enhance the standard of regular day to day existence, which at a later stage can have a generous part in the monetary and social effect at a bigger scale from angles, for example, individual, societal, medicinal, natural and strategic just to name the few.

Industrial Domain: All industrial undertakings encompassing the gainfulness and money related exchanges between ventures, vast corporates, and other related elements can be misused utilizing it. Run of the mill cases would bank area, benefits division, assembling and coordination and middle people. Coordination's and inventory network appended with RFID which can be connected to recognize the materials and stock, be they clothing types, keen furniture, foodstuff, and fluids can be a run of the mill and important illustration of Industrial IoT Application. Lighting that will consolidate with correspondences innovation inside the brilliant building and keen neighborhoods. Sooner rather than later advanced cells will be utilized as a focal evacuate control to employ diverse sorts of smart household applications.

Health welfare domain: The health and medical sector will likewise be influenced by IoT activity and progression, whereby cutting-edge sensors will be conveyed to catch in the nick of time information from various patients, then transmitted the information to the pertinent Doctors, some wearable gadgets will likewise be utilized to unendingly regulate the health of the released understanding and the examples of drug admission. Savvy names will be connected amid operation to limit careless of any operation protest being left inside patient's body after Operation and to clip down on burglary identifying with Hospital equipment's. Moreover, Hospital Beds will be close-fitted with brilliant – touch screen gadgets for both beguilement and instruction administrations e.g., your e-learning contents.

THE CHALLENGES OF IOT

The IoT as a new phenomenon is likewise confronted with many difficulties going from, Data trade inside complex occasion Systems, the genuine mix, collaboration adjustment of uncertain data, data protection, objects wellbeing and security, information confidentiality and encryption and Network security says. Information trade among Complex occasion frameworks and different system components: access to colossal scale arrange components and the interoperability for all articles and sensor gadgets are all essential for the progression of IoT. So the key test in this angle will be: How to make sense of the present consuming issues between the additional immense scale, heterogeneity and the incredible way of its frameworks and Application and the essential for exceedingly proficient information/information trade. Productive joining and communication adjustment of questionable data: Several Smart gadgets or Object inside the physical world are feeling of IoT advancements and Application utilizes different sensors and hubs, setting off a portion of the detected articles (gadgets) ought to eat up appropriate encryption instrument to guarantee the information uprightness at the data handling unit. The IoT administration would controls that are intelligible to see this information, subsequently, it is important to protect the information from facades.

Arrange security: Data originating from sensor Objects (gadgets) is coordinated above wired or remote transmission organize. Besides the transmission framework must be in a position to deal with information from a tremendous amount of sensor protest (gadgets) without inciting any information misfortune because of system blockage, whereby it ensure appropriate safety efforts for the transmitted information and turn away it from external interference or observing.

INTERNET OF THINGS WILL CHANGE INDUSTRY

The Internet has effectively experienced a few phases in its generally short life expectancy. The development has profited people, social causes, governmental issues, business and whole economies by raising connectedness, expelling physical boundaries, and outfitting "Huge Data." The Internet ostensibly is the most transformative and unavoidable driver of progress and improvement in our history.

Smart Assembly: Seeking to lessen detaches between the assembling and undertaking systems, makers are embracing joined keen systems are decreasing downtime by permitting remote access to frameworks and accomplices and conveying exactness, flexibility, and unwavering quality from the plant floor to the enterprise.

The Visual Factory: Manufacturers need better deceivability into hardware execution, asset needs, and security dangers. Developing systems administration and network arrangements empower a dashboard perspective of multi-plant conditions, upgrading effectiveness, security and return on assets.

Plant-wide Visibility: Industrial offices with all-inclusive scattered generation locales require better-incorporated creation frameworks to abbreviate lead times. Web Protocol (IP) arrange innovation associates undertaking applications with gadget level creation information progressively, permitting quicker data streams, speedier choices, and greater market responsiveness.

Plant Alarm and Event Resolution

Plants regularly don't have the ability to issue a nonstop notification when apparatus bombs on hold. Open benchmarks engage clients to interface with sensor-level structures that see breakdowns in a split second (and once in a while before they happen) to make more raised measures of general apparatus (OEE) suitability. Feeling things: Sensor propels Sensors are one of the key building squares of IoT. As all-inclusive systems, they can be sent wherever – from military battle areas to vineyards and redwoods and on the Golden Gate Bridge. They can similarly be implanted under the human skin, in a travel bag or on a shirt. Some can be as meager as four millimeters in size, yet the data they accumulate can be escaped. They supplement human resources and have ended up being principal in innumerable, from social protection to improvement. Sensors have a key favored point of view in that they can anticipate human needs in light of information accumulated about their interesting situation. Their understanding, "copied" by different frameworks, grants them to report about the outside condition, and also to make a move without human intervention.

Inside a cleverly composed structure, sensors play out the components of data contraptions – they fill in as "eyes," get-together information about their condition. Strangely, actuators fill in as yield units – they go about as "hands," executing decisions. Thinking things: Smart advances embedded knowledge in the things themselves can furthermore update the vitality of the framework by relapsing information taking care of capacities to the edges of the framework. Splendid materials join sensors and actuators, as they sense supports and respond properly. At this moment, there are three essential sorts of keen materials.

Uninvolved sharp materials that respond particularly and reliably to help without setting up any of the banner Active splendid materials that can, with a remote controller, senses a banner and choose how to respond; and Independent clever materials that pass on totally joined controllers, sensors, and actuators. Contracting things: nanotechnology focuses on the arrangement, depiction, era, and use of structures and contraptions through the control and depiction of matter at the nanoscale. Potentially favorable circumstances consolidate extended speed and memory limits, and a decline in vitality utilization and, of course, size.

THE BENEFITS AND IMPACT OF IOT

The economic value allied with IoT will be huge and the ROI (Return on venture) will be gigantic for instance it is seen that the US GDP will increment by 2-5% by 2025 with quickened efficiency development and the noteworthy increment as far as Job creation and destitution lightening, The financial effect and advantages of the IoT will be colossal. As per Gartner have estimated that the aggregated esteem and financial benefit of the IoT will outperform $1.9 trillion in the year 2020 alone, besides forecasters at McKinsey and Company (which foreseen in 2012 about the present, and breaking down, shortage of information researchers to fulfill and work with enormous information) have watched IoT wonder and have figure out how to recognize and have overseen and distinguished major benefits that the IoT will derive.

CONCLUSION

IoT Technology and Applications have progressed into various regions with the point of upgrading business, help with making economical savvy urban areas and enhances individuals' nature of lives; additionally, it has contributed in enhancing the connections between the person, condition and questions (gadgets) around them. This article gave a short acquaintance approach with it, laid out the meaning of it from various scholastics, exhibited Application area and structural layers of it examined challenges identified with it and give the anticipated concentrated on the financial effect of it towards explaining the difficulties of urbanization. Sooner rather than later, we will attempt to unload how it can be an empowering agent for brilliant urban areas, make the IoT models for complex occasion administrations disclosure and recommender framework, offer revelation into setting product data joining and administration disclosure for keen urban communities. Our work will help with planning IoT hypothetical structure that will be utilized to create Complex occasion benefit disclosure stages and frameworks for IoT within Smart cities. The Internet of Things systems contains physical gadgets custom hardware, sensors, actuators, preparing units with system network that speak with the cloud framework performing information investigation and handling. Associated with existing systems administration foundation, physical gadgets incorporated into the entire framework send obtained sensor information to the cloud stage, get orders remotely from the cloud and connect with each other over existing foundation. IOT frameworks empower coordinate engagement of end clients with web and additionally portable applications that speak with the cloud framework and offer one of a kind client experience and framework control.

REFERENCES

advancedmp. (n.d.). Retrieved from www.advancedmp.com: http://www.advancedmp.com/environmental-impact-of-iot/.

Atzori, Luigi, Antonio Iera, Giacomo Morabito. (2010). The internet of things: A survey. *Computer networks 54, no. 15*, 2787-2805.

Banafa, Ahmed. (2016). *The Internet of Everything (IoE)*. Retrieved from https://www.bbvaopenmind.com/en/the-internet-of-everything-ioe/.

Debasis Bandyopadhyay, Jaydip Sen. (2011). Internet of things: Applications and challenges in technology and standardization. *Wireless Personal Communications 58, no. 1*, 49-69.

Dieter Uckelmann, M. H. (2011). An architectural approach towards the future internet of things. In M. H. Dieter Uckelmann, *Architecting the internet of things* (pp. 1-24). Berlin Heidelberg: Springer.

Friess, Peter. (2013). *Internet of things: converging technologies for smart environments and integrated ecosystems.* River Publishers.

Gluhak, Alexander, Srdjan Krco, Michele Nati, Dennis Pfisterer, Nathalie Mitton, Tahiry Razafindralambo. (2011). A survey on facilities for experimental internet of things research. *IEEE Communications Magazine 49, no. 11.*

Huang, A. (2016, August 31). *IBM.* Retrieved from www.ibm.com: https://www.ibm.com/blogs/internet-of-things/connected-world-sustainable-planet/.

Huang, A. (2016, August 31). *internet-of-things.* Retrieved from www.ibm.com/blogs/internet-of-things/connected-world-sustainable-planet/: https://www.ibm.com/blogs/internet-of-things/connected-world-sustainable-planet/.

internetofthingsagenda.techtarget. (n.d.). Retrieved from www.internetofthingsagenda.techtarget.com: http://internetofthingsagenda.techtarget.com/definition/Internet-of-Things-IoT.

Jayavardhana Gubbi, Rajkumar Buyya, Slaven Marusic, and Marimuthu Palaniswami. I. (2013). Internet of Things (IoT): A vision, architectural elements, and future directions. *Future generation computer systems 29, no. 7*, 1645-1660.

Jiong Jin, Jayavardhana Gubbi, Slaven Marusic, Marimuthu Palaniswami. (2014). An information framework for creating a smart city through the internet of things. *IEEE Internet of Things Journal 1, no. 2*, 112-121.

Ovidiu Vermesan, Peter Friess, Patrick Guillemin, Sergio Gusmeroli, Harald Sundmaeker, Alessandro Bassi, Ignacio Soler Jubert. (2011). Internet of things strategic research roadmap. *Internet of Things-Global Technological and Societal Trends 1*, 9-52.

Pickett, Dan T.. (2015). *The Internet of Everything Will Impact Everything, Including Your Next Tech Job.* Retrieved from https://www.wired.com/insights/2015/02/internet-of-everything-your-next-tech-job/.

Pinterest, "The IoT Connectivity" https://www.pinterest.com/pin/232850243214237358/?autologin=true.

Rolf H. Weber. (2009). Internet of things–Need for a new legal environment? *Computer law & security review 25, no. 6*, 522-527.

Stromwall, Brent. (2016). *The Internet of Things and Everything — IoT/IoE.* Retrieved from https://polytron.com/blog/the-internet-of-things-and-everything-iotioe.

Telefónica IoT Team. (2016, July 1). *iot.telefonic.* Retrieved from www.iot.telefonica.com: https://iot.telefonica.com/blog/5-ways-the-iot-is-helping-the-environment.

Tracy, P. (2016, November 18). *rcrwireless.com.* Retrieved from www.rcrwireless.com: http://www.rcrwireless.com/20161118/telco-cloud/iot-impact-environment-tag31-tag99.

Wu He, Gongjun Yan, Li Da Xu. (2014). Developing vehicular data cloud services in the IoT environment. *IEEE Transactions on Industrial Informatics 10, no. 2*, 1587-1595.

Chapter 5

THE INTERNET OF THINGS AND 5G WIRELESS NETWORKS

INTRODUCTION

In order to effectively manage the challenges that next generation wireless networks will bring we must consider the very important issues of cost, flexibility, connectivity and the use of artificial intelligence in networking. Before the challenges of next generation wireless arose, we looked at the network infrastructure in segments, software and hardware, local data and remote data. By realizing the challenges ahead we can plan out an infrastructure that will not only be able to handle the data efficiently, it will handle the data properly based on its content.

When addressing next generation wireless networks, the most asked question will likely be how much will this cost? It may not be the question end users ask but the network operators will definitely have to figure out how to pay for the new infrastructure and upgrades to existing infrastructure in order to make 5G or next generation wireless an affordable option for consumers and business alike. Next generation wireless will totally revolutionize the way we do business and how we utilize data, as a result, business will need to be the innovation drivers to make next generation wireless a possibility. The industry has already begun to embrace the possibilities that next generation wireless brings to the IIoT, business and industry leaders realize what truly intelligent networks bring in terms of economic benefits, cost savings and efficiency.

Our current generation wireless networks are not very "flexible," they may have some automated intelligence about them but they are not "flexible" in the sense of being able to adapt to the vast amount of data that will occur due to the huge influx of IoT and Industry IoT (IIoT) devices along with other expect data such as streaming audio, video and VOIP. To address the lack of flexibility, networks will need to become truly intelligent. Being able to see a problem before it happens is great, but with the need of unprecedented uptime that next generation wireless networks may bring we need the problem to be predicted before it occurs. By integrating existing network functions into a soft based network we can create the flexibility we need, the answer is virtualized networks and the possibilities it creates. Network slicing delivers dynamically allocated resources, intelligently and in real time. Not only does network slicing create the "soft" network architecture necessary to deliver real-time analytics it assists in controlling costs by reducing the overhead seen in previous wireless network architectures.

The digital transformation will require access to resources and real-time data, analytics that deep dive into the data and a flexible platform that's business-friendly. The transformation will occur when existing infrastructure and data can be virtualized into a true self-organizing network that is flexible and expandable that is able to meet many different types of endpoint devices and the data requirements presented by that device. Next generation 5G networks will become the most valuable digital asset to the economy as a whole. The digital transformation overall will change how we think about solving problems in business, life and everything in between. Instead of having to search for data, the data is intelligent enough to find its endpoint. Artificial intelligence can identify any real time problem and take healing action. We will be able to meet and solve real-time issues with real-time resolutions.

FUTURE MOBILE NETWORK

The explosion of heterogeneous devices linked through a large-scale and fast internet is a clear indicator that the Internet of Things (IoT) is becoming a reality. Also, several experts and researchers in the field of technology posit that the 5G network will be reliable and efficient enough to boost the deployment of IoT. It is imperative to note that exponential and unprecedented take-up of video and data services spearheaded by the proliferation of social media platform and broad availability of smartphones has made the fifth generation (5G) network inevitable. In fact, 5G resulted both from the increased user application prompting for high bandwidth and throughputs as well as the increasing trend of smart devices that are expected to flood the global market in future. In particular, with increased adoption of motion-based sensors, wearable technology, eye movement sensors, and voice command, the use of 5G networks will be driven by high-reliability requirements and low latency of such sensor-linked Internet of Things devices. 5G adoption is expected to facilitate interaction of millions of smart devices at high Gigabit speeds across various networks within milliseconds. For this reason, the 5G network that connects such devices will require simplified operations and extreme scalability with effective corrective systems. Given that there is minimal human interaction, the availability and reliability expectations of IoT and 5G networks is extremely high. In this regard, this chapter aims at discussing IoT and 5G network by focusing on earlier work, technical and economic analysis, applications and services, scholarly opinion, and feedback on the two technological aspects that have taken the world by storm.

5G should acknowledge that the Internet of Things (IoT) holds the capability of improving our lives via the introduction of the sophisticated wide array of application domains ranging from home appliances, industrial automation, and consumer and healthcare electronics. Presently, there are over ten billion IoT devices that have got connected. Moreover, scenario indicates that with the prevalence of IoT and 5G network, out of fifty billion total connections twenty-four billion are scheduled to be in place within a span of next five years. Primarily, the growth of IoT has been sustained by increasing trend in the use of devices for processing and monitoring the flow of information. An increase in their use is also attributed to their decreasing costs, implying that many individuals can afford and utilize them. However, successful implementation of current IoT solutions requires the adoption of cloud computing services integrated to high speed 5G HetNet mobile networks that are extremely dynamic. However, increasing groups of new customers ranging from distant health care providers, hyper-sensor automotive, and the development of smart cities challenged the service providers. In this consideration, the consumers of such digital services will unbearably have high expectations concerning the push for stringent policy control and Service Level Agreement (SLA) as well as the quality of the services. Thus, several layers of IoT and 5G network ought to be dedicated for use by such customers, prompting the operators to incorporate the use of automation techniques for delivering reliability and the demand for exceptionally high speed. Besides this, it is becoming a common trend for companies offering 5G infrastructures to collaborate with research organizations and service providers for communication to define customized standards for 5G based on articulated cases. It is of the essence to note that 5G network eyes higher availability of spectrum bands ranging from 5GHZ to 60 GHz, thus offering a shorter wavelength for incorporation of Multiple Input-Multiple Output (MIMO) techniques.

It should illustrate that cellular networks for long-range perceived as the probable candidates capable of guaranteeing the internetworking of the Internet of Things devices due to high data rate, enhanced coverage, high spectrum efficiency, and low cost per bit. On a similar note, various standardization and industry bodies have been relentlessly pushing for the fulfillment and accomplishment of the Internet of Things requirements through the adoption of 5G wireless systems. 5G network contended that does not represent the evolution of the existing system generations. In this case, it is perceived that the revolution of Information Communication and Technology (ICT) field, thus adopting a holistic overview with the incorporation of innovative and accommodative network features.

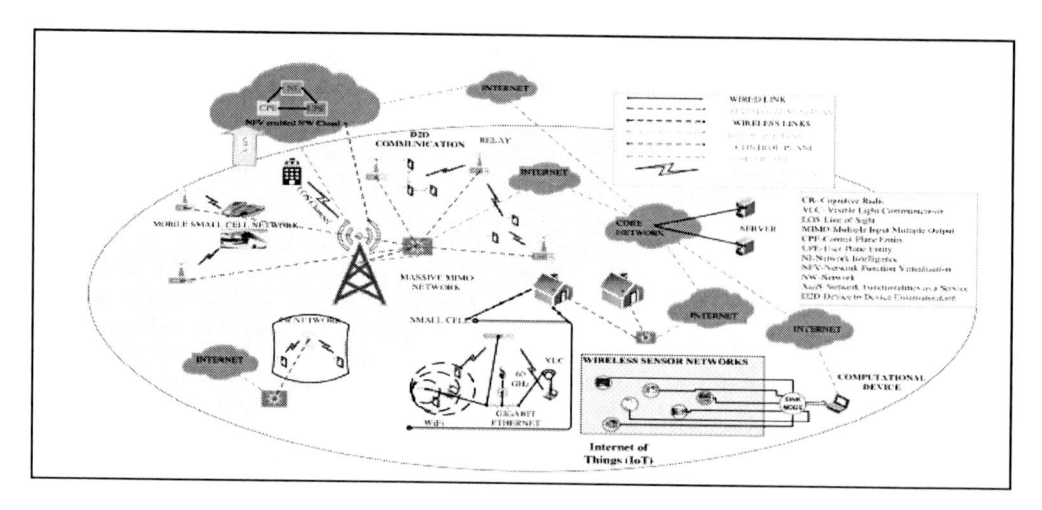

Figure 1. 5G Network Architecture.

In essence, the 5G network is expected to take in business contexts. Spurred by socioeconomic transformations and technological development, the systems characterized by technology, customer, and operator settings. Therefore, with its inception, instant information will be easily fetched due to virtual interconnection with all devices.

Fundamentally, significant technological advancement is characterized by the advent of tablets and smartphones. Given that smartphones are primarily expected to be personal devices. Further, development will be executed by enhancing their capability and performance. However, it is projected that the number of own devices will increase, apart from smartphones and tablets, will increase prompted by devices such as sensors and wearables.

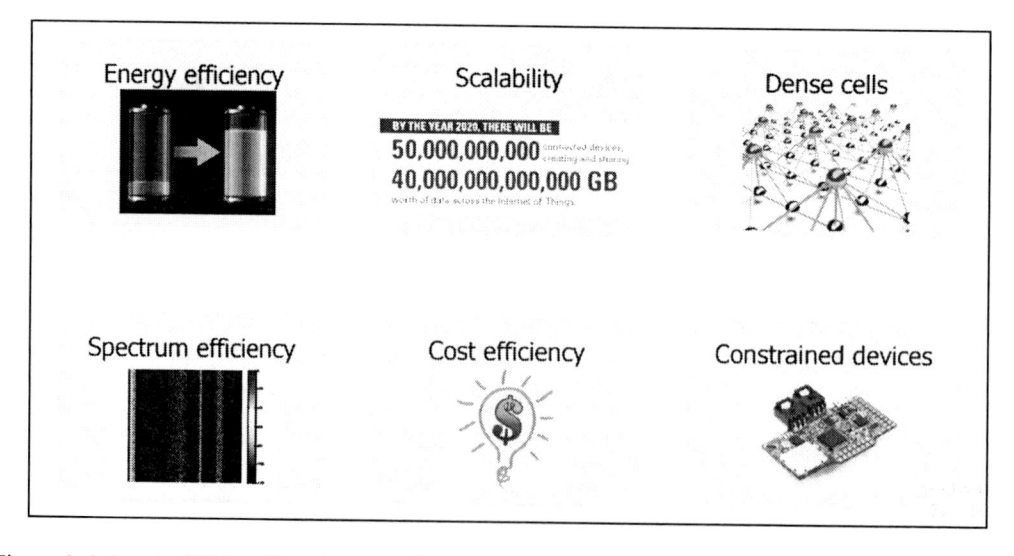

Figure 2. Internet of Things Requirements for 5G Network.

It is expected that personal devices will have extended capabilities concerning cloud gaming, identity proof, payment, content sharing and production, high-quality video, and mobile TV. In this context, those capabilities apply to security, health, social life, and safety.

As per the projections, the context of world businesses beyond 2020 is expected to be different from today's scenario. As such, the emergence of new business models and cases spearheaded by operators and customers' needs will ultimately revolutionize business operations. Therefore, a 5G network is expected to support several emerging cases with divergent variability and applications for various performance attributes. In particular, a 5G network will facilitate lifeline communication, ultra-reliable communication, and real-time communication, massive internet of things, higher-user mobility, broadband access everywhere and broadband access in dense areas.

ACCESS TO BROADBAND IN DENSE AREAS

Principally, there is an increasing need for the development of an intensely connected society. Therefore, 5G network facilitates service availability in dense urban city centers and multi-story buildings that may be densely populated. As such, the system will facilitate communications in areas where thousands of individuals live per square kilometer. It will also support 3D services, multi-user interactions, and other services that will play a crucial role in facilitating the process of communication. In particular, aspects such as HD videos, smart office, and pervasive video will be supported.

BROADBAND ACCESS EVERYWHERE

In essence, a 5G network provides access to the services of broadband to virtually anywhere, with the inclusion of challenging situations such as rural and suburban areas. Therefore, 5G network guarantees consistency among users due to throughput that requires minimal data rate. On an additional note, a 5G network is characterized by aspects such as speed above 50Mbps everywhere and ultra-low-cost systems to facilitate interaction of individuals.

HIGHER USER MOBILITY

Principally, high demand for mobile services in trains, vehicles, and aircraft is expected to be in place by 2020. Despite the fact that some of the services are simply a natural evolution of those that already exist; others may be a complete representation of new scenarios such as broadband communication while on an aircraft. Similarly, there will be demand for improved internet access, in-vehicle entertainment, and enhanced navigation through real-time information. In this consideration, depending on the degree of required mobility, 5G network will effectively offer the platform for their realization.

INTERNET OF THINGS

Due to demand and extensive range of features in devices such as actuators, sensors, and cameras anticipated high usage by 2020. Low cost primarily characterizes the inception of the Internet of Things and represents such as smart wearables, sensor networks, mobile video surveillance, real-time communication, physical internet, and lifeline communication.

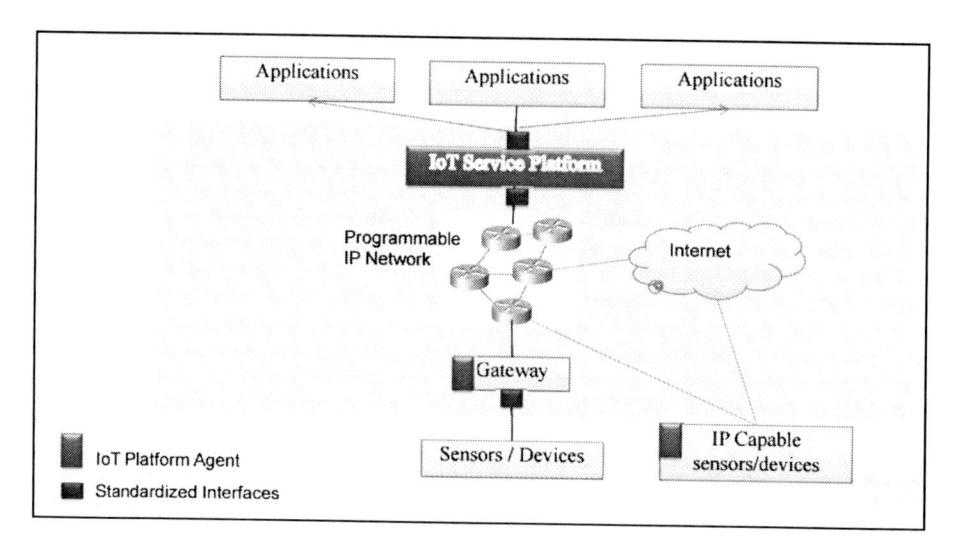

Figure 3. IoT Architecture.

Smart Wearables

Principally, the use of wearables utilizing multiple types of sensors and devices is expected to be the mainstream. In such contexts, Internet of Things comes into necessitate everything. For instance waterproof sensors, less power, and ultra-lights integrated into the clothing by the people. In particular, such sensors can measure attributes such as temperature, pressure, blood pressure, heart rate, breathing rate and volume, body temperature, and skin moisture.

Sensor Networks

Smart services will be pervasive in the urban, suburban, and rural area. Therefore, Internet of Things (IoT) could deploy in metering, city light management, traffic control, monitoring, and other services likely to be offered in smart cities. The aggregation of such services needs an efficient network and high-speed connections through an interworked framework. IoT and 5G network provides such platforms well.

Tactile Internet

Tactile Internet indicates that strong interaction refers to contexts where human beings control virtual and real objects wirelessly. In this context, it requires a real control audio and signal or visual feedback. Therefore, facilitation of such activities will be greatly enhanced by the Internet of Things (IoT) since it is an appropriate platform. Such techniques could incorporate in autonomous cars, remote medical care, and manufacturing.

Automated Driving and Traffic Control

In the next decade, people believe that the world could identify with advancements in safety applications for mitigation of road carnages, improvement of traffic efficiency, and support of the mobility of various emergency vehicles. IoT applications are not limited to infrastructure communication application but also interaction with other road users such as cyclists and pedestrians. Primarily, aspects such as controlled fleet driving require end-to-end ultra-low latency for execution of warning signals and higher data rates for sharing of video information between infrastructure and cars. In such cases, a 5G network will facilitate IoT for the provision of low latency, high reliability, and scalability needed for execution.

TECHNICAL AND ECONOMIC ANALYSIS

A 5G network is an emerging technological improvement hugely utilized in cellular infrastructure. Device-to-device communication (D2D) and multiple input technologies indicate that 5G network will adopt widely in future. According to many conducted research, 5G network perceived that it could incorporate in sharing spectrum with ultra-dense networks, cognitive radio, multi-radio access, millimeter wave situations and duplex communications. As such, research specified that 5G network is the basic framework needed for small access points, D2D, cloud computing and IoT. Moreover, with the use of wave of millimeter spectrum in a densified cell implementation, higher spectral efficiency and more allocated inbound and out-bound spectrum 5G wireless networks provide a platform for IoT connectivity. Based on several conducted types of research, adoption of next generation 5G network and standards would introduce starting early 2020 with staggering numbers of connected devices at different tiers of the network. But, some industries are still skeptic towards the upgrading of a 5G network for fear of new rules that may enforce after that. Despite this, the inception of a 5G network well received in the market according to previously conducted research. For instance, towards the end of 2013, Huawei, the Chinese telecom equipment vendor, said that it had allocated $600 million in extensive research work for 5G network and technologies for a span of next five years.

Principally, unlike the 4G or 3G network platforms, a 5G network is a significant technological advancement that promises to technically and economically benefit most cellular company operators. For instance, the 5G network, which is the key platform for the Internet of Things, will offer exceptional SLA-driven digital services. Operators utilizing 5G network will experience a high influx of customers seeking several digital services. Therefore, such players will be prompted to dedicate a section of their 5G and IoT network to customers to meet all their needs and services. Mainly, this will be earnestly executed with the aid of cloud computing to facilitate prompt execution of commands and responses. It is imperative to note that speed and capacity are important features of a 5G network. Notably, this attributed the fact that it is available in a broad spectrum band ranging from 5GHz to 60 GHz. As such, it can travel over an extremely shorter wavelength to facilitate implementation of MIMO in the whole course of company operations.

Besides this, the 5G network has ultra-dense networks orchestrated heterogeneously due to short range propagations. Therefore, it is able efficiently to manage the real-time end-to-end performance of respective services. It is imperative to note that 5G network aims at evolving the whole concept of communication among cellular service providers, who will be transformed into a digital platform for the provision of their services. In this regard, digital services will be successful in commercial aspect because real-time analytics and high dependency will provide detailed and correlated insights regarding network behaviors and customers.

Furthermore, 5G network and Internet of Things (IoT) identified with maximum reliability and acceptability in the present market. Thus, it can be relied on by various customers for specific needs and services. In particular, customer-centric and insight-driven services offered by the 5G network will play an auspicious role towards upholding the reliability and efficiency of 5G networks. On a different note, 5G networks with sophisticated devices used by people for communication purpose will revolutionize the people's lifestyle.

APPLICATION AND SERVICES

It is imperative to note that Internet of Things (IoT) and 5G networks have a wide array of applications. In particular, 5G network necessitates and facilitates access to broadband in densely populated areas such as city centers. Besides this, IoT and 5G used in higher user mobility, better access to broadband, massive IoT, and lifeline communications. Also, it will enhance ultra-reliable communications, broadcast-like services, and extreme real-time communications. Therefore, its inceptions and applications will guarantee offering of several services aimed at facilitating the operations of operator companies and prompt execution of customers' needs and expectations.

On a different note, Internet of Things (IoT) can be deployed and manifested in several application contexts. In particular, in smart wearables such as clothes, they widely utilized IoT. Furthermore, sensor networks, mobile video surveillance, real-time communication, tactile interaction, lifeline communication, ultra-reliable communication, automated driving and traffic control, and managing network of robots incorporated IoT in their systems. In this consideration, it can be perceived that it offers several services in both domestic and industrial settings.

CONCLUSION

In essence, Internet of Things (IoT) and 5G network are expected to redefine information, communication, and technology. In particular, the high speed and reliability offered by the 5G network will imply that humans can execute many activities that could be virtually tedious presently within a short time. In addition to the everyday use of personal devices such as smartphones and tablets, the inception of IoT and the 5G network will lead to improvement in their efficiency and performance. Also, other devices such as wearables and sensors hugely are deployed in people's life. Therefore, a digital era is in waiting characterized by high speed and reliability. It is additionally scheduled to increase interactions among individuals given that 5G network can support interconnection of billions of devices.

Given that 5G network is expected to be functionally operational by 2020, it should be used as a launching pad for the realization of IoT. Primarily, this is because its high speed of 5GHZ to 60GHZ is fast enough to facilitate the transfer of information, be it video or audio within a millisecond. As such, the evolving business models will compel different companies to adopt them given that they will revolutionize human lifestyle and technology as a whole. However, its implementation should be executed in line with the set policies and standards to avoid it being abused and used for unintended purposes.

Internet of Things (IoT) entails interworked objects containing embedded technological frameworks for communication and interacting with internal and external states of the environment. It should be noted that it is a confluence of improved sensors, efficient wireless protocols, significant capital requirement, and cheaper processors. Fundamentally, IoT is used in sensor networks, smart wearables, video surveillance, tactile interaction, automated driving and traffic control, remote surgery, drones, and public safety to enhance life and delivered services. In this context, it applies to the domestic, commercial, social, and industrial environment. 5G networks, on the other hand, offers massive IoT services, higher mobility, access to broadband everywhere, access to broadband in densely populated areas, real-time communications and offering broadcast-like services. Both infrastructures enhance transfer of data and information in an efficient manner.

REFERENCES

Agarwal, Y., & Dey, A. K. (2016)," Toward Building a Safe, Secure, and Easy-to-Use Internet of Things Infrastructure," *IEEE Computer, 49*(4), 88-91.

Agyapong, P. K., Iwamura, M., Staehle, D., Kiess, W., Benjebbour A., "Design considerations for a 5G network architecture," *IEEE Communications Magazine, 52*(11), 65-75, 2014.

Chen, M., Zhang, Y., Hu, L., Taleb, T., & Sheng, Z., (2015), Cloud-based wireless network: Virtualized, reconfigurable, smart wireless network to enable 5G technologies. *Mobile Networks and Applications, 20*(6), 704-712.

Demestichas, P., Georgakopoulos, A., Karvounas, D., Tsagkaris, K., Stavroulaki, V., Lu, J., & Yao, J. (2013). 5G on the horizon: key challenges for the radio access network. *IEEE Vehicular Technology Magazine, 8*(3), 47-53.

Gubbi, J., Buyya, R., Marusic, S., & Palaniswami, M., (2013), "Internet of Things (IoT): A vision, architectural elements, and future directions," *Future generation computer systems," 29* (7), 1645-1660.

Gupta A., Jha, R. K., (2015), "A survey of 5G network: Architecture and emerging technologies," *IEEE access, 3*, 1206-1232.

Wortmann F., Flüchter K., "Internet of Things." *Business & Information Systems Engineering*, 2015, *57*(3), 221-224.

Chapter 6

CRITICAL ISSUES FACING THE INTERNET OF THINGS (IOT)

INTRODUCTION

The use of information technology among individuals and organizations in the 21st century has become of the essence in realizing set goals and objectives. For the last few decades, the advancement in technology has attributed to increased growth in various industries worldwide. Through technological transformation, there has been increasing demand for various courses being offered by various institutions in order to acquire relevant skills and knowledge related to technology. Through different studies and innovative ideologies, this was attributed to the modernization of technology with various technological devices and systems being developed to enhance more improved communication and storage systems. Through the establishment of Web 2.0, the internet has become essential in the communication industry as applications such as World Wide Web, and WAN has become essential in normal business operations, and in realizing individual goals. The internet, for instance, has made it possible for global connectivity facilitating concepts such a globalization and development of advanced technologies. The possibility of utilizing the internet has however been realized through the emergence and growth of the internet of things. In this case, a review of the Internet of things and challenges facing this concept and systems has been discussed.

The Internet-of-Things or IoT is a trend that is exploding. Devices are becoming more personal and generating more data than ever before. Sensors, monitors, indicators, process controllers, etc. nearly every machine on the planet has some form of interconnectivity with a management system. The data generated and examined by these devices allow for devices to improve functionality while not sacrificing productivity. A study by Gartner Inc. estimates that nearly 20 Billion devices will be on the internet by the year 2020. A new naming protocol is in development URI, or Uniform Resource Identifier is set to be used in parallel to a more traditional means of a DHCP service. IOT is the next big step for technology.

The major challenges that currently face IoT revolve around regulations and standardization. The IEEE or ETF has yet to apply any sort of technical standardization for developers to follow. The result is that many developers are writing rudimentary and proprietary code for their "smart" devices. Take for instance the heating and cooling in your home. If company A makes a system that can heat and cool and company B makes a competitive system, even though both are doing the exact same thing their data would be unrecognizable to one another. Instead of working together to gain market advantage simultaneously, companies are working in secret developing innovations based on the singularity of data their devices provide.

The way these devices connect to one another is another issue facing IoT. Some devices are managed by a mesh network and connect directly to one another. Other devices connect to a remote system hosted in the cloud by services like Microsoft Azure and Amazon Web Services. Some devices may have a smart gateway that they feed and that gateway then relays a pool of data back to a centralized point for analysis and interpretation. Establishing secure and versatile channels is very important to the future of how IOT develops and becomes streamlined into our daily lives.

Privacy and security will always be the #1 challenge that IoT faces. Users are very particular about what data is put out on the web about them. Self-worth will always predetermine the way a user bases their biases on a system. Wearables are changing the way that fitness works in the industry – but publishing too much data about a person can make them feel uncomfortable or weary of themselves. Interpretation will always be at the discretion of the user. A system may be able to analyze and make suggestions based on trends set in data patterns – but it is up to a person to accept or reject the information given. Also, falsified information fed into the world of IoT can provide skewed or misleading data that could flag a system to better check its data and its users. Ensuring that this data is safely and securely sent across the globe is another issue that consumers and developers will face. Exposing something like someone's medical information via an unencrypted channel could spell disaster for business.

Finally, IoT has given us a new world to live in. Our lives are being changed daily and the impact of the devices we sync to the internet is affecting everyone around us. What started as a trend in the early 2000s as having a device that could call or text anyone has now created an environment where lights, appliances, even watches are connected to the internet. They know more about us than we know about ourselves. Our habits, patterns, and distinctive behaviors are nothing more than 1s and 0s to a machine. But big data and data analytics working with IoT are revolutionizing the way we think and live.

HOW DEVICES AND CONNECTIVITY ARE ORGANIZED

The Internet of things is a concept that has continued to attract the attention of various scholars and organizations as many seek to establish more improved systems to enhance efficiency in the transfer and storage of data (Anup & Aniket 9). Similarly, with the increasing technological innovations, the demand for more improved devices in the communication industry has attributed to more improved network systems, software's, and programs. Moreover, in order to enhance effective utilization of the internet, this has led to increased development of structures, and internet infrastructure in different parts of the world (Anup & Aniket, 2017).

Ultimately, this has significantly attributed to the growth of the Internet of Things (IoT). The internet of things, in this case, is described as a concept that involves improved connectivity of devices, systems, programs and services that also involves the use of numerous domains, applications, and protocols. Through the internet of things, this has made it possible effective inter-networking between physical devices, buildings, and vehicles. However, this has been realized through the utilization of various, software's, electronics, sensors and other network connectivity structures, making it possible for the devices to collect and exchange information. Through the IoT, various technological objects can be controlled, detected and sensed remotely through an existing network (Gigli & Koo 17). The efficiency of the Internet of things has also been made possible through the developments of other technologies such as smart cities, smart grids, and intelligent communication. The growth of computerized systems and connectivity with the internet infrastructure has also played a critical role in the expansion of the internet of things operations. Over the years, the investment on technology in various industrial sectors has attributed to the application of the internet of the things in a different type of functions such as home automation, control systems, and wireless sensor network. More importantly, various technologies such as embedded systems, wireless communication, and real-time analytics have attributed to the growth of the Internet of Things (IoT). To date, the internet of things is applied in various fields such as modern homes, hospitals, cyber, offices, businesses, media, transportation and in manufacturing industry (Neha & Priya 16). Through homes and other types of buildings, the IoT devices at applied in controlling and monitoring various used electrical and electronic systems. Similarly, in the transportation sector, IoT is applied through the integration of various transportation systems that enhance control, information processing, and communication. In this case, this has facilitated various functions and operations in the transportation sector including logistics, smart parking, traffic control, fleet management and vehicle control.

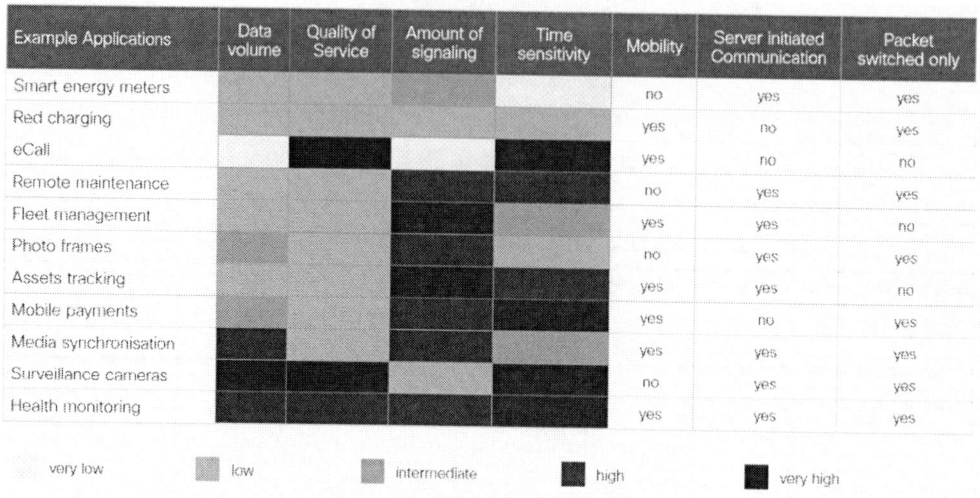

Example Applications	Data volume	Quality of Service	Amount of signaling	Time sensitivity	Mobility	Server initiated Communication	Packet switched only
Smart energy meters					no	yes	yes
Red charging					yes	no	yes
eCall					yes	no	no
Remote maintenance					no	yes	yes
Fleet management					yes	yes	no
Photo frames					no	yes	yes
Assets tracking					yes	yes	no
Mobile payments					yes	no	yes
Media synchronisation					yes	yes	yes
Surveillance cameras					no	yes	yes
Health monitoring					yes	yes	yes

very low — low — intermediate — high — very high

Source: *Handbook: Impacts of M2M Communications & Non-M2M Mobile Data Applications on Mobile Networks*, page 50. ITU (Geneva, 2012). Available at: www.itu.int/md/T09-SG11-120611-TD-GEN-0844/en

Figure 1. Examples of IoT devices already impacting the lives of people across the world.

TRANSMISSION AND COMMUNICATION IS ESTABLISHED BETWEEN DEVICES

Data communication, in this case, is viewed as the process of transferring data from one point to the other or through multipoint channels. Globally, there are numerous channels that have been adopted by firms and individuals for transmission of data including through the optical fibers, wireless communication and through computerized systems (Anup & Aniket 9). The optical fiber, for instance, transmits signals through protons making it possible to speedily transmit the required information. The wireless communication relies on communication satellites and other wireless links critical for transmitting signals. The transmission, in this case, is also achieved through applied frequencies, modulation and through transmission protocols. Mostly, the data is transmitted in the form of electromagnetic signal. This may also be in form of passband or baseband signals that may represent bitstreams. The transmission of data and communication through IoT devices has been articulated by the innovations of various technologies such as the internet infrastructure, computerized systems and other crucial technological devices (Kosmatos, Tselikas & Boucouvalas 65). Mostly, some of the IoT devices may also be classified as wired or wireless. For the wireless devices, they may also be classified as short-range, medium-range, and long-range. Some of the short-range wireless devices may include, blue tooth devices, radio-frequency identification, Wi-Fi, and Thread. The Long-range wireless may include use communication satellite and long-range Wi-Fi connection. The use of fiber optic connections is considered part of the wired technologies of the IoT. Overall, there are numerous types of connectivity applied in the internet of things. Such connectivity may include the local area network (LAN), Personal Area Network (PAN), Wide Area Network (WAN), and Neighborhood Area Network (NAN) (Butler 38). In this case, the IoT devices need to have connections with any of the networks in order to enhance effective transmission of data.

THE PROCESS OF MONITORING AND TRACKING DEVICES

The process of monitoring various IoT devices is essential in enhancing effective transmission of data from one point to the other (Shubhalika & Tanveer 23). This is also critical in enhancing a credible and reliable process of transmitting data. Additionally, through monitoring IoT devices this also promotes an environment where there is a regular checkup on the systems. For business organizations, monitoring IoT devices provides an opportunity for firms to establish mechanisms for ensuring data is not lost due to technical problems with the devices. More importantly, the demand for speedy processing of information and tracking system has also increased the need for monitoring IoT devices among individuals and corporate firms. As part of the management processes within firms, there are numerous approaches that are adopted to help in monitoring IoT devices. For example, through regular checkup on the data being transmitted through various routers, this provides detailed information on technical problems that may exist in the devices (Xian & Zhi 27). Similarly, companies and individuals also have the responsibility of maintaining various devices that are connected to the internet through the selected router. Although the monitoring data usage over a particular period of time can be difficult, it is essential that regular monitoring is made on various devices used for transmitting and receiving data. Such devices, in this case, may include Android phones, Wi-Fi devices, iPads, Smart TVs, Windows PC, Macs, servers, satellites, and iPhone. Through computerized surveillance, companies may also apply this approach to monitor traffic and data on the internet. For corporates, it is also essential to establish management systems for their computers, networks, servers, files, and emails. This can, however, be achieved by ensuring that employees are effectively trained especially the IT experts. Companies that also provide internet services should also take responsivity of monitoring their servers. For example, companies such as Google should ensure that their IoT devices meet high standards and are properly maintained.

There are also numerous technologies that have also been adapted to aid in tracking the IoT operations. Mostly, companies establish tracking systems for the internet of things devices. A tracking system, in this case, play a critical role in observing objects or devices, that then provides the timely position of data for further scrutiny (Razzak 67). There several tracking systems that have been adopted by companies across different parts of the world. Such tracking systems may include the Global Positioning systems, bar-code systems, and Automatic identification (RFID auto-id). There are also tracking systems for devices such as mobile phones including systems such as location-based services. This works in a combination of the systems including cellular locating technologies the GPS systems. Although the GPS systems are frequently used by many companies, the tracking system may sometime fail to provide the needed service based on the location of the IoT devices. In this case, systems such as RFID systems may also be applied for indoor tracking. Other systems may include Real Time Locating Systems that operates through Wireless LAN.

THE MEASUREMENT METRIC FOR PERFORMANCE ANALYSIS AND OPTIMIZATION

The functionality of IoT is essential in numerous business operations and at individual capacity especially if various technological goals are to be realized. The internet of things devices, in this case, may also not reflect effective utilization of the resources especially if the performance is not effectively monitored. With the current diverse use of technology in different sectors such as governments, homes, and enterprises across the board, the demand for improved working IoT devices is significant as this would enhance the growth of business, cities and effective exchange of data globally. In this case, it is essential for individual and organizational users of the IoT devices to frequently conduct an evaluation of the system's performance (Gigli & Koo 17). This may be realized through application of selected metrics of performance that would help keep on check the operations of the IoT devices. By conducting performance analysis for the IoT devices, companies may have an opportunity to improve the functionality of various IoT devices, therefore promoting an environment where there is a speedy transmission of through the IoT devices while also promoting a secure system. Organizations, therefore, have the responsibility of establishing mechanisms and systems that would set standards that would regulate the utilization of IoT devices in order to meet the demand for improved performance. Such standards may involve enhancing security features in the IoT devices and ensuring the quality of technological infrastructure, the adopted devices, and internet connectivity. More importantly, there are numerous approaches and measures that may be adopted in order to enhance the improved performance of the IoT devices. Some of the metrics of performance that may be adopted include evaluation of latency, bandwidth, jitter and error rates. Additionally, it is essential to consider the value of the IoT devices, especially on the basis of efficiency, effectiveness, and speed in transmitting data, level of technology, storage, and network coverage. The value of IoT, in this case, may be assessed through its application in homes, offices, on vehicles, cities, and factories, human, on logistics and on different work sites (Gigli & Koo 17). The economic impact of IoT on the economy is also an important factor to be considered as a metric for performance. For example, it is estimated the IoTs will have a significant impact of up to $3.9 trillion to 11.1 trillion annually in the year 2025. Additionally, cost-effectiveness is also an important metrics for evaluating IoT performance. It is also essential to consider how the IoT is able to transform business process while creating opportunities for business models and business expansion through profitability. The capacity of the sensors and actuators to detect and interpret data from various computing systems is also essential in confirming the fact that the performance of IoT devices is efficient. Other metrics that can also help in administering the Internet of things may include evaluation of traffic on various IoT devices and among various adopted applications. Through an evaluation of various achievement made after utilization of IoT, this is also a critical means by which organizations can also use to examine the performance of this technologies. For example, some of the achievement that may be made through utilization of the internet of things may include increased organizational performance especially in-service delivery, and the communication systems. In this case, companies using technologies such as IoT may experience significant transformation in their business operations such as in production, marketing, and in the storage and retrieving of information. This is essential as different business stakeholders may benefit from improved technologies including customers and the society in general. Subsequently, the evaluation of the various business stakeholders' feedbacks, this can also be used as a measurement matrix of performance for the Internet of things technologies. Through these approaches, companies have the opportunity to use such measurement metrics to evaluate the progress of the installed technologies and whether necessary changes should be done to improve such technologies. By evaluating the performance metrics of the IoT, companies also get an opportunity to establish the weakness of such technologies and take relevant actions in order to improve in critical areas that would improve the firms' operations.

CHALLENGES: SECURITY, PRIVACY, AND INTEGRITY OF DATA

The internet plays a significant role in the transmission of data among individuals and corporate (Gigli & Koo 17). Through the growth of the internet connectivity, this has played a significant role in advancing the concept of globalization. More importantly, through the emergence of various technologies such as mobile phone technologies and other applications such as new media platforms, individuals now the opportunity to communicate and share information from different parts of the world. In the business world, all stakeholders are also regular users of the World Wide Web, including the consumers, suppliers, partners and also the employees. In this case, for instance, consumers use the internet to make purchases online, make inquiries, place orders, and share their feedback with the organizations. Suppliers also utilize the internet for placing orders, reducing their inventories, and tracking various logistics. Suppliers are also able to establish innovative pricing strategies and also access competitive bidding opportunities online. Considering the fact that the internet has a large number of connections globally, the IoT play a significant role in providing physical data, but also enhancing the processing of available data (Anup & Aniket 124). In this case, many firms use this opportunity to provide business insights. The internet of things and the World Wide Web is considered as critical in business operations especially the 21st century. In this case, technology plays an important role in communication and in networking. Within increasing application of internet and other technological advances, consumers are now able to purchase goods and services 24/7 online, many companies have also benefited from a minimized cost of business operation. Subsequently, organizations also have the opportunity for creating good relations with customers while also benefiting from massive storage provided by different types of technologies. The rate of exchanging data through online platforms has also been increased among individuals and firms. This has been achieved through the speedy transmission of data. The advancement of technology and the internet has attributed to the growth of the economy while also enhancing a large number of job opportunities for many. Various business operators have also benefited from advanced technologies through monitoring and tracking their deliveries across different parts of the world. Although the internet of things has been critical in realizing various organizations and individual's goals and objectives, these systems have also been faced with numerous challenges due to immense connectivity across the world. The fact that many of the users lack the relevant skills and knowledge to understand how the IoT works, this has significantly opened opportunities for other users to take advantage of their weaknesses to exploit their systems and create extensive damages to their business operations. Many of the companies across the world have been victims of cyber-crime for instance where they have either suffered a loss of data or damages to their internet of things devices. Subsequently, numerous individuals using various new media's platforms such as social Medias may have also experienced infringement of their applications causing loss of the accounts or disruption effective operations in their account. Additionally, companies in different sectors such as logistics, transport and in manufacturing have also suffered from internet insecurity and damages of the internet of things devices due to mechanical problems or cyber-crime. Many of these challenges have continued to increase in the 21st century due to easy access of different networks where owners have no information about the need to have their IoT devices secured (Anup & Aniket 124). However, companies that have also put some security features have also not been spared with numerous cases of data infringement being reported due cases of cyber-crime. Cases of systems hacking and network interference has also been rampant for the last few decades. This criminal act has been a major threat in different parts of the world especially where government operations are concerned. For instance, due global connectivity through World Wide Web, numerous hackers across the world can access secret information among governments operations in a particular country creating a threat to the nation's security. Regular users of social media platforms such Facebook, Twitter, and Instagram have also been faced with numerous challenges especially when their accounts are hacked. In this case, for instance, some of the social media users have suffered from health conditions such as depression due to hacked accounts where hackers may post videos, messages or images that are demeaning for the user. This has also attributed to individuals image being tarnished especially among celebrity's creating a significant impact on their business operations and opportunities. The World Wide Web is also considered to have been a major contributor to the cyber insecurity as many of IoT devices are interconnected. Additionally, with the existence of wireless applications such as Wi-Fi, information has also become insecure as with single access to such technologies may result in immense loss of data. Subsequently, individual and corporate privacy has also been infringed due to illegal access on the internet of things devices and the available network. In this case, although many governments have put mechanisms and policies to ensure that individual and corporate privacy is secured through a legal framework, over the years, this approach has proved to be complex as it has not stopped illegal hackers from getting access to private data through the internet of things devices. This has continued to be blamed on the increasing advancement in technology and expertise among IT enthusiast. With the increasing training on information communication and technology and networking, many institutions of higher learning have continued to produce IT gurus that have spearheaded the operations of hacking individuals and organizations secured data. Subsequently, innovation in technology especially on the internet of things has also attributed to the challenges on the Internet of Things. As companies compete to develop more advanced technologies, the more illegal applications have continued to be developed by individuals who seek to prove their superiority in IT systems and application. Such individuals have continued to pose a threat to global operations and various internets of things devices across the world (Anup & Aniket 124). For the wired technologies using connection such fiber optic, such cables are also faced with enormous challenges such as cables being cut off through other infrastructure developments in areas such as major cities. These problems have been costly for many organizations that are unable to connect to the internet, therefore distracting the firm's operations. Additionally, such cable may also be exposed to other illegal connection therefore exposing the company's data and information to different risks such as getting to the wrong hands. The internet has also become a source of illegal trade where institutions such as banks have lost huge financial resources to internet criminals. Such cases have been on the rise in both developed and developing countries where such criminals are able access the banks servers and manipulate data hence exposing the banks data including the financial accounts. Moreover, members of the public who own bank accounts are also exposed to similar threats where many have found their accounts drained by hackers therefore losing their hard-earned savings. The internet of things devices used in maintaining vehicle security has also not been left out with many cases of lost and stolen cars being reported in different parts of the world. In some countries for instance, more so in developed countries, cases of stolen cars are reported on daily bases costing the buyers huge losses. These challenges have also been increased by the abilities of hackers to access passwords that are used as security features for different internet of things devices (Gigli & Koo 17). These features have also become of companies losing critical information especially in their computerized systems mostly the passwords are accessed by illegal persons. Subsequently, users of the internet of things are also faced with the challenges of losing their passwords and therefore are unable to access their data or the internet of things devices. For example, with the increasing use of mobile technologies, many people have access to the internet and therefore one can have as many accounts that use passwords to have access. In many cases, this significantly attribute individuals forgetting some passwords there they end up losing important information and data. The process of monitoring the internet of things devices is also a complex process due the number of interconnected devices that demand different type of expertise. The maintenance of servers, satellites, computers and other wired technologies is also a costly affair and damages to these devices would also attribute to firms losing important data (Anup & Aniket 124). The safety of company's data in damaged devices also lies on the maintenance personnel who may also take advantage of owner by gaining access to critical information on such devices while doing the repairs. More importantly, the internet of things devices also consumes a lot of power. In this case, some of the devices rely on batteries such as the mobile devices where cases of drained batteries may attribute inability to utilize such devices. Additionally, devices such as computers, satellites, and Wi-Fi also consume a lot of power and therefore may increase cost for business operations. Ultimately, these in most cases also affect the company's generated revenues. Issues of internet coverage have also been a major challenge for companies that seek to conduct business operations in areas without effective network coverage. For example, logistic companies with global distribution may face challenges in tracing some of their goods when transporting them in places without better network coverage. Vehicles with GPS trackers are also lost without trace when criminals manage to disable the tracking devices or when the vehicles are hidden in places where the GPS tracking system is unable to get signaled from the GPS tracking devices attached on the vehicles (Le-Tien and Phung 46). Such cases are also common with aircraft trackers, asset tracking and among GPS personal tracking devices. The inconsistencies government laws across different countries has also been a major challenge for the installation of some of the internet of things devices. In some countries such as North Korea, installation of the internet of things devices is regulated therefore making it difficult for companies to expand business operations in such countries. North Korea has also put in place policies and other mechanisms that permit the government to infringe any information that is perceived to a threat to the national security. These opportunities are however misused by those in power and therefore such information and the internet of things may frequently be blocked or destroyed before being utilized. In some states such as California, the use of GPS trackers on vehicles by private citizens is regulated through the California Penal Code Section 637.7., where private citizens are required by law to have a warrant for use of such technologies. Due increasing innovation in technology, there have also been a major challenge of compatibility and longevity on the internet of things devices. This has been attributed by the increased manufacturing of non-unified cloud services, diversity in operating and firmware systems across the IoT devices and lack of standardized M2M protocols. With the increased advancement in technology, some of the internet of things devices may in future be declared obsolete forcing companies to seek for other devices that may have compatibility problems that likely to cause damages on other devices. There has also been a major challenge in maintaining high level of standards on the installation of various internet of things devices and technologies including systems such communication protocols, network protocols and data aggression standards. Taking intelligence action against issues that may arise from the use of internet of things devices such as infringement of privacy may also be a complex activity due to challenges resulting from regulations on information security and privacy. Changes in various business environment such as changes in consumer behaviors and demands, has also continued to influence how the consumers makes decision when purchasing various IoT devices where this attributed to the emergence of low quality devices due to increasing demands for more affordable technologies (Anup & Aniket 124). The integrity of data being exchanged across various IoT devices is also compromised due to the risks some of these devices are exposed to. With increasing cases hacking in different parts of the world, there has been increasing cases of information being interfered with before being transmitted to the receiver therefore posing questions on the integrity of data and information being transmitted via the internet. Many of these challenges have continued attract the attention of different institutions, scholars and researchers as they seek to find solutions of securing the internet of things devices. More importantly, many firms and government agencies have also spearheaded various mechanisms of ensuring the internet of things devices are more secured and with minimal challenges.

CONNECTED DEVICES

Both Organizations and individuals have the overall responsibilities of ensuring that the installed internet of things devices is highly maintained in order to enhance efficiency and reliability of such devices (Chang et al., 68). Subsequently, the users of the IoT devices should also ensure that the installed devices are secure from various technological threats such as hacking and other cyber-crimes. By effectively monitoring and maintaining of the internet of things devices, this would have numerous benefits for users including both individual users and organizations. Some of this benefit would include minimized wastage of resources, efficiency in business operations, cost saving, speedy transmission of information and data, more secured IoT devices, and increased profitability, the reliability of the IoT devices and more improved performance in the IoT devices. Taking collective actions on the IoT devices including improved strategies for maintaining and managing many of the IoT devices and technologies is therefore essential in enhancing effective performance and operations of the IoT devices. In this case, there are numerous approaches that may be adopted by companies and other individual internet users as management strategies and IoT maintenance approaches. For example, is essential for companies to promote training programs on the employees in order to equip them with skills and knowledge related to managing IoT devices. In this case, this would play a significant role in ensuring employees understand how various IoT devices operate and the mechanisms that may be adopted to enhance effective management of these devices. This should also include offering training programs on the maintenance of the IoT devices. At a personal level, it is also important for individuals to seek more information about how to use and maintain IoT devices such as smartphones, Bluetooth, internet Web 2.0, GPS, Radio Frequency Identification, Wi-Fi, 802.15.4 and other technologies (Wood, Stankovic & Vironeetal 32). This is important as persons would have the capacity to detect any mechanical problems on the IoT devices and take relevant actions before unrepaired damages occur on the devices. It's also critical for companies to adopt more advanced technological devices that would help in detecting mechanical problems among the IoT devices including when addressing challenges of interconnectivity. Such tools would in most cases help in saving time and resources. Additionally, companies should improve their procurement structures in order to ensure faulty IoT devices are replaced with more genuine ones. This would go along in enhancing the lifespan of such devices while minimizing cases of faulty devices and cost for repair and maintenance. It is also important for companies to recruit technicians that are highly trained to provide their expertise in handling and maintenance of the IoT devices especially when technical support is needed and in repairing faulty devices. Such expatriates may also play a significant role during the installation process of the devices and in the management of installed devices (Chang et al., 68). Both companies and individual users of the IoT devices should also ensure there is corporation among the service providers including the supplier of internet services in order to minimize cases of threats on the IoT devices such as viruses and illegal intrusion on the stored data and information being transmitted through multiple IoT devices.

WHAT NEEDED FOR IoT TO THRIVE?

The concept of IoT over the last couple of years has been critical in understanding the importance various IoT devices and how they operate as a system. The impact of IoT devices and internet connectivity through applications such World Wide Web, among companies and individual users has been eminent in conducting day to day business operations for the last decades. However, although the application of IoT devices has had numerous successes especially in conducting the business operation and in transmitting data, there are numerous challenges that have derailed the efforts of improving the IoT. In this case, there is numerous form of actions that should be put in place in order to facilitate and enhance the IoT concept to thrive. For example, one approach that can be adapted to enhance IoT to thrive is through improvement of the technological infrastructure that supports IoT (Gigli & Koo 17). These efforts, however, can only be realized through close relationship among all stakeholders including government participation in building technological infrastructure in smart cities, while other players such as manufacturers and suppliers should provide the technical support needed in the installation of the IoT devices. Through a well-structured technological infrastructure, this would also minimize challenges in storage or in the transmission of data. This would significantly support the stability of IoT by facilitating increased utilization of the IoT devices. Another approach that can be adopted by companies to improve IoT would be by advocating for laws that would enhance improved protection of data and infringement of privacy. In this case, with tough laws accompanied by heavy penalties, this would instill fear among cyber crimes, therefore, minimizing cases of interference of private data or information. In additions, this approach would also help increase the security of individual data. However, for this to be realized, it is also important to install various security features on the IoT including passwords that cannot be cracked by hackers and other online criminals. Additionally, there also needs to train and educate members of the public on how to manage and maintain the IoT devices and how to deal with numerous global threats the IoT devices might be exposed to. Companies, in this case, should create the awareness among employees about the management approach for IoT devices and processes of protecting the company's data from the external threats. The employees how to use the IoT devices and the means of ensuring company's security features such passwords are acquired by intruders within the system or while at the office. It is also important for organizations to ensure there are individuals such as system administrators that would be held accountable when issues related to IoT emerge. The governments should also create platforms where the public informed on the processes of enhancing secured IoT devices and ensure appropriate maintenance strategies is adopted. Another approach that would enhance IoT to thrive is by having the manufacturers of IoT devices improve in the processes of developing new IoT devices. With IoT devices meeting the required technological standards and quality of devices, this would play a significant role in ensuring a more productive utilization of the IoT. Institutions such as those of higher education should also provide more courses that are related to the concept on the Internet of Things. In this case, companies would benefit from the recruitment of highly trained personnel's. Similarly, individuals that trained through these institutions may also benefit through the acquired skills in operating various personal IoT devices such as Smartphone applications and other effective security features (Gigli & Koo 17). The IoT can also thrive if companies are able to establish effective technological management systems for the IoT devices. With such system companies would benefit to effectiveness in business operations, therefore encouraging other companies to follow suit. The installation of surveillance software would also play an essential role in enhancing security among IoT devices, making it possible for companies to detect any data infringement from unknown sources.

Through Integration of various business stakeholders, there is also a more increased opportunity to improve various technologies that may be adopted by organizations (Afuah & Tucci 17). For example, the internet infrastructure demands the involvement of various government agencies and other stakeholders including private companies. The private companies, for instance, may participate in providing ideas and the needed finances to build such infrastructure. Through such integration, this would also provide an opportunity for more expansion on the internet of things technologies.

DATA STORAGE, MANAGEMENT, INTEGRITY, SECURITY, AND MAINTENANCE

The security of the company's data is considered as one the important factor in ensuring effective utilization of the IoT. More importantly with well implemented technological management systems in a firm, this also plays an important role enhancing the integrity of transmitted data and any other stored data. In the 21st century, organizations have established various mechanisms of ensuring the IoT devices helps in the realization of the organization's goals and objectives. In the storage of data, for instance, many companies have liaised with other firms that help in providing backup for all the company's data, therefore promoting the stability of the company's data. Numerous companies have also installed security features on most of their IoT devices such as the computerized systems in order to ensure the safety of the firm's stored data. Various technological systems and different business models have also been adopted by companies as a means of improving the management approaches for IoT. Subsequently, companies have also ensured various mechanisms such as effective planning, and the establishment of relevant policies is put in place in order to enhance efficiency among employees when interacting with IoT devices. In order to enhance integrity in the IoT systems, different companies have recruited individuals that are well conversant with IoT technologies and people that respect the company's employee's rules and policies. This has significantly improved most of the company's business operations and confidence among the stakeholders that the firm transacts business with due to the level of integrity maintained by the employees. Additionally, many companies have also installed more improved security feature to protect the company's data from being lost or being accessed by unauthorized persons (Guicheng & Bingwu 112). This has been realized through the establishment of separate internal network and router that is only accessible internally by the company's employees. This has significantly played a critical role in enhancing the security and integrity of the company's data. On the maintenance of the installed IoT devices, companies have established mechanisms where in case of mechanical problems the company engages technology specialist and consultants in providing solutions to any mechanical fault in the company's devices. In this case, such companies also their IT staff work with such consulting firm during the maintenance of faulty devices in order to learn more from the experts.

The issue of integrity on the internet of things has also been a concern that has also attracted the attention of different institutions and scholars due to the complexity of the IoT devices (Gigli & Koo 17). However, companies are left with the responsibility of ensuring that the integrity of various technological systems put in place meets the required standards that are in line with firm's values. For many companies, the organization's values play a critical role in providing structures on how the organization should conduct their business operations. This approach has resulted in many companies putting more efforts on ensuring that the installed technological systems work effectively for the benefit of both the end users and the organization. The integrity of the adopted internet of things devices among companies is also maintained by ensuring that the organizational staffs are well trained in using such technologies. This is important as such employees are able to provide the required assistance where required while also ensuring that all technological systems function effectively. More importantly, companies have also put in place various mechanisms that help in regulating and maintaining various forms of technologies that have been adopted by companies. For example, in some companies, there are guiding policies and principles on how technology should use in conducting various business operations. In this case, this help regulates a situation where the employees misuse the firm's technologies causing significant impacts on other stakeholders while compromising the integrity of such systems. On the other hand, companies have also adopted mechanisms of ensuring that the maintenance of various technologies adopted by companies such as the internet of things devices are regularly checked. This has played a significant role in maintaining the integrity of different technologies that are used by companies.

BUSINESS MODELS FOR ORGANIZATIONS AND CONSUMERS

The success of any organization in the 21st century is much more dependent on the strategies and frameworks put in place by the management in order to enhance the realization of the organization's goals. This approach, however, demands participation of all the employees ranging from senior to junior staff. Due to the recently emerging trends, such as the change in consumer's behaviors, and advancement in technology, many organizations have been forced to make adjustments in their business approach and strategies. In this case, companies have begun to adjust their short term and long the goals with the aim of achieving the increasing demands of a business environment. For example, many of the companies have now established a new organizational culture that is in line the organization's mission and vision. This approach is considered critical as it helps the organizations in establishing a framework of disseminating their responsibilities toward their target markets. Subsequently, with an improved organizational culture, companies have also managed to improve their business operations by establishing a favorable working environment that motivates the employees to perform their duties effectively. As a means to enhance successful business operations, many firms have also adopted a business model that is in line with the firm's values, culture, and the set goals and objectives. A business model, in this case, is defined as a framework, strategy, approach, concept or a tradition that is adopted by companies to help in realizing the set goals and objectives (Zott, Amit & Massa 114). This approach has played an important role in transforming organizational operations as the employees are able to focus on achieving the organizational goals through the application of the laid down strategies in the firm's business model. Globally, companies have adopted varying business models. In this case, there are companies that have focused their attention on providing the best services to their consumers. On other firms, their focus may be on improving their business operations, especially in the manufacturing processes. Additionally, there are companies that also focus on improving their service delivery process while others have paid their attention to improving technological processes within the business operation. This kind of business approaches may be considered as business models where companies focus on enhancing their implementation processes. With the increasing changing demands among the consumers that have been attributed to various emerging trends, companies have been left with no alternative but establish and restore their approach to running business operations (Applegate 12). For example, due to recent emerging the business industry such as advancement in technology, changes in consumer behaviors and the growth of concepts such as globalization, companies have been forced to make adjustments on their management approaches in order to fit and meet the demands of the newly emerging trends. Globalization, for instance, has been of a major transformation in the business industry as the concept has attributed to firms having an opportunity to exchange their products and services in different parts of the world without any boundary limits. More importantly, companies also have an opportunity of meeting the demands of rising global competition by improving various processes involved in their business operations. In this case, companies are also focusing on improving their marketing approaches including making adjustments on the company's brand and making improvements on the firm's products and services. Similarly, companies have also increased their efforts towards the implementation of the firm's corporate responsibilities. There are numerous consumer models that have also been adopted by companies to facilitate the realization of improved relations with the consumers. For example, numerous companies have channeled their efforts on examining the changes in consumer behaviors in order to help establish mechanisms of meeting their demands. In this case, companies engage in various approaches such as Customer Relationship Management (CRM) and Corporate Social Responsibility (CRM). These approaches in most cases are guided through the marketing strategies adopted by companies. Subsequently, through marketing strategies, companies are also able to focus on approaches such as marketing research where consumer needs and demands are determined. More importantly, companies also focus on service delivery, distribution strategies, and in promotional strategies. In other marketing strategies, for instance, many companies focus on establishing a marketing mix that is in line with the consumer demands, more so on the 7Ps. The focus on this management approaches within organizations plays a significant role in the establishment of the various business model a firm may prefer to adopt (McGrath 144). With the adoption of various business models, numerous changes are likely to take place in relations to the society, technology, and in business.

Technology

Due to the fact that there have been increasing advancement in technology, companies have been on the front line to provide more improved products and services through the use of modern technologies. In this case, technology has continued to be adopted in various business operations as a means to ensure the organizational goal are realized while the consumer needs and demands are effectively addressed. Although the installation of technologies may be an expensive strategy for many companies, this has not stopped companies from improving systems through modern technologies. For example, in the 21st century, a significant number of companies has adopted technologies such as the Internet of Things. In this case, through the installation of the IoT, many companies are now regular users of technologies such as the social media and social networks. Through the social media platforms, companies have increased their marketing approaches in line with the adopted business models. For example, for through social media platforms, many firms have the opportunity to sell and market their products locally and in the global market. More importantly, companies have also adopted technologies that have been useful in the storage of data, transmission of data and in the management of information. The internet of things, in this case, has been of significant role enhancing the implementation of various adopted business models that exist within companies. Although advancement in technology has had numerous benefits for various firms, technology has also caused numerous challenges for companies (Debasis & Jaydip 25). For example, due to the nature of technologies such as the internet of things, many firms have had to spend a lot of finances to install these technologies. Additionally, companies have also suffered from increasing cost of maintenance for the selected technologies. It has also been a challenge for companies to operate with some of the installed technologies, forcing them to seek for well-trained personnel including the expatriates. With the application of various business and consumer models by companies, this is likely to increase the demand for more advanced technologies. In this case, the demand for more innovative technologies is also likely to transform the technology industry. The fact that companies are in need of more improved business processes such as in the production systems, this provides an opportunity for suppliers and manufacturers to develop more reliable technologies. It is also worth noting that through the use of advanced technology, companies have reaped from various benefits such as efficiency in the delivery of services, speedy provision of services, increased storage of information, more profitability through increased revenues, improved relations with the customers, and effective management approaches. This has significantly played an important role in especially in the realization of the companies set goals. Subsequently, manufacturers of various technologies have also benefited from the increasing demands for more advanced technologies. For example, such firms have increasingly benefited more revenues through increased sales. The used technology has also been perfected by various companies especially in the processes of improving the management and the organization's operations. In this case, companies have established various management systems such as management information systems (MIS) that have played a critical role in enhancing the improved business operations.

Business

The adoption of various business and consumer models is also expected to have a significant influence on business operations. Through the business models, the organizations, in this case, are forced to make several adjustments in their management approach including in areas such as recruitment, marketing approach, logistics, and distribution of information. There have also been increasing changes in the process of developing policies related to management strategies. By adopting a niche business model, companies are also expected to experience numerous changes that would help in the implementation of the selected model. In this case, for companies that use consumer related models, there will be increasing need to develop mechanisms that would help realize the consumer needs and wants (Schiffman 83). For example, in order to effectively realize the consumer needs, companies have to establish systems that would improve efficiency in the delivery of services and in the production of goods. Technology, in this case, may be adapted to make such adjustments while the company may also seek to improve the human resource through empowerment decision-making process or through the recruitment process. In cases where a company is likely to adopt a reliable business model, this may have a significant influence on the firm's goals and objectives based on how the model is applied. The management within the firm may also take different responsibilities with the aim of enhancing the implementation of a selected business model. This is important as the management would use their authority to organize, plan, direct and establish various methods of control and monitoring process that would ease the implementation of the firms selected business model (Simon 51). Companies may also be forced to make adjustments on other factors that would attribute the success of the firm. In this case, it is important for the management to prioritize on areas they would arraign with the set goals and objectives. This influence is essential to any organization that has an existing business model have to ensure that the organizations values and mission is upheld.

Society

With the improved business models, the society is also likely to be affected enormously. In this case, due to the efforts being put in place to streamline various business operations through new business models, this has made many firms improving their operations hence benefiting the end users and the society in general. The society may be considered as a representation of numerous business stakeholders including the consumers. With the improved business models, companies are able to focus their attention on improving various business operations that involve the production of goods and provision of effective service that is beneficial to the end user. In this case, the society benefits from improved products and services. This is frequently attributed to the firms' approach to business. For example, companies have established mechanisms where employees are trained to improve their knowledge and skills, therefore, enhancing the provision of improved services to the end users. Companies have also improved their means of production, therefore, enhancing provision of quality goods where the social benefits through such. In a situation where companies focus on maintaining their corporate social Responsibility's, this has played a significant role in ensuring the social needs are addressed therefore minimizing negative impacts on the society. This approach has also benefited the society as many other concerns have also been addressed. For example, in most of the company's corporate social responsibilities, companies seek to ensure that numerous factors such as the environmental pollution are minimized therefore enhancing sustainable development where the society is part of the beneficiary from such business approach. In this case, companies have also benefited from increased availability of finished goods and improved delivery of services. This has also been attributed the firms' efforts to adopt effective business models that are essential in addressing the needs of the end users and the society in general. The society is however tasked with the responsibility of ensuring that they work closely with companies in order for the firms to realize their goals and objectives. For example, in order to ensure that companies implement effectively their selected business models, the society ought to corporate to some extent with the companies in order to provide essential resources that may be required for the production of goods and services (Teece 73). The society should also provide necessary support that would help the companies to realize their goals and objectives. For example, with a well-skilled society especially in different fields such as on information technology, the organizations may benefit with the availability of labor. In this case, both companies and the society benefit from this approach. Through the advancement of technologies such as the internet of things, the society is also forced to make relevant adjustments in order to effectively access various business platforms that are available online. Due to this, the society has also suffered from the increased cost of technological devices such as the smartphones and other technologies such as the internet of things devices. As companies seek to digitalize their business operations, the society is also feeling the effects of such transformations. However, the society remains as the ultimate beneficially as through such technologies, various business operations are improved, making it possible for the society to easily access company's services swiftly and effectively. In this case, for instance, a member of the society only need to have access to the internet of things devices and is able to access services online including making purchases of goods on various online platforms.

CONCLUSION

In conclusion, although there has been increasing improvement on technologies such as the internet of things, there has been an enormous challenge that has been attributed by the complexity of implementing and maintaining these technologies by companies. The internet of things devices in this case attribute to major challenges associated with these technologies. The cost of maintenance of the internet of things, for instance, has been a major challenge facing these technologies as companies have continued to seek for cheaper alternatives, therefore, creating avenues for purchasing faulty devices among companies. Ultimately, this also opens the opportunity for problems on the internet of things devices, causing companies the security of their business operations. Due to the fact that the security of the internet of things devices is likely to be compromised by hackers, this also poses a challenge to the efficiency of these devices. In this case, companies have the responsibility of ensuring that the adopted technologies meet the minimum standards of quality order enhance integrity and sustainability of such technologies. More importantly, it is also essential for companies to ensure that all the technological systems that are installed are properly maintained in order to realize the organizational goals and objectives. This would help in enhancing the efficiency and integrity of the technological devices put in place with the organization.

REFERENCES

Afuah, A., & Tucci, C. *Internet business models and strategies: Text and cases* (2nd ed.). USA: McGraw-Hill. 2003. Print.

Anup, S. Polgavande, Aniket D. Kulkarni Internet of Things (IoT): A Literature Review. *International Journal of Research in Advent Technology (IJRAT) 2017. Print.*

Applegate, L. M. E-business models: Making sense of the internet business landscape. In L. M. Applegate, G. W. Dickson, & G. DeSanctis (Eds.), *Information technology and the new enterprise: Future models for managers.* USA: Prentice-Hall. 2003. Print.

Butler, Declan. (2020) Computing: Everything, Everywhere. *Nature*, 440, 402-405. http://dx.doi.org/10.1038/440402a.

Chang et al., "Bigtable: A Distributed Storage System for Structured Data," *Proc. 7th Symp. Operating System Design and Implementation,* Usenix Assoc., pp. 205–218. 2006. Print.

Debasis Bandyopadhyay, Jaydip Sen, "Internet of Things - Applications and Challenges in Technology and Standardization" in *Wireless Personal Communications,* Volume 58, Issue 1, pp. 49-69.

Razzak, Faisal. (2012) Spamming the Internet of Things: A Possibility and its probable Solution. *Procedia Computer Science*, 10, 658-665. http://dx.doi.org/10.1016/j.procs.2012.06.084.

Xian. -Yichen. & Zhi.-Gangjin. (2012) Research on Key Technology and Applications for the Internet of Things. *Physics Procedia,* 33,561-566. http://dx.doi.org/10.1016/j.phpro.2012.05.104.

Gigli, Mathew & Koo, Simon. (2011) Internet of Things, Services, and Applications Categorization. *Advances in Internet of Things*, **1**, 27-31. http://dx.doi.org/10.4236/ait.2011.12004.

Guicheng Shen & Bingwu Liu," The visions, technologies, applications and security issues of the Internet of Things," in *E-Business and E-Government (ICEE),* pp. 1-4, 2011. Print.

Kosmatos, Evangelos. A., Tselikas, Nikolaos. D. & Boucouvalas, Anthony. C. (2011) Integrating RFIDs and Smart Objects into a Unified Internet of Things Architecture. *Advances in Internet of Things: Scientific Research*, **1**, 5-12. http://dx.doi.org/10.4236/ait.2011.11002.

Le-Tien T. & Phung V. The, "Routing and Tracking System for Mobile Vehicles in Large Area," *Fifth IEEE International Symposium on Electronic Design, Test and Application,* pp. 297-300, January 2010. Print.

Shubhalika, Dihulia, & Tanveer Farooqui. A Literature Survey on IoT Security Challenges. *International Journal of Computer Applications* (0975–8887) Volume 169–No.4 2017. Print. Retrieved from: http://www.ijcaonline.org/archives/volume169/number4/dihulia-2017-ijca-914616.pdf.

McGrath, R. Business models: A discovery-driven approach. *Long Range Planning*, 43, 247–261. 2010. Print.

Neha Mangla Priya Rathod A Comprehensive Review: Internet of Things (IoT). *IOSR Journal of Computer Engineering (IOSR-JCE).* 2017. Print. Retrieved from: http://www.iosrjournals.org/iosr-jce/papers/Vol19-issue4/Version-3/K1904036272.pdf.

Schiffman, L. G., et al., *Consumer Behavior.* 9th ed. New Jersey: Prentice Hall. 2007. Print.

Simon, H. *Administrative Behavior: A Study of Decision-Making Processes in Administrative Organizations.* 4th ed. ed. New York: The Free Press. 1997. Print.

Teece, D. J. Business models, business strategy, and innovation. *Long Range Planning* 43, 172–194. 2010. Print.

Wood, A. D. Stankovic, J. A. Vironeetal, G., "Context-aware wireless sensor networks for assisted living and residential monitoring," *IEEE Network*, vol. 22, no. 4, pp. 26–33, 2008. Print.

Zinkhan, G. M. Human Nature, and Models of Consumer Decision Making. *Journal of Advertising,* 21, (4) II-III. 1992. Print.

Zott, C., Amit, R., & Massa, L. The business model: Recent developments and future research. *Journal of Management*, 37(4), 1019–1042. 2011. Print.

Chapter 7

SECURITY AND PRIVACY ISSUES ON THE INTERNET OF THINGS

INTRODUCTION

Security phase has been brought up in a multitude of sectors with a myriad of feelings backing it. Those in the IT field will typically harbor mixed emotions about security for a good reason. With the advent of the internet, society has shifted towards dynamic where we want as much information as possible with high speed. With this ideology and the ever-growing field of big-data, we've come to a market-dictated solution known as the Internet of Things or for those more accustomed to the alphabet soup of the IT industry, IoT.

A fundamental element of IoT is simply a device with an internet connection. It generates traffic involving data very personal to the owners. These devices range from Mother, a simple motion tracking object used to help maintain a constant routine, to Alexa, Amazon's Always-listening personal assistant; IoT devices utilized in lifesaving devices such as insulin pumps and pacemakers.

These devices integral part of our lives as the internet is, the devices that interact with it have taken a backseat when it comes to security. The IT world is on fire related to security and what it means to security, and with good reason.

The three states of digital data can be useful in defining security requirements for IoT. These three states are data at rest, data in use and data in motion. Data at rest refers to data stored on a device such as a hard drive or offsite cloud backup that is not currently being transmitted, read or processed. Data in use, on the other hand, is data that is in the process of being generated, updated, appended or erased by one more application. Data in motion is defined as data that is in the process of traveling across a network. Many companies that haven't yet developed a single IoT application are already exposed to these risks. The Shoran web index, which slithers the Internet searching for associated gadgets, has just listed more than 500 million associated gadgets including control frameworks for industrial facilities, hockey arenas, auto washes, activity lights, surveillance cameras and even an atomic plant. These gadgets were commonly associated with the Internet through an interior application gave by the maker or by outsiders so now and again the proprietor of the gadget may not know that it is associated. As you may expect, these gadgets frequently have just simple security capacities. A significant number of these gadgets require no secret word to associate with them and numerous others utilize "administrator" as their client name and "1234" as their watchword. 70% of the gadgets convey in plain content so softening up is simple regardless of the possibility that they utilize a safe secret key.

Furthermore, millions of devices are running very old versions of their operating systems with many known vulnerabilities that a hacker could use to gain access to the system. In the first place, associations should fuse security with their contraptions toward the start, instead of as a touch of insight into the past. As a noteworthy part of the security by design process, associations should consider: (1) driving an insurance or security peril assessment; (2) restricting the data they assemble and hold; and (3) testing their wellbeing endeavors before impelling their things. Second, as to staff sharpens, associations ought to set up all specialists for extraordinary security, and certification State-of-the-art IoT platforms provide a highly granular system of permissions and visibility that can be implemented without coding. These platforms make it possible to grant or deny both design time and run time permissions at a range of different levels. In the case of a conflict, the most restrictive security setting is honored. Access control can be granted at the most granular level such as specific read or write access to a single property of a single thing. Or, the ability to read all properties of all things in the system can be granted much more broadly at the collection level. Likewise, multiple property services, subscriptions, and events can be combined in a template to which permissions can be granted. Another approach is to structure things and people into hierarchical structures which might be based on organizational units, function, geography or business process and assign permissions and visibility based on this structure.

While Commission staff urges Congress to consider protection and security enactment, we will keep on using our current instruments to guarantee that IoT organizations keep on consider security and protection issues as they grow new gadgets and administrations. Classified information very still ought to be encoded on IoT applications and cloud administrations to avoid information breaks and utmost the downstream effect of a traded off application. Specifically, framework passwords and keys ought to dependably be put away encoded and client passwords must be hashed both at the edge parts and at the IoT stage. Generally, memory preparing on a PC isn't secured for information being used. The alleviating controls ensuring the machine are viewed as satisfactory for information preparing. Cryptographic capacity preparing some of the time keeps running in a Trusted Platform Module (TPM) which is a devoted microcontroller for secure crypto calculation. Your association ought to decide whether the expenses of such an answer are essential for the application that you are planning. Information on movement ought to likewise be encoded so it can't be blocked or controlled while making a trip to its goal. The present business models are AES 128 or 256 for symmetric key encryption and RSA 2048 for lopsided or open key encryption. Information on movement encryption ought to be considered for the information transmitted crosswise over systems and for information inside a system for example between a gadget and door or perhaps between a sensor and gadget. Obviously, there are a few examples where the equipment does not have the handling energy to have the capacity to perform encryption exercises. In these cases, organize observing and other alleviating security controls ought to be set up.

IoT stages created utilizing these structures have a more develop security pose and are more secure as well as can adjust to a consistently changing security scene. For instance, Open SAMM rules give a system to security administration, development, confirmation, and organization. Each of these business capacities has a subset of security hones related to them. Confirmation, for example, incorporates configuration surveys, code audits, and security testing. While numerous assessments concentrate on the pen testing part of security testing, one can perceive how the Open SAMM structure has a significantly more extensive arrangement of contemplations and in this way pushes associations to comprehensively build up their IoT applications. Not exclusively do these systems help to alleviate security issues yet they likewise can bring down advancement costs. It's significantly less costly to settle issues ahead of schedule in the improvement procedure than after the product has been conveyed to the field.

The potential for considerable execution and cost enhancements is rousing numerous associations to create a large number of new shrewd, associated items. With the quantity of associated gadgets and applications expanding at an exponential rate, it's a given that the security dangers related to these gadgets and applications are likewise soaring. The number and assortment of these gadgets exhibit a wide assault surface that joined with the nonappearance as a rule of human administrators postures fundamentally critical security challenges. This white paper has delineated security best practices that can be connected at the gadget and application level by associations that are arranging or planning savvy associated items to guarantee the security of their IoT gadgets and arrangements.

WHY IS IOT SECURITY IMPORTANT?

Internet of Things can be defined as the network of physical devices, home equipment as well as other items that may have the software, actuators, sensors and network connectivity embedded in their structure to enable them link and exchange data with one another(Mattern and Floerkemeier). IoT is a means by which technology can manage to integrate the physical world that we experience into computer-based systems. The term "things" in IoT can refer to a wide range of devices like automobiles, field operation devices, air purifiers, cameras, mobile phones and heart monitoring implants among many others.

With IoT spreading its use and influence to almost all sectors of human life, it is important to ensure that all IoT devices are guided by a number of elements (Noto La Diego and Walden). These key elements increase the quality assurance of the IoT devices as well as safeguard the interests of the users. When a client is making decisions to make use of an IoT device, there are a number of things that they consider from cost, return on investment and the security, privacy and ethical considerations by the manufacturer (Singh, Pasquier, and Bacon).

Key Elements of IoT

There has been consumer concerns raised that most IoT devices are developed in a rush without careful considerations for their privacy and security elements (Singh, Pasquier, and Bacon). According to a survey carried out by Business Insider Intelligence, in the last quarter of the year 2014, 39% of the survey respondents felt that security was their biggest concern when considering using new IoT technology. Security and privacy are part of the key elements that determine the effectiveness of IoT devices.

Security: Consumers have expressed concerns mostly about the handlers of big packets of data. This data is harvested in large quantities and stored over a long period of time. In case of a high profile hack, it is possible that consumer details could be brought to light and used inappropriately. Most IoT devices are sold to customers with unpatched software and operating systems. Aside from this overlooked mistake, some consumers forget to change the original password after purchasing their smart devices.

Privacy: IoT privacy involves protecting consumer information from exposure to the IoT environment (Rouse, IoT Privacy). Data transmitted from more than one endpoint when collected and analyzed can give rise to sensitive information. Consumer concerns on privacy have been plagued with notions that it would be impossible for infrastructures that deal with big data like IoT to consider privacy. Some of these IoT devices have been labeled to invade public space.

As technology advances, we as a society are using the information generated by the technology to improve our lives. While the notion and ideology are sound, but we have to tackle potential of the abuse. The methods we use to enrich our lives should be tried, tested, and secured. Several companies have started shifting their models to accommodate this change in ideas, but as it stands; the IT community still lives in a 'wild west' mentality.

In just 2016, Cyber attacks in the healthcare industry have risen over 60%. Credit card processing systems, as well as 3.6 million patient records of Banner Health, 3.4 million patient files, were taken from Newkirk Products, and even a worst case that the FBI had to alert 21st Century Oncology of their breach, which affected 2.2 million people.

These are three of the biggest incidents to happen in 2016. Three compromises of the integrity of three companies put millions of people at risk. Now the inability to secure the IoT environment vastly expands the ability for malicious intent. We've started to see just a glimpse of the harm that could come from the lackadaisical approach to the development of the Internet of Things, such as the attack on the ISP Dyn late 2016.

In October of 2016, hackers initiated a DDoS or Distributed-Denial-of-Service attack in which multiple compromised network-connected systems try to take a service offline by bombarding it with traffic, directed at that facility's resources; against the Internet Service Provider (ISP) Dyn. The devices responsible devices compromised by using malware Mirai, which allows the compromise of old Linux and turning them into bots that can perform large-scale network attacks. The DNS server was knocked out; it affected customers ranged from private individuals to big-name players such as Amazon, Spotify, Netflix, and Paypal.

Technical Analysis

Data protection has been an issue since the first two computers were connected. As the Internet evolved, concerns for security also grew to include personal privacy and threats from cyber theft. In the case of IoT security is synonymous with safety. With a regular computer device, when you get hacked you might lose some money. There's no doubt that can have devastating effects. However, when there is interference with a pacemaker or a nuclear reactor, it poses a threat to human life.

The evolution of security has grown in parallel with networks. First, there were the packet filtering firewalls in the late 1980s. From there they progressed to the more sophisticated firewalls that were protocol and application-aware which are introducing intrusion detection and prevention systems and security incident and event management solutions. These were designed to attempt to keep malicious activity off of a network. However, if they did gain access, these controls would detect them if a firewall was breached by malware, antivirus, using signature matching and blacklisting to identify and fix the problem.

As malware grew and detection techniques advanced, blacklisting was replaced by whitelisting techniques. Correspondingly, many different access control systems were developed as more and more devices started coming onto corporate networks. These systems authenticated devices and users as well as authorizing those users for specific actions.

Concerns over software authenticity and intellectual property protection, resulted in various software verification and attestation techniques, sometimes referred to as trusted or measured boot. Data confidentiality has always been the primary concern. Controls like physical media encryption and VPNs were created so that data in motion could be secured.

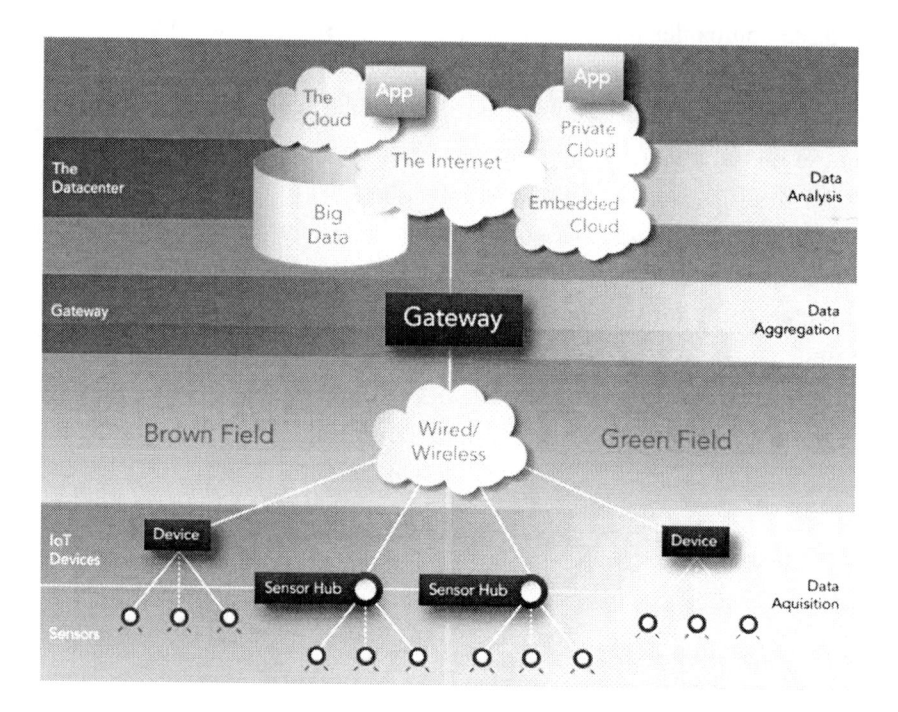

Figure 1. IoT system Infrastructure.

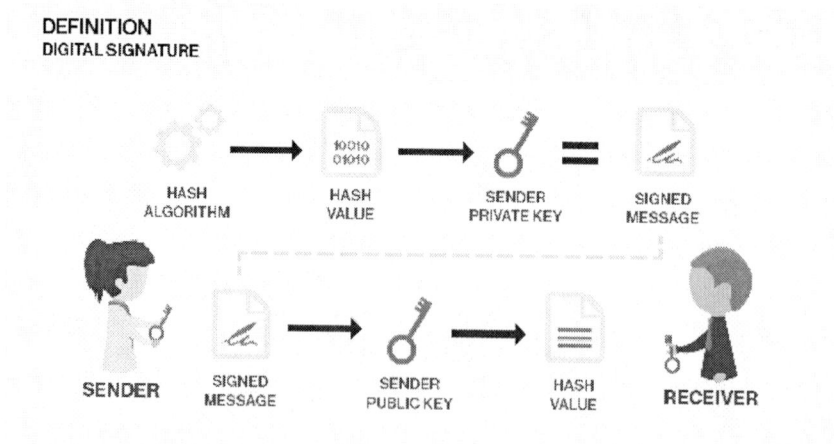

Figure 2. A typical digital signature.

With all these security controls and techniques, one would think it wouldn't be too difficult to apply a variant of them to in the IoT world. However, in order to do that, considerable re-engineering would be required in order to address device constraints. For example, blacklisting which is very successful on a regular network requires too much disk space to be a practical solution for IoT application. IoT devices often have limited connectivity and are designed for low power consumption. Customarily, their processing power and memory are limited to only as much as they need to perform their task. To add to the challenge, most are "headless" devices, meaning that there is no human operating them. This eliminates the possibility of someone inputting authentication credentials or decide if an application should be trusted. In our absence, the device must decide on its own whether to accept a command or execute a task.

Because there are numerous IoT applications, there are just as many security challenges to go with them. For example, the control systems for nuclear reactors are attached to infrastructure. These systems need consistent updates and patches in a timely manner to work properly, but how can they receive them without impairing functional safety. As another example, consider smart meters for your home. These meters collect data like energy usage to send to the utility company. But that information must be protected. The data showing that power usage has dropped could indicate that a home is empty, making it a target for burglars.

With so many different challenges to overcome, it's no wonder why this problem has yet to be solved. However, many people have ideas on how to address this. The most popular solution proposed is a multi-layered approach that starts from the bottom up. This approach would start with secure booting. When the device is first given power, the software on the device is verified for authenticity and integrity using cryptographically generated digital signatures. A digital signature looks something like this:

In the case of IoT security, the digital signature would be attached to a software image and then the device would verify it to make sure the software has been authorized to run on that particular device and signed by the entity that authorized it, can be loaded. This establishes a foundation of trust to start.

The next step would be applying different forms of access control. These controls would be built into the operating system and could be either role-based or mandatory. These controls limit the privileges of device applications and components so that they only access the resources they need to do their jobs. In the event that a component is compromised, access control can ensure that the intruders' access is minimized to other system parts.

After access control, the next step would be Device authentication. This means that prior to receiving or transmitting any data, a device should authenticate itself as soon as it is plugged into the network. Similar to user authentication which allows a user to a network based on credentials that user provides, device authentication works the same with a set of credentials stored in a secure storage area.

After device authentication, firewalls and IPS are the next layers to securing IoT devices. These firewalls will inspect and control traffic that is destined to end at the device. These are necessary even though network-based appliances are in place because deeply embedded devices are unique to themselves, independent from enterprise IT protocols. Industry-specific protocol filtering and deep-packet inspection capabilities are important to have in order to identify malicious payloads hiding in non-IT protocols. With these in place, a device won't have worry about filtering higher-level common internet traffic, but it does still need to filter the specific data destined to terminate on that device.

The last layer in this solution is simply updates and patches. The patches that operators need to roll out should be authenticated by the device in a way that doesn't harm the functional safety of the device or consume bandwidth.

This solution starts at the very beginning. Security should not be an afterthought adds on to a device, but an integral part of devices functioning. The solution does not start at any one place but should be implemented up through the layer to be effective. The internet of things may never be 100 percent secure but through collaboration across stakeholders in hardware, software, network, and cloud, we can be prepared.

Economic Analysis

The security of the Internet of Things is a huge issue. While the devices you have in your home pose a certain security risk, the repercussions of those devices getting hacked would be significantly less devastating to the population than a device in the electrical grid. Attacks in the last few years on places like the Ukrainian power grid have highlighted the increasing need for security.

One of the biggest challenges in security is money and the questions are always who should be responsible for the costs. Back to the example of power grids, should private owners be responsible for the major investments? It is, after all, to their advantage to invest in security, at least up to the point of their own losses, mostly loss in revenue. However, there is also a much greater cost to our society if there were to be a major electrical outage. This justifies much greater spending to manage the security risks of a sophisticated attack. For these types of attacks, it is possible that private investments will not be enough. It's because of this reason that the government wants to institute some form of security oversight on critical infrastructures. This asymmetry of cost means that we cannot put too much faith that a free market system will optimize the outcome.

Cost asymmetry is part of a larger field commonly referred to as security economics. New to the economic discipline, it focuses on understanding security incentives and the cost misalignments. There are a few different elements with this field. Software being at the center of the cybersecurity problem Non-adhesion contracts absolves a vendor from any liability, such as security vulnerabilities. These contracts are wide-spread, giving the software vendors very little incentive to concern themselves with security.

Though some liability should be attached to security failures if we want better security outcomes, it's unreasonable to expect vendors to shoulder the blame and full cost of every security failure. With the technology we have today, no product can ever be 100 percent secure; there are many best practices that can greatly reduce vulnerabilities. It is true; however, that security can slow down software development making vendors risk the speed of innovation with the added expense.

At this point, the question becomes how we find a middle ground between no liability and full liability so that we can improve the outcome for the entire system, and not just software companies' share price. A great example that could be used as a model is the automotive industry. As the technology for self-driving cars becomes more prevalent and mainstream, many have questioned its liability. Automotive manufacturers have always been held to a higher standard than software companies due to nature and dangers their product brings. To ensure the safety and security of their product, automotive manufacturers are working side-by-side with regulator and security companies like BlackBerry to ensure that their systems are adequately secure. This partnerships regulations and industry practices could be used as the example to establish liability guidelines for other IoT devices.

In today's market, being a first mover in a burgeoning market means some significant advantages for the seller. These first movers often gain a foothold in such markets and experience exponential customer growth, which gives them the dominant position in that market. In this case, time-to-market is vital to the success of the business.

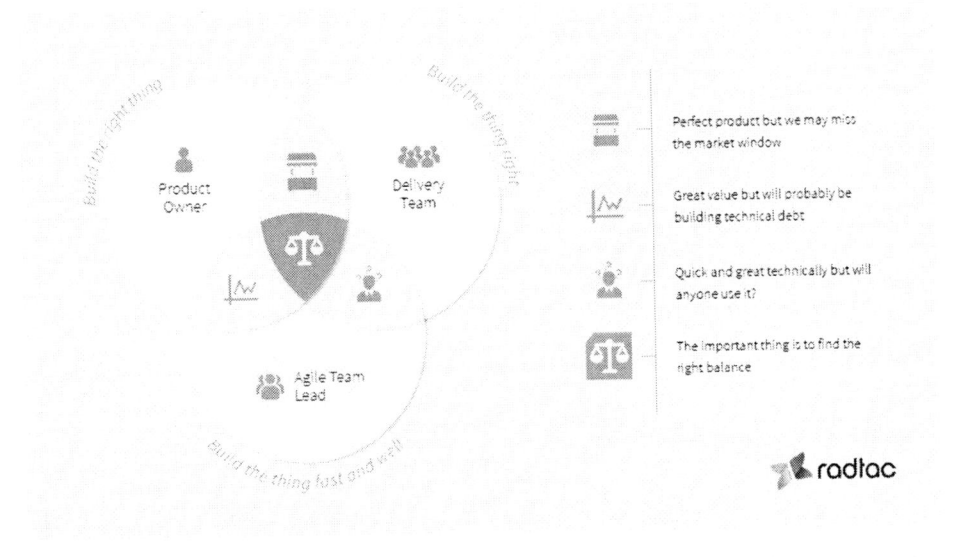

Figure 3. Time to market consideration.

The lack of liability and the hazy nature of security during the buying process has generally lead to the shipment of products with all the required features first, leaving security to be worried about later. Historically, this has caused companies that delay time-to-market for the sake of security to be penalized. This dynamic, however, is unnecessary in the IoT market. Operating system defects and design issues are responsible for many security concerns. With the new IoT devices, many of these issues are invisible to the user. It is for this reason that leveraging third-party embedded system platforms as a starting point for product development could be advantageous for vendors. This would allow their products to be more secure and stable as well as allowing a faster time-to-market.

While the technology and processes for security in the Internet of things will be important in the coming years, some of the battles fought on this subject won't be about technology at all. Instead, they will be about the economics of security incentives. Who is liable and who's not. Economics will be a driving force in the evolution of security in IoT.

VAULT 7: FBI'S ARMAMENT UNLEASHED

On March 7th, 2017 WikiLeaks posted individual activities and capabilities of the Central Intelligence Agency in the areas of Cyberwarfare. Of these files were details of homegrown software capabilities, attack vectors against operating systems of many smart devices including the compromises that can compromise standard operating systems such as Current versions of Microsoft's Windows, Mac OS X, and certain distros of Linux.

The release from WikiLeaks came in 10 parts:

Year Zero – Lays out over 7800+ web pages detailing exploits and capabilities of software supposedly written by the Center for Cyber Intelligence.

Dark Matter – Documented the CIA's efforts to hack iOS and macOS at both the software and hardware level.

Marble – Contained a little fewer than 700 source code files for the framework designed to obfuscate to evade current malware detection techniques.

Grasshopper – Framework used in building persistence malware payloads for Microsoft's Windows operating systems geared towards avoiding standard antivirus solutions including Microsoft's own Security Essentials Suite.

HIVE – This acts as a CIA malware suite with a public-facing HTTPS interface. Using a masking agent to maintain its presence behind public domains (program dubbed "Switchblade") allows the transfer of information and opens the compromised devices up for directions for tasks.

Weeping Angel – Joint product ventured by CIA and MI5, allows televisions with built-in microphones and possibly video cameras to record and transmit even when they turned off.

Scribbles – Contained source code of a tool that generates documents with web-beacon tags dedicated to tracking document leaks (How Ironic).

Archimedes – Redirected browser sessions to a different computer (MITM or Man in the Middle).

After Midnight & Assassin – Malware disguised as DLL's that upon reboot, allowed sets up a connection with the host. Assassin does something similar but disguises itself as a windows process.

Athena & Hera – This two hijack both remote access service and DNS caching service. Both affect all current versions of Windows 10 and could potentially affect Windows Server 2012.

The majority of these were zero-day exploits, meaning that these were not previously known vulnerabilities. The CIA had these leaked and already developed behind closed doors. The idea is that the devices that we utilize on a day to day basis could use, exploit and compromise to the extent that you wind up on the 11 o'clock news.

Wannacry

On Friday, 12 of May 2017, first mass weaponized attack from the Vault 7 leak. The WannaCry ransomware crypto-worm utilizes EternalBlue, an exploit in SMB protocol. The popularity of the incident went viral when discovered from a weaponized exploit that the NSA had, but didn't report it to Microsoft; within less than four days, 230,000 machines infected in over 150 countries.

WannaCry was just one worm that comprised of several exploits that affected windows machines. Roughly 11% of medical devices are windows based, and of that 11%, almost 99% of them are running on an XP system.

The idea is that we're going into an age where security needs to be an after-thought. It's come to the point where we need to set standards for IoT that can allow peace of mind, but this can easily attribute to a mindset. Producers have to inspect their products better, before releasing it to the public.

The next step analysis of the situation shows us analogy "be the calm before the storm." IoT holds a pretty significant chink in the armor that we try to uphold in the everyday struggle of information technology. Since the beginning, we installed the devices to maintain the CIA triad: Confidentiality, Integrity, and availability. There is a multitude of pros and cons to each subject of the Triad. The mindset has to start at the beginning of the project with incentives to upgrade and to keep things at the standard required for the internet of things.

Many organizations utilize the CIA model when creating their information security policies as a method of staying ahead of the evolving cyber-threat. Following the payment card industry, security standards council is a sure-fire way to get started to changing the mindset of your organization to prepare yourself against cyber threats.

PCI sets the baseline of technical and operational instances that practice a "defense-in-depth" approach, especially to cardholder data but can be implemented in all areas of a business to protect a multitude of assets. Maintaining PCI compliance addresses confidentiality through the scrutinization of insecure protocols and the assets it encounters; protocols and services like FTP, Telnet, and various email protocols (PoP3, IMAP, and SNMP).

The idea is to understand what's going in and out and being able to minimize the risk by doing as much as you can to mitigate the worst-case scenario. It becomes a mindset as it sets a standard that to follow, repeat, and secure. This applies to IoT from the beginning of development to software to the services that run on the device.

The Mindset securing the Internet of Things will require the thorough knowledge and strenuous testing of possible vulnerabilities following the OSI model. Here is a brief reminder of the seven-layer system.

Layer 1: Physical – How could the device be physically compromised?
Layer 2: Data Link – how could the connection between two devices be compromised?
Layer 3: Network Layer – How could the machine be compromised from a Network perspective?
Layer 4: Transport Layer – How are we securing the data transmitted between connected devices?
Layer 5: Session Layer – How are we handling remote access?
Layer 6: Presentation Layer – Could the device's interface be abused?
Layer 7: Application Layer – How could someone abuse the service we provide with malicious intent?

Cisco's Idea

Cisco is proposing their framework that allows for the development of a policy to address their perceived threats involving IoT. They developed an encompassing strategy revolving around Authentication, Authorization, Network Enforced Policy, and Secure Analytics.

Authentication

At the core of this framework is Authentication. IoT infrastructure can be accessed with a trust established between devices; an example would be Active Directory Authentication. There are other protocols laid out in IEEE 802.1X utilized as a standard for CPU and memory allocation for credential storage. With this distribution, it allows the ability to establish through X.509 certificates, further advancing cryptographic capabilities for low-grade public-key operation.

Authorization

Using current policy mechanisms, we can control a device's access throughout a network; it works pretty well through enterprise networks by segmenting the traffic which is simple with technology, already implemented in most corporate environments. Trusts could potentially form from exchanges between devices. Cisco uses cars for their example. Say a car builds a trust with a shop, the car could share its authorization to an on-site worker for readings of the odometer, last maintenance records, etc.

Network Enforced Policy

Once again established policies are well suited to elements involving routing and transportation of traffic securely over the infrastructure.

Secure Analytics Visibility and Control

Secure analytics laid out the services that utilized in an IoT ecosystem. Network analytics used for monitoring a deployment of a massive parallel database that allows for the processing of large volumes of data in near real time. Threat mitigation could vary from shutting down to isolation for further investigation.

Is this a silver bullet? No, in the IT world there isn't a clean cut answer for everything as there are all kinds of variables that have to work around. It's up to us to remain as secure as possible.

Recommendation

Most IoT devices will require the collection, analysis, and transmissions of sensitive data. It is of the most importance that this data is adequately protected at all times, also that users are aware of what private data is being processed. I have compiled a list of concerns that should ultimately be applied to devices.

- The device should be designed with security, appropriate to the threat and device capability.

Security architectures for devices and networks should be developed at the same time as the device rather than implemented later.
- Offer appropriate protection for all devices

Sensitive data may also be exposed to other connected systems. Consider how the security of the data will be covered throughout the network.
- Be sure users are informed of what private data is required for the device to operate.

Many users want to take advantage of the opportunities offered by IoT but they also want to ensure their privacy is taken into consideration and protected.

- Audit security products to be sure sensitive data is being protected.

Implement local security policies for handling private data.
- Manage encryption key securely

Consider the lifecycle of encryption keys, decommissioning when necessary.

Data needs to be protected from tampering or modification while in motion from one location to another. If it is not, you may have a malicious attacker lying in wait for that data to come across. It is too late at that point. Security conditions to consider include the following:

- Be sure your software is verified (e.g., Secure boot)

This ensures that only known and trusted software are allowed to run on the device.
- The device or system should only use a hardware-rooted trust chain

This protects against sophisticated low-level software attacks.

- Data must have authentication and integrity protection.
- Remove any compromised or malfunctioning devices.

If a hacker recognizes any device that is malfunctioning, it is then much easier for them to take over the system and in many instances, take over a network since they would have a way in the front door.

- Minimize which systems have access to important data.
- Test system integrity on a regular basis.

In order to avoid any vulnerability exploitation of device due to the operation of the device under an out-of-date Software upgrading software is a must and can be done within different scenarios.

- Vendor update and management process

Security patches/updates should be applied as soon as they are available.

- Only install patches/updates from the manufacturer or another authenticated source allowing unauthorized patches/updates could potentially pave the way for hackers.

Conclusion

Information technology is a mindset that has to be compatible across all facets of IT. The methods we use to design, implement, and maintain our networks are supposed to be transparent, easily navigated, and appropriately managed. The Internet of Things (IoT) is another hurdle thrown at users, and it's up to users to analyze the problems with this innovation, adapt to the issues, and overcome them with well thought and documented solutions. Internet of things is a pretty substantial hurdle that has given the potential outcomes. It's up to users to alter the mindset towards IoT security, and the IT community has to adapt to these security issues. Researched ideologies have a pretty good grasp on their benefits and effects in the corporate environment, but some professionals deal with this on a day-to-day basis. The struggle is, educating the populace who don't interact and deal with technology every day. Lack of awareness of security threats is the main reason for policy existence, and the policies hold some pretty good ideas to persuade the issues.

References

Bauer, Harald. "*Security in the Internet of Things.*" McKinsey & Company, McKinsey & Company, 1 May 2017, www.mckinsey.com/industries/semiconductors/our-insights/security-in-the-internet-of-things.

Borza, M. (2017, May 16). *How PCI compliance is the first step in achieving the "CIA Triad."* Retrieved from http://www.bobsguide.com/guide/news/2017/May/16/how-pci-compliance-is-the-first-step-in-achieving-the-cia-triad/.

Cisco. (2016, December 16). *Securing the Internet of Things: A Proposed Framework.* Retrieved from https://www.cisco.com/c/en/us/about/security-center/secure-iot-proposed-framework.html#9.

Dhanjani, Nitesh. *Abusing the Internet of Things: Blackouts, Freakouts, and Stakeouts.* 1st ed., O'Reilly, 2015.

Dickson, Ben. "Why IoT Security Is So Critical." TechCrunch, TechCrunch, 24 Oct. 2015, techcrunch.com/2015/10/24/why-iot-security-is-so-critical/.

Drolet, M. (2016, June 20). *8 tips to secure those IoT devices.* Retrieved June 01, 2017, from http://www.networkworld.com/article/3085607/internet-of-things/8-tips-to-secure-those-not-devices.html.

Foxhoven, P. (2016, November 08). *Security risks from the internet of things.* Retrieved from http://internetofthingsagenda.techtarget.com/blog/IoT-Agenda/Security-risks-from-the-internet-of-things.

Hajdarbegovic, N. (2015). *Are We Creating An Insecure Internet of Things (IoT)? Security Challenges and Concerns.* Retrieved from https://www.toptal.com/it/are-we-creating-an-insecure-internet-of-things.

Hajdarbegovic, Nermin. "Are We Creating An Insecure Internet of Things (IoT)? Security Challenges and Concerns." Toptal Engineering Blog, Toptal, www.toptal.com/it/are-we-creating-an-insecure-internet-of-things.

Industry News. (2017, January 25). *3 Big Information Security Stories in 2016.* Retrieved from https://www.capella.edu/infosec/year-in-review-sixteen/.

INFOSECINSTITUTE. (2015, November 30). *Security Challenges in the Internet of Things (IoT).* Retrieved from http://resources.infosecinstitute.com/security-challenges-in-the-internet-of-things-iot/.

Losey, R. (2014, April 28). *The CIA Cyber Security Triad and 9ec4c12949a4f31474f299058ce2b22a.* Retrieved from https://e-discoveryteam.com/2014/04/27/the-cia-cyber-security-triad-and-9ec4c12949a4f31474f299058ce2b22a/.

Meola, Andrew. "What Is the Internet of Things (IoT)?" Business Insider, Business Insider, 19 Dec. 2016, www.businessinsider.com/what-is-the-internet-of-things-definition-2016-8.

Network, CIO. "Security Surprises Arising from the Internet of Things (IoT)." Forbes, Forbes Magazine, 8 May 2017, www.forbes.com/sites/ciocentral/2017/05/08/security-surprises-arising-from-the-internet-of-things-iot/#401fc4d42495.

Porup J. M. (UK) - Jan 23, 2016, 3:30 pm UTC. "'Internet of Things' security is hilariously broken and getting worse," *Ars Technica*, 23 Jan. 2016, arstechnica.com/information-technology/2016/01/how-to-search-the-internet-of-things-for-photos-of-sleeping-babies/.

Rouse, Margaret. *"IoT Privacy."* 2015. Print.

Rouse, Margaret. "What Is IoT Security (Internet of Things Security)? - Definition from WhatIs.com." *IoT Agenda,* TechTarget, Sept. 2015, internetofthingsagenda.techtarget.com/definition/IoT-security-Internet-of-Things-security.

"Securing the Internet of Things." *Securing the Internet of Things | Homeland Security,* www.dhs.gov/securingtheIoT.

"Security in the Internet of Things." *WindRiver,* www.windriver.com/whitepapers/security-in-the-internet-of-things/wr_security-in-the-internet-of-things.pdf.

Samani, R. (2016, June 06). *3 key security challenges for the Internet of Things.* Retrieved August 21, 2017, from https://securingtomorrow.mcafee.com/business/3-key-security-challenges-internet-things/.

Schneier, Bruce. "Schneier on Security." *Schneier on Security,* 1 Feb. 2017, www.schneier.com/blog/archives/2017/02/security_and_th.html.

Schneier, Bruce. "The Internet of Things Is Wildly Insecure - And Often Unpatchable." *Wired,* Conde Nast, 3 June 2017, www.wired.com/2014/01/theres-no-good-way-to-patch-the-internet-of-things-and-thats-a-huge-problem/.

Singh, Jatinder, et al., "Twenty Cloud Security Considerations for Supporting the Internet of Things." *IEEE Internet of Things Journal* (2015): 1. Print.

"The Cost of Connectivity: How Will Security Economics Influence IoT Security?" *Inside BlackBerry,* blogs.blackberry.com/2016/03/the-cost-of-connectivity-how-will-security-economics-influence-iot-security/.

"The Internet of Secure Things – What Is Really Needed to Secure the Internet of Things?" *The Internet of Secure Things – What Is Really Needed to Secure the Internet of Things? |* Icon Labs, Icon Labs, www.iconlabs.com/prod/internet-secure-things-%E2%80%93-what-really-needed-secure-internet-things.

Talluri, Raj. "The Fight to Defend the Internet of Things." *Network World,* Network World, 22 June 2017, www.networkworld.com/article/3202767/internet-of-things/the-fight-to-defend-the-internet-of-things.html.

Vault 7. (2017, May 31). *Wikipedia.* Retrieved June 02, 2017, from https://en.wikipedia.org/wiki/Vault_7.

Chapter 8

APPLICATION AND SERVICES IN IOT

INTRODUCTION

The Internet of Things (IoT) has been a very prevalent and engaging force in our world over the past few years; devices now have some form of connection to the outside world and can change how we operate on a day to day basis. These devices use applications that allow us to perform many different tasks like setting reminders, tracking our health and wellness and provide information on a plethora of subjects. Every day new applications are created, and older applications are updated or replaced; applications considered as a driving force in the effort to change and improve the ever-evolving world of (IoT) and helps in managing our lifestyles. Applications provide the ability for people to create new and different things, allow new markets and economic opportunities to open up, and to continue the further advancement of technology and communication.

The predecessors to the applications that we use every day started with the creation of the home computer and the internet. Those two inventions played a pivotal role in allowing the creation of millions of applications like programs, websites and other services ingrained in our daily lives. Those inventions themselves were thought of, created, and then eventually transformed into an ever-evolving form that sees constant changes and improvements. It's important to understand how massive to scale the number of developed applications. Perez (2016) stated that by the year 2020 the apple app store would reach over 5 million apps. The article mentions that "despite the fact that people seem to limit the number of applications they regularly use to just a small handful. Developers keep building, so the apps keep coming." Figure 1 shows the metric for apps and how they've been rapidly increasing for almost a decade. Applications can come in all variations and provide many different features and functions. The importance of applications does not only exist in what they do but also in their reason for existing. Applications now can do everything from helping you balance your diet, to providing entertainment and social connections and also personal management like calendars and notifications. All of these applications were created to benefit someone somewhere. In a world where everything is becoming more automated and efficient, it's understandable that applications would try to implement in different areas.

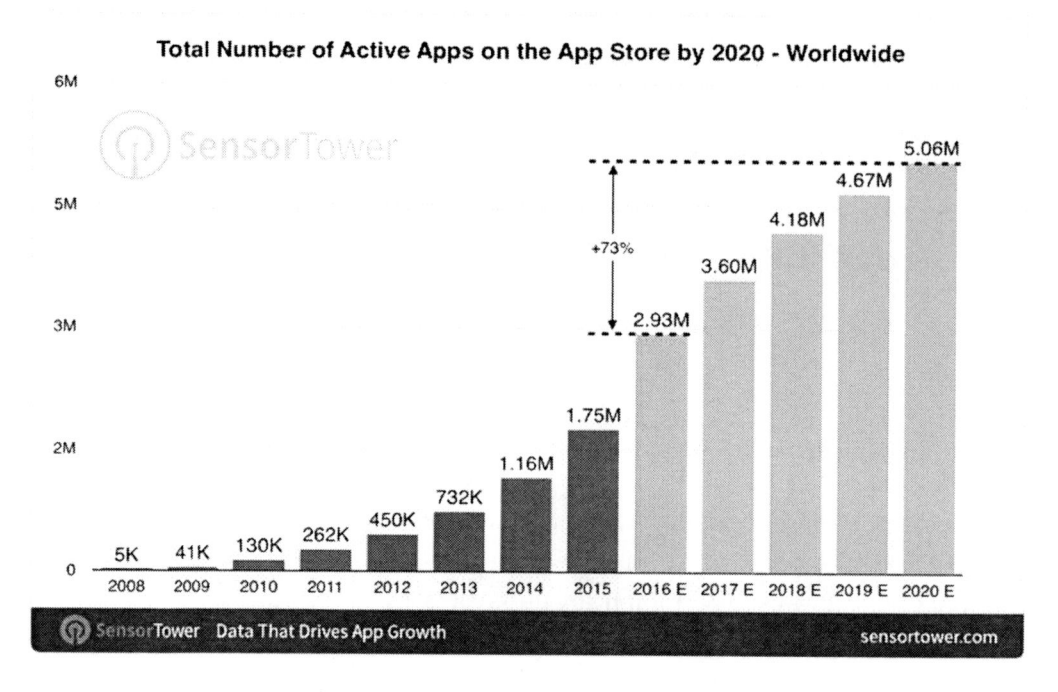

Total Number of Active Apps on the App Store by 2020 - Worldwide

Year	Apps
2008	5K
2009	41K
2010	130K
2011	262K
2012	450K
2013	732K
2014	1.16M
2015	1.75M
2016 E	2.93M
2017 E	3.60M
2018 E	4.18M
2019 E	4.67M
2020 E	5.06M

SensorTower Data That Drives App Growth — sensortower.com

Figure 1. Increase of Active Apps by 2020.

To become more efficient, users are now using many different devices that impact their daily lives. Almost everyone has a device that allows them to text, send e-mails, watch videos, and access the web. In an article written by Kirk Borne, he theorizes the number of devices that might connect to the IoT network. He states that "The number of connected devices on the IoT network will be huge. One estimate says that the number will be nearly 40 billion, which is approximately 30 devices for every active social network user in the world." Besides the common user devices like phones and tablets, other devices are beginning or already integrated applications that connect to the ever-expanding IoT network. Figure 2 is a graph showing the most popular types of IoT applications and gives insight into what is being talked about and used. The most popular type of application is that of the smart home. Smart home features include smart thermostats, connected lights, smart fridges, and smart door locks. These examples are a just small group of services controlled manually but have been integrated to make life easier. Eventually, the smart technology could integrate all functions of your home; the benefits being that you can control what is on and allow you to reduce your utility bills. The second most popular application is smart wearables. A wearable can be anything from a watch to glasses and even things like earphones and rings. These devices can keep you mobile working by keeping you updated with many different notification and communication services. The importance of applications cannot be measured. Applications will continue to develop and will fill almost any roll in human life. The creative aspect of applications should also not go unnoticed; the capabilities are there for almost anyone to create an app for any reason or purpose. When you search for apps, you can find a plethora of different apps for almost any situation.

Figure 3 gives an idea what the most popular types (for the google play store) of mobile apps available. The apps available for the categories like education, lifestyle and entertainment don't always have to be of a specific age or nationality. The universal aspect of applications is what makes them so appealing and numerous. Not all apps used in the United States are popular or even available to people in other countries. A person in another country may have similar apps, but those apps could also be very different in phrases, images, and other colloquial properties but still, maintain a similar look and feel to our applications that we use here. Apps that are developed and deployed in these countries, as well as in the United States shows that we may speak other languages and have different meanings and phrases for things that everyone should have the ability to the same type of apps that provide essential services for the day to day routine. The IoT network should not be tethered to one nationality or language and should be available to everyone and anyone.

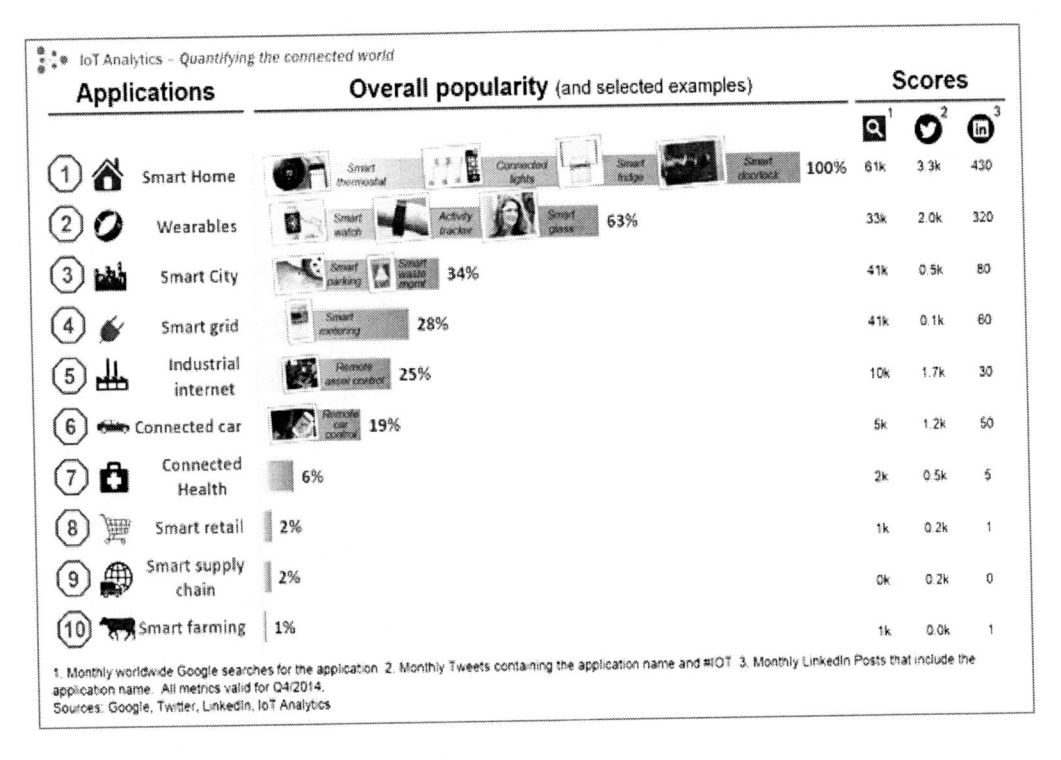

Figure 2. IoT Applications in different sectors.

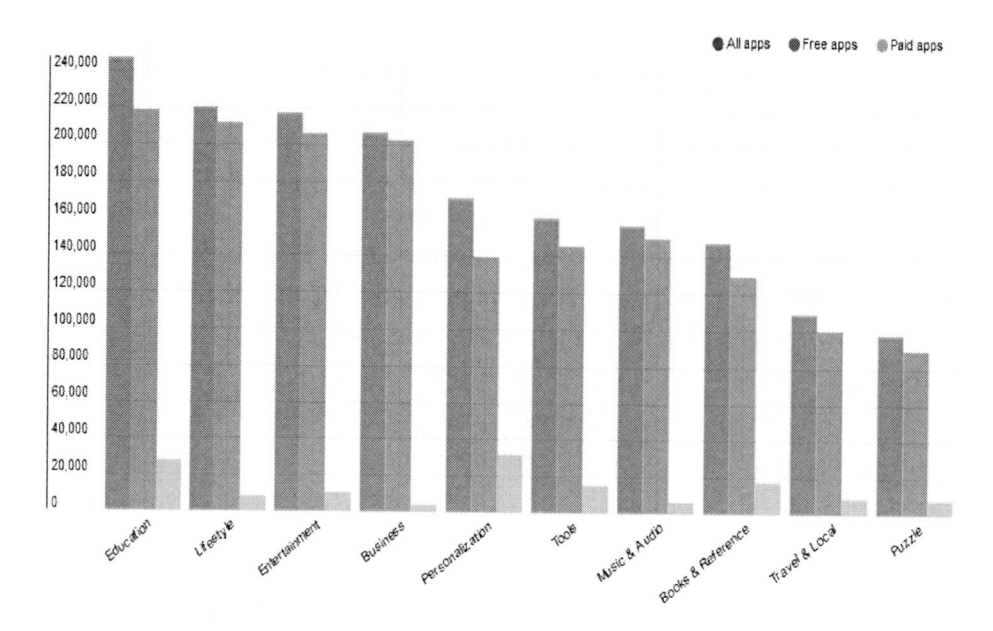

Figure 3. Popular Types of Mobile Apps.

Applications do not only provide a creative outlet for people's ideas; applications provide a structural foundation for businesses and markets that sell goods and services. Applications can facilitate information and conduct transactions between business to business and customer to the firm. Applications can also provide opportunities for businesses to communicate with their clients; offering services like coupons and sales that are easier and potentially more efficient because they are easily viewable online. Applications benefit global businesses as well as local businesses. Anyone can go online and view goods and services in their area, and most if not all businesses have some form of online presence. Local businesses can have access to many different types of applications that make their day to day operation easier and more effective. Padia.K (2015), he explains the benefits that mobile apps provide to small businesses. He writes "From calculating expenses to providing event timelines to processing credit cards, mobile apps have significantly changed the way many small businesses engage with technology." Padia also mentions that "Building your mobile app is not at all expensive and cumbersome a challenge as it was just a few years ago." which is good news for people wanting to integrate their businesses online, and for app developers creating those apps. Local businesses can benefit from having more access to their goods and services and app developers can benefit from having the work from the businesses. Not only can local businesses benefit from increased visibility and possible increased revenue, but apps can also track analytical data and employee engagement. Data analytics are very important and can drastically change how you operate your business. Apps can monitor spending, revenue and other factors that can positively affect business life down to a day to day scale.

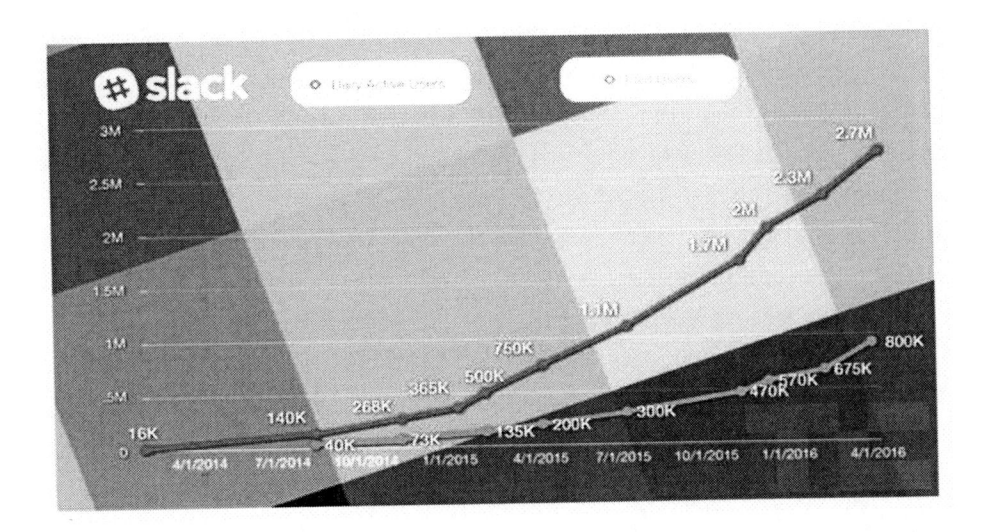

Figure 4. Increase of the Users in Slack.

Applications not only affect long-standing local businesses, but they also can help new, upstart businesses reach local, national, and even global recognition. Whatever your goal is, applications can contribute to achieving them. A recent example of a growing upstart business is slack. Slack is a messaging service that consolidates services into software that businesses use to communicate. Slack has been in the news recently for their enormous growth. Constine (2016), states that Slack's "daily user count and its paid seat count are up 3.5x in just a year."

Figure 4 gives a historical number of Slack's user base since its inception in 2014. The graph shows a huge jump in some users from October of 2015 to April of 2016 with an increase of about 1 million users. Although Slack had a substantial growth period in late 2016, it stalled resulting in about 1.25 million paying subscribers. While the app is new and people are still figuring out how to use it, there could be issues regarding its intended purpose. Apps that are newer could take more time and effort to understand and utilize completely, and it may be a deterrent to potential "paying" customers. Constine (2016) wrote that "Slack may need to find a way to defeat its greatest foe: human nature…The way Slack facilitates procrastination and low-value socializing that could interfere with actually getting work done might be scaring off customers." Regardless, this is a primary example of an application that was born on the internet and has had success from achieving a balance of old communication ideas with new technology and services.

If you have the benefit of having a business that has global recognition, then apps are crucial to your businesses' survival. Applications allow you to connect with your user base all over the world and have unlimited potential increasing your revenue and notoriety. Websites and services like USPS, UPS, and FedEx are constantly trying to improve their businesses structure by increasing employee and site productivity, means of production and marketing presence. All of these factor increases are in no small part due to their integration into the IoT applications and services. All of these companies now have mobile apps, online tracking and other essential services that benefit the company in data and productivity, and the consumer in ease of use and convenience. These applications are crucial for business growth who and trying to remain one step ahead of their incumbent in the market. Data analytics provided by these applications can provide so much useful information; where and when the most orders are coming in, are online services working to optimal efficiency, are the customers happy with our services, and what is the average size or weight of a package? All of these factors play a huge role in informing the company how to react and operate accordingly.

Those companies were just a few examples of competition in the digital world. Other corporations and services that have similar counterparts also face similar struggles and issues. Online shopping services like Amazon and eBay are in competition and other numerous online sellers sell products similar to Amazon and eBay but may not have as much of a selection or only sell one type of product. Applications help these kinds of companies manage their orders, properly calculate revenue, control means of production, monitor inventory and many other services that are crucial in the fast-paced world of online shopping. These applications help the companies stay competitive by understanding what is popular, what is not and what the price of the market is for these products so that they can sell them efficiently. Figure 5 and Figure 6 display the shopping habits in India and how important online shopping is to their way of life. Figure 5 shows the regularity of monthly shopping and indicates that over 60 percent of online shoppers in India shop online at least a couple of times a month. Regardless of what is purchased, the thought that over half of the population of India shops online for goods is astounding, and it will only grow with the addition and improvement of online application

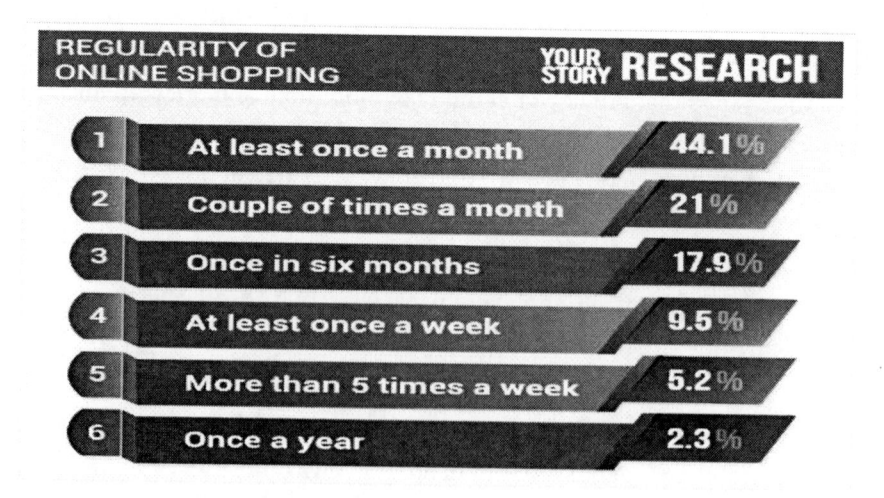

Regularity of Online Shopping		
1	At least once a month	44.1%
2	Couple of times a month	21%
3	Once in six months	17.9%
4	At least once a week	9.5%
5	More than 5 times a week	5.2%
6	Once a year	2.3%

Figure 5. Regularity of Monthly Shopping.

Figure 6 shows what is popular and what is selling. This figure is what would be included from applications that monitor data analytics. The companies could use this information to start branching out to other products or try to adjust their methods to sell their products more efficiently.

Applications are crucial to the development and productivity of companies. It is more important than ever to have an online presence and be willing and able to provide the best quality service at an efficient rate. Applications assist companies in knowing what to sell when to sell, and how to sell. Enterprises that do not alter their business structure or methods of production are almost always doomed to fall behind other companies that are actively trying to out-pace and out-sell you. Applications will continue to evolve and will further benefit companies that take the time to understand their purpose and believe in the data analytics that they provide. The results have shown by the effort that companies put in and how active they are in accepting new ideas and contributions. The internet is not going away and companies need to realize that to be successful.

Applications were born from technology; they serve to use our devices easier and more efficient. Currently, technology being pushed to its limits to meet the needs of the applications we use every day. Communication between individuals has also changed; communicating with someone across the world is as easy as communicating with someone next door. Applications like 3D modeling software, virtual platforms, games, and other required technology to be equipped to deal with the input and output of these applications and programs supply. Tech devices are transforming to take advantage of these applications properly; phones and tablets for mobile gaming and multimedia purposes (pictures, videos) integrated with more powerful processors and cameras for maintaining efficient use of these programs.

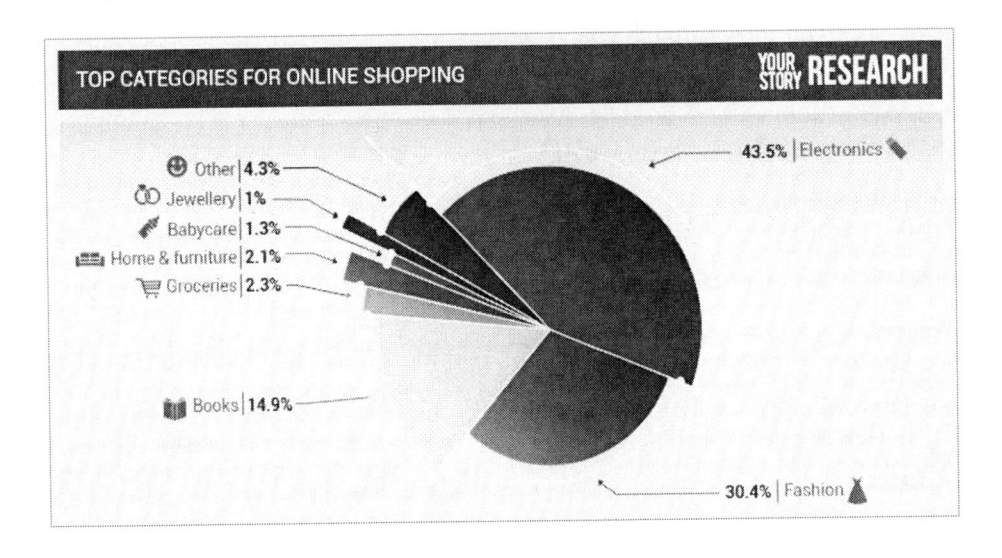

Figure 6. Popular Goods Sold by Online Shopping.

Computers can be altered to fit application trends, tablet-computers have gained significant popularity in the past few years by allowing users to have the processing power of a computer while having the travel functionality of a tablet. Currently, applications are almost as important as the devices. Certain types of applications like 3D modeling software require a lot of processing and memory services to function properly. Most 3D modeling software programs allow you to design the smallest detail and create massive structures that eventually help developing things like sports stadiums, apartment complexes, and schools. A blog hosted on smartgeometrics.com explains the benefits that 3D modeling has for engineers and architects. The blog states that "3D modeling has been used by architects around the world for many years to improve efficiency and aesthetic of their designs." 3D modeling applications have allowed engineers and architects to have certain advantages over old 2D applications. The blog lists these as speed, precision and control, scenario visualization, and reduced lead times. One of the significant advantages that achieved with 3D applications is that they can provide scenario visualization. The website "smartgeometrics.com" describes that architects and engineers can also manipulate 3D models in a way to validate their plans and design quality that couldn't perform by 2D. These types of benefits and services would not be available if they are not aimed at the advancement and improvement of applications.

Applications have also provided a means for people to communicate with other people for business and personal reasons by way of virtual platforms. Virtual platforms can include anything from social media services to software and collaboration tools. Social media applications and services have exploded over the past couple of years and only seem to be growing with every app that comes out that offers something different. Social media applications allow users to do almost anything available in the virtual world, including face to face conversations, uploading pictures and videos and conversing back and forth through chat programs. By far, the most important apps in the past few years are those that allow you to share pictures and videos with anyone and everyone. Applications like YouTube, Facebook, and Instagram, have an enormous user base. Figure 7 shows how many users each of the top 15 sites have and it's astounding to see the numbers.

Facebook leading the charge should not be surprising, but it's interesting to see other social media services that fall under it, but also put up massive numbers in their right. It's also worth noting that as time has gone forward, social media sites have integrated services like VOIP, live streaming, video and mobile applications to compete with other niche social media sites and services. The evolution of these types of applications is probably the fiercest in the IoT network and will continue to be for the very near future.

While applications viewed as social, it doesn't always have to be for people exchanging videos or chatting about their weekend; applications can also provide a way for different platforms and services that involved. Virtual platforms and cloud computing (Software, Infrastructure, Platform as a Service) applications are top-rated now and are

Application and Services in IoT 151

good tools for exchanging everything from online tools, programs/software code and general knowledge and support. These applications have massive potential and have allowed users to do a plethora of things. A Perfect example of the virtual platform is Github. It's a web-based internet hosting and code repository website. Github allows users to upload their code so that other members of their team can provide changes and support. The site also hosts your code, giving you a place to store your code so that it can be easily accessible. Github is just one example of a virtual platform that has allowed users to create and maintain their inventions and ideas. Figure 8 shows how cloud computing works in a public cloud environment that would allow users to access these services online and have them deployed from the vendor.

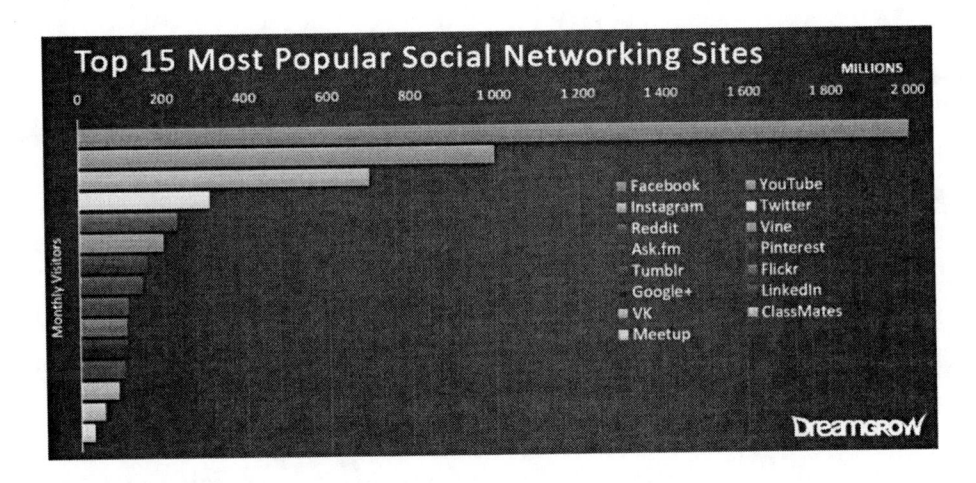

Figure 7. Popular Social Networking Sites.

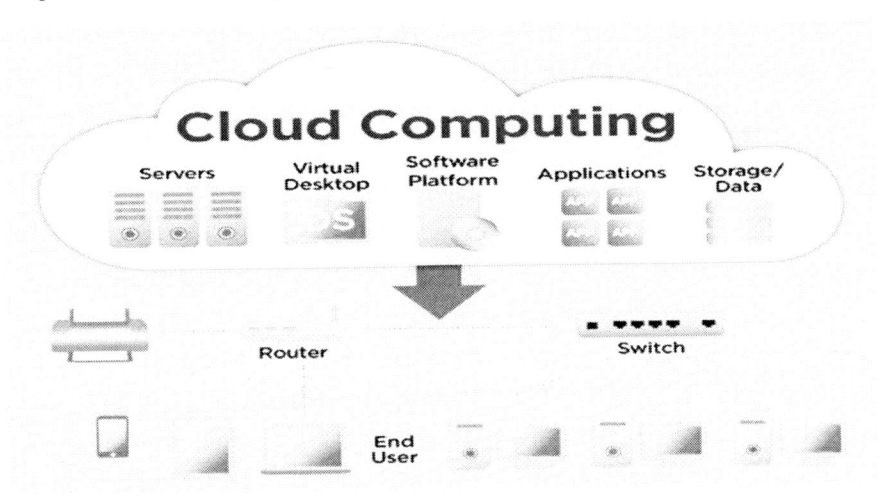

Figure 8. Cloud Computing in Public Cloud Environment.

Emerging Cloud Computing Ecosystem

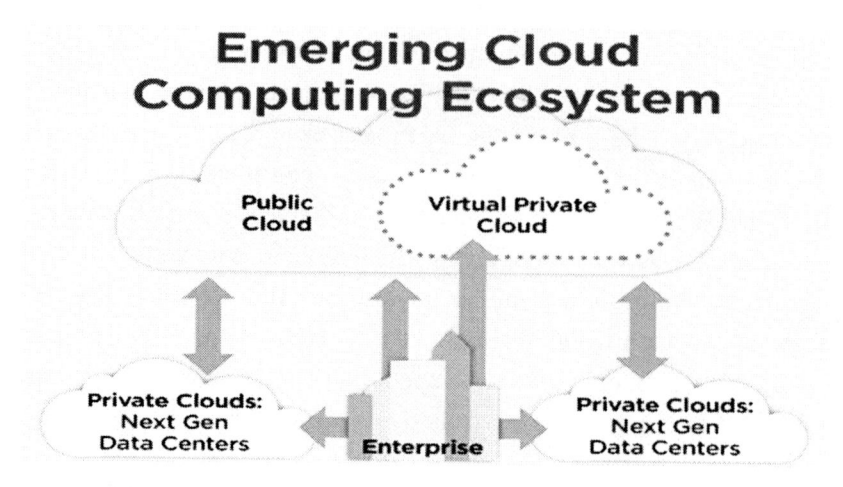

Figure 9. Cloud Computing in Private Cloud Environment.

Cloud computing has also been very successful in the past few years; cloud computing can offer many different services that can fill almost any role or need. Cynthia Harvey, in an article written on cloud computing, wrote that "Most technology experts list cloud computing as one of the most influential IT trends of the twenty-first century." And that "cloud computing has revolutionized enterprise IT to the point where most organizations now take a "cloud-first" approach to their technology needs." The importance of cloud computing goes far beyond the idea that we can just access a service online; it allows us to perform almost any task in a virtual environment effectively.

Figure 9 shows how cloud computing implemented in a private cloud system; private cloud systems are usually handled by the organization or company and allows for dedicated service and scalability that a public cloud infrastructure cannot offer. Cloud computing has taken control over software deployment and could eventually replace the need for physical servers. As applications are rapidly growing-in development and scale, that will push the need for these virtual and cloud computing platforms further and make them more relevant.

Games and gaming applications have been on a steady climb since their creation back in the arcade days. Games have evolved from a few pixels on a screen, to high-definition, motion captured creations. Mobile gaming has also been retaining popularity, with new mobile games entering the apps stores every day. Every year it seems like video games are becoming more and more realistic and blurring the line between game and reality. As the games continue to grow so too does technology develops that plays them. The newest gaming trend that has entered the market has been virtual reality applications. Virtual reality is the definition of combining reality and fantasy. These applications allow the user to physically control aspects of the game while immersing them in the world and the game itself. Virtual reality applications and their technology have grown in popularity over the past few years and have had success in finding a market. Online services like Steam and Origin have been able to provide users with virtual reality games that support different types of virtual reality tech. Although the technology is available and there are software applications in place for these devices, the cost is still too much, and the service not in huge demand so far. Virtual reality and its applications will hopefully find success within the IoT network. These applications have the ability to expand the already expansive IoT network, and possibly take it where it's never been before regarding development and deployment.

One of the most popular forms of gaming now is mobile gaming. Mobile gaming allows you to play almost anywhere and it's significantly cheaper than other means of gaming. Mobile applications have been in constant demand and games are no exception. Takahashi (2017) states that "Mobile games hit a new record by generating more than $40.6 billion in worldwide revenue in 2016, up 18 percent from a year ago." 18 percent is a huge jump for any service. Figure 10 shows the U.S is not the only country that accesses these applications and they are not top investors in the gaming industry.

Mobile gaming's success has been in no small part to their accessibility and strategy. Games are typically free, paid services within the game allow the player to gain items quicker by paying instead of playing longer to get the item. The initial "free" opportunity is usually enough to gain a few million downloads. The growth of mobile games has not halted either.

McDonald (2017) highlights that "Mobile is the most lucrative segment, with smartphone and tablet gaming growing 19% year over year to $46.1 billion, claiming 42% of the market." It's important to highlight as well that everyone around the world has an access to a mobile device able to access these mobile applications. Gaming and its applications may not be the first thing you think of when considering applications in the IoT network, but they are just as important in their contribution to the IoT network as much as a social media application or a virtual platform.

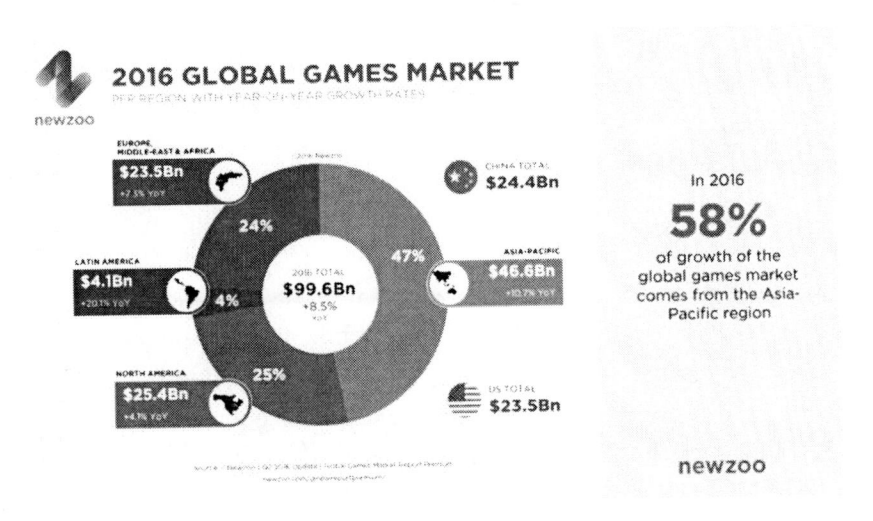

Figure 10. Growth rate of Global Games Market.

In conclusion, applications and their services are critical to the IoT network not only because they provide users with a majority of users and services, they also provide a reason to keep building upon the framework of the internet. Applications allow users all over the world to create and bring new ideas and inventions into the world. Applications have beneficial values for different types of companies and businesses, giving them an online platform to grow and develop their market and allow them to benefit from increased revenue and exposure. Applications help in future development of technology; new devices and services are sprouting every day and making constant improvements to existing technology. Applications are crucial to the development and the survival of the internet, IoT network will become a driving force in almost all developmental aspects.

REFERENCES

Borne, K. (2014, August 06), *14 Benefits and Forces That Are Driving The Internet of Things*. Retrieved from https://mapr.com/blog/14-benefits-and-forces-are-driving-internet-things/.

Constine, J. (2016, April 01). *Slack's growth is insane, with daily user count up 3.5X in a year.* Retrieved from https://techcrunch.com/2016/04/01/rocketship-emoji/.

Constine, J. (2016, October 20). *Slack's rapid growth slows as it hits 1.25M paying work chatters.* Retrieved from https://techcrunch.com/2016/10/20/slunk/.

Harvey, C. (2017, March 27), "*Cloud Computing*" Retrieved from http://www.datamation.com/cloud-computing/what-is-cloud-computing.html.

McDonald, E. (2017, April 20). "*The Global Games Market 2017 | Per Region & Segment,*" Retrieved from https://newzoo.com/insights/articles/the-global-games-market-will-reach-108-9-billion-in-2017-with-mobile-taking-42/.

Nair, R. P. (2015, August 17). *YS Research: India's favorite online shopping brand revealed.* Retrieved from https://yourstory.com/2015/08/indias-favourite-online-shopping-brand/.

Nelson, R. (2016, August 10). *Apple's App Store Will Hit 5 Million Apps by 2020, More Than Doubling Its Current Size.* Retrieved from https://sensortower.com/blog/app-store-growth-forecast-2020.

Padia, K. (2015, July 28*).* "*6 Ways Mobile Apps Can Fuel Business Growth,*" Retrieved from https://www.semrush.com/blog/6-ways-mobile-apps-can-fuel-business-growth/.

Perez, S. (2016, August 10). "*App Store to reach 5 million apps by 2020, with games leading the way,*" Retrieved from https://techcrunch.com/2016/08/10/app-store-to-reach-5-million-apps-by-2020-with-games-leading-the-way/.

Takahashi, D. (2017, February 01). *SuperData: Mobile games hit $40.6 billion in 2016, matching world box office numbers.* Retrieved from https://venturebeat.com/2017/

02/01/superdata-mobile-games-hit-40-6-billion-in-2016-matching-world-box-office-numbers/.

Top 15 Most Popular Social Networking Sites (2017, May). *Digital image.* Available from https://i1.wp.com/www.dreamgrow.com/wp-content/uploads/2017/05/top-most-popular-social-networking-sites-graph.jpg?ssl=1.

"Top categories on Google Play – AppBrain" *AppBrain Best Android Apps.* Retrieved from https://www.appbrain.com/stats/android-market-app-categories.

Weins, K. (2014, April 02). *Cloud Computing Trends: 2014 State of the Cloud Survey.* Retrieved from https://www.rightscale.com/blog/cloud-industry-insights/cloud-computing-trends-2014-state-cloud-survey.

"Benefits of 3D modeling for Architects and Engineers" *SmartGeoMetrics,* 2014, Available from: http://www.smartgeometrics.com/blog/engineering/4-benefits-of-3d-modeling-for-architects-and-engineers/.

Chapter 9

INDUSTRIAL INTERNET OF THINGS (IIOT)

INTRODUCTION

The Industrial Internet of Things (IIoT) is an industrial revolution that represents the future of computing and automation. The potential of IIoT lies in the ability to connect the enterprise planning and product lifecycle management with the IIoT operation decision-making system. The IIoT has been acclaimed primarily as the way to improve company operations, but nowadays companies are finding it as a tool for achieving unexpected growth by using these three approaches: creating new business models, transforming the workforce, and exploiting the intelligent technologies to boost productions. This chapter discusses how IIoT can be implemented to enable higher business control.

Often viewed as a technological and industrial revolution, the Industrial Internet of Things (IIoT) has been under development for the past two decades, and will possibly require another two decades to achieve its optimum potential. IIoT imagines a world based on smart manufacturing enterprises, in which smart devices and objects are connected to each other to form a system, and consequently, through the interconnections, become a part of the larger, more pervasive systems. What makes these devices or object smart is their possession of an intellectual faculty that enables them to sense their surroundings and gather data, manipulate their surroundings, and take independent decision. An intelligent faculty is at the crux of these individual smart devices, and through this intelligence, they connect to make the smart network of devices that comprise the smart manufacturing enterprise. Multiple devices can access these smart network systems securely, information collected and processed through their foundation of cloud and internet technologies. This also permits an advanced analysis of the obtained data which increases the commercial value of other mobile technologies, which results in increased profits and efficiency, enhanced security and safety, innovations and a reduction in the impact of carbon dioxide emissions.

While the progress of IIoT is slow, it will also change the face of industries, for it will enable industry owners to invest in technically enhanced machinery which will be the result of IoT. Industrial operations and businesses will be more controllable by IIoT, and will result in a smart manufacturing enterprise, for the introduction of self-fixing smart machines will reduce expenditure, generate a safe working and sustainable environment. While the integration of IoT with industries and its estimated impact has resulted in both confused as well as hopeful industrial stakeholders and investors, the main challenge for comprehending the impact of IoT on different sectors is the plethora of IoT applications. For instance, as mentioned earlier, a smart manufacturing enterprise will be created by self-fixing machines, and the same devices will also be programmed to manufacture customized goods on a large scale. On the other hand, overall business performance will get enhanced, and delivery time reduced, by the efficient collection and analysis of data by intelligent sensors. The dynamic collection and processing of data will also simplify the smart manufacturing, thereby increasing profits, and a new era of human-augmented machines will result in the development of even more advanced technologies. The implementation of these changes, either long-term or short-term, will depend on the type of industry and the role of the consumers in the same, and the establishment of the international standards of Industrial Internet of Things (Conway, 2015).

BRIEF REVIEW

Despite the hindrances in predicting the specific course of the development of IIoT and its impact in the long run, it is certain that the emergence of the smart enterprise is incumbent upon the following three managerial environments:

- Connected Enterprise Control
- Asset Performance
- Augmented Operators

Though the three managerial environments are different, they are like each other in a few aspects and are even interdependent to a certain extent, for their functioning. A detailed explanation of these three managerial environments is as follows:

1. Connected Enterprise Control

The connected smart components and machines will be closely combined through IIoT resulting in a broader enterprise, enhanced flexibility, efficiency and profits in manufacturing. Though beneficial in the long run, the implementation of smart enterprise control is complicated enough that for the amalgamation of IT and OT systems, new standards must be generated.

The next generation of a smart IoT system advocates breaking down the various enterprise systems to enable an inter-dependent functioning that will enhance the efficiency gain of the enterprises by at least thirty percent. As explained in the following figure, such a holistic approach will closely integrate EPR systems, production systems, PLM (Product Life Management) systems, CRM (Customer Relationship Management) systems and SCM (Supply Chain Management) systems.

Smart enterprise control will connect the automation systems currently used in the value chain, lifecycle and enterprise systems, rather than replacing the currently used system with a new one. The result of this will be a highly controllable business and the optimizing of the complete business enterprise. This control of the entire business on an actual time scale will encompass non-physical as well physical parameters, while the closer integration will result in increased efficiency and profits due to more quick responsiveness and heightened agility to the inconstant and unpredictable conditions of the market. Increase in innovation, better management of safety, the impact on the environment and performance and enhanced cybersecurity will be the potential benefits of such an integration and heightened control.

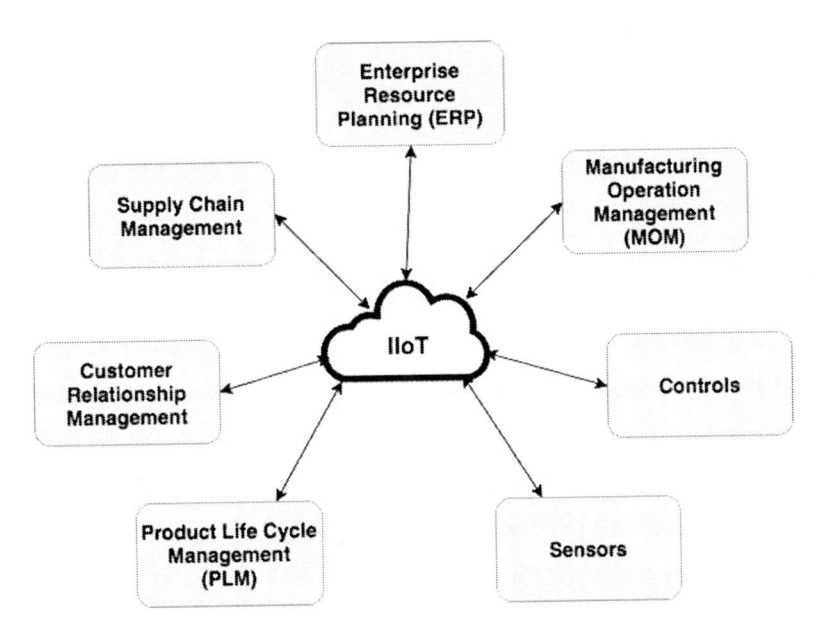

Figure 1. IIoT Control Areas.

The examples of smart enterprise control include the large-scale production of customized products, early identification of defects in products, size reduction in production recalls, elimination of root causes by product modification, planning production alike with the weather forecast, modifying the manufacturing of products in accordance with the market value of their raw materials, etc.

2. Asset Performance Management

The performance of the assets will be enhanced by the implementation of open cloud connections, economical and equally efficient wireless sensors, and data analytics, which will easily enable to collect useful data from the surrounding environment and processing of the same on a real-time scale, resulting in futuristic and educated decisions.

The cloud-based infrastructure of the new systems and the wireless IP connections will reduce the highly expensive costs of the implementation of asset performance management applications by introduction new economical and simple sensors, thereby enabling a delivery of highly advanced technological solutions, which is currently restricted due to the high costs of physical and logical connectivity. The next generation of IIoT systems will result in a significant reduction of unnecessary expenditure. For instance, the currently high-cost of equipment maintenance will be reduced with the introduction of conditional monitoring and self-repairing equipment. The following figure describes the extent of technologically advanced solutions in asset performance.

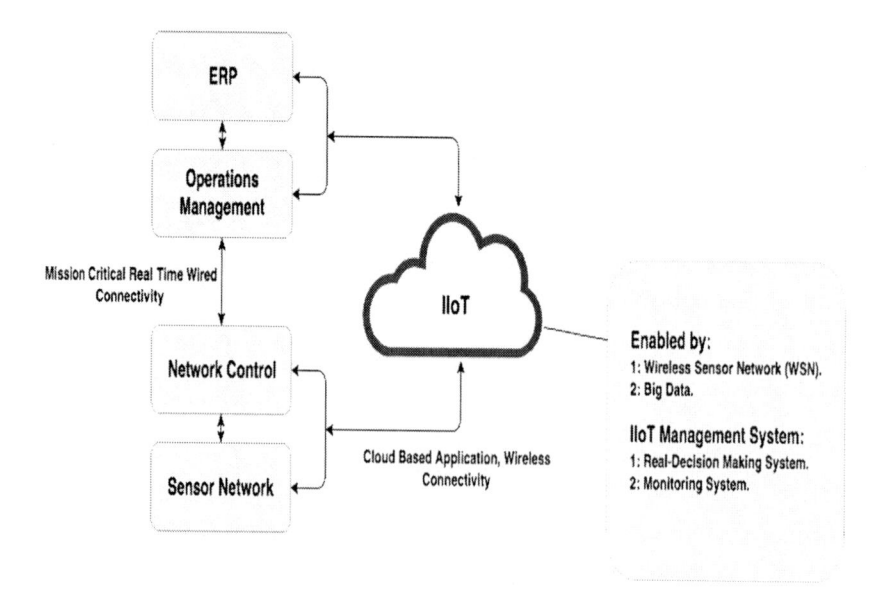

Figure 2. IIoT Cloud-Based Infrastructure.

3. Augmented Operators

To increase productivity, employees will use augmented reality, mobile devices, data analytics and transparency in network connections. Because there will be a reduction in the human workforce, workers with only exceptional skill are employed at the industrial plants. The quick information needed by these workers will be delivered to them in a worker-friendly way on a real-time scale, therefore making the plant centered on the operation of the workers rather than machines.

The functioning of the operators will be transformed by the increased usage of tablets, smart-phones, wearables, etc. which constitute the mobile HMI (Human Machine Interface) technologies and the IP-access to augmented reality and analytical information while the operators can currently access data only from the automation systems. In future, with the implementation of IIoT systems, the operators will be able to access and manage the efficiency and performance of information from every enterprise system, resulting in increased profits. As described in the following figure, the capacities of mobile wireless devices will be expanded, the operator experience will be improved, and the augmented operator will be rendered increasingly productive due to technologies such as dynamic QR codes.

While the implementation of this next generation smart enterprise manufacturing system will yield numerous benefits. To adapt the IIoT systems by the manufacturing plants and industries, several industrial and technological obstacles need to be overcome, such as modification of industrial standards accompanying with IIoT, adapting the human workforce to work by IIoT and developing their required skills, and protection from cyber threats or liabilities. The overcoming of these obstacles will further thin the line between the material and virtual reality, which will result in a more agile system of obtaining machine and process information that will enable ergonomic systems founded on the standards of the internet, by dodging inflexible automation infrastructures.

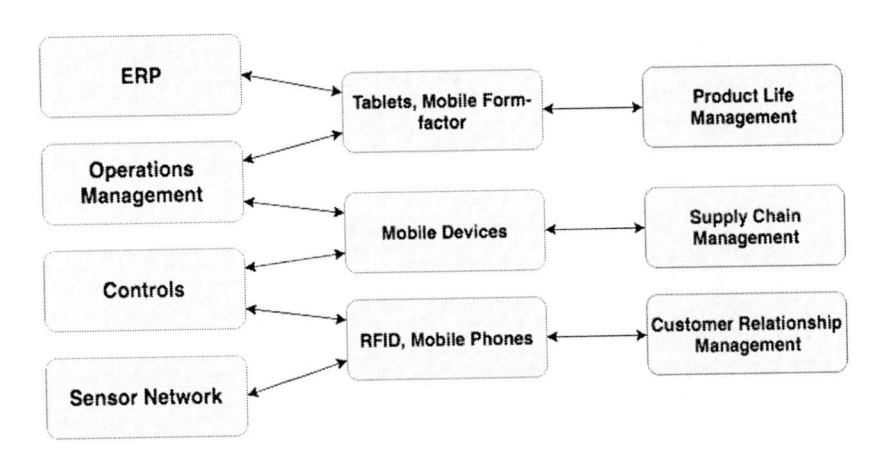

Figure 3. IIoT Mobile HMI.

Though data collection and generation is an integral aspect of IIoT, other components such as the conveyance of IIoT specific interconnected smart devices, edge gateway, digitalized services and applications and the availability of a common platform, also need to be considered for achieving the optimum potential of IIoT. The conveyance of IIoT specific interconnected smart devices implies that the technologies of the internet, such as internet services and WiFi are inherently integrated into the smart devices to deliver a technologically enhanced sensory system for the generating data from the data processing that occurs initially within the device. The system-inherent technologies are crucial for supporting the optimization of the process. On the other hand, an edge gateway is essential for the aggregation of the collected data and delivering the processed solution of the same on a real-time scale and to the correct people. An edge gateway is also a mediating link between the virtual and the material reality; it contributes independent and essential services to the entire system. An edge gateway remedies the crucial requirements of the common platform of IIoT by ensuring an advanced degree of system connectivity and performance (Shahid Ahmed, 2016).

Two other crucial requirements to the success of IIoT customers are the digitalized services and applications, which will extend the scope of data collection to encompass data analytics, therefore conveying relevant and productive information related to both technology and business. The information will be relayed on a collaborative and open platform to enable the selected business investors to generate specific services and applications that provide the optimum services that have been promised by IIoT. Developing a stable environment with efficient management and processing will result in an effortless amalgamation of IoT and IIoT platforms and change the face of industrial businesses and technology.

FRONTEND SERVICES

The provided Frontend services include the delivery of specific services, such as those listed below, for applications and data analytics, data processing, network communication, devices and integrated circuits (IC) respectively:

1. Applications and Data Analytics

The services provided under applications and data analytics include Software as a Service (SaaS) and Real-Time Operational Analytics. SaaS is a paid subscription service which involves prime management of software and provides programs like API (Application Programming Interfaces) which make the software adaptable to various applications. On the other hand, real-time operational analytics combines the operating systems and the analytical system, and runs them simultaneously, to deliver data analysis on a real-time scale. Companies like Google, Microsoft, IBM, Red Hat, SAP, Amazon, and Oracle are going to provide these services (Derek O'Halloran, 2015).

2. Data Processing

Data Processing will offer services like Platform as a Service (PaaS), Infrastructure as a Service (IaaS), Data Management and Data Storage Platform. The PaaS provides customers the tools they need to develop application-specific software, to supply various levels of scalability, iterative development, etc. On the other hand, IaaS is a third-party service to third-party companies that provide different controlled services like allocation of bandwidth, warehousing the data, etc. to conserve the company's funds, distribute resources evenly, etc. The data management and storage platform service will be provided through cloud storage and cloud management with various types of storage systems for securing the data. Companies like Cisco, Arista, HP, NetApp are going to provide these services (Abdulrahman Yarali, 2017).

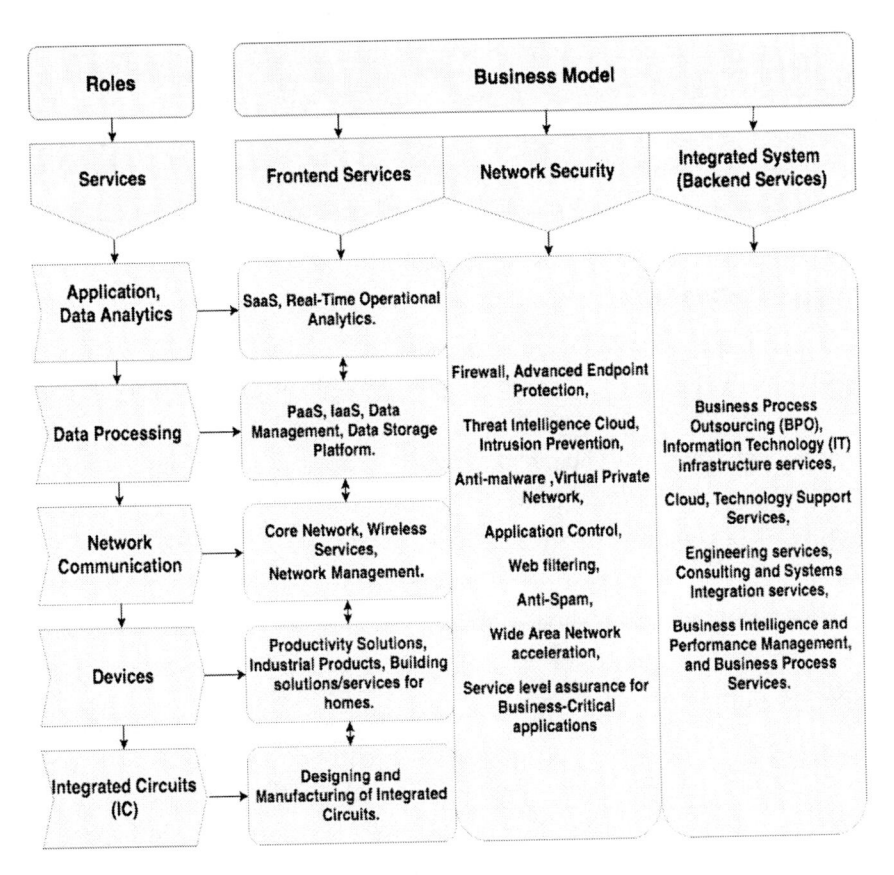

Figure 4. IIoT Business Model.

3. Network Communication

Network Communication will include services like core network, wireless services, and network management. Core Networks services include the essential services for facilitating the hardware, software, and devices within the company's IoT system. On the other hand, wireless services include providers who offer internet transmission services for devices that support wireless network such as laptops, mobile phones, etc. Network management involves the efficient managing of core network services and wireless network services. Companies like AT&T, Dell, Nokia, Juniper, Verizon, Cisco, are going to provide these services.

4. Devices

Devices, in frontend services, include productivity solutions, industrial products, building solutions, services for homes, etc. Industrial products include smart machinery and other equipment required for manufacturing, packaging and delivering products. Building solutions and services for homes, on the other hand, include small devices like pervasive and interconnected Bluetooth devices, smart gadgets and home appliances, etc. Both the types- industrial devices as well as devices for homes- serve to increase efficiency and productivity. Companies like ABB, Bosch, Schneider, Honeywell, and Siemens are going to provide these services (Kirk Bloede, 2017).

5. Integrated Circuits (IC)

Integrated circuits include the designing and manufacturing of the microchips which consist of all various electronic components such as capacitors, resistors, transistors, etc. The microchips, regardless of whether they are microcontrollers or microprocessors, are all integrated circuits by nature and are the crux of every single circuit currently used. Companies like Qualcomm, Intel, Texas Instruments, Microchip are going to provide these services.

6. Network Security

Network security offers services such as Firewalls, Advanced Endpoint Protection, Threat Intelligence Cloud, Intrusion Prevention, Anti-malware, Virtual Private Network, Application Control, Web filtering, Anti-Spam, Wide Area Network Acceleration and Service level assurance for business-critical applications, for securing the network and preventing hackers into the company's network and accessing confidential information. While some services, like anti-malware, anti-spam services, etc. perform a specific function. Other functions like Web-filtering and Firewall perform operations in a broad way, but the ultimate service provided is the same: enhanced protection against threats and foolproof network security. Companies like Check Point, Cisco, Fire Eye, Dell EMC, and Symantec are going to provide these services (Kotian).

7. Integrated System

Integrated systems provide backend services like business process outsourcing (BPO), information technology infrastructural services, cloud, and technology support services, engineering services, consulting and systems integration services, business intelligence and performance management services and business process services. Through these various services, the process-specific business responsibilities of the integrated systems are contracted to third party service providers to increase the efficiency of the entire system. The backend services of the integrated system aimed at increasing the overall consumer experience through call centers, customized helplines, etc. Companies like IBM, Cognizant, HCL, TATA, and Wipro are providing these services.

MARKET ANALYSIS

1. Industrial IoT vs Consumer IoT

The introduction of the Internet of Things (IoT) and the consequent technological advancements therein was predicted to change the face of networking and technology, like the predictions made regarding the Industrial Internet of Things, which is said to change the face of industrial businesses in addition to technology. The concepts of IoT and IIoT are interrelated, and with the progression of advanced development in both IoT and IIoT, the differences between the two become unclear. However, the starting point of differences between the two is that IoT comprises of elements that are influenced by IIoT.

The IoT is composed of big data, analytics, and cloud components, while IIoT is estimated to transform the methods of obtaining and processing this big data- which is the chief constituent of IoT and even the architecture of the system. While data collection is an integral part of IoT, but it is not restricted to industrial plants that constitute the IIoT: IoT sensors collect data from every kind of surroundings and environments, and therefore the data obtained through IIoT is merely a part of the greater IoT system. The data is collected and processed by IoT to increase the productivity and efficiency, of not just manufacturing industries, but also of the general lives of the consumers. On the other hand, IIoT is specifically concerned with increasing the efficiency and productivity of the manufacturing process and increasing profits (Hoske, 2015).

The necessity of data collection, processing and relaying of information on a real-time scale is important for both IoT and IIoT, but more so for the latter, especially with the introduction of self-fixing machines, which require a constant flow of information to function smoothly and avoid breaking down. On the other hand, since IoT is more environments and consumer-centered while the transportation of data is not though it is an inherent part of the system. For instance, if the flow of data collection, processing and information halts in a manufacturing plant, the machine might cease to function, stopping the production line and resulting in varying degrees of loss. However, if the flow of information and data processing stops in an IoT powered device, such a mobile phone, or a tablet, the only result will be that the customer using the device will have to exert him/her more to achieve the result.

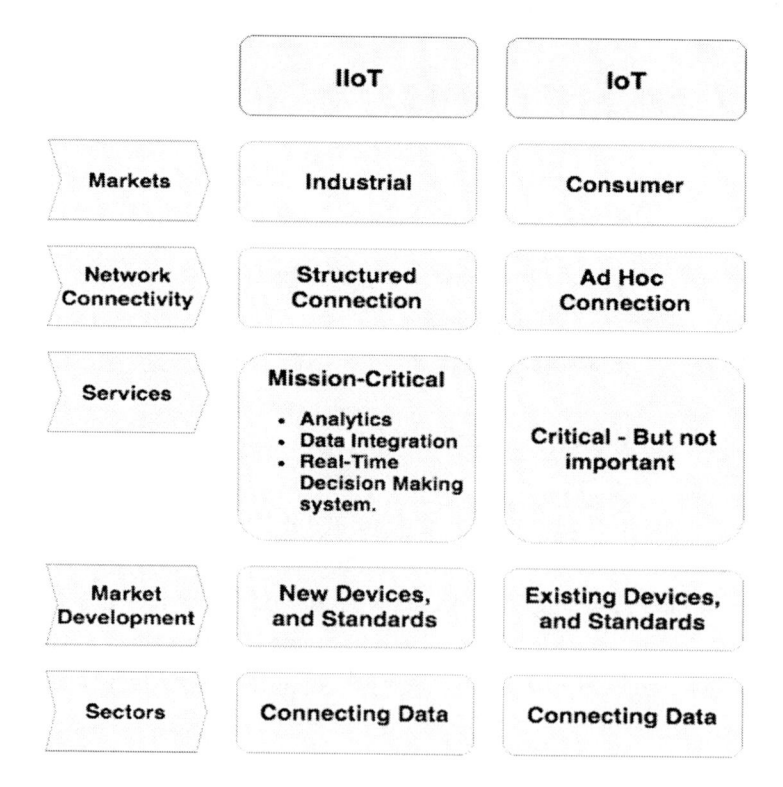

	IIoT	IoT
Markets	Industrial	Consumer
Network Connectivity	Structured Connection	Ad Hoc Connection
Services	Mission-Critical • Analytics • Data Integration • Real-Time Decision Making system.	Critical - But not important
Market Development	New Devices, and Standards	Existing Devices, and Standards
Sectors	Connecting Data	Connecting Data

Figure 5. IIoT vs IoT.

While particular platforms are an amalgamation of IoT and IIoT, such as manufacturing plants, smart cities, etc. since they focus on enhanced productivity and efficiency, as well as increased security, IoT is undoubtedly more pervasive than IoT and more consumer-centered. The development of an independent network through IoT aimed at enhancing not just for industrial production, but also the lifestyle of the consumer, their security, and privacy while opening avenues that aren't currently feasible due to restrictions in the resources available to humans. In such scenarios, IoT rather than IIoT will be more efficient, where IIoT will help in manufacturing the material form of ideas, IoT will be crucial for generating virtual ideas that will become a reality.

Figure 5 shows the differences between IoT and IIoT, which are palpable, but also evident that IIoT further develops the features of IoT, thereby implying that the difference between the two is more than just that of consumer-centered and manufacturing-centered, but rather, the difference between generation and actualization.

APPLICATIONS

With the integration of IoT in the industrial sector, the face of industries and business is changing. Machine to Machine interaction on a real-time scale, self-fixing machines, automated machines and big data are increasing the efficiency and the productivity of various industries. As such, multiple industries, like the following are implementing IIoT:

1. Flight and Aviation Industries

The implementation of IIoT in flight and aviation industries, including commercial airlines as well as research-based aerospace and aeronautical industries to enhance the performance of their systems, and increase the security of the airplanes. The machine to machine (M2M) interaction is essential in aeronautical and other aviation industries for the information needs to be obtained and processed on a real-time scale in a very brief amount of time, and, the self-fixing machines will help eliminate the chances of an aircraft malfunctioning, thereby preventing accidents. Also, in case of research-oriented aviation industries, IIoT will ensure the delivery of authentic and verified data, reducing errors in scientific studies, etc.

2. Defense and Security Industries

Implementing IIoT in the defense and security industries will enhance the methods of defense, and also enable the production of machines programmed to defend or protect against all kinds of attacks, and even eliminate or curb potential threats within and outside the borders of the nations. On a smaller scale, the machine to machine interaction will ensure complete security in residential complexes, protecting against crimes and burglaries, and even disasters like fires, etc. because the data will be processed and communicated on a real-time scale.

3. Healthcare Industries

The implementation of IIoT in the health services and well-being industries will reduce the costs of different medical treatments and make various essential things, like surgical tools, medicines, etc. easily accessible. The automated machines will also make robotic surgeries a reality. The increased accessibility of medical supplies and the accuracy of the treatment will help save more lives. With the implementation of IIoT, general well-being's instruments like treadmills and other healthcare equipment will provide authentic data about the user's heart rate, and other conditions, while automatically considering the person's BMI, age, sex, etc.

4. Energy Industries

Implementing IIoT will help energy industries generate energy from various sources and preserve to utilize it efficiently. IIoT will enhance the functioning of hydro-electric plants, windmills, and even solar energy plants to generate more energy and using it efficiently to improve the living standards of the people. IIoT will also help in energy conservation. Machines, with their autonomy and even the ability to repair and heal problems in themselves, will save a tremendous energy. Perhaps, the implementation of IIoT will even lead to the discovery of new sources of energy and their generation, for instance, generating energy from lightning bolts.

5. Transportation Industries

The implementation of IIoT in the transportation sector will result in the creation of smart and economical public transport, automated cars, trains, buses, etc. While increasing the efficiency of the transportation system, will also enhance the safety of transporting from one place to another. Also, using IIoT in the transportation industry will reduce the chances of accidents, and even lead to the substitution of gas in vehicles with electricity, or maybe even create solar-powered automobiles, etc.

CONCLUSION

Despite the changes and profits promised by it, IIoT is still under development and therefore, isn't a revolution. The IIoT potential optimization requires not just funds for development, but also the replacement of old machinery with new and smart production equipment. While the business or industrial plant owners are lulled into investing in IIoT, they are still resisting the introduction of new and smart machinery, as it results in increased expenditure. Moreover, industrial owners are reluctant to use smart, self-fixing and autonomous machines in view of facing any risks that might incur losses, despite the promise of profits.

Further development and its actualization are necessitated for reaching the zenith of IIoT. Yet, even the conceptual form of IIoT, with its potential developments that increase efficiency, productivity and profits are potent enough that upon its development and gradual evolution will transform the working of the production industry, and every company or industry. The industry will be forced to adopt IIoT if it wishes to retain its status and profits in the competitive business. Already, companies are leaning towards IIoT not only because of the rosy picture that it paints of the future but also because the costs of sensors, pervasive network systems, etc. are dropping dramatically as the companies gradually implementing IoT. This investment is estimated to grow double of what it currently is, in the next three to six year. Additionally, with an increased implementation of IIoT by manufacturing industries, a safe and sustainable work environment will be created, that will significantly reduce the production risks, as well as the risks to human life in industrial plants. Therefore, the aim is risk-free, and cost-efficient, but productive environment promised by IIoT, will be achieved.

REFERENCES

Conway, J. (2015). *The Industrial Internet of Things: An Evolution to a Smart Manufacturing Enterprise*. Retrieved from http://www.mcrockcapital.com/uploads/1/0/9/6/10961847/schneider-an_evolution_to_a_smart_manufacturing_enterprise.pdf.

Derek O'Halloran, E. K. (2015). *Industrial Internet of Things: Unleashing the Potential of Connected Products and Services*, World Economic Forum. Retrieved from: http://www3.weforum.org/docs/WEFUSA_IndustrialInternet_Report2015.pdf

Hoske, M. T. (2015, June): *Industrial Internet of Things 4.0 Control Engineering.*

Kirk Bloede, G. M, *"The Industrial Internet Of Things Making Factories Smart For The Next Industrial Revolution."* Woodside," Capital Partners, London Retrieved from http://www.woodsidecap.com/wp-content/uploads/2017/04/WCP-IIoT-Report-Spring-2017-1.pdf.

Kotian, R. (n.d.). *REALIZE Industrial Internet of Things Security Best Practices.* Retrieved from https://emcworldonline.com/2017/connect/fileDownload/session/4CA7C5562DF3168973CFAD90E04E5FED/DellEMCWorld_Security_Best_Practices-Final.pdf.

Shahid Ahmed, R. C. (2016). *"The Industrial Internet of Things"* Retrieved from https://www.pwchk.com/en/migration/pdf/tmt-industrial-internet-may2016.pdf.

Yarali, A. (2017). *5G Infrastructures: Sensors and Internet of Things.*

Yarali, A. (2016). *5G Mobile: From Research and Innovations to Deployment Aspects.* (pp. 251-270). Hauppauge, NY: Nova Publishers.

Chapter 10

IOT: A NEW TRENDS IN ENTERPRISE

INTRODUCTION

In this chapter, we describe the meaning of Internet of Things (IoT) and detailed how it will affect enterprises globally and change the way of operating and interacting the businesses. Along with changes to the industry, the chapter addresses some issues that affecting industries more than others will have to solve to move towards IoT generation. I will also detail some opportunities that the internet of things offers that businesses will be capitalizing on in the next few years. Above all, the chapter describes the implication of all these effects to express about future.

The internet had no precedent where there is an evolution of TV, radio, and the telegraph but none of those compare to the internet evolution. In the past, when looking to future, predictions were not always on point. No, there are no flying cars, nor robots that serve humans in their day to day lives. The internet of things though enables some of those once ridiculous possibilities to be a reality. In a nutshell, the internet of things is a network of internet-enabled devices, nodes, and sensors that collect information and interact with each other. So, there may not be robots, but it is now possible to have a home that can be almost fully controlled by the thermostat to refrigerator through a smartphone. The future is now, what people think of as smartphones were released less than ten years ago, these smart appliances just come out in the last few years, and now self-driving cars are being tested by companies like Google. With over twenty-five billion internet connected devices expected by 2020 and close to two trillion of economic benefit [1], like the internet, these technologies are not fads and will dramatically increase in usage over the coming years. There is a reason why the internet of things has been hyped up by the media; this will affect all aspects of life. One focus that people may not realize changes the way of doing business. Businesses run differently depending on location and culture, but this will change them all just as much as the internet has in current times.

TRANSFORMATION PHASES

There are 4 phases of future IoT development for businesses; the first step is called operational efficiency and consists of "asset utilization, operational costs reduction, and worker productivity" [5]. The goal is to achieve phase one in the near-term future. The second phase of the short-term future is called new products and services in which "pay-per-use products, software-based services, and data monetization" is used [5]. The two remaining phases are designated for the long-term future. The third stage is called outcome economy, and it consists of "pay per result, newly connected ecosystems, and platform enabled marketplace." The fourth stage is called autonomous pull economy, and it consists of "continuous demand sensing, end-to-end automation, and resources optimization and waste reduction."

Phase one has been achieved simply. Since there will be little to no delay in the time that it takes to notify an employee of a problem or a situation, there will a huge increase in productivity. There will also be lack of misinformation which will lead to less tedious work and will improve employee morale. As said earlier, there would be a significant reduction in operating cost. When everyone at the company is in sync with each other, there will be a massive increase in asset utilization.

At the same time, these phases are just ideas and not set in stone, for better or worse. So while phase 1 is achieved, other phases are being accomplished, or at the very least being initialized. So, as much as going chronologically though this would make sense, some topics have to be highlighted before others. Make a note that this outline is a general business outline and as such, many topics are not relevant to this.

For that reason, the fourth phase is the next step in the outline the possibility of determining the level of demand in real-time and highly automated and flexible production networks. It means with continuous demand sensing manufacturers, and distributors will know instantly what the demand is and can make adjustments in production and price depending on the result. For an end to end automation, without any human assistance, there will be robots that will make the product, determine defects, and then packed for delivery. For resource optimization and waste reduction this is very straightforward with the combination of automation and the constant sense of demand, when there is a decrease in demand, there will be a decline in production, and there will be very few deadstock products not sell in stores.

Many of the factories and infrastructure in the world largely maintained and monitors by manual laborers. Automation is the next step in the evolution of factories. Many factories are already utilizing robotics. Much like modern-day data centers have only a handful of employees, this will be the future of factories where sensors monitor the work environment remotely. There are so many benefits that will reap through this technology. Among those benefits are: "Better optimization and coordination of single processes or process chains and complete plants and sites, significantly improved resource efficiency. Better coordinated control loops in one process chain give higher process yields which result in better material efficiency, waste reduction, less energy use and reduction of pollution. Improved product quality through better process control and smart quality control, will increase utilization of equipment. New collaborative solutions with integrated information management offer new possibilities for supply chain management including the price-based coordination or optimized market mechanisms. Safer operation of plants due to improved control and shut-down procedures more opportunities to integrate multiple processes.

As shown, there are so many benefits to explain that are of tedious experience, but the point is that automation is a technology with overwhelming benefits and few negatives such as unemployment. Automation will be achieved through M2M technology, though there are quite a few technologies that will have to put in place at the backend for the best possible deployment. The needs for "the appropriate embedded processors include connectivity, storage, and packet processing to support M2M gateways and infrastructure." Figure 1 shows the industrial IoT infrastructure model [2]. The automation systems will be cloud-based automation systems with a possibility of centralized or distributed control architecture for the network [8]. Since some of the places where sensors implemented along the roadway and other various infrastructure that isn't going to have fiber laid down for the backbone, they will most likely use a wireless network using the future 5G network. For example, there is a railway in Scandinavia called Heathrow terminal 5, and it alone has five million connected points. Another example is the London railway; it has several million bearings. These millions of bearings will support the monitoring of the condition of the bearings as well as the monitoring of the condition of the railway wagons.

To fulfill the other prediction of phase four, demand in real-time, and more; another industry that will be changed by the internet of things is retail stores. Currently, on the internet, if someone looks at one product there are services such as googles analytics and Adsense services that track what you look at so that other websites can target ads toward a certain person. In the future, through sensors and displays that communicate with these sensors through technology such as Bluetooth. A person could be looking at an item and through eye tracking have that product shown to them on a nearby display that they could then interact with using NFC (near field communication) by swiping their smartphone or smartwatch past and then finding out more about the items they are interested. Another more devious way this could work out is if someone is looking at an item in a store the store could track them and store the data of their interest in a database. That information used to attract them to similar items or sell that data to the third party, and in effect, everything that a person would look at could be specifically targeted at them, which could be good or bad depending on usage of data. Either way, this would lead to a vast improvement in analytics. Lightly touching on phase four of the outline, manufacturers will know what to sell and what doesn't and comparing the data about the product they are selling.

On the topic of retail, the internet of things and its sensor technology can help curve shoplifting. With current technology and magnetic strips, there can be a passive sensor on goods above a certain MSRP. Then there can be a sensor on the register that deactivates this sensor through EMR (electromagnetic resistance) once scanned, sort of like how styluses work. If the sensor hasn't been scanned and deactivated, then there can be a sensor on the door that will go off if it senses a stolen good.

RFID is critical to multiple business operations. RFID technology is essentially a microchip that used for identification of an object [10]. The technology that currently has great uses but if it combined with an IoT that would expand greatly. The advantage of RFID is to read wirelessly without the need of a line of sight. There only needs to be a minimum of one reader and there can be several chips. There are three types of RFID tags: passive tags, semi-passive tags, and active tags. The differences are: passive tags have very limited capabilities when it comes to computing, and they cannot communicate with any other tags, which mean that they only respond to communication with the reader. Semi-passive tags are tags that have a battery built into them so that they can communicate with other RFID tags. Passive tags can communicate with other RFID tags, but they can also detect collisions and sense with channel they are on. They can operate at frequencies ranging from 100 kHz all the way up to 5.8 GHz.

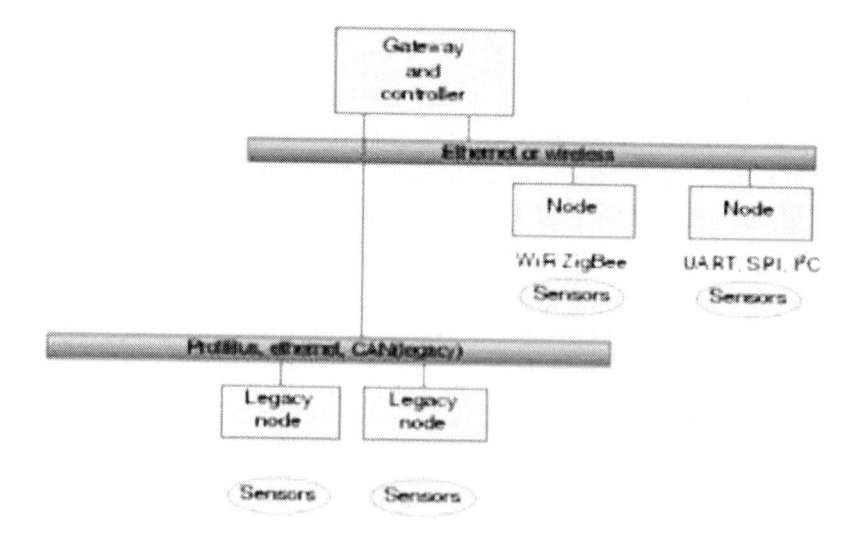

Figure 1. M2M Industrial Infrastructure.

The best use of RFID technology for the use of any business is for inventory and asset accountability operations. No longer will companies have to spend thousands of work hours to consider all merchandise in the store. Neither will college students working tech support have to spend four hours just to find a printer which is not used for a couple of years. There are many other uses such as credit cards that have previously been using magnetic strips that have been in use since the 1960s. There are also uses for keys and various items. Recently they have an increased prevalence in sensitive matters like passports and driver's licenses. Even automobile collisions could avoid when there are multiple automobiles enabled with this technology, it is one of the technologies that have 'unlimited' users and can only improve by integrating with the internet of things.

To reiterate, when it comes to business, consumption and productions are just two sides of the same coin. Internet of Things (IoT) will change how businesses and marketing are done. For phase 2, physical devices can be phased out and replaced with software-based services. New products that come from technology companies, in particular, can be pay per use services. What most users don't realize is that the IoT has not yet realized, but it is here and has been advancing in small steps over the last few years. With streaming services becoming popular and there being an ever-increasing reliance on cellular data, people's consumptions habits have changed and definition of ownership has altered whereas in the past if a user would buy a physical compact disc (CD), he would own it for 'life'. Several years ago a service called iTunes started changed the way for users to listen to music, and the iPod came out and took the music industry by storm. No longer did people have to buy a whole album to listen to a select few 'hits.' Some artists tried to resist, but it just leads to decreased sales among their fan base. However, it leads to people being able to enjoy a more diverse library of music. Transition to a few years ago, people start paying a subscription fee and now have access to a vast library of music and videos. They do not own this music, but they are constantly streaming the most current music and movies to enjoy. Figure 2 shows streaming is being adopted faster than ever and quickly overtaking physical media and even downloads. Therefore, people no longer tied down by physical media, and no longer they are paying to own a product but paying to use a service which means that phase two has already been fulfilled, at least in the music and video industry.

Along with these software dependent services, there is a need to address more consumer based business services. Microsoft just recently went with a software-based service subscription plan for their office suite called Office 365. The same service applied for Adobe, and their software suite now called the creative cloud, which is very popular and same as streaming services. People can pay twenty dollars a month instead of the ridiculous multi-thousand dollar prices paid previously. The true benefit of software as a service (SaaS) is through virtual machines, and this is used to provide a variety of services that can be accessed simply by logging into a web client and management critical services.

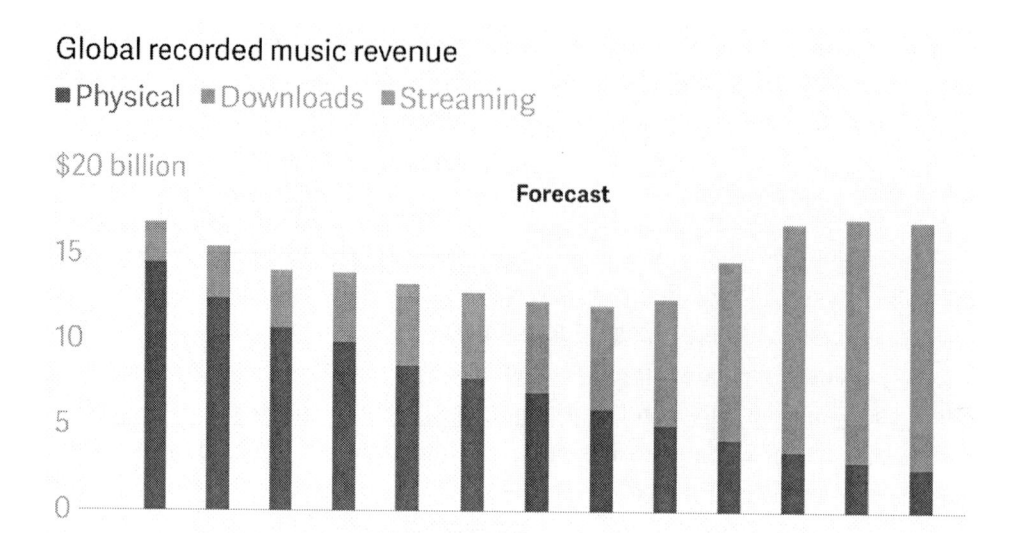

Figure 2. Music Revenue generated globally [11].

On an individual outlook in the enterprise, with the introduction of all these new technologies and devices, as well as automation, there will be a broad number of new jobs that will be created just to manage these new challenges. Most of these jobs will be in the information technology sector and within that most will be focused on different subsets of data analytics. Not all of the analytics could analyze by human hands, results in implementing machine learning. There will be computers that take all the data that has been compiled and then proceed to process it and make the needed changes. Not a popular example, but a current one could be during the times of day when there are more people buying gas the price will go up, and when there are fewer people buying gas, the price would in effect go down.

Currently, there is a shortage of people with the skillset needed for the current need for information technology dependent jobs. In the future, this will be even more of a problem. Not all data is alike and practically every industry will have so many different types of data that they need to be analyzed. There will be a need for specialized services and companies to handle the demand. It is only natural that not all of these services can provide local and that the demand has to fulfill in some way, which can be achieved by outsourcing; this is the only solution that can completely solve the problem. Traditionally, outsourcing indicates a negative connotation, but this is the wrong way of thinking. Economically, outsourcing is needed because people have to put their time to best use and to put it simply: some people do things better than others. "IoT marketplaces provide a one-stop shop to build an IoT solution where the enterprise then typically runs and manages its connected equipment. But in some cases, it may make sense for an enterprise to outsource IoT activities, including building, running and managing a suite of connected things" [3]. Again, this only frees up other people to do other needed services, and this is what makes the enterprise work.

Presently, there are many technology-oriented startup companies, but the internet of things will revolutionize startup companies and not just in the technology sector. Currently, if someone were to start a business dependent on a niche market, there would be a difficulty even finding out how to market it to consumers let alone all the operations that are needed to continue running it. With outsourcing and readily available data analytics from people that are willing to give away all their profile information to any application platform, or in the new future reality, any building they walk into, there will be an excess of data. Knowledge is power, and there will be many companies willing to aggregate all of this data so that these start-up companies can know who to market. As for operations, these are not even the primary cost of any start-up. The main expenses for a startup are research expenses, advertising expenses, technological expenses, and employee expenses [4]. When looking at advertising costs, analytics play a key role, because analytics is a two-way street with a huge number of businesses competing with business. Customers have new ways to see the advertisements that cost low, and in a situation where privacy is all but dead. The company would need only a very minimal presence and broadcast their products to their market efficiently no matter how small. To be clear though, most of these services will have a minimal human presence bringing down the cost to receiving companies, and will speed up the response to start-up companies that can go from just an idea to being a tangible product. With outsourcing, these start-up enterprises minimize the expenses that can eliminate the majority of the employee expenses. About technological costs, most of these costs outsourced in current times, but third-party companies are eliminating their cost and getting more business, leads to a reduction in outsourcing cost.

As mentioned, before a company requires a heavy amount of information sharing and collaboration needed for devices, people, and companies. Sharing of critical information recommended for situational awareness, and there needs to be no delay in the sharing of it. The question is how does this come about when there are a vast number of different industries needing to communicate all at once. In the ideal situation to eliminate overhead between devices nearby, there would need to be technology such as Bluetooth to transfer the information. But when different sectors are communicating and when data needs to store there will need to be open access to most business' information, currently it becomes a security concern. There will be an AAA server in practically every business along with a considerable information security presence. There will be data centers to hold general information that any business can use for a price. General information in this future is anything from traffic analysis to consumer habits that goes back to the second phase and data monetization as well as pay per use model. There can be any number of ways to monetize this information because to a company that needs to know their subscriber base and they no longer need independent studies but can just get the raw data.

A subscription model would be popular with smaller businesses while a lump sum contract model would better fit larger companies which may demand more data at a regular frequency or more detailed information.

The third phase is essentially when quantitative technology becomes so advanced that forecasted trends and measurable outcomes are common to predict. When this happens, these companies paid for each of their predictions. With these newly connected ecosystems, there will be massive data that if it is analyzed, it wouldn't be that difficult to give a precise prediction of future events. As for a platform enabled marketplace that covered earlier with business cataloging an advertising service that knows what a person's purchases and interests are and then directing advertisements at what a person may want.

Like with the other phases there are already present examples of phase three coming to fruition? Most would say that the future cannot be predicted accurately through just various sensors. There is an instance of humans predicting future events as unlikely as that is. In 2016, there was this swarm AI that accurately predicted the outcome of the Kentucky Derby and turned one dollar into over five hundred dollars. [6] A swarm AI is a system that links together many people in a real-time system and uses their joint consensus to predict the correct answer. Now, this isn't too different than what people have been doing for thousands of years with deciding upon a consensus and deciding upon that, for example, democracy. The creators of the AI first got twenty people with supposed knowledge of horse racing to choose the top four winners of the derby. Then they had the swarm AI determine the order of the top four, the swarm AI has an accuracy of 73%, and that is higher than any of the experts that paid to predict the results accurately [6]. So as shown the AI isn't that advanced, though it will outperform individuals? But if there can be a swarm AI with humans and their inherent biases, then if there was to be a swarm AI with just sensors and computer and pure information then just think how much more accurate would that be.

In the process of achieving true outcome economy, there has to be a platform-enabled marketplace, and this is in a beta phase to say as of now. Figure 3 shows the effects of new businesses and products in the society. The following changes lead to new communities supporting that technology as well as more advanced technology building off that technology to lead another business then refining that technology to repeat the cycle all over again. It is stating that the community and the business depend upon each other for growth and change.

As the issue related to the marketplace, community and economy are continued to discuss there has been a noticeable trend over the last thirty years of a change in how products make, or at the very least how they made to operate after a certain amount of time. There are products such as microwaves and various home appliances that made that still to this day work and have no defect. Still, today, if someone were to buy a similar product would it last the same amount of time? Products today are made in a way that makes a person upgrade every few years. Electronics are no different, in fact, they are even worse. Cell phones are practically made to replace every couple of years. On the opposite end of the spectrum, if there were devices that were very old, there would be legacy services that would limit the potentials of new technologies and compromise some services. Legacy is a major problem in many businesses with some even using insecure and outdated operating systems like Windows XP. Therefore, in the future, with technology advancing at an unknown rate, and other technology becoming outdated, the life cycles of products will become even shorter to encourage people to adopt the latest technology.

There is more to a business's income than just purchases of new technologies. Future business models will be based on a modified servitization model which means that "the point of sale is not the end of a transaction, but the beginning of a customer relationship that provides high margin revenue to the manufacturer - as well as ongoing responsibility for product performance and maintenance to the customer" [9]. But instead of maintaining the product, it is just replaced with a new product at a subsidized cost. In the previous paragraph, a decrease in the amount of time a person would own a product decreased. Well, in this model, the manufacturer mainly profits from the services that their product provides and it offers an incentive to sell their products at a lower price. However, there may be a further encourage adoption of the product and upgrading to maximize their usage and from that profits that come from those services.

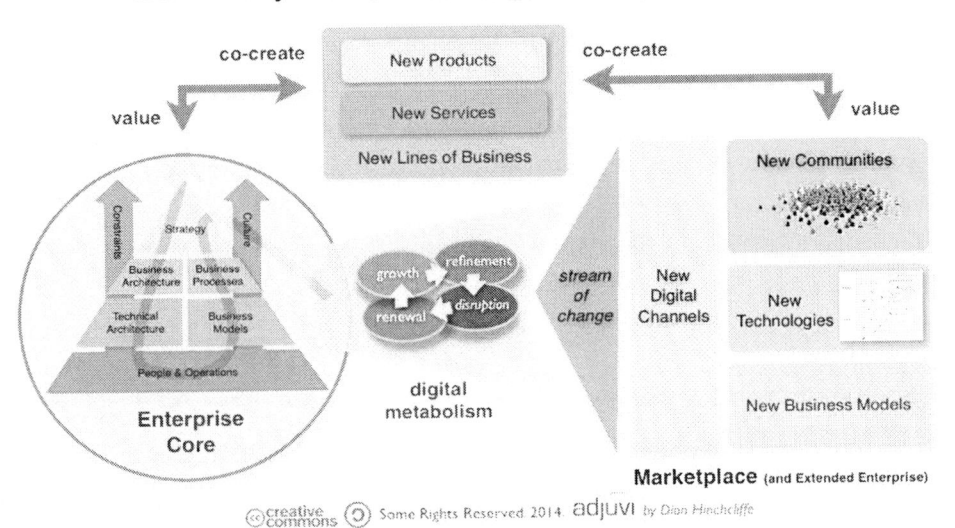

Figure 3. The effects of new business and products in the society [7].

CONCLUSION

The theme is that these trends and changes are in part a byproduct of changes and trends that have been happening over the course of the last ten years. The internet of things is just like any other technology as a tool to help facilitate these changes. But like in all changes they do not come all at once, and there are steps and gradual evolution. The 4-steps or phases of future IoT development for businesses are, an Operational efficiency which consists of asset utilization, an Operational costs reduction, and quality enhancement and worker productivity. Also, new products and services in which "pay-per-use products, software-based services, and data monetization" are used. Outcome economy and it consists of "pay per result, newly connected ecosystems, and platform enabled marketplace." Autonomous pull economy and it consists of "continuous demand sensing, end-to-end automation, and resources optimization and waste reduction" [5]. These four steps are just benchmarks for progress since progress doesn't follow a set course and all of these steps are happening in a non-sequential order. There are technologies crucial to the internet of things such as sensors and RFID chips. The ways of implementing business practices need to be changed beyond the normal thinking of an individual. What may have worked just a few years ago may not work today. Just as technology adapts as time goes on, people should change to benefit the most from it. Even though every business is different the internet of things will change them all just as much as the internet has in current times.

REFERENCES

[1] Pettey, C. (2015, August 31). *The Internet of Things and the Enterprise.* Retrieved from http://www.gartner.com/smarterwithgartner/the-internet-of-things-and-the-enterprise/.

[2] Behmann, F., & Wu, K. (2015). *Collaborative internet of things (C-IoT): For future smart connected life and business.* Somerset: John Wiley & Sons.

[3] *Driving The IoT Journey: 10 Trends To Watch.* 2016. Ebook. New York: ABI Research.

[4] Morah, C. (2017, June 28). *Business Startup Costs: It's In The Details.* Retrieved from http://www.investopedia.com/articles/pf/09/business-startup-costs.asp.

[5] Gierej, S. (2017). The framework of a business model in the context of Industrial Internet of Things. *Procedia Engineering, 182,* 206-212.doi:10.1016/j.proeng.2017.03.166.

[6] Reese, H. (2016, May 06). *Swarm AI predicts the 2016 Kentucky Derby*. Retrieved from http://www.techrepublic.com/article/swarm-ai-predicts-the-2016-kentucky-derby/.

[7] Hinchcliffe, D. (2014, May 28). *Going Beyond 'Bolt-On' Digital Transformation*. Retrieved from https://dionhinchcliffe.com/2014/05/28/going-beyond-bolt-on-digital-transformation/.

[8] Delsing, J. (2015, September 8). Building automation systems from the Internet of Things. In *IEEE International Conference on Emerging Technologies and Factory Automation:* Retrieved fromhttp://ltu.divaportal.org/smash/get/diva2:1004934/FULLTEXT01.pdf.

[9] Smith, L. (2014, March 07). *Outcomes-based Services: How the Internet of Things Is Driving the Future of Manufacturing*. Retrieved from http://www.industryweek.com/technology/outcomes-based-services-how-internet-things-driving-future-manufacturing.

[10] Maharjan, S. (2010). *RFID and IOT: An overview*. The Simula Research Laboratory University of Oslo. Retrieved from http://www.uio.no/studier/emner/matnat/ifi/INF5910CPS/h10/undervisningsmateriale/RFID-IoT.pdf.

[11] McDuling, J. (2015, March 23). *The music industry wants to fight the internet again—and it's probably going to lose*. Retrieved from https://qz.com/360002/the-music-industry-is-going-to-fight-the-internet-again-and-its-probably-going-to-lose/.

Chapter 11

IoT: Smart Cities and Smarter Citizens

Introduction

Creating appliances that connect the end users to the Internet of Things (IoT) will be essential in implementing it in the cities around the world. It requires more attention to implement this idea when IoT reaches a tipping point where no individual can be separated from it and still operate within the limits of a city, the systems that connect them need to be reliable and useful.

As it stands, citizens of any living condition are already somewhat employed in IoT, without knowing it in many cases. People enroll their lives in apps such as Uber or Lyft, Connecting to the web with shopping websites like Amazon, and are finding their city functions integrated with the internet. Socially, citizens have found an IoT ready and willing to incorporate them on a personal level. The success of non-commercial IoT systems will likely fall to the idea how well they stack up to their commercial counterparts.

Citizens are capable of operating in an industrial IoT. Paying for a good or service or generating ad revenue comes a lot more comfortable than dealing with IoT personalized systems developed by a government force. Why? The answer is simple but necessary to address adequately.

IoT Systems and Privacy

Personalized Internet of Things (IoT) systems and networks are going to require the users to sacrifice some amount of personal privacy to function completely and fully. While individuals already spread personal information knowingly on commercially viable apps without recoiling, they will be hesitant to share the same information with government bodies. When dealing with commercial IoT systems that connect individuals, the user can choose to remove the app or stop using it if he or she is dissatisfied with the way it functions.

As it stands, there is no requirement to own a social media account. There is no need for every person to use the Uber app. A system that is designed to interact with the user if designed from the standpoint of a city, may prove to be required by governing body for its citizens to use. IoT is useless without large quantities of information; this includes personal user information that will be like currency for governing bodies. Obviously, there is something like a double standard present in this answer. The governing body of any developed nation already possesses an immense amount of information on its citizens.

In the prevailing political climate, the user will face personal opposition to govern IoT systems even if they would desire to share similar or more information with commercial apps. For example, insurance companies like progressive offer devices could determine how fast a car is going, how quickly it stops, and the driving behaviors of the person behind the wheel. For some users, this could be a potential service to monitor the use of their car or to secure potential insurance deals. Progressive does not, however, require all of its users to partake in this program. Any user is dissatisfied with what the product does can get rid of it at any time.

However, within a fully integrated citywide IoT, a similar device may not be optional. If the city uses a particular tracking on cars to regulate traffic flow, users will not have a choice. Suddenly, individuals will find their driving information sacrificed for the greater good. If those systems fail, then the users will question the actual need to monitor their driving habits. In this context, an insurance company gives customers the luxury of choice in this regard. If someone perceived that progressive was learning too much about their habits, then they could find to work with another agency. In a city, this would likely be impossible without moving out of the city, an example that related to present scenario. It exposes the double standard, either imagined or valid that people will hold against governing IoT over industrial IoT. Cities are going to build up a condition of trust and security before employing personalized IoT devices. Citizen involvement will be essential for IoT cities to function.

Moreover, the governing body of a city will need to produce strict rules in handling the information gathered from its citizens. Trust will be built up in a few areas that will allow cities to regulate and collect information from various sources. Personalized IoT systems need a launch-pad that strictly benefits the users or citizens. When looking at what a successful IoT city will be judged by, the answer can be found.

IoT Personalized Systems and Healthcare

Giving citizens avenues for receiving personalized health care will be essential in building trust for governing IoT customized systems. With healthcare, citizens are already willing to give up personal information that will lead to proper treatment. Again, commercially available IoT systems are already in their infancy in the commercial field. Pharmacies have some systems in place to quickly receive and treat patients. Individuals are willing to give up this information as dealing with sickness well outweighs the loss of personal information to a commercial body. This attitude will transfer over to governing bodies trying to produce reliable healthcare; it relies on cities integrating commercially owned hospitals into governing bodies, something that has already occurred in developed countries.

Moreover, the services provided by emergency rooms are a personal asset. Medical records are available for patients as well, but only if they have a record within the institution itself. Here is an opportunity for governing bodies to produce apps or IoT sources to integrate citizen's health issues, it could be something mandatory for health physicals or uploading information on past health problems or conditions in the family. These would work independently of insurance companies so that the government could ensure total commercial removal of these apps. Citizens would be more comfortable with this and produce a wealth of information for IoT hospital systems, which in turn will provide a more capable health care system. When the public recognizes the net gain of this personalized IoT system, then the door will be open for other elements to secure confidential information. Government forces will, again, find competition with commercial IoT systems. However, this is their chance to excel in quality over the commercial bodies. Citizens will likely be willing to do double duty when inputting information and will recognize that their private information being siphoned by two separate organizations as an issue. Healthcare IoT systems currently not up to an outstanding level, and distinct corporations operating with different systems, the government has an opportunity to become the leading source for healthcare IoT. The market could mostly corner, and users will choose to integrate themselves in public IoT systems as they produce the best results. In turn, governing IoT systems could share correct information with private bodies if the user desires. The system that described here is already somewhat in play. However, in countries like America, the involvement of the government in healthcare will prove to be the largest roadblock. Individual cities may find ways to maneuver around this, but will likely find problems in sharing information reliably on a national scale. In European countries, where government involvement in healthcare is already an often accepted norm, IoT cities will have a much easier time of it.

The question will be if the success of these cities will prompt American or other global bodies to relent on government action. IoT cities will be defined by how effectively they handle their healthcare. America may not want to find itself behind when foreign cities begin excelling in the care of their citizens. In any event, the integration of personalized IoT systems and health care will be essential to produce large-scale, functioning, IoT cities.

The collection of healthcare data may prove to come from commercial sources in American IoT cities. Apple has recently made significant steps in collecting health data from its users. iPhones are now capable of judging the sleeping habits of their users, listening to the sounds made during sleep to decide when users are experiencing REM sleep and adjusting potential sleep schedules to maximize the restfulness of any given night. In addition to this, users can opt to have Apple watches or other products gauge heart rate during exercise to produce more useful work out routines. This package of health care related functions has become rolled in with every new iOS update. This information, or similar avenues of information-gaining, could prove to be essential in the more capitalistic world of America.

In this case, governing bodies will find the use of commercial information to be important. However, companies like Apple may choose to operate off of public opinion when selling or sharing this information. Apple, in this case, holds both a leverage of power over the government and a wealth of potentially insecure information on citizens; it opens up another point of privacy that leads to conflict citizens in other American IoT cities. Information on this scale will likely find itself a publicly traded commodity. If Apple is not willing to play ball with this information, another company may do so. It is currently impossible to judge the public reaction to a potential war over their health information. Healthcare is already a billion-dollar industry; the market is there for personalized IoT systems.

The American government may find that it will need to step to regulate the situation, again provoking potential ire from its citizens. Healthcare will prove to be essential when designing active IoT personalized systems. The situation described above will likely prove to be an uphill battle for American cities and a major hurdle to overcome. In any event, resolving this issue will be required if American IoT cities hope to keep up with the world that has already resolved this issue.

American IoT systems, may find an easy route to develop governing personalized systems in another way. When exploring a capitalistic society, the option is always available to make buying goods more efficiently.

Governing IoT Systems and Marketing

A successful institution is a benefit to any city. A mall that brings in customers from across a wide area can bolster the tax revenue of a town. A notable restaurant can become a source of pride for a town. When IoT systems already exist that drive marketing for customers, why can't IoT cities take advantage of this? Researching shopping trends and developing resource gathering tools to bolster the city's intuitions could be handled without the risk of invading the privacy of citizens. Any citizen shops and that purchasing goods or services create a paper trail that is open to both commercial and governing bodies. The customer agrees to this sharing of information as he or she needs to purchase whatever good or service. Using credit cards, paying taxes, regulating personal finance, are all things interacted by citizens. When these individuals shop at online retailers, those companies will often employ algorithms to suggest potential products for that customer to buy.

Search histories are combed for the major wards to produce more effective advertising. In the world of online shopping, currency is exchanged and moved to a wide variety of places. In many states, internet goods are not taxed, and some cities are even finding their local retailers crushed under the competitive force of Amazon or other online stores. While many companies with physical storefronts are currently taking steps to combat this, why is there not a governing IoT system employed to promote local business? An IoT system that tracks the spending information of citizens within a town can be designed to suggest local stores or restaurants. Imagine an app, developed by a city body that displays users' local deals and potential places to shop, where the local business community could engage in competition with each other rather than massive internet bodies. Customers would be more engaged in their local shopping scenes, gives more potential to strengthen local business in a town and create a stronger tax base. The caveat here is that this might be more successful in a larger town with a more robust infrastructure system. A town with less diverse shopping areas may still find itself losing out to internet companies in this regard. However, creating an IoT system like this could install both good faith in businesses and the community.

Interest in designing a better town is present in every citizen in any city. A company that operates as franchises may see inherent stability in the towns that show this level of dedication to building a secure base for them. For small cities, IoT city marketing channels could prove to be a developmental area to draw in new citizens and companies, while protecting their investments in the system.

A larger city may find the ecosystem of its shopping districts served to great effect by an IoT system. Shoppers could be happier that, their shopping information handled by secure source than faceless marketing companies. Individuals may be alienated when they see products relevant to recent searches popping up on their Facebook feed. However, a city could do well to make a bright and functional system intent on helping the local community. Besides, IoT cities employing this kind of system may find an easy avenue to producing more invasive IoT systems. The governing body could learn the difficulties and challenges without risking something as dangerous as the public health. For American cities, combining capitalism with IoT systems may pave the way to the future.

Personalized IoT Systems and the Future of Cities

This chapter has gone to lengths to discuss the importance of effective and robust personalized IoT systems. IoT designed cities will, at some level, be reliant on personalized IoT systems. The elements of privacy, data sharing, and trade will come to affect the outcome. Cultural differences in how these are viewed will decide which cities or countries produce more effective systems.

In future, where interconnectivity will decide the economic and public success of cities, it will be important to produce smooth transitions for citizens. The key to this, of course, is to produce systems that are at first minimally invasive related to what kind of information is collected. IoT cities will need to use every drop of information effectively to secure the trust of their citizens. Commercial providers of personalized IoT systems may come out on top when government bodies attempt to produce their content will be one that will be navigated by both governing bodies and the private citizen.

In current times, people enjoy their personalized apps. The potential for making wise shopping choices is blossoming every day. The market available to the current consumers is significantly greater than the one available just ten years ago. In this way, consumers have made the first steps to institutionalize IoT systems. Consumers reluctantly switch from commercial systems to government systems may prove to be a hurdle for them doing so. Cities are requiring more and more personal information in their systems. There is potential in addressing personalized IoT systems before tackling more massive projects to gain the trust of the public. Some countries will find themselves with an advantage over others in some fields. Personalized systems and their Implementation may even shape the face of cities. Countries may produce unique ways of interactivity to cope with the needs and demands of their citizens. Where the technology and the person have closer engagements the cities will find their futures. Consumers have already proved themselves willing participants in the commercial IoT market. Citizens may find themselves willing to cooperate with their governments if the systems are trustworthy and reliable. That is why there is a need for the initial personalized IoT systems to be minimally invasive and maximally useful to the user. There needs to be little risk in the event of a failure on either end. A perfect IoT system may prove to be unachievable as a perfect government, which is not a major issue for consumers, but the real issue is how sharing their privacy will benefit them if the cost is worth the reward.

SMART HOME

This paper provides a background into how home automation has progressed throughout the years, how the technology that is used and incorporated works together to make your home "smart," and the future of home automation and what we can expect to see. This is an exciting time to be involved in technology, and our society now can turn old science fiction tv show ideas into real possibilities. The market for items that will make your home "smarter" is growing at an extremely rapid pace.

Before diving into those new tech advances, one has to look at where we all came from. The idea of home automation has been around for an extremely long time. The level of technology that was needed was not there to make some of those dreams a reality. These were included in science-fiction novels and shows from many years ago. One such that sticks out in my mind is that of the Jetsons. Another famous author that has written about the future was Ray Bradburn in his short story, "There Will Come Soft Rains." One of the first automation was actually invented by the famous Nikola Tesla, and it was a remote-control boat in the year 1898. In the coming years, technology had to catch up to the ideas of the inventors. The phrase, "Smart Home," finally came about in the year 1984. The next large step in automation was an engine powered vacuum cleaner in 1901, and an electrically powered vacuum 6 years later.

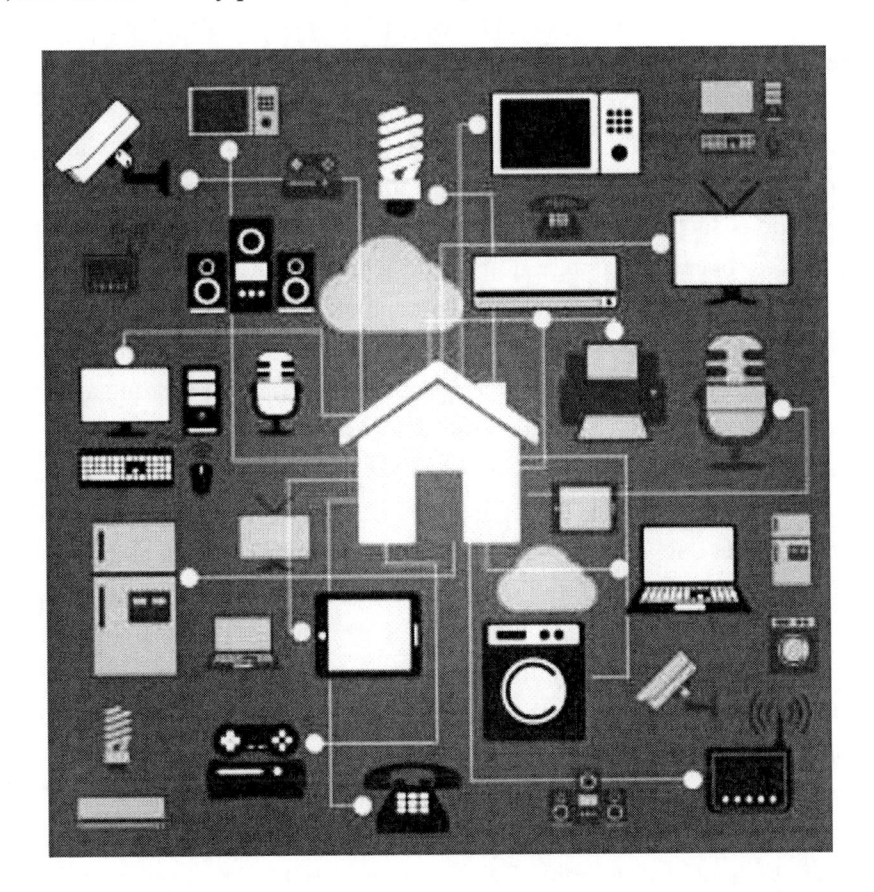

Figure 1. A smart home connectivity.

For the next two decades, there was a revolution of new technologies such as refrigerators, clothes dryers, washing machines, irons, and toasters. There were extreme luxury items that could only be afforded by the wealthy.

Moving on through history, a company named Pico Electronics from Scotland was the first group to really revolutionize the idea of home automation. The company began in 1970 and was first known for developing a single integrated circuit calculator. During this time, most calculators had five chips or more. The next big invention from this company was a record changer that could select tracks. It was called "The Accutrac," and it worked by a remote control that would use ultrasonic signals to change the tracks. In 1975, a project was developed called the X10 project. The idea behind the project was that signals could be transmitted over already present AC. The project was continually worked on over the next years, and finally had a huge bit of success in 1984 with the production of the GE Homeminder. This Homeminder was a box that connected to your TV the same way a cable box does. You could operate the box with an IR remote and your monitor as your TV screen. Through this, the user could control their entire home. It also was accessible through an outside telephone line. It is hard to believe that the X10 from the past is still used today to network the appliances and lighting in a home network for easy access. The X10 is mainly used in the type of home automation where the items can respond to command based protocol. It is still mainly used in home networking. It can perform actions such as: turning on and off the lights around your house, operating certain appliances, operating garage doors, and even security systems. It can basically talk to any device that will recognize simple commands. The X10 system has evolved into a wireless technology also. Now, you have a device that you plug into your wall somewhere in the house. Then, with a wireless device capable of sending a signal to the X10 receiver, you can push a button on your device, for instance, for a ceiling fan. This then sends a signal to the X10 unit; the unit then sends a signal through the X10 system to the ceiling fan. In researching the X10 unit, I found some specific applications that could be used in our current day and age. The first deals with your morning alarm routine. You can synchronize your alarm clock to the X10 system so that when the alarm goes off, the lights slowly begin to brighten, and the coffee maker in the kitchen turns on auto and begins to brew a pot of coffee. Yes, this sounds like something out of a Jetsons episode, but it is indeed possible. There are other uses such as you can have your porch or outdoor lights set on a sensor so that when a specific darkness or time is reached each day, they turn on and off. Sadly, with new technology, come new competitors for the X10 systems. The future's not looking too good for X10. Although it was a revolutionary system that was breaking the mold of normal things a home could do, there are other newer technologies that offer more than the X10 does. It was a relatively cheap system compared to its competitors, but it was also the slowest and the least reliable. In 2005, the company Smartlabs launched a product called Insteon.

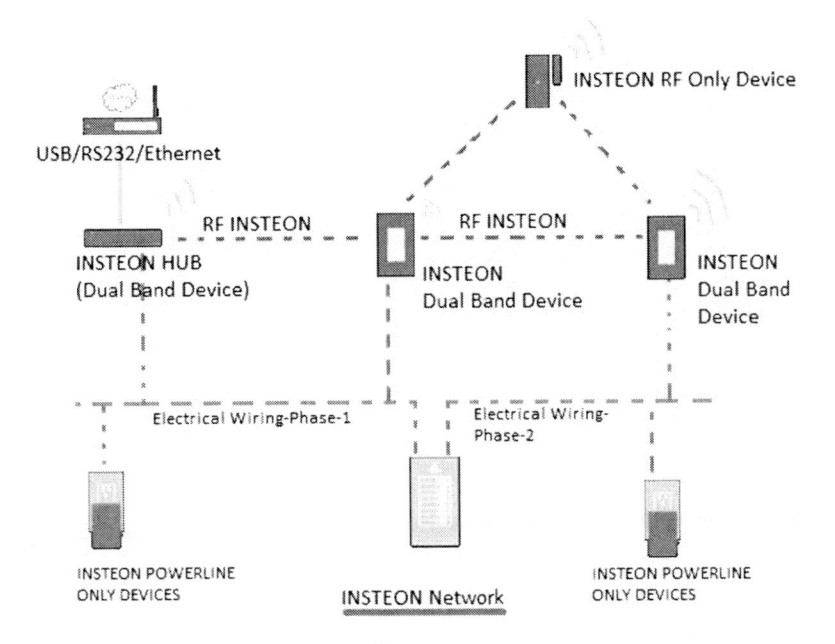

Figure 2. A sample home automation configuration.

Insteon is a home automation technology that enables things such as thermostats, remote controls, motion sensors, lights, or other electronically powered devices to be controlled. It is different from older technologies such as the X10 system in that it not only uses power lines to communicate with devices but also uses radio frequencies (RF) to communicate. This is called using a dual-mesh networking topology. The existing electrical wiring becomes a backup transmission protocol for any RF interference. Insteon is the bestselling and most reliable wireless home automation networking technology around today. The thing that makes these devices so unique is that each one of Insteon devices you install in your home acts as a repeater. When a signal is sent from the base controller, every device the signal hits undergoes error detection and correction. The signal is then boosted after being cleaned and then retransmitted to improve its strength. By doing this on every device, the RF dead zones are basically eliminated. With the power line transmissions, phase-line keying is used. For the radio frequency messaging, frequency-key shifting is used. Since this is only a peer-to-peer network, all of these devices do not require network supervision or routing tables. With Insteon, the entire system can actually function without a central controller, although most times you would want one. You can manage your system with things such as tablets and smartphones. If desired, you can purchase a USB/Serial Powerline Modem, and connect a PC to the network. The modem would serve as a bridge to the Insteon network. To keep neighbors and outside intruders from accessing your personal network, linking control security is enabled. This basically means that other users cannot link to your network unless they have physical control of your device and know the individual ID of the device.

When it comes to home automation, there are many different things one can do. The main thing one has to do is decide what exactly they want to accomplish. Some of the things you can do are to convert your home into a home theatre. You can set it up to distribute your music around your house. You could control your lighting in the house with a single device. It can be used to conserve energy, or it can also be used to enhance your home security. You can also set your home for different settings during the night or during the day. In the following sections, each of the different types will be covered.

If you are a movie fan, one cool thing you can do is turn your home into a home theatre system. I know a huge pain in my home, is the plethora of remotes in the basket next to the chair. At the moment, there is a television remote, sound bar remote, blue ray player remote, fire stick remote, and cable box remote. If one were to say there is a possibility to ditch all these remote for one, you would be silly not to jump at the idea. This is the power that IoT offers. With this, someone can control all their devices from one single remote of the tablet. My wife and I are in the process of building our first home together. Luckily, we will get to plan everything that is going to go into this. I plan on heavily incorporating IoT into the home. One thing I will be doing is to have an entertainment tablet. Below is an image of the Logitech Harmony Home Hub. It allows you to connect up to 8 smart home devices to this hub, and control them via a free app. You can either control this from a tablet or even a smartphone. So this means that if you cannot find your tablet, say your two years old has decided to take it and hide it in their room, one always has their cell phone, so you can quickly and easily pull it out and control anything you need to.

There are other devices also that perform the same tasks. One popular choice is to use Alexa or the new Google home. We will discuss there more in depth later in the paper.

The next section that will be discussed is similar to the home theatre system, but a different type. The idea is that of home music. When you want to play a song in your home, before, there really was no way to push it out across the entire house unless you had speakers running cabled to each room or area you want the music. This could lead to a logistic nightmare when you have to worry about the length, type, and distance the cables need to be run. Sometimes you don't want to have to drill holes in the walls and run cables through all these extra spaces. Now, with home automation, you can place speakers anywhere you want, and connect to them remotely to play the same song all over your house. This can be done simply by using a wireless sound system and some Bluetooth speakers. At my home, we have the Polk, smart home sound bar. This sound bar acts as a sound hub. I can remotely connect to it via my smartphone or tablet via an app. This lets me do a few different things. One main thing is to of course control the volume that is going to come from the speaker. Another nice feature is the ability to start up a streaming service like Pandora. Since I bought the higher end sound bar system, in the beginning, it has the available feature to act as the smart hub. This means that I can add even more speakers to this and they will connect to the hug via Bluetooth; all without cables and cords running everywhere. You can add as many speakers you want to make your home area as surround sound as you would like. One nice feature is to also have the ability to take these wireless speakers outside. When we have guests over or are entertaining outside, we can take one or two of the remote speakers to the porch and they play whatever the soundbar is playing. This way, the sound is not only playing in the living room from the main sound bar, but it is also playing from the two remote speakers outside. This is a wonderful source of entertainment, and truly evidence that the IoT is a great tool to have in one's home. The next section is one of more convenience than of new cutting-edge technology. This is using a smart device to control the lighting and light effects of your house. If I had a dime for every time my wife asked me if I turned off the lights in the kitchen after settling into the perfect spot in bed I would be a rich man. Now, if I had that same question asked with an IoT smart home, it would not be a big deal. With a smart device and IoT home, you can take your normal light switches, and have them wirelessly talk to a hub in your home. With this, you can control them using a smart-enabled device. Today, the technology goes much farther than just a simple on and off. Now, you can control the dimness and even set an on and off timer. Today's technology has also pushed the limit even farther by having smart bulbs which can even change color! Want to change the season colors in your house easily? No problem with the new LED color changing bulbs. When looking online at some prices for the different bulbs, it is looking like our local Walmart has some for as low as $19.99. Granted, this is quite a larger investment than the normal 98 cent bulbs we are used for purchasing. But with time and cheaper materials, I believe that these type of things are going to start coming standard.

The most beneficial type of IoT technology that I have in my home is a home security system. In my home, we have the Vivint security system. Different types of alarm systems may use different technologies. For ours, it is connecting using the Z-wave systems. It has a central hub that is a tad larger than the other side panel located in the bedroom. From this main panel, you can see all of the system diagnostics, and if needed, you can arm anything you need. From this main hub, all other things in the house are connected. Unlike the old days when you would have to have a manual cord or wire running from each window and device to the main hub, everything through this system is run wirelessly. We have small sensors put on each window with only a simply 3M strip. These things create a closed circuit when the window is closed. When the window is opened, an alert will sound, letting us know that the window is open with a verbal message from the hub and the small panel in our bedroom. The same is true for all the doors in the house. Each of the doors also has a sensor on them with their own name. Each one will alert us verbally when the door is opened. I can still remember when our five-year-old was only two; we were all in the living room and heard an alert that our garage door was opened. When we explored this, we found the child in the garage about to get into things he probably shouldn't have and could have been hurt. That by itself warranted the cost of upgrading to this wireless system. Another time that this system has come in handy was during a long vacation. Not only does this type of system alert you with a verbal cue in the house, if your alarm is set to away and a window or door is opened, a service is called. This service acts as a call center to handle emergencies such as police, fire, and EMS. When we took a family vacation to Florida, we were about two states away at a rest stop when the phone rang. Apparently, one of our windows had been opened. Since we knew it was not any of us, we were immediately worried. We called neighbors immediately after getting off the phone with them, and the neighbor was getting ready to go over there and check it out. Luckily for us, before the neighbor could even get outside, a police cruiser pulled up to our house. Together they walked around the house and saw that nothing was wrong. Apparently, the house had settled and one of the windows popped up from its locked setting. Using the phone app, we were able to see exactly which window it was and where it was in the house. When we were finally home, we were relieved to see that nothing was stolen. Granted, we did check every inch of the house to make sure no one was waiting. The home security system makes a log of every single door open, lock attempt, and window pull that has happened. Therefore, we knew for sure that no one had entered or left the house. It is a nice tool to use also to check when exactly the housekeeper arrives and leaves compared to the time she is charging us for! The application can be different for different companies, but the one from Vivint is very good. With it, I can assign passcodes to different users, or also set up something that I would have never thought of to incorporate into an alarm system. Not only did each one of my doors come with an installed smart lock that I can control my phone, computer, or keypad, this alarm system also deals with your house's energy. The package came with a smart thermostat for the upstairs and downstairs. With this, we can control the fans and temperatures from our smart devices. A neat feature that has been added to this is also that the thermostat communicates with the hub to check the current weather conditions. With this, if a heat wave is coming, or the temperature is going to bottom out, the thermostat can make the decision to change the temperature on its own. If in the middle of the night, you decide that it is cold, there is no more getting out of bed to go to the living room the adjust the temperature. With the newest technology also come new advances. We had our system installed about 5 years ago. Now, in the newest packages, there are more capabilities that we did not have the opportunity to install. You can have cameras in your home that can track any movement, but also be watched from your smartphone. Also, there is a doorbell that has a camera built into it. Then, when someone rings it, you will immediately know who it is that is ringing. The doorbell has great features like night vision. There won't be that uneasy feeling anymore when it is time to go check the door at night. I know from experience, that if the lights are on inside your home, it is almost impossible to tell who is at the door when it is dark outside. This doorbell can remedy that problem quite simply.

You can control your garage door from the smart hub also. We only have the sensor on ours that tells us that it is open or closed. With the software on their side, you can write specific rules. I have written one that if the garage door is not closed by 9 PM, my wife receives a text on her phone that says the door is open. This happens quite often and has saved us from leaving the door open overnight many times. Are all these things needed in a home? Of course not, but, the fact that they are there can make some people feel more secure. At the moment, our security system is being used as more of a home automation system then it is for security. Since it is using the Z-wave technology, you can now install electrical outlets that sync up to your hub. This means that I can manually turn on and off the power to certain outlets that I name anything I want. We can control lights from on vacation to turn them on and off. We can set the Christmas tree to turn on at a certain time if we so choose. The possibilities are endless when one really starts looking at what you can connect to a smart outlet. The ability to have all of your lights turn on in certain parts of your house when the garage door opens is just amazing. In our new home, this will definitely be one of the main things we put in. The plan is to have a large panel or hub in the entrance from the garage that will be the main base for everything. Similar to our current house, but more centrally located. This way, you can manage your alerts, passcodes, and device management all from one place. There will also most likely be additional panels on each level; One specifically in our bedroom to alert us to an open door or window in the middle of the night. This will also help in a few years when our two boys become teenagers. No more saying you got home at a specific time when there is a data log to tell differently. Another new addition that is making waves is smart blinds. Basically, there is a sensor that tells you when it is getting sunny out, and you can have the blinds close automatically. This will not only stop the house from getting warm but will also save you money. It can save money by closing when the temperature in your house is going to heat up. This will then cause your air to not have to kick on as much or as long. In the end, these blinds would definitely pay for themselves.

This next section dives into a newer product on the market, but one that greatly affects how your home will run using home automation. It is the smart home assistant. Currently, the top ones that come to mind are Alexa, from Amazon, and google home. These small wireless devices can become a member of the family it seems. The first one we will be looking at is the Alexa device. You can pick up and Amazon Echo at Home Depot for about $99. One not so known feature of the Alexa is that is can almost be considered a landline telephone. You can make calls to other Alexa devices in other homes. It functions almost the same as the 90's answering machines in that you can even leave a message. It was covered before, but the Alexa can also control your smart home. You can ask Alexa to turn the lights on or off. You can even request that it changes the color of the bulbs if you went with that feature of bulbs like we talked about earlier. Some models of garage doors can even be opened with a voice command. If it is too hot or cold in the house, you can also have your Alexa change the temperature to the desired level. I think one of the best features for the Alexa is that it is hands-free. I cannot tell how many times I have been trying to cook something and forget how many tablespoons convert into a quarter cup or some other measurement. Now with a simple, "Alexa, how many tablespoons are in a half-cup?" The device will look up the information for you. There is no more washing your hands, dry your hands, then pulling out your smartphone so you can check and see how much is required. You can query Alexa to find your recipes or give you step by step instructions for cooking. I think that having one of these devices can really impress the family with the newfound cooking skills! Instead of having to clear the timer on the microwave, you can also use Alexa to set a timer. If bored while cooking, you can also hand free have the device play a specific song or playlist. Outside of the kitchen, you can get quick news brief of everything that has happened in the world. For your children, the Alexa model can also entertain them. It comes loaded with a few fun games for them to play and is preloaded with a bunch of answers to those kids and their silly questions. One of the neat features of Alexa is something called skills. If it does not come with a certain function you want it to out of the box, the community of owners have come up with certain codes that will program your device to do what you want. There are a ton of resources out on the internet that can give examples of what these are. Like other devices, Alexa can control your TV. There is an additional step for this to work though. You either have to have a special type of remote like the Logitech Harmony Remote, or you can buy the hub so you have your Alexa start, stop and pause Netflix hands-free! The default music program is Amazon music which is not that good, but with some settings reworked, you can change the default music to use Spotify.

The main competition to the Amazon Echo or Alexa, as previously discussed is the Google Home. The difference here is that the Google home integrates with Google itself, not Amazon. So, while Alexa is great at ordering things from Amazon like extra toilet paper, it is not so great at telling you what movies are out today. This is where the google home shines. One great feature is that you can control your Google Chromecast with your voice. It also lets you use google search if you have a question to ask it. One neat feature that this one has is that it allows you to access your Google calendar and Gmail. Unlike the Alexa, it cannot control as many home automation devices. And the ones that it can do, it does not use them as efficiently as the Amazon version. The Echo also comes with more apps, with the input from the community, but hopefully, that will be remedied later. When the head to head comparison is broken down to which to choose you to have to take into consideration what exactly these things will be used for. Simply put, if you want something that is great for controlling your home, go with the amazon echo. If you want a device that is great for answering your questions, you will want to go to the Google home. In my own opinion, there is not really a need to control all of your home automation with voice. I plan on having a tablet or two around the house, and plenty of smart hubs that I will not need to call out to lower the temperature in an odd voice so the Alexa can pick it up. Just pull out a phone, grab a tablet, or walk to a hub and change it.

The thing I like most about them is the answers to questions. Like the cooking example earlier, I think that the Google home will really come out on top for me. The Alexa device was released in 2015, and the Google home was just released last fall. It still has some growth to make, but when it does I think it will be a much more powerful device for home automation and inquiry. With Black Friday deals, both of the devices are looking to be in the $79 dollar price range.

The future of IoT is looking amazing. When one stops to think about what else could they possibly develop or deploy, you never really realize how cool of an idea that is until you see that new tech on the shelf and wonder how you ever lived without it. Sensors are becoming smarter and smarter. With this, we get newer ideas and technology. One new item that will be hitting the market soon is a sensor that communicates with your thermostat and HVAC to automatically Febreze your house. That is correct, there will now be a robot out there that knows when your house stinks and the optimal time to dispense the fragrance. For those people who really worry about water consumption, there is a new shower head coming out that actually measures the amount of water you use while you shower. The shower head has built in LED's that change as the amount of water you use is measured. Along with the theme of water and sensors, new sensors also are out that detects if it is going to rain, and stop your lawn from being watered. Things like the Roomba robot floor vacuum are only going to get smarter, and your devices used for cooking are only going to get more efficient. My most recent smart cooking apparatus was the Anova Bluetooth machine that cooks food Sous Vide by setting the water to a perfect temperature and cooking the food in the moving water. It is all controlled by my phone and I get texts when the food is ready. As the years go by, we will be able to connect more and more things to our smart home. Looking at the chart below, you can see just how much the Internet of things is growing.

In conclusion, I myself am really looking forward to the new age of the IoT. There are many more things that just cool tricks you can do for your home. These types of things can not only save you time and money but can also make you safe. I know that outside of the home, one neat thing I enjoy is having my truck hooked up to my cellphone. During a hot sunny day, I can start my truck from my phone about 10 minutes before I get outside after work. If auto starts the AC in there also so you are not unable to breathe when opening the door. These kinds of small tricks do not seem like much to some, but considering where we have come from; there is no telling what the future has in store for us with the IoT. In this paper, we have covered the history of IoT, from where it began, to where it is now. We also discussed some of the new features you can have at your home to bring it up to today's IoT standards. And we also looked at the celebrities of the IoT community the Amazon Echo and the Google home. Finally, we discussed where the future may take us with the IoT. Thank you for taking the time to read through this write-up, and I hope you all learned something interesting.

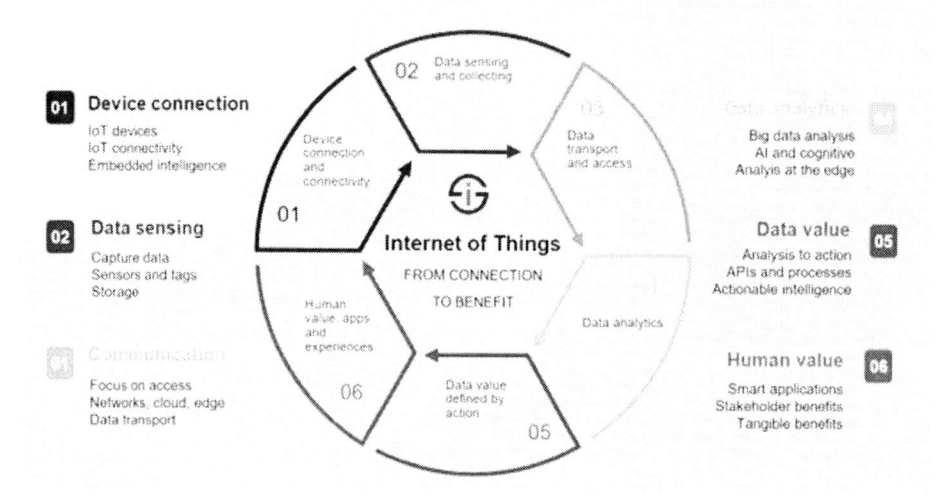

Figure 3. The Internet of Things redefined – from connecting devices to creating value.

REFERENCES

"*Amazon Alexa*" Google Images.com, www.google.com.

"*GE LED Color Changing Bulb.*" Google Images.com, www.google.com.

"*Google home*" Google Images.com, www.google.com.

"*Harmony Hub*" Google Images.com, www.google.com.

Imler, Kathryn. "*History of X10*" X10 Communications, Nov. 2008, https://sites.google.com/site/x10communication/Home.

"*IOT Growth Chart*" Google Images.com, www.google.com.

"*Vivint Home Automation*" Vivint Smart Home Security Systems, 2017.

Mod, Shreepanjali, *Samsung backs IoT platform for Smart Home and much more*, https://www.engineersgarage.com/news/samsung-backs-iot-platform-smart-home-and-much-more, (Accessed December 2, 2017).

https://www.i-scoop.eu/internet-of-things/.

Chapter 12

IoT: ARCHITECTURE AND VIRTUALIZATION

INTRODUCTION

The Internet of Things (IoT) is the term coined to encompass the way connected devices and technology are growing. The Internet began as a system to connect people with devices on a single network around the world. The intelligence of these devices and technologies has grown to the point that devices could communicate and share the information each other without any human involvement. IoT devices continue to enter the market from a large assortment of manufacturers and the big question moving forward is how we are going to build a system that will allow these devices to connect with each other now and with future devices. Building a network should evaluate future growth and deploy of new devices is a challenge that will be addressing in this chapter. This chapter discusses the possible solutions, describes the technical architecture and also the use of Network Function Virtualization (NFV) to handle scaling and promoting longevity of end devices and the network as a whole.

We have seen a lot of advancement in the past few years when it comes to connected devices. Connectivity and network architecture with embedded algorithms and artificial intelligence makes IoT devices as "Smart" devices.

Architecture is the design and plan of a structure. Architecture with respect to IoT system is to connect devices along with the way they exchange the information at different levels and tiers of networks. When dealing with so many devices which are all from different manufacturers a lot of times with their own proprietary software, designing an architecture can be very difficult, to address this issue with a viable solution that offers scalability, reliability, and ease of use.

In this chapter, we will be going over why the Network Function Virtualization (NFV) is an answer for advanced networking functions–and is done by a centralized common hardware device that shares all network functions of a system. NFV can be implemented in each device using software, this makes the network scalable and reliable without the need for an additional purchase and maintenance of hardware and control each end -device.

This chapter also looks at SDN (Software Defined Networking) usage in conjunction with NFV to provide the best structure for IoT architecture and backend control.

The Internet of Things (IoT) is the next generation of an internet that is driving the evolution of network architecture to adapt to the growing needs while keeping an already established infrastructure viable and keeping the cost low for consumers and companies. The cost for IoT devices is relatively small with advanced technology but the cost to connect and maintain these devices can be high due to the fact that a company might have to upgrade existing hardware to support the influx of all these new devices on to their network load. We live in a time of big data and to support the mass flow of data these data centers have been being pushed to their limits and beyond to handle the amount of information traffic. Software solutions can handle massive data, but at some point, new hardware upgrade and cost incurred can be the breaking point for some companies.

Looking at the numbers to compare the amount that data usage and the amount of IoT devices, the expected number of IoT devices is going to keep increasing exponentially through the years. Figure 1 gives the growth of objects connected to the IoT by 2020.

With IoT devices entering the market at the rate at which they are going to make sure any IoT infrastructure that can handle the growth in devices and the data that is collected and transferred while making certain security practices mandatory.

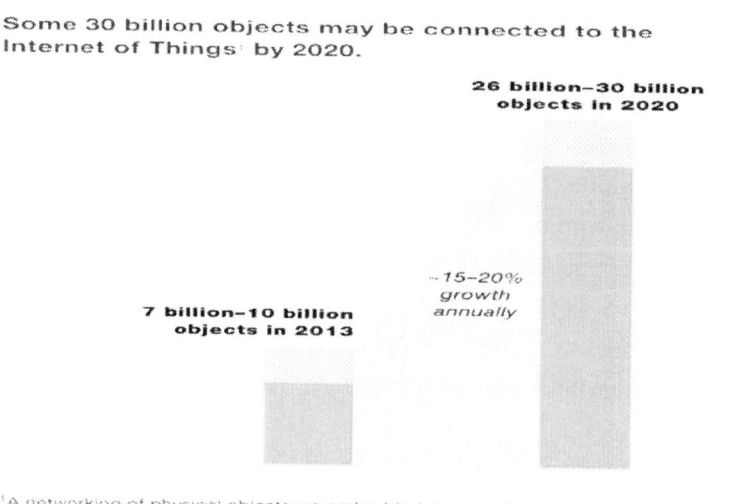

Figure 1. The Increase of objects connected to IoT by 2020.

This chapter started by introducing the Network Function Virtualization (NFV) which is one of the key concepts that will be discussed as a solution when it comes to IoT architecture. Another concept emphasizing in the chapter is Software Defined Networking (SDN) which is the process of controlling networking protocols through software to allow for hot changes without sacrificing service caused by downtime. Building an IoT system with these two concepts will accomplish the goals we need the system to meet.

The system has to meet the goals in terms of scalability, sustainability, security, and simplicity to be able to handle the increasing load and also be compatible with current and future advanced devices.

Figure 2 shows expected growth of devices is around 15 – 20% annually which rounds out to be in the ballpark of about 10- 15 billion more devices added every year.

Network Function Virtualization (NFV) and Software Defined Networking (SDN) can be used in conjunction with one another to meet the system's objective. NFV (Network Function Virtualization) is a standalone system and would work fine in achieving most its goals. But, SDN adds long-lasting scalability and sustainability. It allows the ability to push network protocol updates and flexibility for a system administrator to change the networking of the system without taking anything offline and losing uptime.

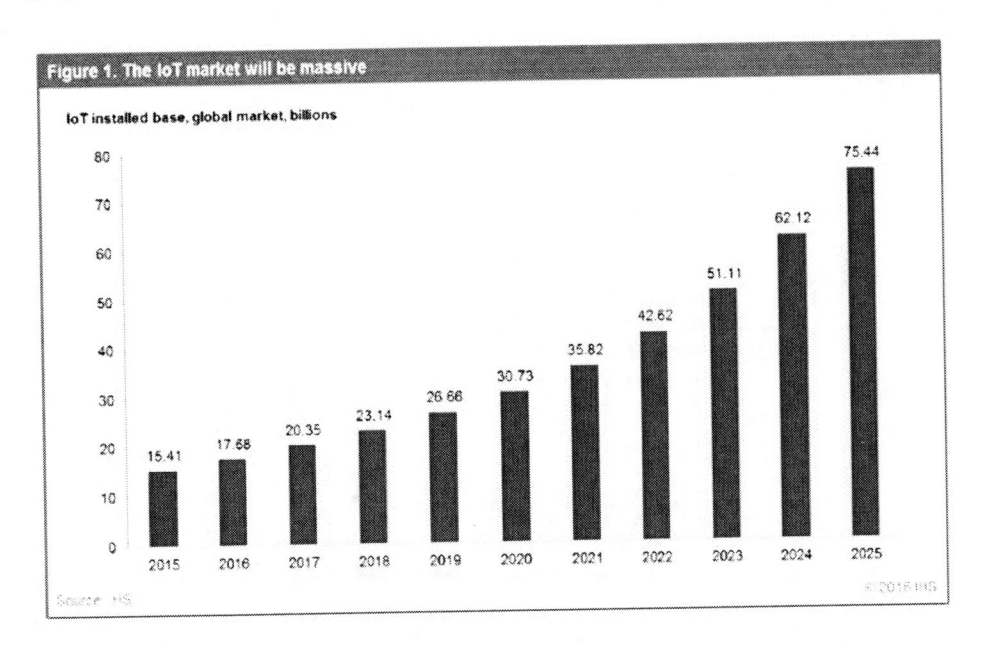

Figure 2. The Growth of IoT Devices in Billions.

Security and simplicity are the other two goals to accomplish with NFV and SDN. SDN accomplish both goals by allowing for network protocol change and security while NFV would keep handling the networking load and data from the individual devices, providing security would be easy and straightforward when compared to conventional devices. The devices entering the market are from many manufacturers with proprietary software on the device. But when using NFV it wouldn't matter since the centralized device could be open source and integrate with all the devices that make the system agile to tailor itself for adaptivity. However, an administrator would want the system to run. Figure 3 shows NFV back-end architecture that supports IoT Gateway.

The figure shows how each device connected to the IP network through an IoT gateway to the data center where you can see virtualized layer behind the hardware layer. Virtualized layer contains different IoT apps which allow for getting and pushing out the latest updates from the manufacturers. It also allows the system to communicate and collect data from all the different IoT devices even though they contain their proprietary software.

SDN comes to back up this virtualized system in the form of a middleware that can implement hardware changes through software which allows for the changing of protocols and ports on the first two OSI layers. The system will be easy to maintain and scale to fit the needs of the administrator regardless of the deploying environment. This architecture meets all the goals mentioned earlier and while there are many ways to set up an IoT system by using these two concepts it allows for the easiest building and maintaining of the system while offering superior reliability.

Data flow and handling is still the biggest issue but with this solution, implementation of physical machines or even a cloud-based infrastructure which would allow for greater scalability and ease of maintenance for your backend data center. AWS or Microsoft Azure would offer the services needed to build the backend infrastructure without the cost of physical equipment and could relieve cost for businesses and individuals while also allowing integration with their current infrastructure.

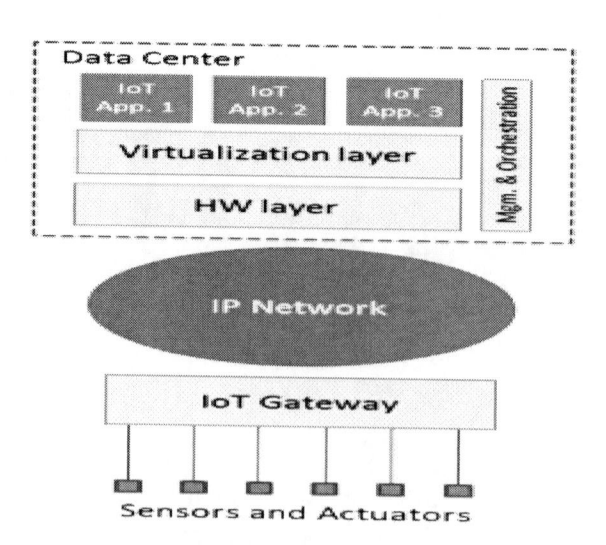

Figure 3. NFV Backend Architecture supporting IoT Gateway.

CONCLUSION

The Internet of Things (IoT) is a collection of devices connected to a network that collects information to be stored and analyzed. To make up the backend architecture for the system to meet the goals of system sustainability, scalability, security, and simplicity, it is recommended to have an IoT system that uses NFV and an SDN. The system architecture meets all of these goals and makes the system very flexible for end devices and the backend. The backend can be built on physical machines, or a cloud-hosted system depending on the resources and need of the administrator implementing the system on their network.

The architecture using NFV and SDN allows the integration of all the different IoT devices on one network with a centralized data center to handle all of the network traffic and load processing. Therefore, the end devices only required sending the data they collect over the network where the data center will handle all the processes. This procedure saves the life of the end devices by having the heavy logic and network processing handled by the main device.

The SDN would take care of layer one and two protocols on the network, by making them easily changeable and allowing for the less downtime of the system since it allows for changes the networking logic and protocol. This makes SDN a flexible solution for IoT infrastructure that helps to build and maintain a sustainable, scalable, secure, and simple system for all IoT devices on a new network or existing infrastructure can be cost-effective and easily done for a system administrator.

REFERENCES

Cisco. (2017, June 07). *The Zettabyte Era: Trends and Analysis*. Retrieved from https://www.cisco.com/c/en/us/solutions/collateral/service-provider/visual-networking-index-vni/vni-hyperconnectivity-wp.html.

Miladinovic, I., & Schefer-Wenzl, S. (2017). A highly scalable IoT architecture through network function virtualization. *Open Journal of Internet Of Things (OJIOT)*, *3*(1), 127-135. Retrieved from https://www.ronpub.com/OJIOT_2017v3i1n11_Miladinovic.pdf.

Martin. (2017, February 23). *Internet of Things of Statistics*. Retrieved from http://informationmatters.net/internet-of-things-statistics/.

The 4 stages of an IoT architecture. Retrieved from https://techbeacon.com/4-stages-iot-architecture.

Chapter 13

THE INTERNET OF THINGS: A MORE CONNECTED WORLD

INTRODUCTION

The Internet of Things (IoT) recognizes the connectivity of the future for humans. It envisions the world where devices can integrate information to the extent that it creates a new paradigm in human interactivity. It is not a sci-fi concept that would easily found in a movie. The IoT identifies are things that research and money are currently being put forward to discover trends. Communication is already essential to use the internet. It created a program that would allow for data to flow from human users across vast areas.

Since its creation, which was not very long ago relatively, the way that devices integrate connectivity has become a new mold for how it interacts with the internet. Humans are very sociable and will always strive for new ways to close the barrier between interactivity and communication. Humanity loves interactivity and automation. Our obsession with creating tools is part of what found our ability to create civilizations. The movement toward IoT has already created:

- Easier to use interfaces on computers.
- Interactively minded designs for smartphones.
- Cell phone technologies in general.
- Monitors and high-resolution displays.
- Monitoring devices for healthcare and finance.
- Numerous household appliances and upgrades to dated products.
- Immense and always expanding stores of applications for consumers.

The exciting part is that the trends identified in IoT signal the coming of automated process that would allow for better services in the medical field and the prevention of human casualty in industry and improvements to home life. In addition to that, there is potential for creating smarter and more widespread communication grids. These would expand the ability to communicate across the globe efficiently and cheaply in the future.

Before getting into the more complex areas of the IoT world, we must first look at the environment that developed after the creation of the internet. Before the widespread, commercial use of the internet people regulated to use slower communication means to express complex information. While the phone line had existed for nearly a century before the internet, it does not produce a written document when used to relay information. Additionally, limitations in using a phone to communicate would make companies and business have to maintain a high paper network that relied on slower delivery methods. The consumer would have to look at magazines and catalogs, and then have to wait for their orders to receive through the mail, and they would have to wait for the company to deliver the order after.

In internal business use, the lack of electronic cataloging meant that relevant business info would store in vast libraries at the expense of the business itself. These could quickly become unorganized and would be vulnerable to fire damage.

Disorganization in business always leads to some amount of loss of productivity. Valuable information, or important communication between customer and producer, would always rely on slower communication methods. It is important to recognize how key this is to the current development of IoT. Why should this be considered more important that communication and interactivity?

The drive of business and making money is second only to war in what evolves the paradigm of communication technology. World War Two created the foundations for a broad range of technologies and even set the stage for the importance of computation machines in the world. Before that, the telegraph lines created a new paradigm of global interactivity with the trans-Atlantic line. With the inception of the internet businesses suddenly had a massive new store space.

When good companies find a way to make even more money off of consumers, they go for it wholesale. While that thought helped contribute to the "dot-com" bubble of the early 2000s, it also leads to the commercialization and expansion of the internet. Some businesses specialized in providing the internet to people, businesses who specialized in rich applications and workstations for a huge new demand for personal computers. The companies that sold products suddenly found that they could reach customers country or even worldwide.

Then new businesses sprung up to deliver packages and act as a middleman for the client. When the infrastructure for the internet became stronger, and more customers achieved greater bandwidth capabilities, dozens of companies sprung to life to provide customers with streaming video content. Cable companies and traditional content providers also jumped on board as to not lose all their customers to this quicker and more convenient content.

The prospect of creating faster internet speeds drove to charge at more premium rates led some companies and researchers to essentially "pave the way" for businesses to take advantage of those speeds, now regular for many customers, to provide more varied content.

Regarding interactivity and business forcing the paradigm forward we just need to look at the smartphones. The technologies that exist just to use it, the simple touch screen that is present on most smartphones and tablets, was developed to a consumer grade just over a decade ago. Companies recognized the human attraction to interacting with POS, Push on Screen, devices and capitalized on a market of communication.

As they developed new and cheaper methods to create touchscreen devices, many companies integrated those ideas into home desktops. From there, more precise touch interface devices suddenly found themselves in every aspect of consumerism. Touch interface phones got their significance, touch interfaces found themselves in cars, air conditioning and household appliances, security devices, and fast food and shipment services.

On the production side, touch interface screens integrated into every aspect of heavy machinery and chemical production. Workers can be more easily trained to interact with devices that have touch interface devices. In this aspect, the IoT has already somewhat arrived. However, this is the foundation for a future with total integration. The need for businesses to drive forward the ability to connect with more and more consumers has founded this revolution in the tech industry.

There are military applications for these devices currently, but it can easily assume that everything listed above developed with a sense of consumer-grade qualities. Why is this important? The flow of computational devices from inception to commercial grade started with computers being only viable for military use.

The development power of the army at that time eclipsed the power of the general public. This new wave of technology, not founded by military involvement and independent of that, shows that the technological ability of private companies and individuals can keep pace with military development, except a few cases.

Obviously, there are restrictions on military grade hardware, like drones with offensive abilities, for general use. But the importance of communication and the globalization of business villages is the 'big bang' for the IoT environment.

Commercial grade developers mean that new cutting-edge products are being received by consumers quicker. There are"t extended periods of time where the technology is only allowed to use by specific groups in the military or government. In the past, those periods of time could prove to be decades long.

There is a slight negative to this new paradigm of consumer technology. The marketplace that people find themselves in has been tuned to deliver products or goods at a quick rate. Technologies are becoming outdated faster and potentially harmful, or 'junk' devices have invaded the marketplace.

While not exactly tied to the user interface and IoT, consider the recent case of exploding batteries in the Samsung Galaxy line of phones. Samsung, before the problem became apparent, were working on the standard business model of pushing out a product alongside or faster than the competition, primarily Apple. The real demand for Samsung's device meant that a massive amount of these devices shipped with faulty batteries. The point here is that Samsung may have been able to catch the issue or develop a more resilient battery pack if they were competing to be the cutting edge of cell phone technology.

Consider that an era of the country or worldwide marketplace there have been a vast amount of 'junk' products. Things that exist to fulfill a consumer demand for cheaper devices or to capitalize on a consumer disregard for quality. An example of this might be a faulty line of cars, low-quality audio devices, or insufficient computer hardware.

Where one company leads the field in consumer grade products, other companies come along to ride the coattails and pick up the business of customers who cannot afford to purchase, or just do not wish to purchase, those higher quality products. Why is this important to consider before heading into a more researched idea of IoT in the future?

In a world where interconnectivity is a king, there are bound to be tons and tons of companies that try to capitalize on consumers who are either on the outliers of the reach of IoT systems or are unable to buy the products required to take advantage of IoT. While IoT theory does suggest that interactivity will become a global thing that is accessible by all there will certainly be a period where devices that allow those connections sold at a premium. During this period there will also be an immense amount of competition, likely comparable to the PC rush of the 90's, that will create a massive amount of dangerous products from both well-known and obscure companies, leads to the largest issue in approaching the world of IoT. Consider even our current world and its ability to connect to the internet freely. At a college campus, we enjoy the use of the high-speed internet. In cities that house tech centers, Sacramento or Houston for example, even residential consumers can enjoy tens of megabytes of download capability- some even up to a gigabyte per second, at a reasonable cost.

Now consider how much of the world is still shut off to these speeds. Rural areas that have deemed 'unmarketable' for companies to extend their services to either have to rely on phone lines, the 'old school' dial-up some of us remember, or unreliable and expensive satellite internet. Both those options impose huge limitations in comparison to the previous internet options. These people have been limited and may find participating in a high bandwidth field of interactivity completely impossible.

In the growing field of interconnectivity, we must consider how the business centered wave of development is going to affect people who decide or must live in rural areas. These individuals will likely have to wait until the cost of expanding internet technologies become 'commercially viable,' or more quickly known as cheap enough, to extend to these areas. The questions that are currently hard to answer with conclusive research are;

- If communication speeds will reach rural areas quick enough to integrate them into the IoT.
- If communication speeds will be good enough to interact with technologies that will likely develop with more urbanized areas in mind.

Individuals who live in the countryside, even people who live in less developed countries, are unfortunately poised to be left behind by urban areas in regards to IoT. While the future of what businesses may find profitable enough to pursue can be guessed with evidence, the damage can be discovered that separating these areas from more integrated systems.

Once IoT becomes a staple in urban areas it will quickly outpace the productivity and living standards of areas without it. Those underdeveloped areas will face an ever-growing hill to catch up to these markets. Businesses who recognize that their productivity will be more efficient in developed areas will not even consider expanding out to underdeveloped areas if the profit margins for doing so do not prove to be sufficient.

There are a lot of reasons for this cost, and before addressing what will likely be the first steps of creating IoT centered urban spaces, I will examine the cost and importance of developing rural zones. The FCC has within the last few years set forward initiatives to get broadband internet, internet with speeds of 4.0 Mbps down, to more and more rural and 'tribal' Americans. The FCC has also stepped up the requirements for what 'broadband' can be called, likely in anticipation of the data speeds an IoT environment will require and have made information available to the public.

Figure 1 is taken from the FCC website [1] and demonstrates that there is an appreciable gap between rural and urban areas for internet access. The access to high-speed internet for urban areas is at 98%. Compare that to the highlighted 60.75 percent of people in the countryside are unable to access those programs. That represents a huge population gap, a difference of nearly 38%, of people that cannot access that same amount of bandwidth. The FCC started this initiative to expand internet capability in rural areas in 2010, so even seven years later there remains a huge gap.

This will likely demonstrate the gap between people who can take advantage of IoT and its usefulness and those who cannot; it will likely become a concern for voters in these areas and will likely influence government at a national level. It is the responsibility of the US government to get rural citizens on board with the stronger network environment unless they want to lose their citizens to the technological gap.

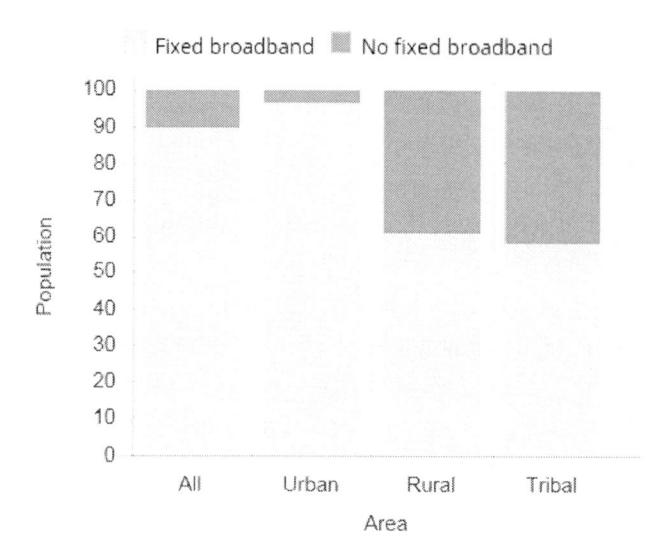

Figure 1. Morphology Broadband Coverage [1].

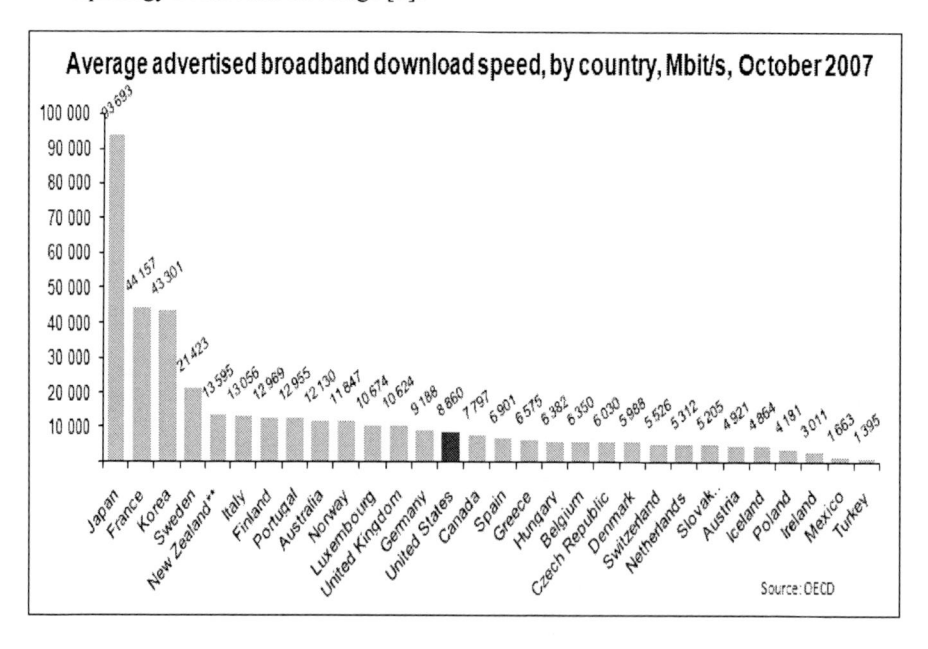

Figure 2. Global Average Broadband Speed [2].

The other and more pressing concern that line of thoughts opens up are how countries that have general inability to access the fast internet will compete in the IoT environment. Obviously more technologically or fiscally sound countries will lead the charge here. That has been the usual way of development in the past, but the ideas of the IoT represent to deal with new issues for the world. Interconnectivity is something that will lead to mass production increases, and countries that cannot keep up with those speeds are going to fall significantly behind.

To that extent, the United States will not automatically be the top player in the world. IoT and the development of interconnected cities will flourish in countries that already have dedicated extensive infrastructure to maintaining connectivity in the modern era. More radically, consider the cultural viewpoint of sharing that kind of space and interactivity with other people. Will the US be able to compete with European countries in that regard? Will nations with higher population densities suddenly come out on top thanks to their already integrated nature? This is our first step to consider before going into IoT cities.

Above Figure, from ten years ago, has been chosen as a background for my point [2]. Here we find that the US is in the middle of the fastest average speeds, but is nowhere near even the fourth place country, Sweden. The graph demonstrates that the average speed for the US was around 1.0 MB/s. Compare that to the rates in the geographically smaller country of Japan, which enjoyed around 10.0 MB/s in 2007. Japan, a country which has a much higher population density than the US, has a natural need to produce and maintain more top quality infrastructure to satisfy the needs and demands of the population.

The other countries to keep an eye on here are Italy and France. European countries are much smaller in legal landmass when compared to the US, but France certainly has its rural areas. However, the country has an average speed that knocks on the door of Japan and smashes the US's rates. Italy will become important later in the paper in regards to IoT cities, so notice how even that country enjoys a slight but appreciable increase over the US.

These countries either through recognizing the importance or through the natural growth of their populations expanded the internet speeds. These countries have a stronger foundation for employing complicated and efficient IoT paradigms even before they realized their capability. Now let's examine a more recent chart [3].

Figure 3 shows commercial subscriptions to internet speeds by charting speed of the bandwidth. This is a good look into the infrastructure in the countries as it signals how robust the communication systems are overall. France and Korea have overtaken Japan, who still enjoys a much stronger infrastructure than the US.

Moreover, we find that there are suddenly several new, and somewhat surprising, arrivals to the graph that were not even present in the previous graph. Countries like Malta have rocketed to the top of the graph in their capability to provide the internet to their citizens.

Malta is a small island country in the Mediterranean Sea, so how have they come so far? The answer is right there- and it should not be surprising why smaller countries are becoming the leaders in interconnectivity. There is simply a more condensed population in a smaller landmass. Even if the governments of those countries do not possess the same economic powers of larger countries, they don't need to.

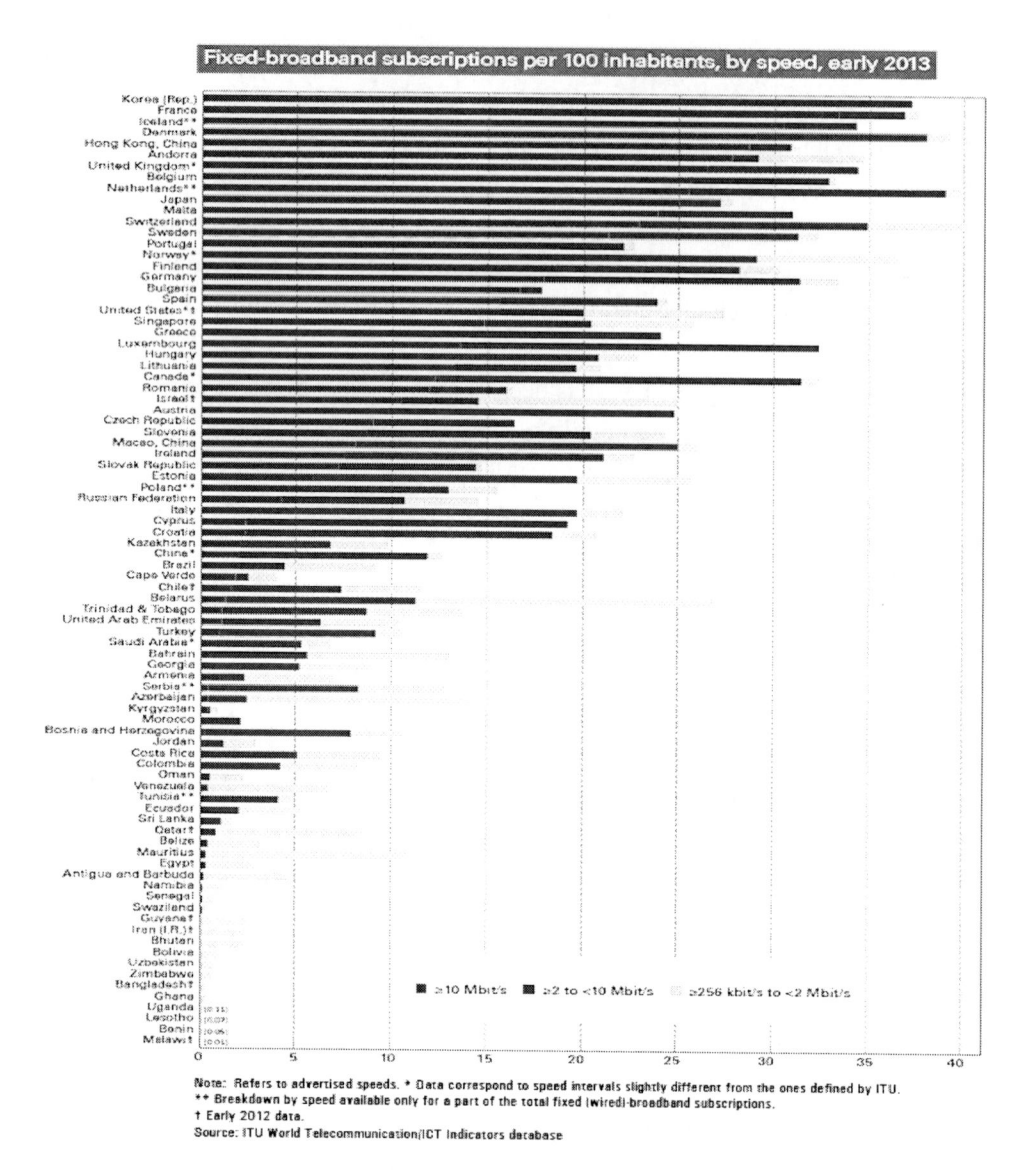

Figure 3. Global Speed of Internet [3].

The cost to allow access to high speeds of the internet to all their citizens is tiny. The time to which it would take to build that infrastructure, in some countries from the ground up, would take very little time at all compared to the effort that would be needed to link a country the size of the US together. As a bonus to building entirely new infrastructure, there is no cost in replacing outdated or insufficient wires or towers.

The technology to build the best infrastructure possible is commercially viable and easy to find. Any business would be ready and willing to accept a contract to assist a government in the construction of infrastructure. In a global marketplace with wildly shared ideas, the country of Malta could have had access to the best they could afford.

Malta demonstrates a strange bond between the natural world and the developing technological landscape. Where there are smaller land masses, more condensed populations, there is greater potential to start up new systems of interactivity. Residents used to share the communal spirit that comes with living in proximity and sharing a country would be more easily willing to interact in an IoT environment.

Malta is the greatest example of this as it proves to be one of the quickest to develop to expand its internet connectivity to its population. An article, [4], list that Malta's growth of internet use was the highest in the world, with New Zealand and Iceland right behind it. It is interesting to see that those other two countries are themselves smaller island countries with smaller or denser populations than the US. Malta is also of a smaller landmass than either.

Could that natural connection prove to be extremely important in the growth of IoT communities? Even if those countries lack the raw industrial power to take advantage of interconnectivity they could still become markets for tourism and attractive places to live for new citizens.

The ideas behind designing an IoT city seems to follow already planning the city like an island of infrastructure, where everything maintained within the bubble of the city. An island, or smaller country, might prove to be the perfect proving grounds for interconnected cities. As communication abilities are developed in the present, world governments are taking notice.

Figure 4 developed by the International Telecom Union, shows that while the developing world is still under the number of citizens provided with the internet regarding developed countries, underdeveloped countries have still but substantial gains in that regard.

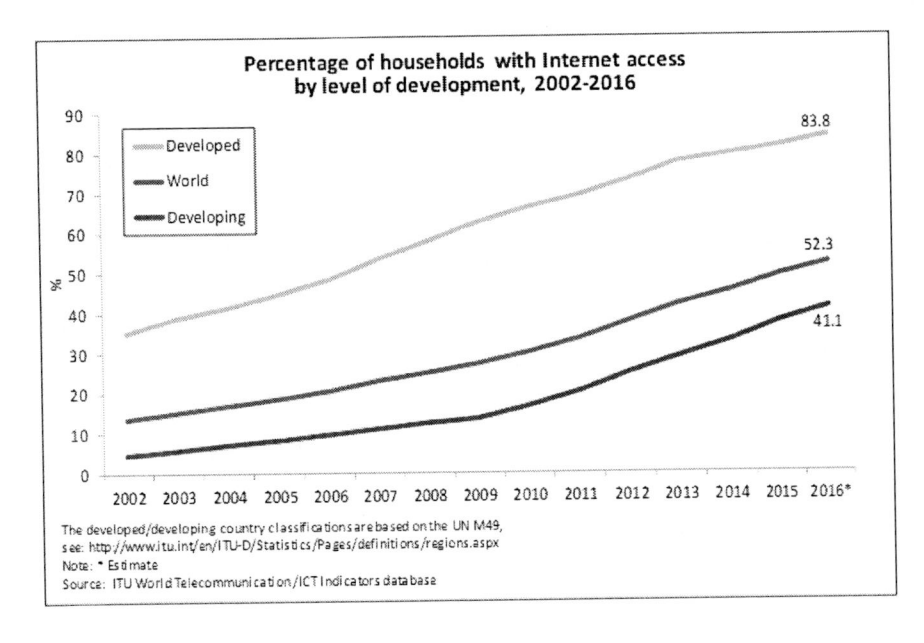

Figure 4. Household Internet access percentage (ITU).

Island countries, like Malta, may start to find themselves in the position to suddenly arrive at the forefront of technological standards where they previously could not. Obviously, this ignores the countries that are landlocked and are not able to share internet use to all their citizens, will perhaps prove to be another gap between countries of different developmental levels in the coming era of IoT systems. It will be an exciting new reality that island countries will have to explore. They will also find themselves in direct competition with smaller countries that have already implemented massive communication infrastructure and already compete in a global marketplace.

Countries like Japan or Korea are poised to turn their urban centers into 'islands' of IoT interactivity and become world leaders for those designs. Other countries, notably China, may be more than willing to forgo the needs of rural citizens if it means that certain cities, like Hong Kong, can be propelled into productive powerhouses. Entire economies are going to leverage on how efficiently IoT systems implemented into place.

The geographic locations are so important to consider and will likely become a point of contention when IoT systems arrive in force. The chapter mentioned earlier about the gap that already exists between urban and rural areas. And while some smaller countries find themselves at a sudden advantage in producing new infrastructures, bigger countries may decide to sacrifice the productivity of their underdeveloped zones to elevate their cities.

Governments will likely look at the scientific models of building IoT and real-world models of island-based infrastructure to develop plans to create their own. What this could mean for population growth and the transfer of populations into urban areas can likely be figured out in previous developments in urbanization.

Interconnectivity is becoming a greater and greater draw for consumers into a manner of new marketplaces. The desire, created by both consumerism and need, to be on the forefront of technology will attract new populations to urban areas. The less and fewer tolerance people have for being left out of the faster speeds of internet interconnectivity will lead to more people integrated into IoT systems.

The higher production capabilities and current economic values of IoT cities will also create a new job market that will require employees. Just as industrialization and office work brought people to live in the suburbs and grow cities decades ago, interconnectivity and operating in a global marketplace will attract people to live in cities.

How this will 'grow' an island of IoT systems will likely depend on the ability of the country and citizens to operate in a high population dense city. At this point, we likely find that current cities lack the proper foundation to deal with this new kind of interconnectivity. It is almost a matter of architecture, but modern cities built under the blueprint of satisfying traffic flow and organizing districts into commercial and residential zones. The ideas work for current needs but will likely prove to be too old to keep up with IoT designs.

Another example of how geography might help island or smaller countries competes with globally influential countries. They have potential to develop modern infrastructure and plan their cities to take full advantage of IoT designs. They can also do that without the immense cost it would take to revolutionize a town like New York or Hong Kong to benefit from these IoT systems fully.

It seems that larger countries have already recognized the impossibility of redesigning whole cities to meet every need a 'smart city' requires. They instead seek to outspend smaller countries in the fields of web infrastructure and research. In the last decade, all developed countries have started to spend freely and massively on trying to upgrade their internet capabilities. Smaller countries cannot spend a vast amount of money on research to keep up and currently rely on being able to use commercially available contractors.

While Malta demonstrates that a country can produce a level of internet connectivity that outshines larger countries, it does not take into account the ability of more major countries to work inwardly and build a stronger infrastructure. Countries that rely on 'importing' or contracting internet services from somewhere else may eventually find themselves outmatched by larger countries. The cost of keeping up with buying commercial contracts may prove to be too expensive to maintain a sufficient IoT structure. See Figure 5.

Exhibit D: Change in R&D Spending by Industry, 2014–15

Software and Internet companies increased spending by 27.4 percent — roughly three times the percentage increase of industrials.

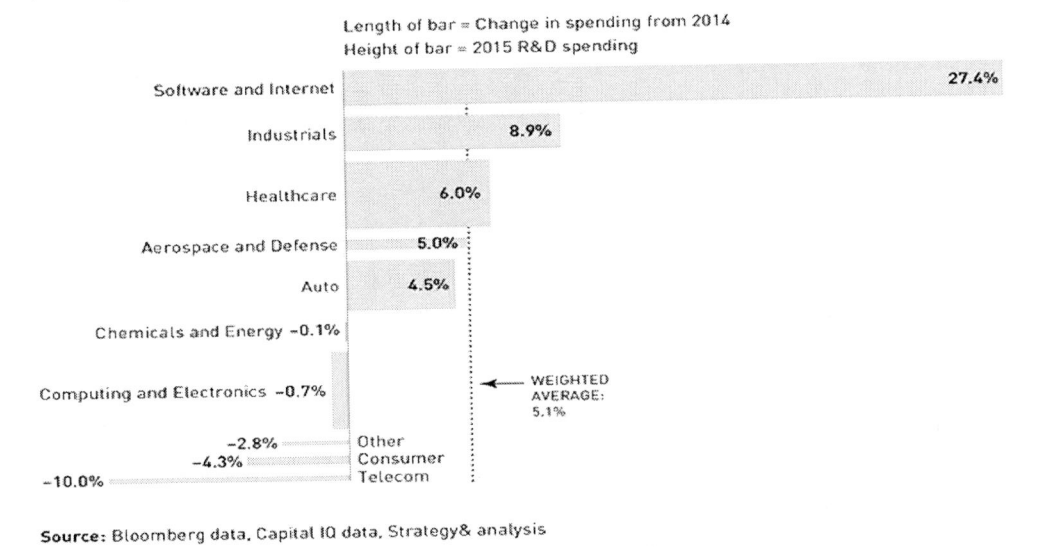

Length of bar = Change in spending from 2014
Height of bar = 2015 R&D spending

Industry	%
Software and Internet	27.4%
Industrials	8.9%
Healthcare	6.0%
Aerospace and Defense	5.0%
Auto	4.5%
Chemicals and Energy	-0.1%
Computing and Electronics	-0.7%
Other	-2.8%
Consumer	-4.3%
Telecom	-10.0%

WEIGHTED AVERAGE: 5.1%

Source: Bloomberg data, Capital IQ data, Strategy& analysis

Figure 5. Different Fields Invested in Research & Development [5].

The above chart, provided by Strategy Business [5], shows that American spending on software development research and development has far eclipsed other areas even with the last two years. With the oncoming prospect of IoT designs, it is likely that all developed countries are either experiencing or looking into invest money into technologies to develop their infrastructure. What does this mean? This could very well turn into a new form of global competition, not between businesses, but between governments.

Consider the space race in the 1950.s. While there were commercial enterprises involved, namely in the US, the space race was a technological race that propelled both computational power, engineering, and even global communication networks. The ideas and people behind each country.s space program became commodities. When one country advanced the others into space, it did not share the specifics of that achievement; the ways to produce a manned space module and create a safe to use the rocket for manned flight.

The technology itself was a weapon that used in a war. This same situation will likely happen with regards to IoT technologies and the development of cities. As the infrastructures of cities are improved then the secrets and ways that they improved will likely become a manner of national importance. To maintain an edge in a global marketplace, the governments of the world will probably find it to be in their interests to not share the technologies that operate their systems.

Countries who can spend money on research will hold an advantage here. It might assume that faster and more precise technology developed inwardly will cover up the limitations that cities will encounter when first being integrated into IoT systems.

When these technologies become a matter of national importance, then it will likely be hard to impossible for those technologies to share with countries that may not be a threat to a global marketplace. It is probable that in the future globally minded cities will experience a similar difference in development levels as they do now. Where widely interconnected populations are the norm and the complex structure that maintains that interconnectivity is the factor that decides a developed city. Internet speeds could prove to be significantly faster in the towns with infrastructure that has been developed by government forces. Countries that once relied on buying their infrastructure may leave with inferior supplies from business contractors.

This competition is very likely going to happen, but where those lines of completion will be drawn can only be guessed on from current policies. It could assume that the US will find its strongest competitor in China. But will it find global allies in the EU or Japan or Korea? Will those countries be able to develop an integrated system that is far superior to the US.s and China.s and decide that they will take up the charge over those countries? Contrary to the space race, every single developed country is poised to compete in the marketplace of the globe trying to guess the lines of competition might be impossible. Or be wrong to assume. Technology is being worked on by any country at all times. While

IoT does dictate the oncoming age of interconnectivity, it does not account for the distinct differences that systems between countries may entail.

The socioeconomic impact of designing IoT cities cannot be ignored. What some countries may deem acceptable for creating a functioning system may not be acceptable for others. Where some countries may find no issue with integrating citizens into interconnected lives, other countries may encounter large problems. Some countries may design the IoT systems to accommodate certain aspects of the industry that may not force in the other countries.

The template to create an IoT city, an efficient one, may prove to be unique to every case. There are, however, individual impacts that considered in each instance that would have to deal with every country. Socioeconomically speaking multiple aspects need to be satisfied that prove to be universal in their need.

Fulfilling the humanistic requirements of the citizens may turn out to be the success of longevity for these cities. Interconnectivity is relevant and fresh desire for citizens, but other needs need to be accounted for to maintain these urban areas.

These include robust job markets, housing, adherence to the cultural norms, education, civic pride, understanding of good traffic flow, beautification. And for each country, those needs will mean different things. One country may find integrating government activities to be necessary.

Another country may consider linking the entertainment industry necessary. Some citizens may require industrial jobs while others may desire to work in commercial areas.

Cultural norms may dictate how compact the residential areas can be before citizens no longer want to put up with the density. Other countries may find that they have natural strengths in their citizen's ability to live near each other.

As discussed earlier, this is the strength of literal island countries. However, countries who have maintained dense urban areas, Japan, Korea, China, could very easily take advantage of that aspect. For other countries, this might be something to consider when designing IoT cities.

It is necessary to consider the consequences represented in Figure 6 and figure 7. The figure shows the necessary consequences of land impact. While we can safely ignore the agricultural side of the graph, as we focused on central cities and not large urban landscapes, we must recognize the impact of constructing a smart city IoT system on the environment.

Some European designs, which will be researched in full later on in this chapter, suggest designing a city around green methods of energy. However, in countries looking to upgrade current cities to IoT systems, they will likely not have the luxury or desire to develop green technologies that could provide power and functionality to a city. While maintaining the electric power for interconnected systems does not have a large environmental impact, the things surrounding it do.

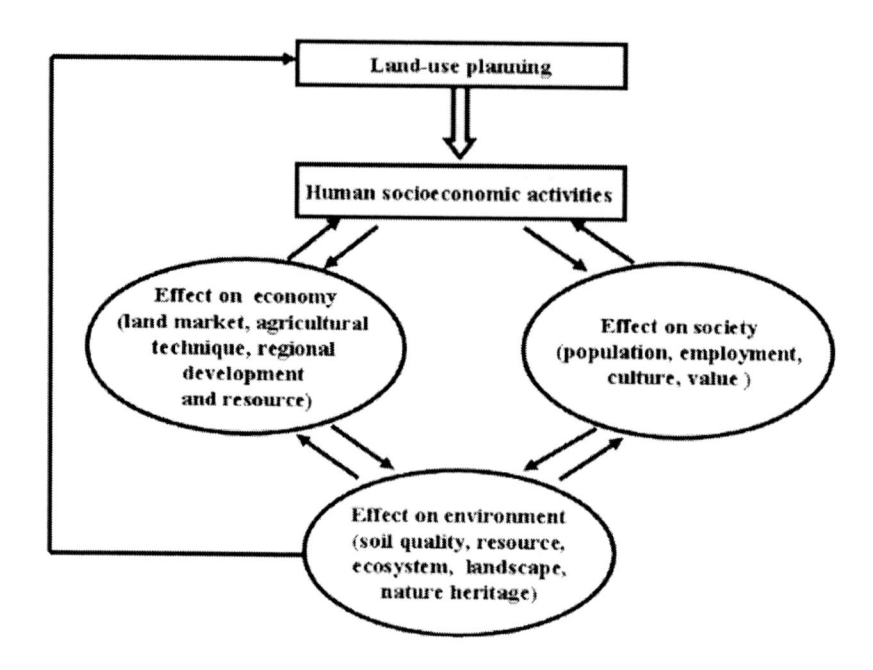

Figure 6. Environmental Impact Mechanism in Land-Use Planning [6].

Imagine the traffic in a city that has invited in thousands of new citizens. The waste output by the many individuals that will make up an interconnected city will need to go somewhere. The industrial need to keep up with those populations will produce waste, but proper land use planning can counter these things, but where cities already exist the money may not be there to change it.

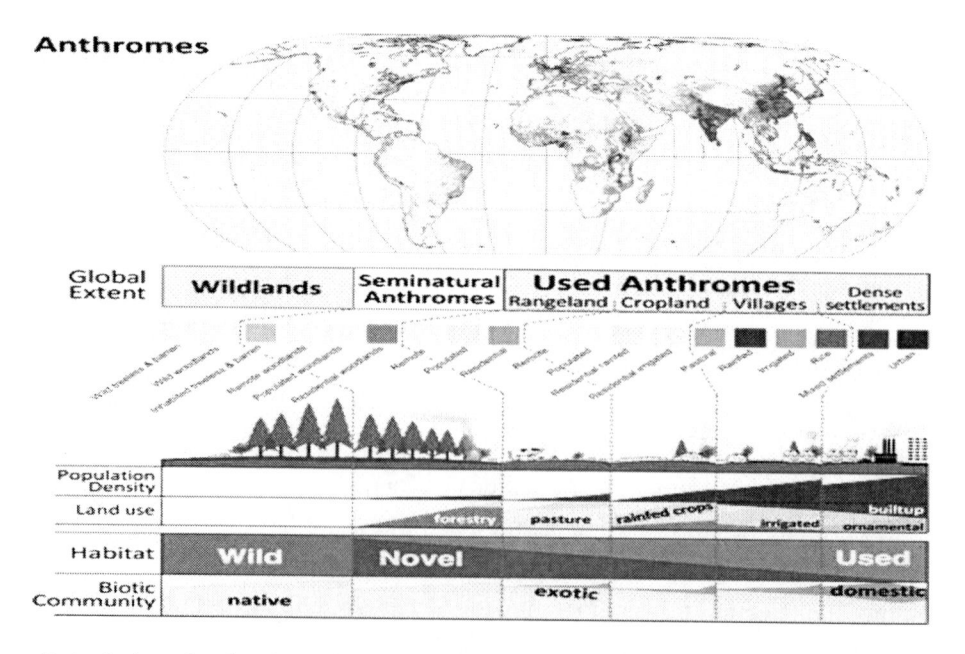

Figure 7. Agriculture Land and Population Density [2].

Figure 7 demonstrates both the agricultural makeup and population density of the world. It shows where humanity has inhabited the world the most and where areas are more or less unusable for human inhabitation. This graph may be a demonstration of where IoT cities are most viable to place for developed countries.

Unsurprisingly, those areas are already places where cities exist, and population densities are strongest. This socioeconomic growth also needs to think of one more thing regarding population density Reproduction. The increase of population centers has fueled the rise in human reproduction.

Consider the difference of estimated global populations before and after the industrial age [8].

The creation of the major urban areas drastically fueled the growth of humanity. Much of that growth started before even the inception of the internet. Even just by having people living nearby, in towns that could support them, the population of the world exploded.

Now consider the effects of a city that is interconnected. Where being linked socially to everyone around is the norm. Where the previous population growth relied on proximity and stability, this could provide an entirely new layer of contact. How IoT could affect future population growth is easy to guess. It would be well within the realm of speculation to see population surges in urban centers that people have gravitated to for their interconnectivity.

Also, the quality of life that an IoT system could impact on a population could easily carry a brand new community. This community, which would be born and developed in IoT cities, would, in turn, bolster the population further.

With the city being a comfortable and natural place to grow up and raise families, the factor would increase significantly in birth rates, something that modern cities converted into IoT smart cities. If a city is unable to bear the weight of a population growth that is sure to happen, then the city will fail to operate efficiently.

Those citizens, used to enjoy the benefits of an interconnected system, will likely go to find another one that is more suited to their needs. Whether they will be willing to cross the boundaries of countries is arguable. However, it is already very common people moving between cities to accommodate their needs within their own countries.

Hypothesize that integrating health care systems into a robust IoT city system will be critical in both ensuring sustained population growth and increasing the socio-economic value of a city. Healthcare is becoming a huge concern across the world for a verity of reasons. Even health care is expensive; it is becoming more important as population densities rise. People living in proximity communicate diseases more often. The spreading of diseases is something that cities deal with regularly and have been struggling with for the past century.

220   Abdulrahman Yarali

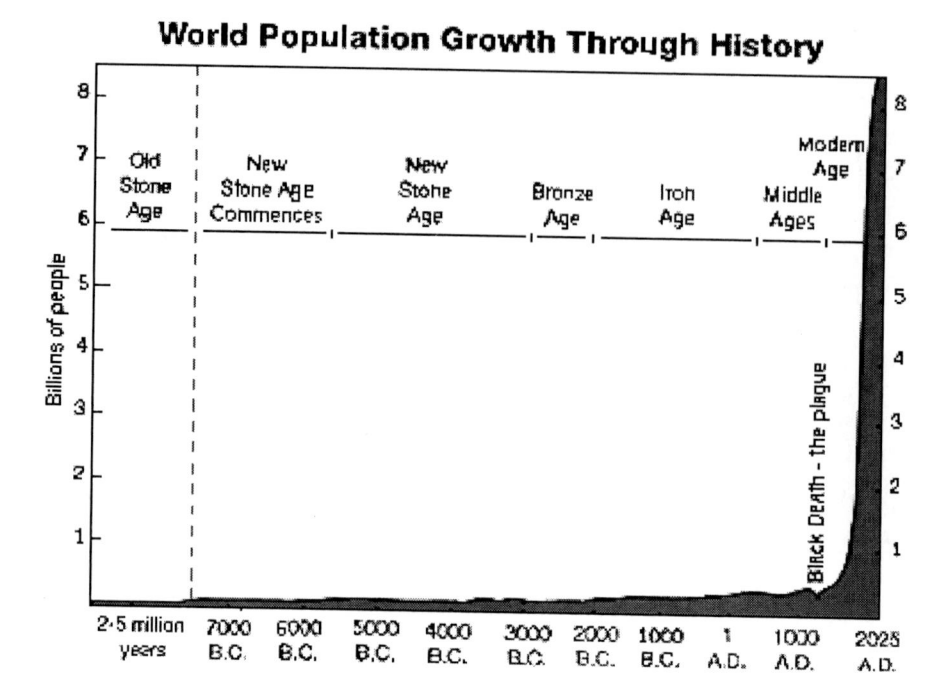

Figure 8. World Population Growth [8].

Figure 9. IoT Implementation in Healthcare Industry [9].

The healthcare market could take advantage of an interconnected populace to track disease vectors and common germs. Hospitals could be optimized to take in patients and treat them regularly. The image above [9] depicts a hospital operating at the forefront of optimization in this system. The potentials of a hospital using this design are almost up to one's imagination. A hospital could track common diseases occurring in one neighborhood and be ready to treat them or contact local government to look into the situation before an epidemic arises.

Healthcare closely monitored for citizens, and previous visits and issues could be tracked to see how to treat a patient best. The hospital could connect its inventory with other hospitals, or even manage the flow of patients in the case of an emergency.

There are many uses of the hospital in an IoT smart city. A well-operating hospital is going to be essential for when population growth starts to balloon in interconnected systems.

Figure 10 shows the potential for expansive new populations in urban areas. If IoT cities don't prove to be as explosive to population growth as predicted; they will still need to be able to counter the health issues that will come with the natural population growth of humanity. Caring for the sick, and counteracting diseases, will likely prove to be a significant draw for people to live in IoT cities. Healthcare that can be made available to many citizens is going to be a high draw and a foundation for building larger populations.

The healthcare systems that IoT cities may be able to provide will likely revolutionize the medical field. Possibly to the extent those hospitals themselves will have to redesign in similar ways to a smart city. Figure 11 shows a hospital which may be something similar to what a 'smart' hospital will become; a building structured around the intake and flow of patients through the building, rather than just being a storage place for the patients that will easily reach capacity. These hospitals will likely experience a flow of patients than the current one; connected systems must be designed to monitor the health of the populace, they may choose to visit the hospital for something considered relatively minor today.

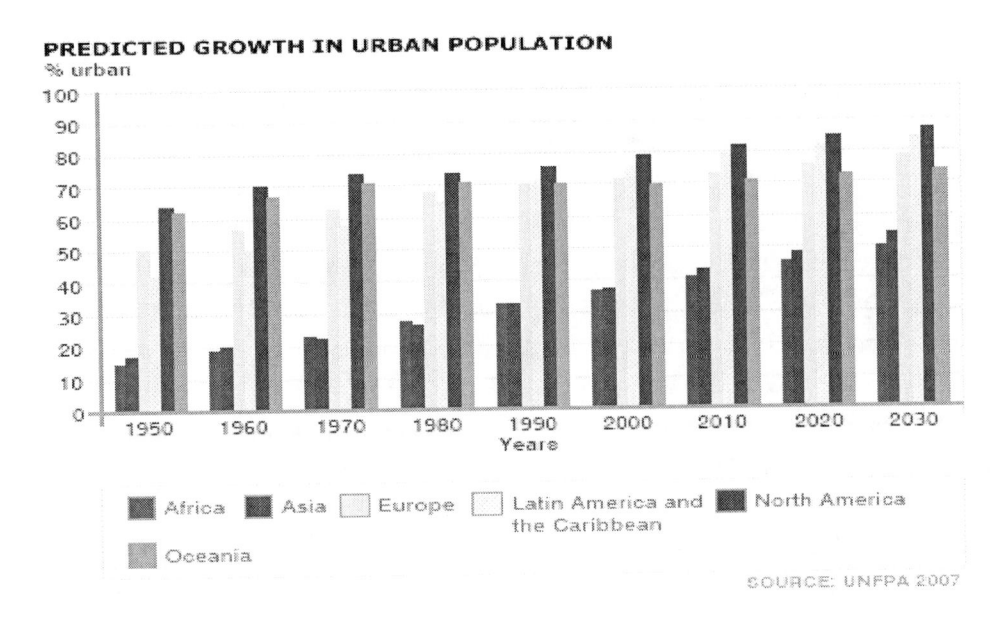

Figure 10. Predicted Growth in Urban Population [10].

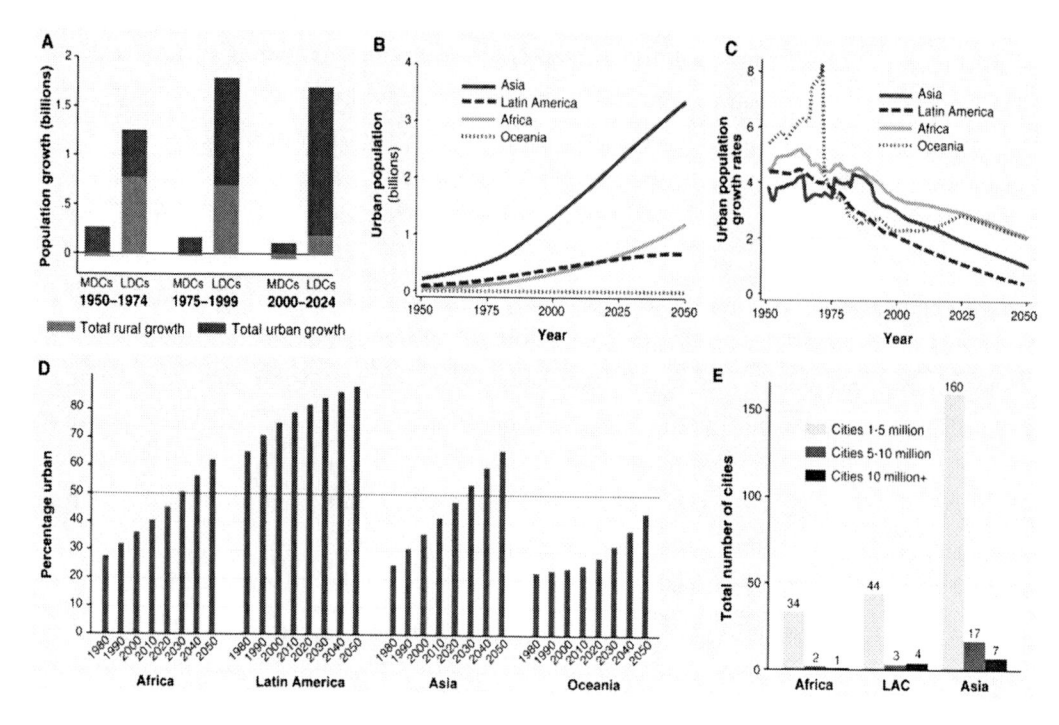

Figure 11. Urban Population Growth in Different Continents [11].

An efficient hospital may even be able to diagnose patients with not life threating issues away from the hospital. And those patients could go to pick up medication from pharmacies without taking up space in hospitals dedicated to more in need patients. To the credit of IoT's thinking, these systems already exist in small forms for doctors and pharmacies. However, they are there to help individuals who do not wish and have the ability to pay for the service.

A hospital operating on the grounds of serving an entire city would need to extend quick and around the clock access to services like these to every citizen within the connection of the city. Figure 12 shows some of how IoT has already positively affected healthcare [12].

Interconnectivity has already helped in monitoring disease, that element of the graph represents the largest section and possibly most important. It demonstrates that people can access medical help for issues efficiently and get accurate diagnoses.

The systems of service in an IoT centered city are going to be the aspects for which the city assessed outside of its economic capability. Population demands will put a few elements of city service in the highlight, and health care will prove to be the most important.

A city that breaks down due to an outbreak of disease will be very harmful to the model of IoT smart cities. It is something that cities converted into smart cities will likely encounter. Cities that developed into this are liable to develop stronger health care principals to combat those issues.

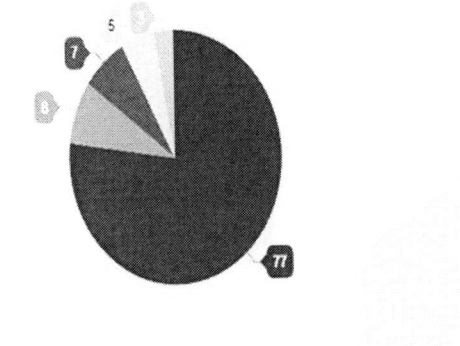

Figure 12. IoT usage in Various Aspects of Healthcare Sector [12].

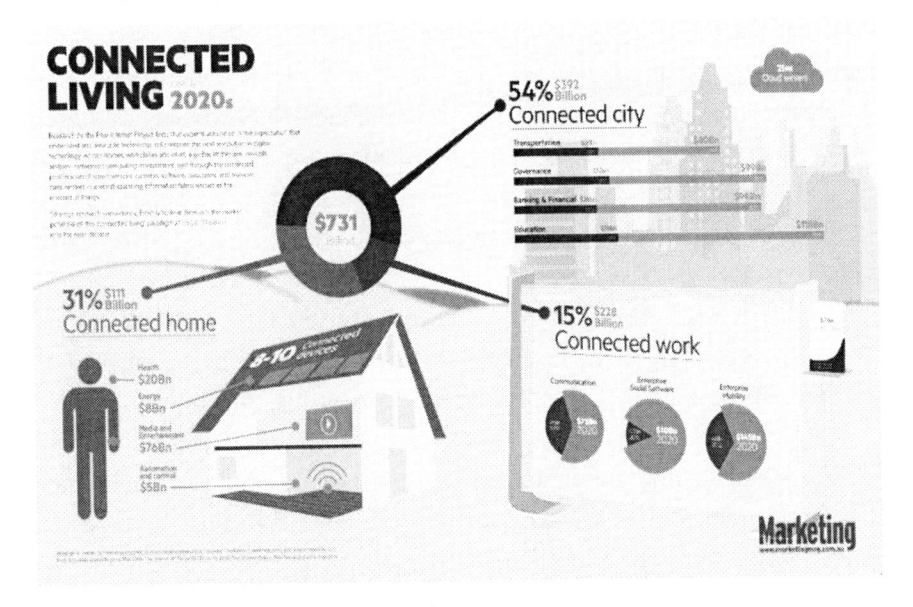

Figure 13. Estimated Investments in Various Sectors for IoT by 2020 [13].

Population growth will happen, and the degree to which interconnectivity will multiply it remains. However, it may be important for humanity as a whole for cities to maintain a stable standard of healthcare, even if those measures are independent of the city to city or country to country.

Interconnected cities are likely to, at some point, lead to tightly connected global communities. Even with such substantial gains in technology humanity cannot forget how vulnerable it can be to disease and the spread of viruses.

Healthcare is not the only aspect of an interconnected city that needs to be considered before moving forward. Interconnectivity also stands to improve the education systems of many countries that implement connected systems.

A new dedication to education will be essential to maintaining and developing an interconnected society. The standard by which people will need to educate will need to change and be elevated. However, the expansion of education is a natural aspect of increasing connectivity. The Internet once considered as a tool for researchers to share information and ideas.

Now think of how the internet is used to link students to classes. Colleges now maintain vast social networks and programs that allow students to be educated from their screen as well as in the classroom. The ability for students to produce research, connect with students globally, be exposed to new ideas, or even to turn in homework has expanded significantly.

Figure 14 shows, the money that education produces for an economy can be positively affected by how to connect the populace is to the modes of education. As the demands of technology rise, and will likely multiply under interconnected urban areas, people will need to educate under new principles and understandings. However, so too will the earning potential of citizens living in that population increase.

Understanding the technologies and being able to produce products and content in this environment efficiently will only serve to strengthen the economy. Where there is more money produced by businesses, more population to pay taxes, there is ever more money invested in schools? What may prove to be an interesting change is if technical schools explode in population to accommodate the need for specialized workers to maintain these systems.

Colleges already handle a lot of students who are pursuing technical fields. These students are, of course, able to function within the ever-changing technical field; even developing new and immersive new technologies to propel the future. Much like the businesses that popped up in the wake of the internet bubble earlier in this chapter, it would not be outside reality for education systems to be made to accommodate the maintenance needs of smart cities. The deciding factor may come when one country decides to take that step and start to outpace other countries. The college system in America and around the world may face revamping in the way they funded.

If IoT produces a huge need for technically proficient workers, then governments may decide that more money needs to go to educating students in that field. I suspect that the IoT systems and smart cities will produce children who are very interested in learning how the world around them works and provide a feedback loop of workers who want to live in these systems and can also maintain them. With more people able to keep up with technologies, those systems will be expanded and developed.

The IoT seems to be able to build upon itself only to the limits of human capacity. Therefore, this chapter listed health care above education, believe that the health of a population is the underlying principle that keeps a city running.

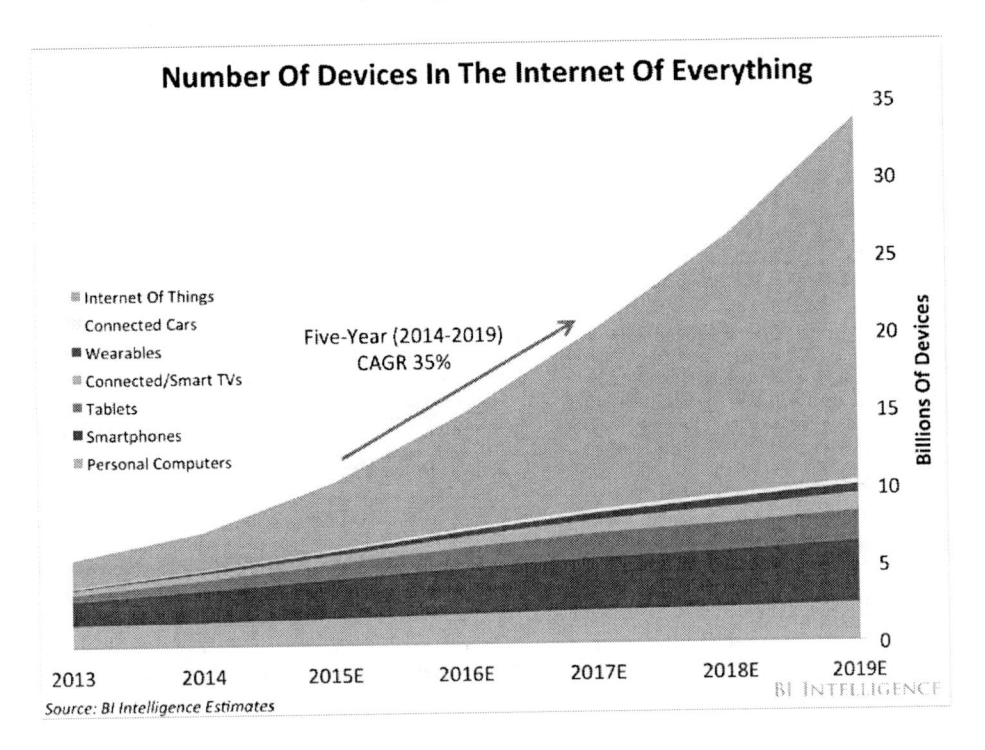

Figure 14. Increase of number of devices in IoT [14].

Technical colleges may also provide students from lower income areas to participate in the field of their choice. Just as technical colleges now allow students to take up a craft or aspect of engineering without having to go to a college, the realm of technical upbeat could become a 'trade.' Dealing with computer technologies could lose its stigma for being only very intelligent that it has today. With integrated cities normalizing the mass use of technology, people will find that there is nothing to fear with trying to learn more about the systems they use in their everyday lives.

To that extent, an individual would not surprise, if technology maintenance, coding or even hardware studies, made their way into the public school systems in America. Within a smart city, the importance of understanding technologies might prove to be very important to the people that decide curriculum. In this way, a city can also attract businesses into the city by demonstrating their commitment to developing more capable workers. That may cause a further gap between cities and rural areas, however. Consider that curriculum for a city is often decided by the state, and those guidelines might extend to children in the countryside.

While that education could prove to be an asset for those students, it may also alienate them as they have no reason to care about the city they do not live in, that comprised of integrated technologies. In this event, cities may have an independent curriculum that could be seen as favoritism for people in that city.

In this chapter, we discussed the divide that interconnectivity might create between individuals in a city and people in more rural areas regarding internet availability. Here we must examine how someone living outside the city could be underserved regarding education and healthcare, and see if that is morally acceptable.

People may live outside the city where they are at for many reasons. Family, jobs, or simple desire or love of the area does not mean that people can be disserved. People who work agriculture are vital to feeding people in cities and across the nation. In this way, smart cities must find a balance in how they dictate the future of states and governments.

Farms will likely not be immune to the furthering of technology, however. Equipment on the fields will probably start to integrate with mass communication devices that detect weather patterns or even evaluate crop growth.

Education, the children of farmers on the ways to maintain technology, could produce efficient and self-sustaining communities of farmers. Much like a smart city can build on its successes, agriculture has nothing to lose by integrating technology into the fields.

This shift in paradigm, like any other significant change in society, will likely come when newer generations are given a stronger understanding of technology. In this way, education could be specialized from local to local. It would also ensure that the advancements in education made in IoT centered cities could spread to areas outside of the city itself.

The state or country could only benefit from having a more educated workforce. Students would have a more diverse knowledge portfolio that would prove to be attractive to international businesses and would strengthen the economy of the local area and beyond. Of course, this would rely on how dedicated either companies or the government of any country is to expanding broadband internet to areas outside of cities, which is hypothetical and little optimistic. However, I think that a country focused on preserving its populace and maintaining a strong global presence will be likely to pursue that course of action.

This chart from Business Insider [13] shows the number of devices estimated to be a part of the IoT within the next few years. The interconnectivity talked about in the earlier parts of this chapter did not touch on the degrading of the privacy barrier between people and businesses.

We may be willing to turn over personal information to health care providers to ensure that we receive care, but how comfortable are we with our personal information spread as a commodity? Personal info is bound to be something of a product shortly. It is now, in the sense of advertising preference and shopping habits. This chapter will ignore the 'commercial viability' of identity fraud as discussing the black-market of information trade is not helpful. The security measures needed to protect people from identity theft in a more interconnected world will need to be more significant.

The real question that needs to determine is, how much a business or company should be able to trade personal information for money. An interconnected city will likely face this issue, and the opinions of what to do about it will come from the citizens within. In countries where citizens have very little autonomy in their government, they will likely face the threat of having personal information traded freely. In more democratic countries citizens may express concern with this prospect, while companies will likely try to capitalize on this market.

The generations going into a more integrated world do not appreciate this trade of information. It is seen as an invasion of privacy committed in the name of making a dollar. In an interconnected city, people may find surprising aspects of the individual information traded freely. It may be important to educate citizens on evaluating who they give their information to before they do.

The government may need to step in and create guidelines or organizations that exist solely to counteract the trade of individual's information. If a hospital were trading the details of their patients on the side to other companies to make money, this could easily be a gross invasion of privacy against people who relied on the hospital for care. If the trust in the hospital breaks down, people might be hesitant to visit that, and other hospitals lead to a breakdown in public health and safety. To that end, we must examine how much and city system can be allowed to know about its citizens.

Information given in confidence cannot be allowed to trade commercially, there must be an element of respect by city systems for the people they serve. Imagine if a police force sold the crime stats of individual people to a public market, and those statistics used to target people. Imagine if a hospital sold health records to pharma companies that then used that information to charge more for medicine particularly on a specific person.

IoT systems serve to generate a more connected world but do not seem to have any fundamental protections for the people living in them. It would be naive to assume that the system could only be used positively and to help the citizens living in the city. The potential for invading the privacy of citizens is there, and there will be individuals that will take advantage. Those people do not need to be a place of importance within city systems.

People in healthcare, law enforcement, government, are just a few of the examples. As the profitability of the IoT increases drastically over time, the potential for a massive market of information selling becomes more and more likely. The free sharing of information is bound to break down security measures that exist today. Unless radical new electronic security measures introduced, then the loss of personal information may become widespread. To that point, this need for the safety would expand the market that exists today to protect consumers.

While it is impossible to predict exactly how personal information may be cracked and stolen in a smart city environment, it is easily assumed that companies will be there to provide a security service to protect consumers. Additionally, businesses might find a point of promotion in securing customer records from cyber-attacks. In this new market, customers might be willing to pay a premium to protect their information.

228   *Abdulrahman Yarali*

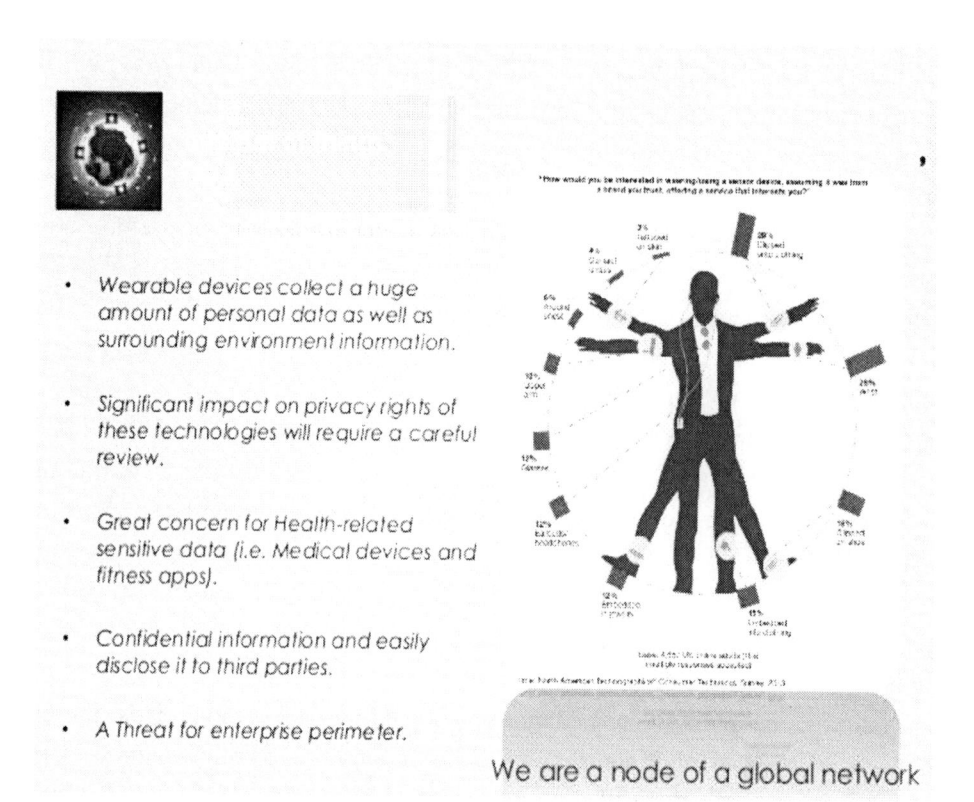

- Wearable devices collect a huge amount of personal data as well as surrounding environment information.

- Significant impact on privacy rights of these technologies will require a careful review.

- Great concern for Health-related sensitive data (i.e. Medical devices and fitness apps).

- Confidential information and easily disclose it to third parties.

- A Threat for enterprise perimeter.

We are a node of a global network

Figure 15. Risks due to Internet of Things [15].

Figure 15 demonstrates how even simple devices can collect personal information. Notice how these do not require being integrated into the systems of a smart city to gather data. This chapter previously mentioned how institutions could collect data and sell it as part of the IoT city. However, we must take a look at security risks that are independent of a hypothetical city and exist with us today. iPhones integrated with a health app, and the rise of bracelets that monitor the health of users are available to any consumer.

Companies who do not secure these devices put their customers at the risk of losing personal information. Looking back to a previous point in this chapter, the rise of junk products in a new market, the fact can be noted that malicious devices can be sold with the sole intent of collecting personal information. It would not take very long for these companies, if they are unmonitored, to collect a vast amount of information on users. Once this information reaches a marketplace, it might prove to be impossible to recover. Even if a business caught in the act, it would not require a lot of effort to send out the information.

The chart also points out that our use of these products makes us part of the IoT. The tradeoff seems logically sound. We agree to use devices that integrate themselves into global communication. However, the moral implications of making oneself part of this system could be problematic to some. The input of data requires a user willing to be comfortable with sharing some amount of data to potentially anyone. We may find ourselves ready to share a lot of things on social media, but we need to take a step back before sharing any information to a place where data sold to anyone globally.

Figure 16 represents the simple idea of a smart city in the IoT. Information is transferred freely across several aspects of city services to produce a more coherent environment. Interestingly, the flow of information seems to assist with the flow of traffic and automation of public transport.

If we can compare the delivery of data packets on the internet to the delivery of workers and commuters on the smart city's roads and railway, we can find a logical if not coincidental need for a smart city. The flow of people to and from workplaces, for example, is significant in maintaining the health of a city. While this chapter has focused on the strengths of individual aspects in a smart city, it has until now not reviewed the aspect of physical transportation in a smart city.

Transportation is a unique issue for every city, something that again could be a problem in addressing with cities that have the long-standing infrastructure for roads and trains. The grid systems on which cities are built were designed to be efficient movers of people and traffic, but they will prove to be a complication when trying to implement automated and smart city designs.

Tracking the flow of traffic down to the individual car will either require a new paradigm in vehicle manufacturers or for drivers to carry trackers on their vehicles, treated as an invasion of privacy. Additionally, the inclusion of city-wide security measures has already faced much criticism from citizens in certain cities. London has made massive steps in implementing city-wide security, led the citizens are becoming more concerned with how much their governments are observing them.

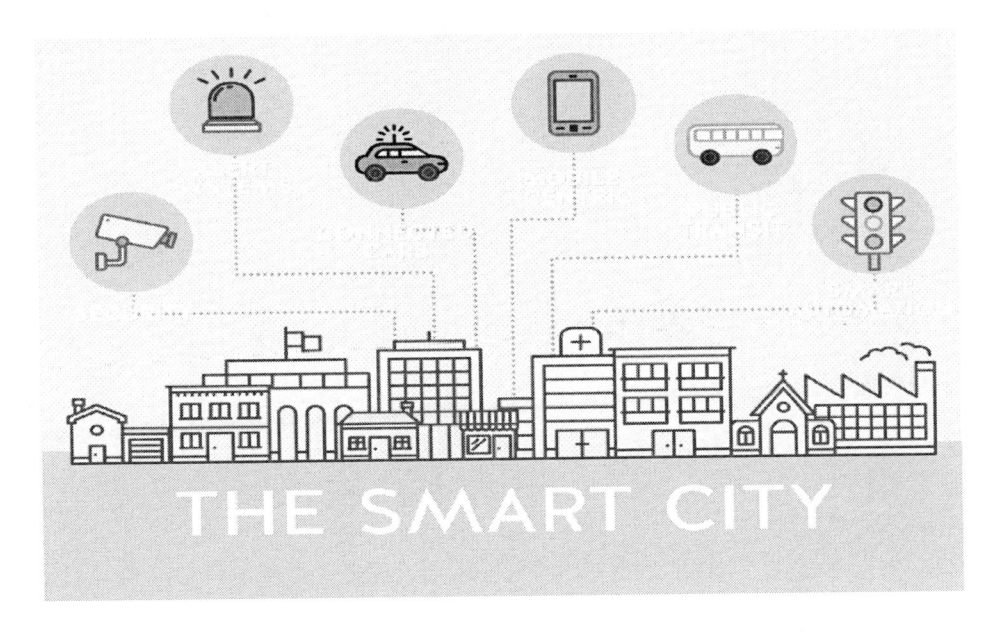

Figure 16. Smart City Model in IoT [16].

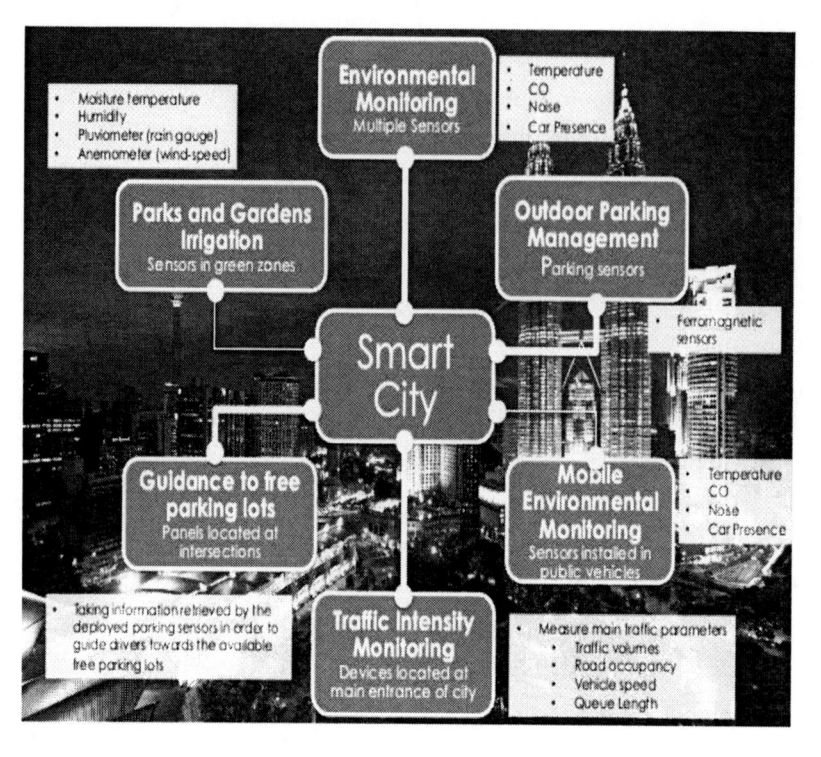

Figure 17. Features Comprised of Smart City [17].

Smart cities may find difficulties in convincing citizens to allow their cars to become part of the information flow. While cities already can map traffic to the minute, a lot more could happen if we could track the information from vehicles. The smart city would have to prove the worth of tracking cars over the need and desire for privacy to its civilians. Some bonuses to vehicle monitoring judged in the graphic below [17].

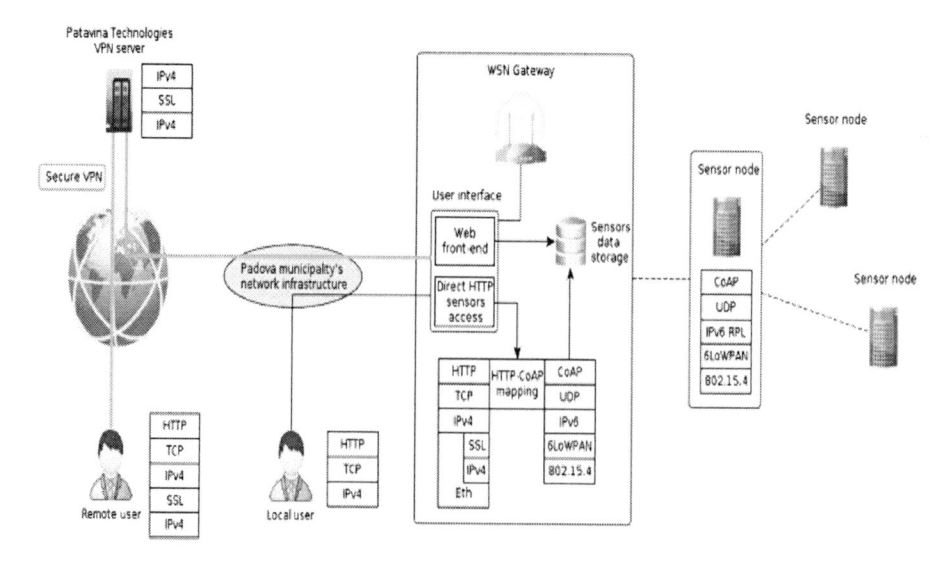

Figure 18. System Architecture of Padova Smart City [18].

While the potential of an IoT smart city can be up for debate, the existence of the mechanics that drive the city is very much a real thing. The ability to connect systems through sensor nodes and wireless gateways was proven by students in a hypothetical smart city design at the University of Padova, seen here [18].

The system used to demonstrate to figure out traffic congestion through chemicals in the air and weather patterns through humidity. The principals of building a smart city from the ground up a little more convoluted. However, smart European Cities identifies six key fields of development, which will be discussed and analyzed here [18];

Smart Economy

The principles of making a healthy and functioning city have already been discussed in detail previously in this chapter. However, in the smart cities guide there are points for city image that haven't addressed so far. For a smart city looking to lead the way in technological advancement, the image may prove to be everything. The first cities will have to cultivate a healthy civic image to attract business and people. For older cities looking to upgrade, this fresh new look may prove to be vitalizing for tourism and self-promotion.

Smart Mobility

As discussed above, smart cities are poised to excel in the realm of mobilizing workers and traffic. The implementation of that technology may prove to be the most challenging aspect. Convincing drivers to turn over their location while on the road constantly may be a hard pill for them to swallow.

Smart Environment

This step involves a smart city leaving a tiny or zero carbon footprint on the surrounding area. This is a task that is likely to prove impossible for metropolises today. While steps have been taken to reduce carbon emissions, stamping them out is undoable for many cities. To this degree, smart cities need to have this in mind from their very beginnings. Cities could use interconnectivity to create less impact on the environment.

Smart People

Aside from the aspect of education we discussed earlier, smart people include cultivating a diverse and open-minded populace. This something that interconnectivity could surely help. Citizens who share a bonded communal spirit are more likely to be open to the concept of accepting differing religions or races.

Smart Living

Smart living scores the highest on the smart cities guide and corresponds to some of the longest areas of research within this paper. Elements including health, education, the standard of living, and communal pride are all in Smart Living. These things are essential to the foundation of a smart city and can all be improved by the Internet of Things. When these needs are satisfied any city can go a long way towards becoming a smart city on its right.

Smart Government

The government has been touched on lightly in this chapter. Smart cities list that a government should be aware of the issues present in a smart city, be efficient and transparent, and promote public services.

The integration between city functions and the Internet of Things is a paradigm shift that is bound to happen. This paper presents a lot of positives in examining how a city, and the lives of the individual, could be improved by integration. The Internet of Things (IoT) represents the natural progression of humanity and its relationship with technology.

As users demand more and more friendly content and availability, they must also expect to give up individual security for those goals. Civic structures and governments are now focusing on the potential for integrating running a city and keeping an eye on its populace. The desire for more mobile and stronger technologies will continue to drive the market forward into the era of IoT. When businesses start to gain traction from the immense earning potential of the IoT, consumers need to expect to integration start to appear in all of the workings of life.

It is the time to evaluate how much we as a society want to integrate ourselves into our communications or sacrifice the part of our identity required to exist on the edge of communication technology.

While the integration of technologies is invincible, and its implementation is still within the control of the engaged users, there needs to be a healthy balance between achieving sufficient data flow and giving out personal information.

Internet of Things (IoT) describes a reality that is already a part of the connection between us and our devices and the web of information. Our ideas may have to change when walking into a more integrated future, and even the ideas that the generations after us may decide the course humanity takes in regards to how embraced the IoT becomes.

This chapter also points out to be mindful of the people who may not be able to participate in the integrated societies and cities shortly. Making technology accessible to everyone needs to be the primary goal for IoT minded individuals quickly.

There is so much to be gained and learned from this new frontier. There is also no escaping it if you live in the developed world. How companies and governments use this new level of integration may fall to the respects of the civilians under their care. IoT is ripe to be abused for profit, but it can also prove to be an important step in developing human society.

REFERENCES

[1] *Federal Communications Commission GIS Program.* (2016, June). Retrieved from https://www.fcc.gov/maps/fixed-broadband-deployment-data/#lat=38.82&lon=-94.96&zoom=4.

[2] OECD (2007). *Average advertised broadband download speed, by country.* Retrieved from http://www.websiteoptimization.com/bw/0711/oecd-broadband-speed-country.png.

[3] Jackson, M. (2014, May 6). *ITU Ranks UK 7th Globally for Fixed Broadband Subscriptions by Speed.* Retrieved from http://www.ispreview.co.uk/index.php/2014/05/itu-ranks-UK-7th-globally-fixed-line-broadband-speeds.html.

[4] Malta Independent (2006, January 10). *Malta Top of the world in internet penetration and growth rates.* Retrieved from http://www.independent.com.mt/articles/2006-01-10/local-news/Malta-Top-of-the-world-in-internet-penetration-and-growth-rates-85790.

[5] Jaruzelski, B., Schwartz, K., & Staack, V. (2015, November). *Innovations New World Order.* Retrieved from https://www.strategy-business.com/feature/00370?gko=e606a.

[6] Lai et al, (2003). *Environmental Impact Mechanism in land-use planning.* Retrieved from https://mastereia.files.wordpress.com/2015/02/lai-et-al.png.

[7] Quinn, J. E., Johnson, R. J., & Brandle, J. R. (2014). Identifying opportunities for conservation embedded in cropland anthromes. *Landscape Ecology*, 29(10), 1811-1819. doi:10.1007/s10980-014-0098-8.

[8] *Support U.S. Population Stabilization.* Retrieved from http://www.susps.org/images/worldpopgr.gif.

[9] StampedeCon Follow. (2016, August 09). *Using The Internet of Things for Population Health Management.* Retrieved from https://www.slideshare.net/StampedeCon/using-the-internet-of-things-for-population-health-management-stampedecon-2016.

[10] BBC (2017). *Predicted Growth in Urban Population.* Retrieved from http://newsimg.bbc.co.uk/media/images/42430000/gif/_42430816_population416x306.gif.

[11] Montgomery, M. R. (2008, February 08). *The Urban Transformation of the Developing World.* Retrieved from http://science.sciencemag.org/content/319/5864/761.full.

[12] Klubnikin, A. (2016, October 04). *3 Ways Internet of Things Impacts Healthcare - R-Style Labs.* Retrieved from http://r-stylelab.com/company/blog/iot/3-ways-internet-of-things-impacts-healthcare.

[13] Roper, P. (2015, March 27). *Connected Living 2020: the market potential of the internet of things.* Retrieved from https://www.marketingmag.com.au/hubs-c/internet-of-things-market-potential-infographic/.

[14] Greenough, J. (2015, April 08). *The Internet of Everything:* 2015 [SLIDE DECK]. Retrieved September 06, 2017, from http://www.businessinsider.com/internet-of-everything-2015-bi-2014-12.

[15] Paganini, P. (2014, December 13). *Internet of Things-Privacy and Security Issues.* pp. 9. Retrieved from https://www.slideshare.net/paganinip/io-t-42674396.

[16] *12 Awesome Features Smart Cities India Will Have.* Retrieved from http://www.15august.in/2015/06/features-smart-cities-india.html

[17] Abbas, M., Dr. (2015, August 26). *Internet of Things - Connecting and Aggregating the Innovative Minds.* pp. 52. Retrieved from https://www.slideshare.net/mazlan1/internet-of-things-connecting-and-aggregating-the-innovative-minds.

[18] Zanella, A., Bui, N., Castellani, A., Vangelista, L., & Zorzi, M. (2014). Internet of things for smart cities. *IEEE Internet of Things Journal*, 1(1), 22-32. Retrieved from http://ieeexplore.ieee.org/document/6740844/.

Chapter 14

INTEGRATION OF IoT AND AI

INTRODUCTION

A multi-billion dollar enterprise, the Internet of Things (IoT) is creating new opportunities, both in business and in enhancing the lives of the general population. Artificial Intelligence (AI) is a technology still under development, but with the potential of growing exponentially and changing the face of business as well the employment sector. The integration of IoT with AI will lead to the development of a smart ecosystem. However, the proposed architecture for this integration is still flawed, and therefore, is hampering the future development of AI. This paper seeks to examine the interaction between the IoT and AI to propose an architectural model for the amalgamation of the same, which will result in the optimum development of AI and create enhanced technological and business opportunities.

New opportunities are continually being created, both in the field of business and in the enhancement of the lives of the general population, by the Internet of Things (IoT) which is now evolving into a multi-billion dollar enterprise. Businesses around the globe are efficiently generating new avenues by manufacturing new products and providing abundant customer-centered services using the Internet of Things (IoT). However, to realize their optimum potential and reach their zenith, in addition to the IoT, companies need to implement the current technologies founded by, and based on, Artificial Intelligence (AI). The implementation of the swiftly developing AI technology by the companies will eliminate human error and the need for human direction; the machines will be made intelligent, consequently empowering them to make learned decisions and function independently. Even today, the amalgamation of IoT and AI is required to be successful and earn profits in the digital ecosystem, explicating why businesses are developing expeditious techniques in this ongoing progression in technology.

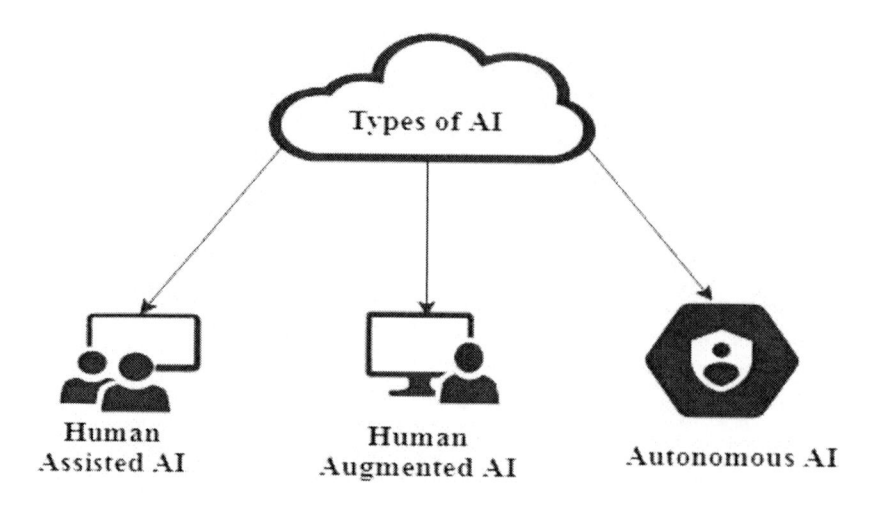

Figure 1. Different types of Artificial Intelligence (AI).

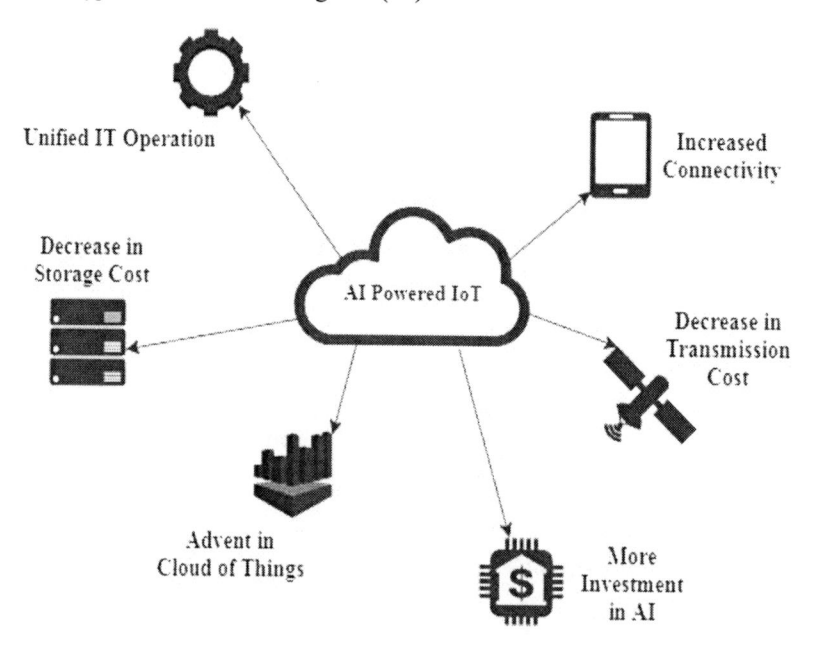

Figure 2. AI features benefitting IoT.

The profits to be reaped in future by the businesses highlighted by the fact that despite lacking an accurate course of development, AI is still taking precedence and is largely being implemented. The most crucial function of AI is inducing a smart operating system in machines to empower them with intelligence. IoT is necessitated in AI to create an intelligent network by linking every single machine or device involved in the system of smart operation. In the primitive stages of AI, human assistance was essential because AI wasn't equipped to perform a higher level of activity and combat all scenarios with uniform efficiency. Since then, however, AI has evolved to be actively empowered and engaged with intelligence, to function as intelligently, as or even better than a human, in actual-time. The rapid equipping of machines and devices with AI will offset an entire generation of intelligent machines.

From performing rudimentary and recurring exercises in its initial stages, the current AI applications for various devices and machines have progressed to functioning in diverse and constantly altering situations, thereby enabling effective and efficient execution of circuitous applications.

The current advancement in AI categorized into three different stages: Human Assisted Artificial Intelligence, Human Augmented Artificial Intelligence, and Autonomous Artificial Intelligence. A variety of factors like the optimum development of intrinsic and fundamental technological aspects, balancing of the nuances in the technology-finance relations- have affected this advancement in AI (Raman Chitkara, 2017).

Smart and significant opportunities will be created in diverse fields by the continuous evolution and advancement of AI and its increasing application to machines and devices. In the first stage, rudimentary comprehensive and physical operations shall undergo automation for the provision of Human Assisted Artificial Intelligence. In the second stage, AI will supply Human Augmented decisions in composite scenarios that necessitate the accuracy of human judgment. The final stage, the machines, and devices empowered with their intelligence by being taught and educated will enable to make intelligent decisions, and educated actions, independently.

The current development in Artificial Intelligence (AI) is resulting in an amalgamation of AI with IoT, and the combination is so potent and powerful, that AI is becoming necessitated for IoT. Intelligence or smartness will be made a prerequisite in every machine and device by the three crucial elements of IoT- sensory data, connectivity and automated mechanics (automatons). Consequently, AI will become essential for IoT. With the continuance of this amalgamation, various factors like the diminishing costs of device and cloud components, the burgeoning of machines and devices, etc. will affect the future developments in IoT. The emergence and increasing use of cloud, however, will be the most prominent factor affecting this development.

The continual development of IoT and AI has resulted in the growth of linked devices to form a dense network with the internet. A number of connected devices will rise from 13 million in 2017 to 90 million in 2030, promoting an immense data size of 195 zettabytes annually, from 5.5 zettabytes in 2014 to 55 zettabytes in 2020. Consequently, businesses around the globe will face some trials from this torrent of data, including, but not limited to:

- Stabilizing the imbalance between the isolation of data for retaining the user's privacy and data customization
- Ascertaining a way to generate significant knowledge from the data and analyze and organize it

- Maintaining the equilibrium in data circulation
- Sustaining the momentum and precision of data inspection
- Preserving the security despite the increasing amount of digital, and virtual, attacks and other perils

With various businesses increasingly incorporating Internet of Things (IoT), Artificial Intelligence (AI) is being necessitated by default, to combat the future policy-making, strategizing to sieve through the data, and retaining only the data that can be further utilized. The panacea of IoT will be influenced by AI in two ways so that predictive sequences can be gradually derived from the data, and real-time reactions and feedbacks will be permitted. By performing these actions, AI will equip applications functioning on IoT to analyze, predict, prescribe, and adapt data. Alternatively, due to its ability to provide real-time feedback, IoT will also be made necessary for AI, permitting AI to learn, evolve and resolve systematic errors, if any. The IoT-AI amalgamation will enable intelligent application of sensors, resulting in data prediction, prescription, and adaption discussed in more detail shown below.

- *Data Prediction:* Scrutinizing and analysis of data will occur on an actual time-scale, avoiding any possible setbacks or failures by enterprising intercession; for example, Flight data collection.
- *Data Prescription:* Instant reactions and the problem-solving mechanism will be enabled by intelligent sensors, consequently preventing any possible fiascos. For example, the technology used in automobiles to keep them in the center of the lane.
- *Data Adaption:* The sensors will enable the system to assimilate knowledge including, but not limited to, precise reactions and feedbacks, situational differences, etc., thereby equipping the system to make independent decisions. For example, devices used for constant monitoring of insulin levels in the blood, self-driving automobiles, etc.

It is estimated that AI will generate a multitude of new markets and ventures which will gradually grow exponentially as AI develops from Human Assisted Artificial Intelligence to Human Augmented Artificial Intelligence and to Autonomous Artificial Intelligence (Jonathan Holdowsky, 2015). As the incorporation of AI in IoT, and consequently businesses, increases, a few important changes will occur in the domain of business:

- *Elevated Profit and Income:* The direct profits of the IoT-AI combination reaped by the manufacturers of devices and machines, the suppliers of internet-based information and data, and the agencies that offer applications and programs run by intelligent sensors to the customers (Raman Chitkara, 2017).

- *Increased Security:* Any possible setbacks and fiascos will be averted by the observation and comprehension of data in real-time. Moreover, AI will be equipped with the knowledge to differentiate between various species and even automatons, thereby enhancing the security of the people as well as programs.
- *Diminished Expenditure:* The amount of money spent by customers on home appliances, gadgets, and other devices will be reduced by the intelligent analyzing of data by a smart network. Additionally, intelligent management of the obtained data will diminish possible threats to the customers, as well as the damage to the material goods and property.
- *Elevated Consumer Catering:* Equipped with AI, the intelligent sensors will be able to customize themselves according to the needs and wants of the customers, adding a heightened sense of comfort and luxury to their lives.

LITERATURE REVIEW

The technology used for incorporating intelligent devices and machines into IoT must be amenable to the provision of the adequate framework, by the continual necessity for global communication, and the multifariousness of machines and devices. Though the infrastructural organization of IoT cannot be specified, the following factors determine the requisite architecture: any moment, any location, and any device.

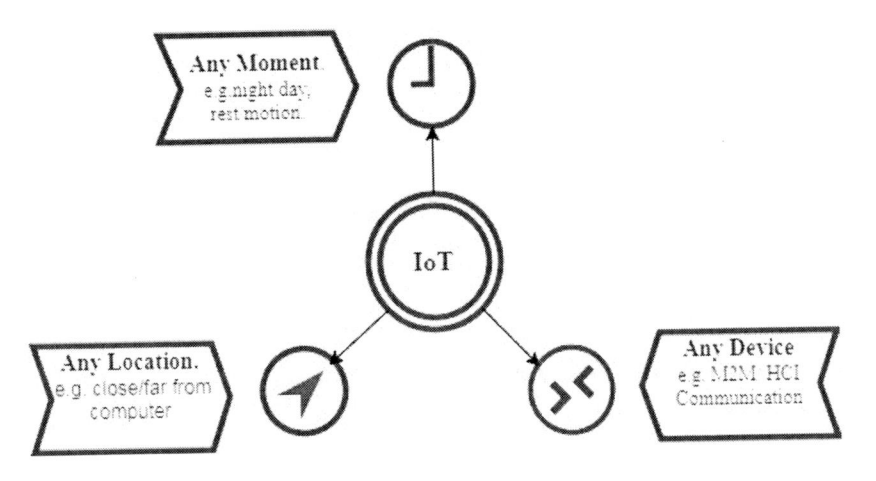

Figure 3. Three main factors for IoT Communication.

Considering these three determining factors simplifies the creation of an appropriate model for IoT; additional features, such as customization, can be added later according to these three factors. The incorporation of IoT-based systems necessitates a pervasive perusal of the structural organization, with the highest level presenting customized applications to the users, and the lowest level engaging in data collection from the sensors.

THE THREE LAYER INFRASTRUCTURE

The three-layer infrastructure is the most basic infrastructure of the Internet of Things (IoT) and can be implemented even in the most unsophisticated systems. The following are the layers of the three layer architecture:

1. *The Sensory Layer:* The first and the lowest layer- consist of a variety of sensors and is responsible for the collection of the information from the actual environment and integrating it into the virtual environment.
2. *The Network Layer:* The second layer of the architecture functions almost like the network formed by the neurons in the brain, and involves the processing of the information obtained by the Sensory Layer, and transmitting that processed information to the next layer of this infrastructure.

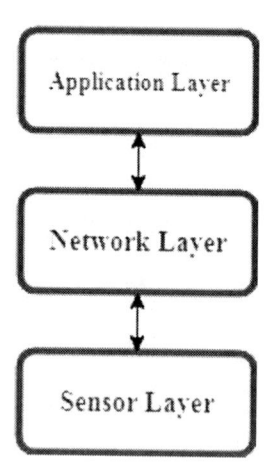

Figure 4. Three Layer IoT Model.

3. The Application Layer: The final layer is the most comprehensive and substantial layer of this infrastructure, and is responsible for delivering the various applications and other services to the customers. Its core function is the provision of a rostrum for smooth and uninterrupted collection and examination of

information, at this moment establishing a secure correspondence between the network, the services provided and the customers (Miao Wu, 2010).

THE FIVE LAYER INFRASTRUCTURE

This infrastructure consists of five layers which enhance the three-layer infrastructure. The following are the layers of the five-layer infrastructure:

1. *The Sensor Layer:* The first layer of this infrastructure is composed of infinite sensors whose primary function is to sense and identify the physical characteristics such as mass, temperature, position, of different entities in the surrounding environment, and digitizing the information obtained for the transfer of data through the sensory network. The sensory layer is composed of location trackers, two-dimensional scanners and identifiers, cameras, a sensor network and the RFID software.
2. *The Transport Layer:* The second layer of this infrastructure, also called the Network Layer, uses different networks, such as Cable or wireless networks or even the LAN (Local Area Network) to forward the data obtained from the Sensor Layer to the processing hub. The main technologies implemented in this layer are the 3G, ZigBee, FTTX, UMB, infrared, WiFi, etc. For quick and efficient transportation, various protocols incorporated in this layer, such as the Internet Protocol (IP) crucial for handling and managing infinite things.
3. *The Processing Layer:* The main function of the third layer- the processing layer- is to receive the information from the transportation layer, and process, scrutinize and store it. This layer is derived from, and yet distinct from other layers because scrutinizing and storing a large amount of data is a complicated and difficult process. The technologies of smart processing, cloud as well as universally pervasive computing and database are crucial to this layer.
4. *The Application Layer:* The next layer of this architecture is primarily responsible for creating various industry-specific IoT applications for the execution of the information processed by the processing layer like smart networking and transportation, enhancing security and privacy, validating identities, smart services based on the position of the device or the object, etc. This layer is essential because the continual development and implementation of applications that occur in this layer are essential for the optimum evolution and development of AI-IoT.
5. *Business Layer:* Business layer is the final and the highest layer of this architecture. It is not only responsible for the security, privacy, management, control of applications and businesses, but also for researching the scope of every

single business model and the profits to be earned from it. Because the optimum development of any technology, full utilization of potential, and success in the market, is determined by its business model. Therefore, continual research and evolution are necessary for the integration of AI-IoT technology (Miao Wu, 2010).

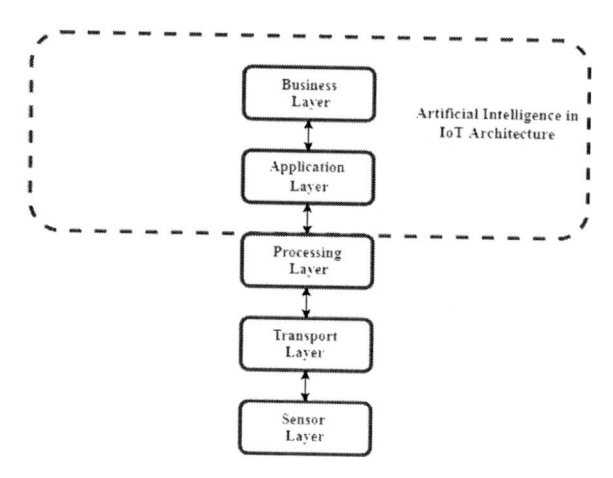

Figure 5. Artificial Intelligence (AI) in IoT Architecture.

Due to being a single entity of intelligent devices, and also due to the diversity it provides in information collection and processing, IoT's current development has made it an essential element of various technologies. Depending on the data transmission within the system, three essential constituents of IoT can be categorized: data apprehension, data summation, and data examination and processing. The data is apprehended from the surrounding environment by the sensors and is examined by the device itself, before being sent to the IoT network, thereby establishing a primary interaction within the system. The data summation occurs within the IoT after the apprehended data is transmitted. This data is examined and processed once more, before being transmitted to the getaway and being delivered to various information hubs by the Internet. Following this, a detailed data analysis and examination (sometimes conducted in purpose-built servers) take place, and later, the data presented to the customers with proper applications. The data is then re-sent to the source device for the generation of an appropriate response. The customers or the device users can manipulate the devices connected to the IoT by the nature of the functions or actions they perform on the devices.

Though IoT is being designed and modified to cater to the customers and make their lives easier, the myriad systems of IoT are so vast and compound that they are bound to confront many problems. The multifariousness of the systems itself is an important problem, since the numerous devices are, in addition to being interconnected to each other, also connected to the internet. Hence, the consequent data collection and transmission, and its processing become an immense and compound process with many possible flaws and increased chances of system failures. However, since this continual procedure is necessary for the acquisition of new information, the system infrastructure needs to be sound, with well-defined protocols.

Another challenge is presented by the location, configuration, and management of the acquired data. Because finding the source of the data is easy, but maintaining the confidentiality of the data and protecting the users' privacy is a complicated process because the users don't always comprehend the multitudinous, interconnected, self-identifying systems, thereby making themselves susceptible to frauds. As data collection and transmission are a crucial part of IoT, it is necessary to ensure the privacy of the data, as well as the device users, to prevent data exploitation.

The complexity of the IoT is such that it is built, not only on the foundation of rudimentary sensors that transmit data calculated through statistical records and mathematics, but also a more advanced technology integrated into a system itself, such as Artificial Intelligence (AI). AI enables the system to make quick decisions finding and considering a solution to individual problems or daily activities, rather than just providing generalized results derived from mathematical equations. The incorporation of AI into IoT is also to ensure the autonomy of devices and machines which enables them to function on an actual-time frequency. Though complete autonomy of the machines and devices has not yet been achieved and it is also currently unadvisable, it is necessary to ensure the functioning of the devices without human supervision or interference, to maximize their usage potential and output. The implementation of Artificial Intelligence (AI) ensures the customer-device interaction is convenient and that the device is capable of following orders, and evaluating them correctly to cater to the customers' needs.

The key challenge in incorporating Artificial Intelligence (AI) in the IoT operation is its placement in the system infrastructure, since the amount of received data needs adequate space in the system to be processed and stored, and accommodating of the knowledge unit of the entire system is not possible in any of the three, or five, layers described earlier. The most plausible place for the incorporation of AI into IoT is in the servers, due to their evaluation capacity. Additionally, incorporating AI into the servers maximizes the output potential because it amalgamates the functioning of the servers with the data stored and analyzed, which enables effective learning within the system itself.

Figure 6 describes a standard speculation for the amalgamated infrastructure of AI-IoT. The three important constituents of the system hierarchy are:

1. *Precursory Interaction:* This includes acquiring data from the actual environment to deliver to the other organizations within IoT. The data is acquired by the IoT-based devices and is pre-processed to ensure transparency in the entire system. The data is then either distributed between the various devices connected to the system or imparted to the chief IoT system via the internet for the acquisition of

more information. Once the data is securely within the system and it is being processed with specific reference, it is assembled to undergo AI processing, a procedure which might necessitate the selection of adequate data to process the system's command and provide the correct solution.

2. *Referential Communication:* This includes active decision making in real-time, based on the processed and selected information. Definitive solutions are provided by the system to IoT devices and machines that enables to take further action. Therefore, IoT devices and machines should be connected to the knowledge unit in the IoT system infrastructure, to comprehend the decision provided by AI correctly to implement it. This aspect of the system can be labeled as autonomous intelligent decision making. The data that has undergone correct processing and evaluation transmitted further to the relevant devices for the generation of an appropriate response. In situations, where the destination of the processed data is different from the source, AI employs device identification to ensure correct and efficient delivery of the data, and to execute the right action as per the command. Furthermore, by device identification, AI is also able to identify the various threats to the devices and the systems, and consequently, deploy countermeasures to eliminate the threat.

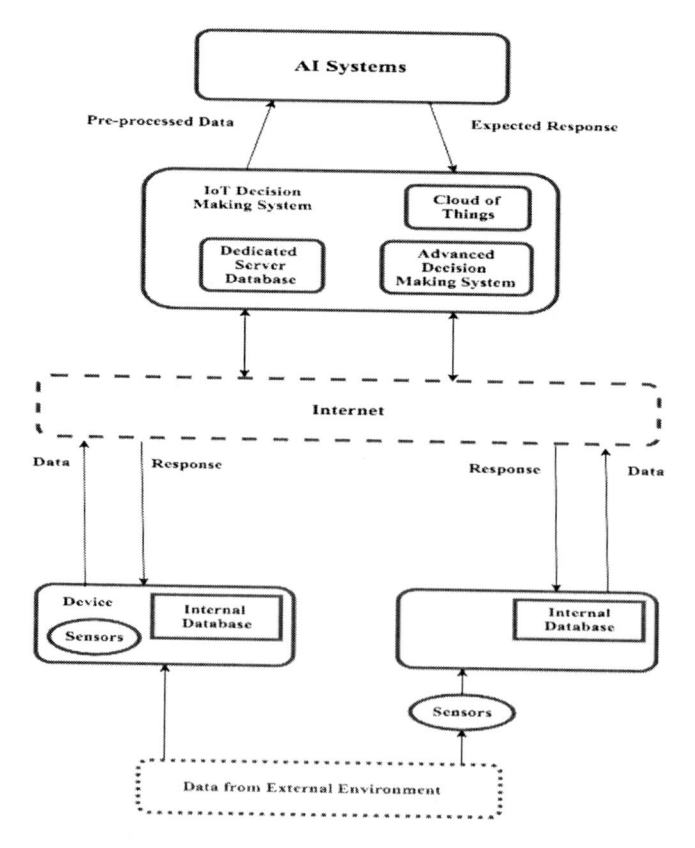

Figure 6. AI-IoT Decision Making System.

3. *Intramural interaction:* This involves a supplementary path for intelligent interaction between smart devices and machines. The intramural interaction can occur in precursory interaction itself, to enhance the data collection and transmission to the higher layers of the system, as well as later, in referential interaction, to facilitate the simultaneous functioning of a multitude of devices that have been provided with definitive solutions by the system. The amalgamation of AI and intramural interaction can intensify the autonomy of the devices by making them more intelligent.

THE CURRENT STATUS OF AI DEVELOPMENT

The previous, as well as current developments in the field of Artificial Intelligence (AI), have led AI being used diversely in a variety of applications and avenues, almost all of which simultaneously enhance both the scope of AI as well as the efficiency and the impact of its applications. Currently, AI is being developed into Narrow AI and General AI, while the various applications of AI range from Machine Learning, Deep Learning, Automation, and Autonomy, to Human-Machine Teaming.

Narrow Artificial Intelligence

The current development in Artificial Intelligence (AI) has progressed enough to allow for Narrow AI, which is artificial intelligence at its most primary level, and therefore, it is limited in its scope. Circuitous tasks, cognitive as well as physical in nature, are performed by Narrow AI, such as processing and translating languages, identification of images, detection of face and voice, predicting the weather, etc. Though also termed Weak Artificial Intelligence due to its elementary functioning, it is effective enough already to eliminate the need for human effort and intervention in certain tasks like planning travel, diagnosing medical disorders and diseases, education and research with its smart classrooms, etc., therefore contributing to the benefit and advancement of the society.

General Artificial Intelligence

General Artificial Intelligence also termed as Assisted or Human Artificial Intelligence (AI) due to its capability of functioning as well as a human, with the added benefit of rapid processing and analyzing of data and offering solutions. Though it is yet to be completely developed, the proposed model of General AI will equip machines and devices with the full potential of human cognitive processes, enabling the machines to exhibit intelligence equal to that of humans. In such scenario, computers or other devices, and not humans, will be able to generate original ideas and implementing these inventions in reality. Consequently, resulting in the optimum development of AI- Super Artificial Intelligence- in which machines will be more intelligent than humans in every possible area and even control every single system- technical, educational, etc. - that is essential to humans.

Machine Learning

Machine Learning (ML) is a systematic procedure that involves teaching the machines to learn from the acquired and accumulated data, it is used as an application and approach where machine learning achieved by expert technicians integrating the data into the software of the machine or the device. The Embedded data has a definite aim and parameters and is divided into instructional data and assessment data. The instructional section of the data alters the parameters to optimize the aim, while the assessment section implements the data to scenarios and tries different methods for effectiveness. It also generates parameters to utilize the obtained knowledge in future to other unpredictable scenarios, which is advantageous, because the combination of its systematic analytical procedure and limited scenario-specific alteration capacity, enables the implementation of machine learning in problems that are understandable, and yet cannot be fathomable or easily solvable by humans, such as detecting forged signatures, or any sudden changes in the pulse rate, etc. On the other hand, the constantly altering parameters make the system inherently complex, thereby making it difficult to provide substantial proof for any action used by the machine or device, or the result supplied by it (Jonathan Holdowsky, 2015).

Deep Learning

Induced by the neural network in a human brain, deep learning functions as a structural network which advances the functioning of machine learning. As opposed to machine learning, which is implemented under human supervision, deep learning requires supervision only till certain stages, after which it can function partially under supervision, or even independently. Multiple tasks are undertaken and performed by deep learning: the embedded codes allow diversity of aim as well as function, so that deep learning is inferior only to the human mind, and in some scenarios, even equivalent to it. Since different sets of fresh and accumulated data are linked by the deep neural network, deep learning equips machines and devices to perform complex tasks like speech, face and even species recognition, following verbal commands rather than just the commands of the embedded codes, processing and auto-translating languages, identifying substances, especially in the field of medicine, etc.

Automation and Autonomy

The application of Artificial Intelligence (AI) to everyday-systems that are essential to humans, because of its ability to generate as well as control and contain physical changes and actions, brings about automation, as well as the autonomy of machines and devices. Automation takes places when a human is replaced by a machine to perform tasks that previously required human skill and effort, either cognitive or physical. This reduces the need for human labor and changes the status quo of employment and employee classification and it also eliminates human error and potential human inefficiency. Finally, autonomy refers to the independent operation of a system by means of Artificial Intelligence (AI). Human guidance, supervision, and control are rendered unnecessary due to autonomous devices, even regarding identification of potential problems within the software or the hardware of the devices, their repair, and maintenance, thereby reducing costs and increasing profits of businesses.

Human-Machine Teaming

Human-Machine teaming involves the co-operation of human and a machine, not as a means of guidance, control or supervision, but as an effort to compensate for and overcome the shortcomings of each individual one. This can involve the use of human cognition by the machine, in addition to its data and analysis procedure to arrive at a solution, or even the machine operating on behalf of a human. A few examples of the human-machine teaming are customer service and help desks on online shopping websites, or online navigation protocols, etc. Human-Machine teaming, due to its utilization of both the human as well as mechanical, artificial potential, reduces the chances, as well as the risks of erroneous solutions and false interpretations of data. Hence, its extensively used in science, research, as well as daily lives of humans.

FUTURE IMPACT

The implementation of Artificial Intelligence (AI) through the Internet of Things (IoT) in different sectors of human life will have a significant impact in the field of business and job employment. It is estimated that at least 40% of the human workforce worldwide will be replaced by machines equipped with AI. With its data acquisition and retention capacity, and its ability to generate real-time, customer- or situation-specific solutions, AI will be superior to humans, and will only fall short regarding creativity and innovation, at least till it achieves complete autonomy. Products- household appliances and gadgets, as well as heavy equipment and machinery- will be made intelligent with AI to develop a smart ecosystem. A few examples of the elements constituting this intelligent ecosystem are smart classrooms, smart homes, automatic automobiles, robot-operated surgeries, enhanced security systems for homes, institutions, as well as countries, etc.

The integration of Artificial Intelligence (AI) and the Internet of Things (IoT) will also result in AI controlling and managing the Cloud of Things (CoT). The services provided by CoT- Software as a Service (SaaS), Platform as a Service (PaaS), and Infrastructure as a Service (IaaS). Consequently, it will be developed and enhanced to function independently, rather than with human assistance, which is a current scenario. The human effort, as well as interference in each of the services, will be rendered unnecessary: the financial transactions and resource distribution (IaaS), deployment and provision of new services (PaaS), and the management of the cloud software and its access (SaaS), will be handled autonomously and efficiently by AI as the IoT networks will result in the dominion of AI over the digital domain (Abdulrahman Yarali, 2017).

The costs, however, of such an intelligent development and digitalized takeover, are enormous even though they will result in a profitable future in long-term. Also, while some businesses may very well opt for a traditional method of production to retain their employees, it will be at the risk of losing their value and market. Eventually, however, with the developments in deep learning, and deep neural networks, it is estimated that the autonomous AI will be able to invent software or machines superior to those invented or designed by humans.

While there is considerable risk in ceding control to Super Intelligent or Singular AI, it will effectively eliminate any need for human effort and labor. The rapid development of the intellectual capacity of AI will also enable humans to develop and expand their capacities as well, both in terms of intelligence and a better lifestyle. Humans will finally have a chance to experience and enjoy a higher quality of life with the replacement of humans with machines in business and employment sectors.

APPLICATIONS

Due to the immense scope of opportunities presented, a multitude of companies is implementing the AI-IoT amalgamation to avail the advantageous facilities. The following are a few examples of the same:

Airplane Companies

The conditions and functioning mechanism of the multiple systems on aircrafts is constantly observed by the sensors, thereby detecting the subsisting, as well as the future, flaws, and bugs in the system that may prove detrimental to the flight of the aircraft. Consequently, the implementation of AI-IoT integration by the airplane companies helps to increase the security of the aircrafts and ensures smooth and hassle-free flights.

Oil Companies

The machines and the heavy equipment used for oil drilling are susceptible to damage drilling oil are prone to get damaged, or even exploding, due to the pressure encountered when the drills pierce a gas pocket. The affixation of intelligent sensors on the drilling machines and equipment can help to constantly evaluate the amount of resistive pressure encountered by the drills, thereby warning the system operator, or directly shutting down the system in case of a pressure overload, preventing explosions and even damage to expensive machines.

Production Companies

Production based companies and industries that manufacture a variety of things- from heavy machinery to household devices- are now affixing intelligent sensors to their production machinery to enable continual servicing and maintenance of the machines, preventing machine failure or collapsing due to overheating.

Intelligent Architecture

The buildings affixed with intelligent sensors are secured against, and better equipped to deal with any accidents such as fires or natural disasters such as earthquakes and floods. In addition to offering protection against disasters, the sensors also increase the environmental effects of the building by adjusting the room temperature in accordance with a number of people in the room, etc., and by helping with the maintenance of the building premises.

Interactive Homes

Residences or homes equipped with intelligent sensors provide security against burglaries and even natural disasters. Additionally, the intelligent sensors customize the homes according to the health conditions of the occupants, their preferences of room temperature, etc., while also effectively conserving energy and reducing the power consumption costs incurred. Moreover, the sensors help maintain the property and provide updates on any failure or defect in the household electrical or gas systems.

Wearables

Intelligent wearable sensors observe health and other physical activities and help detect certain health problems or disorders. Moreover, the sensors can also help monitor heart-rate by predicting any anomaly or possible heart conditions. Additionally, the sensors are also convenient for people who exercise daily, as they help keep track of the calories required, burned, etc. Also, the wearable sensors can help increase productivity in companies by estimating the working capacity of each worker, therefore helping avoid overloading of work on any single worker.

CONCLUSION

The current development in the field of technology that integrates Artificial Intelligence (AI) and the Internet of Things (IoT) is essential for further development of both business and technology. AI can change the face of business as well as employment by making devices and machines smart and equipping them with almost human potential, both cognitive and physical. IoT can enhance the potential of AI by supplying it with the structural networks. Since the IoT itself is a network, integrating IoT into AI will connect every smart device and machine to enable a free exchange of information on a real-time frequency. The function of the intelligent network will be akin to the function of the neural network in the human brain. IoT-AI combination will result in a smart ecosystem and even a super-intelligent AI.

While the current development in AI has been enormous, still stays at a rudimentary level compared to the potential development that can be accomplished. While AI functions with human assistance currently, the smart networking functions of IoT and CoT will enhance the capacity of machine learning and deep learning to help AI evolvement into autonomous AI increasing the benefits in productivity and quality. The IoT and CoT networks will enable intelligent application of sensors through the prediction, prescription, and adaption of data resulting in enhanced benefits like self-fixing, maintaining equipment, enhanced security of businesses and people, enhanced privacy and personal security through AI wearables, increased profit from efficient and innovation production and even reduced expenditure from the lack of human labor.

Integration of IoT with AI (AI-IoT) is not only essential for a brighter and advanced future but also enhances the current standards and for more future development.

REFERENCES

Chitkara, R., Rao, A., & Yaung, D. (2017) *Leveraging the upcoming disruptions, from AI and IoT*. Retrieved October 15, 2017, from https://www.pwc.com/gx/en/industries/communications/assets/pwc-ai-and-iot.pdf.

Holdowsky, J., Mahto, M., Raynor, M. E., & Cotteleer, M. (2015) *Inside the Internet of Things (IoT)*. Retrieved May 30, 2017, from https://dupress.deloitte.com/content/dam/dup-us-en/articles/iot-primer-iot-technologies-applications/DUP_1102_InsideTheInternetOfThings.pdf.

OSTP, *Preparing for the Future of Artificial Intelligence*: Retrieved from: https://obamawhitehouse.archives.gov/sites/default/files/whitehouse_files/microsites/ostp/NSTC/preparing_for_the_future_of_ai.pdf.

Wu, M., Lu, T., & Ling, F. Research on the architecture of Internet of Things View Document: *International Conference on Advanced Computer Theory and Engineering*, 5, 484-487. doi:10.1109/ICACTE.2010.5579493.

Yarali, A. (2017). *5G mobile: from research and innovations to deployment aspects*. New York: Nova Science.

Chapter 15

THE INTERNET OF THINGS: MACHINE LEARNING, ARTIFICIAL INTELLIGENCE, AND AUTOMATION

INTRODUCTION

The internet of things can be said to be a genre of services and technologies that have been created to focus on creating a network of technological objects. The internet of things includes almost everything. Over the recent years, it has become almost impossible to try and focus on the future of technology in the world, the internet, and different industries without mentioning the phrase, the internet of things. What this means is that there is an increasing and ever-expanding network of things, characterized by a greater and broader internet that is filled with many connected devices that go beyond Smartphones, laptops, and desktops. In the internet of things, these devices are connected together so that they can communicate and track with enablement of cloud storage (Waher, 2015). The intern of things is so vast and to better understand it, it is important to first understand its three broad aspects on which the internet of things is based. The three main aspect of the internet of things is machine learning, artificial intelligence, and automation.

There are a lot of things that have been enabled by the internet of things. A car, for example, will very soon be able to drive itself around the estate and in town and there will be no need for pedals or steering wheels. What will enable such technologies to operate in such a manner that the improved artificial intelligence and sensor technologies that have the capability of surveying the environment and making accurate positioning using other technologies such as GPS (ICSITA et al., 2014). Thereafter, the car will be able to make decisions like the human brain and take the direction it should. The result of all this will be a safer and more efficient transportation system that has reduced costs.

The internet of things basically works to make life easier for man. With it, things can be achieved over very short periods where the human brain could take hours to process.

One unique aspect of the internet of things is that it involves almost everything, including wearable devices. Devices that are worn on the body, including smartwatches, can easily connect t other devices such as mobile phones and home security systems via such technologies as Bluetooth which enable the watch to receive data from the cloud. The number of steps one makes, the number of heartbeats one has in a day and the quality of sleep that one gets can easily be recorded and stored in the cloud so that the information can be accessed by other devices from almost everywhere in the world (ICSITA et al., 2014).

IoT and Consumers

The internet of things basically means benefits to the consumers. Thanks to the internet of things, for example, homes are safer. The interconnected devices in the house or in a room can be sued to tell the number of people in a house, the house curtains and windows can be programmed to close and lock with the setting of the sun and the air conditioning systems can be programmed to cool or heat the house whenever the meters rise or fall. For the many homeowners, for example, in the United States, the internet of things related technologies are already efficiently running and they work quite positively. For example, the smart electrify meters have completely replaced the old-fashioned mechanical meters which had to be read and recorded by the technicians at the end of every month for bills (ICSITA et al., 2014). The electricity meters have made it easy for electricity consumers to keep up to date with their electricity bill status.

Industrial Revolution

The internet of things has also revolutionized the industries of the world. In industries, the internet of things has increased efficiency. The internet of things technologies can power and run heavy machinery as well as gather and collect important information about different happenings in the production environment. There are a lot of technologies, for example, sensors that can check on the efficiency of a production machine and recommend changes, servicing or a replacement of parts. A lot of data can be shared between different control rooms where individuals can control and monitor production processes from the beginning to the end.

Another area where the internet of things has greatly been used is an area of security. Internet of things technologies has been sued to develop home security systems that have become widely applied and availed with integrated into cloud and applications that monitor door and alarm systems remotely from mobile phones and other devices. To make it simple, the internet of things has been so helpful to human beings and it is the best and most simple way that the intent can be described. The internet of things is an environment where mobile phones, laptop, tablets and other gadgets including cars and machinery can communicate to each other in order to ease human life (IEEEWFIOT, 2014). Since it was coined by information technology researchers, the internet of things has been recently observed to emerge as one of the mainstreams of human life. Some researchers and technology enthusiasts say that the internet of things will soon transform everything, including the functionality of the current 21st-century technologies as well as the technologies of the future for about 100 years to come (Waher, 2015). It is a representation of the generalized concept where interconnected network devices can collect and analyzed data around the world and share the data with other connected devices where it can be differently analyzed for different functions and usability.

The internet of thing can interchangeably be used with industrial internet which simply means the interconnected devices and applications in the manufacturing world. However, the internet of things it cannot be limited to manufacturing alone.

Abilities of the Internet of Things

While most of the future projection and predictions for the use and development of the internet of things may seem like science fiction, some of the technologies that seem as unrealistic some 20 years ago are currently in the application (IEEEWFIOT, 2014). Some of the future applications of the internet of things that may seem like science fiction include:

- Self-driven vehicles
- Detection of physical danger by wearable Iota devices
- Automatic tracking of daily physical activities
- Automatic ordering of home supplies and groceries

The Internet of Things and Network Devices

Almost all the home appliances and gadgets can be changed or rather, modified to work with the internet of things, Motion sensors, Wi-Fi adaptors, microphones and cameras among other appliances can be embedded in the internet of things devices. Some of the home automation systems have already applied some of the primitive concepts of the internet of things including light bulbs and blood pressure sensors. There are some wearable devices such as spectacles that have been envisioned to be part of the internet of things in the future.

Issues around IoT

Immediately the internet was invented, questions started arising bout the privacy information, especially personal and confidential information. There is a lot of information that can be accessed and used against the people who are connected to the internet of things. Whether it is real-time data or updates about medical issues, financial information or social information, there is an issue of security with the increase in the internet of things.

Power is another issue that has been puzzling the internet of things. Supplying power to almost all the devices that are connected to the internet of things can be logically difficult and expensive. Some of the portable devices that are connected to the internet of things have to use batteries which must be replaced after some time. Although most of the devices have been optimized sue very little power, the energy cost that will be incurred with the increased in the allocations and devices in the internet of things will always be running high. As much as the internet of things may have its disadvantages many businesses across the world have latched onto the phenomenon to try and take advantage of any opportunity that they may have that may arise from the internet of things (ICSITA et al., 2014).

As much as competition in the market is healthy as it helps to reduce the prices of goods and services, in the most undesired case, it may lead to a lot of confusion and inflated claims about the services of a product. The internet of things has the assumptions that some of the devices and equipment as well as other related technologies have the ability to ruin on themselves either partially or automatically, for example, keeping mobile phones, tablets, and computers connected to the internet can be as difficult as trying to make these devices smarter. There are different people in the world that may have diverse needs some of which might force the internet of things to be configured or to adapt to many preferences and situations. All in all, even if the challenges brought with the internet of things are manageable, individuals have become too reliant on the intent of things–which is not so robust as any technical issues with the systems can result to immeasurable financial or physical damage.

The Importance of IoT

It may be surprising to learn of the number of things that are connected to the intern and how much benefit, social and economic that can be derived from the internet of things as a result of interconnected streams of data (Waher, 2015). Some of the examples of why the internet of thing is important to include:

- The intelligent transportation systems, that have been enabled with the internet of things speed up the flow of traffic and reduces fuel consumption.
- The smart electricity grids are more efficient since they have been connected with renewable sources of energy which has in general improved the reliability of the grid system
- Data based systems have been incorporated into cities transportation and infrastructure systems leading to the creation of smart cities which makes it easy for the city municipalities to manage things such as waste and garbage in the cities.
- Law enforcement systems have been reinforced with the internet of things devices that help the authorities do their jobs better.

The benefits that the internet of things offers to human beings are so many.

MACHINE LEARNING

The world has come to a point where it operates on machine learning (ML) and artificial intelligence. There are already three driverless car companies which are Uber, GM, and Google that revolve around the Citrix Octoblue on a daily basis. There era some cognitive artificial intelligence systems such as the IBM Watson that is working to collect all sorts of data while freely interacting with people and in the process they get to learn new things in a reasonable scale.

Machine learning is one of the aspects of the internet of things and it focuses on the creation of technological systems and application that have the ability to access data and using the data to learn and make improvements in the systems without being improved or upgraded.

Machine Learning and Artificial Intelligence

Artificial intelligence can be said to be the development of applications and technological system that are able to perform tasks that may require human intelligence. Therefore, it is basically creating a system that works more or less like the human brain.

However, there is a difference between machine learning and artificial intelligence as machine learning can be said to be a subset of artificial intelligence. With more precise, machine learning can be said to be the learning process of artificial intelligence. While the artificial intelligence is applied in machine learning, these systems are first rained on how to solve problems (Waher, 2015). Artificial intelligence is important when the machines are being programs to copy the process through which the human brain goes to make good decisions and carry out tasks in a more humane way.

There are basically only two types of artificial intelligence and these are applied artificial intelligence and generalized artificial intelligence. Generalized artificial intelligence tends to be more informational while applied artificial intelligence tends to be more actionable (Jalali, Licht & Nataraj, 2012). For example, there those systems that have been trained to trade shares and stock and drive driverless vehicles and these will be categorized under the applied artificial intelligence. The transformation that is taking place in the digital business is driving real-time automation, data collection and data analysis in a very fast rate and companies that realized the importance and saw an opportunity in machine learning and artificial intelligence have positioned themselves at a better competitive positioning than those that have not adopted machine learning.

Machine learning can, therefore, be said to be a branch of artificial intelligence that collect data and analyses it for the automation of devices on the internet of things. It is based on the concept that machinery and internet devices should adapt and learn through experiences.

Machine Learning Evolution

Because of the ever-advancing computer technologies, machine learning has been evolving and the machine learning of the past is not like machine learning in the present day. Machine learning (ML) was enabled with the aspect that machines can perform and learn how to perform a certain task without being programmed to perform some tasks. The technology enthusiasts who came up with artificial intelligence and machine learning wanted to study of computing can identify trends and learn from a data set. The importance of the interactive form of machine learning can be realized when the models are exposed to vast and different data since they are able to adapt quickly and independently. They declared from the previous researches and data to come up with reputable and reliable results and currently, it is a science that has gained fresh and strong momentum (Jalali, Licht & Nataraj, 2012).

As much as there have been so many artificial learning algorithms from a long time ago, the ability to apply the complex calculations to the big data sets from time to time with incredible speeds is one of the most recent achievements. Some of the commonly used machines learning applications in the world are:

- The self-driven vehicles which are an essence of machine learning
- Online offers and recommendation that are used by companies such as Netflix and Amazon
- Understanding customers' needs through such platforms as Twitter which works on the basis of a combination of linguistic rules and machine learning
- Fraud detection

The Importance of Machine Learning

The resurgent interest that has been developing over machine learning is because of the factors that have popularized the Bayesian analysis and data mining. Such issues come as the growing volumes of raw and processed data with many variables, computerized processing which has been cheaper and cheaper over the years as well as the low costs of data storage. All these factors only mean one thing and that is a quick and automatic production of data analysis models that can be sued to analyze very large sets of complex data and come up with a more accurate result even on an hourly basis.

Machine Learning Users

Most of the companies in large industries that collect large sets of data have realized the importance of machine learning and how it can be beneficial to its business. By using the data, real-time companies and organizations are able to work more efficiently and gain a competitive advantage over their competitors. Some of the industries where machine learning has been greatly explored and applied are the finance industry, healthcare, government, transportation among other industries.

Finance Industry

Businesses such as banks and financial institutions have started using machine learning for two specific reasons one of which is to identify insights from data and the other one is to avoid cases of fraud. The data insights can be identified specifically to identify opportunities for investment and to help the potential inventors to understand the dates when it is most profitable to trade (ICITA et al., 2016). Data mining can also be used by the same financial institutions to analyze customers and client profiles and identify the high risks profiles. The companies can also use the data to pinpoint fraud and warning signs.

Government

Government bodies and agencies can use machine learning in very many ways. Some of the government agencies have specific needs for machine learning because they already have large sets of data that can be used for insights. These agencies can analyze information such as the sensor data to identify the ways in which the government can increase service efficiency while saving on expenses. Some government agencies can also use machine learning to identify theft and minimize cases of fraud.

Healthcare

Over the recent years, machine learning has been growing in popularity in the healthcare industry. Because of the wearable intent of things devices such as neuron censors, doctors can easily check on the status of their patients in real time even when they are not physically with them (ICITA et al., 2016). The machine learning techniques can also be sued by medical practitioners to analyze different sets of data and identify trends that can act as a red flag which ultimately improves healthcare provision.

Sales and Marketing

Companies have realized that machine learning can be used to promote sales. For example, those companies that make recommendations for the items that the customer may want based on the previous requests and purchases use machine learning to analyze the purchasing patterns of the consumers. Basing on the items that the consumer purchases, the companies make recommendations on the items that the consumer may be interested in. the future of reality lies in the ability of machine learning to collect data, analyze it and use it to improve the shopping experience for the consumers.

Gas and Oil Production and Sale

Machine learning has been used in the oil and gas industry from time. The machines can be used to find new sources of energy by analyzing the underground minerals. The machines have the ability to predict the failures of the machinery sensors. Therefore, the application of machine learning in the oil and gas industry has made the service less costly and more efficient. The numbers of machine learning technologies that are being applied in oil and gas production are so many.

Transportation

An analysis of the trends and patterns is one of the keys contributes to the success of the transportation industry which basically relies on making traveling programs, plans and schedules with the aim of making profits. Machine learning has been applied in the transportation industry to identify a trend in traveling and come up with schedules that suit the schedules of different people. The delivery industry, together with the transportation industry have used machine learning to increase their profitability and improve service delivery.

Methods of Machine Learning

There are basically two widely applied methods of ML that have been applied by companies all over the world. The two basic methods of machine learning are:

- Supervised machine learning
- Unsupervised machine learning

However, there are other methods of machine learning just that they are not widely adopted like these two.

Supervised Machine Learning

Supervised machine learning applies algorithms that have been trained to use examples that have been labeled such as the inputs where the developers understand the desired outputs. For example, a machine can be programmed to have two sets of data points like success or fail. The algorithms from which the machines learn receive the data inputs together with the outputs and the machines learns by making a comparison of the actual output and three output that it has given to determine the errors and the sources of the error. After the identification of the errors, the machine thereafter makes changes and models itself correctly. The machine uses such methods as regressions, classification, gradient boosting and predictions on the data that has not been labeled. Supervised machine learning is commonly applied in making machine applications where the previous data has been proven to predict the future outcomes. For example, if the machine detects, based on previous data that a credit card transactions may be fraudulent, the machine automatically sends an error code and it may also file a claim.

When Inductive Learning Can Be Applied

There are some situations where machine learning cannot be applied effectively. Some of the areas where inductive learning can be applied include:

- When solving where there are not human experts
- Where humans can take up the task but there are no people who can describe how the tasks are completed
- When solving problems where the desired outcomes are variable
- When solving problems where the needs of the users are customized

Unsupervised Learning

Unsupervised learning is the kind of machine learning where there is no historical able on a data set. The machine is therefore not informed of the right answer and the algorithms that have been used are forced to figure out for themselves the implication of the data that is being fed. The major aim of using unsupervised learning is to identify structures within a set of data and it is mostly used in transactional data. A good example of unsupervised learning can be the identification of customers who may have similar taste and presences as well as similar shipping habits. Therefore, the machine learning can be used to come up with marketing and promotions strategies that are aimed at reaching out to these kinds of people. In the same example, the unsupervised machine learning can be sued to identify the differences that customers have amongst themselves. The algorithms in unsupervised learning can also be used in text topics, identify data outliers and recommend items to customers and clients.

Apart from these two major types of machine learning, there are other machine learning methods which are:

- Semi-supervised learning
- Reinforcement learning

Semi-Supervised Learning

Semi-supervised learning can be used in the same applications that are developed using supervised learning. However, semi-supervised learning makes use of both labeled and unlabeled datasets for the training. Typically, it uses very small quantities if labeled data with huge amounts of unlabeled data usually bascule the unlabeled data sets to be cheaper compared to the labeled data. Semi-supervised learning can be sued in such methods as a prediction, regression, and classification. Semis supervised learning is most appropriate when the costs of machine learning have been speculated to be very high in order to allow a labeled training process. One of the applications of semi-supervised machine learning is the face detection technologies that have been applied to several technologies including mobile phones and cameras.

Reinforcement Learning

Reinforcement learning is commonly used in navigation, gaming and in robotics. Reinforcement learning applies the methods of trial and errors in the development of the algorithms and makes use of the action for which the yields are greatest. Reinforcement learning has three major components which are the environment which is everything that interacts with the agents. The second component is the agent who is the decision maker and also the learner. The third component is the action and it refers to the activities that the agent can perform. The purpose of reinforcement learning is for the agent to make the decision and chose the action that fully maximizes the rewards over the specified amount of time. To reach the good decision, the agent must make use of the policies and for that matter, the best policies. Therefore, the major objective of reinforcement learning is to grasp the ideal policy.

Machine Learning in Relation to Data Mining and Deep Learning

Although machine learning, data mining and deep learning have the same goal which is to collected data, analyses the data and identify relationships, they tend to have different abilities and approaches to how they manage to do this.

Data Mining

Data mining can be said to be a superset of different methods of data insights extraction. Data mining may involve some traditional methods of machine learning and statistical data methods what data mining does is the application of data from different areas so that it can identify previously established and non-established data patterns. Data mining makes use of machine learning, time series analysis, statistical algorithms among other data analysis areas. Data mining also involves the practice of adapt manipulation and storage.

Machine Learning

The major difference between ML and data mining is that like in statistics the major purpose is to identify patterns in the data by identifying structures in the data. Therefore, with the statistical data models, there are theories that can be used to mathematically prove the existence of relationships but the disadvantage is that it has to make use of strong assumptions. Machine learning has been developing on the basis of the ability of computers to probe data even when there is no theory that describes the structure of the datasets. Most times in machine learning, the machine learns by validating the existing database on the previous tests that have resulted in the invalidity of the data. Therefore, since machine learning is mostly applied in an iterative approach, the process of learning can easily be automated. The passes are made on the data several times until when the pattern has been identified and recorded.

Deep Learning

Deep learning makes use of both neural networks and the computing power of machines to learn some of the most complicated patterns in large and complex sets of data. The deep leaning technologies are currently being widely applied in the identification of sounds, words, and objects on some images. Technological researchers are currently researching on how deep leaning can be applied in the recognition of more complicated tasks which may include automatic sound translation from one language to another, automatic medical diagnosis and other important social businesses.

Traditional Programming and Machine Learning

ML tends to be more of a process that uses algorithms as the catalysis, the data, and the developers and processors.

- Machine learning: the output and the data are passed through the computers so that a program can be created. The program develops can be applied in traditional programming
- Traditional programming: the output and the data are fed into the computers to give output as the end result.

Key Elements of Machine Learning

There are millions of algorithms that already exist that are sued in machine learning and new ones are developed each day. However, there are some basic components of machine learning algorithms that must be present for it to be an algorithm. Some of the key elements of machine learning algorithms are:

- Evaluations: this refers to the way in which the hypothesis which refers to the candidate programs, are evaluated. Some the evaluation processes test on the accuracy, the squared hood, the costs, the posterior probability and the prediction as well as the recall
- Representation: this refers to the way in which the knowledge is represented. Some of t representation methods include a set of rules, tree decision diagrams, graphical models, vector machines among other methods
- Optimization: this refers to the process through which the candidate programs are generated. Some of the optimization methods include convex optimization, constrained optimization, and combinatorial optimization.

All the machine learning algorithms work through a combination of these components that serve as the framework for understanding all machine learning algorithms.

Traditional Programming Conceptual Framework

Program, Data → Computer → Output

Machine Learning Conceptual Framework

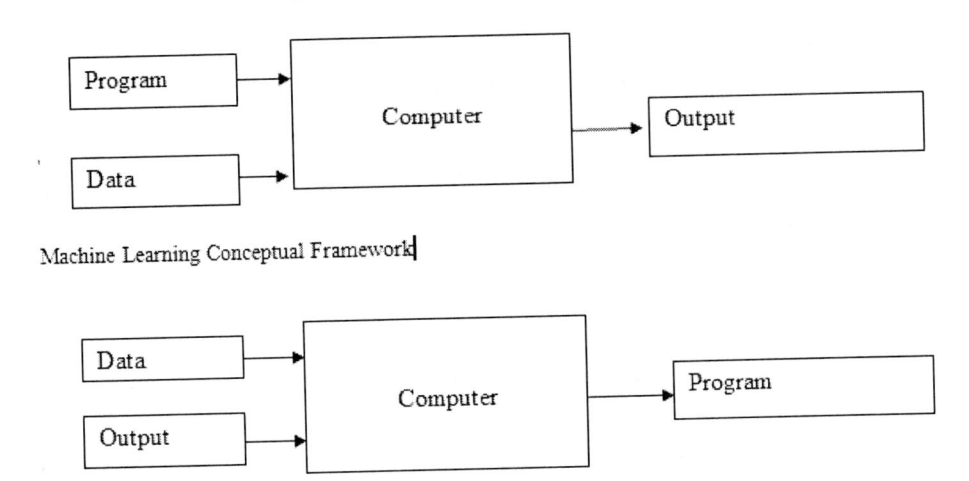

Data, Output → Computer → Program

Figure 1. Framework of traditional conceptual Framework.

Machine Learning Processes in Practice

The algorithms that are used tend to be a very small proportion of the whole process so machine learning. The typical process of machine learning tends to happen in loops that may look like:

1. *Initial loop*
   - An understanding of the domain, the goals, and the previous knowledge. The experts usually talk and consult the domain experts. Usually, the goals of machine learning are very unclear I the initial stages. The developers usually have very many things that they can develop and implement
   - Data selection, integration, procession and learning: this tends to be the most tie consuming process and it is important for the developers to have very accurate data for this process. The more the data that is used, the more difficult the process because the data is usually large, disorganized and dirty. Therefore, the principle of garbage in garbage out may apply here.
   - Result interpretations: sometimes in machine learning, the process that is fowled onto matter as long as the desired result s are achieved. Some domains, however, may require that there is an understanding of the model as the developers are likely to be challenged by the experts in domains
   - Deployment and consolidation of the knowledge. Most of the projects that tend to be successful in the laboratory are not implemented as it is usually very difficult to find something that has ready worked and has been used.
2. *End Loop*

The end loop is not a strep based process since it is more of a cyclical process. The developers have to run the loop many times till they achieved the desired results. Moreover, in each of the loops, the data must be changed in every new loop.

The Essence of Machine Learning

The main purpose of all machine learning programs is to reduce the cases of errors and differences between the predicted values and the real outcomes. It is through the process through which the correct correlations between different figures and features are used to determine the accuracy and increase the accuracy of a machine learning model especially on the part of training.

Machine Learning Workflow

A typical workflow of an ML process can be illustrated as below. The following is a detailed explanation of ML Workflow:

- 1a: this sit eh process where the original data set is split into smaller and different subsets to facilitate learning and training
- 1b: a consideration is made of the smaller data sets for learning
- 2a the data that is used for training is passed through the machine learning process through a linear regression
- 2b: the data set that is used for testing is populated and transferred in preparation for evaluation
- 3a: the algorithms to be tested is applied on each of the data sets as training takes place
- 3b: the different parameters are applied in testing the data set to determine the outcome
- 3c: the repetition of process 3b until the generated values are closer to the data that is used for testing
- 4: the right parameter are sued to come up with the final model for the specific dataset
- 5: the model developed is applied in predicting the outcomes of new data sets.

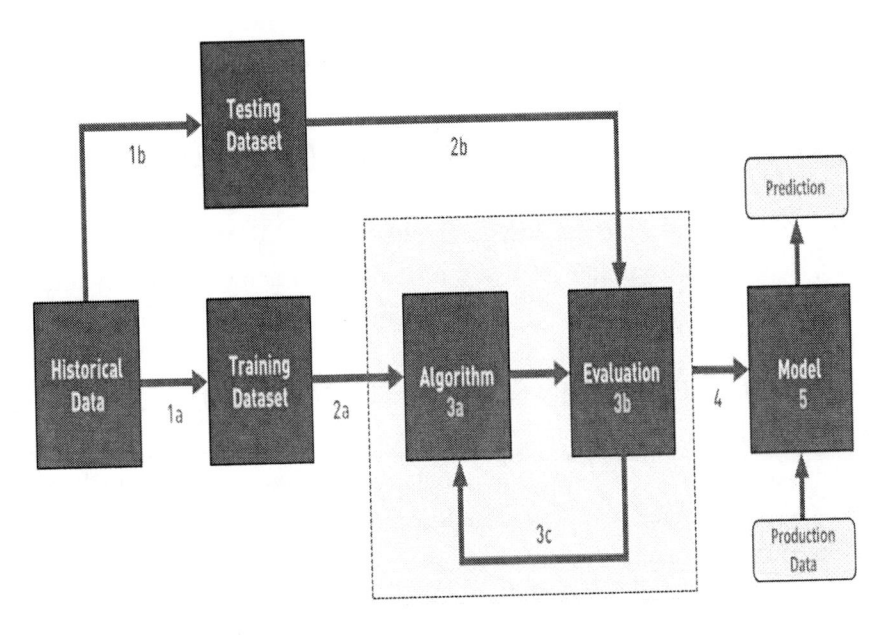

Figure 2. Machine Learning Workflow.

As evidenced from the process, machine learning is basically what happens in the third step because once the algorithm to be used has been chosen; they are finely tuned in accordance with the different data sets so that accurate predictions can be made. The entire process represents what basically happens in the learning part of machine learning. The algorithms that are learned can be transferred into a model that can be used to predict occurrences and produce data.

Apart from the process of linear regression, there are other millions of algorithms that can be used in machine learning some of which include the Bayes algorithm, the logistic regression, and the K, meaning clustering algorithms, other methods and algorithms include the supportive vector algorithms, the nearest neighbor algorism the artificial networks algorism the random forecast and the appropriate algorithm. Each of the algorithms that are used in machine learning is designed to either classify data or to predict the outcome basing on the data set. For example, when the logistic algorithm is being applied, it can be used to find a value that may result in two outcomes which may be true or false. Linear regression is also used in certain cases, as seen and it is mostly used where the outcome to be predicted is a value like a number. The other algorisms that are used in machine learning are best used in cases of data classification. However, regardless soft the nature of the algorism used, the goal of machine learning is to determine accurate parameters that may be used to design the final model.

Artificial Intelligence

Artificial intelligence (AI), like machine learning, is a technology that is already affecting and impacting the way things are done and how users of technology interact with it. Moreover, it focuses so much on the benefits of the internet and how the internet has worked to sharpen human life by easing the manner in which certain things are done. The impacts of artificial learning are likely to increase in the near future. Artificial intelligence, to a great extent, has shaped the way human beings interact with each other and with the internet to only in the digitalized world but throughout the human networks and the socioeconomic institutions for good and for bad. The importance of artificial intelligence to human life can only rely on if all the stakeholders in the phenomenon participate in the various discussions and debates surrounding artificial intelligence. If the different stakeholders in artificial intelligence come out and bring their different viewpoints and experiences, the benefits and the disadvantages of artificial intelligence are more likely to be realized.

There is a rapid growth of artificial intelligence and its application. Thanks to the internet, the speed of artificial intelligence has reached to some of the most remote regions of the world and sooner or later, artificial intelligence may have a great impact to the everyday life of man. Artificially, intelligence simply means the creation of an intelligence system that more likely function like the human brain meaning that the system can reason, think, perceive, plan and process things in different languages. In fact, to some extent, the artificial intelligence may be accurate and better than the human brain especially when such as aspects of multitasking and analysis set in (Jalali, Licht & Nataraj, 2012). What has led to the rapid growth and application of artificial intelligence are the many benefits that artificial intelligence has brought to man especially in the spheres of defense and economic prosperity. Artificial intelligence has brought to man so many opportunities some of which may be social and it has also helped human beings solve some of the social and economic challenges that did not previously have solutions.

Because artificial intelligence is an internet-based technology, the internet society has come to understand the challenges and the opportunities that are associated with artificial intelligence. Since internet users already trust the internet, there is no reason why human begins can doubt artificial intelligence. Because machine learning is ready being used in the provisions of services and products, there are a lot of considerations that have to be made when it comes to artificial learning and the trust that people have for the internet. There are several issues that must be considered when addressing artificial intelligence and these are such things as the social impact, the economic impact, the cultural impact, then after of the artificial intelligence actions to human beings in the world and the ethical issues that are connected to the application of artificial intelligence. Another impact issue to be considered is how the artificial intelligence can impact the ecosystem and lead to the generation of another different ecosystem than there is currently.

At the same time, in the complexity of the artificial intelligence, there are some challenges that are facing the application of artificial intelligence some of which may include the interpretability of the processes and applications, the transparency of the application and the issues of data quality and the chances of databases. Security and safety issues are also important to consider as well as their implications (Jalali, Licht & Nataraj, 2012). Other considerations have to be made on accountability, the potentially disruptive effects and impact and the effect on the social and economic structures and systems.

To better analyze and evaluate the various challenges involved in artificial learning, there are some principles and systems that have been set by the internet society in reference to what has been termed as the abilities of the artificial intelligence and the usage of artificial intelligence with reference to the internet and its abilities. There is no doubt that artificial intelligence has continued to be popular among human beings for the many benefits it has but recent trends point to the importance the internet with regard to the development and usage of artificial intelligence.

Artificial intelligence has been receiving a lot of attention in the recent years and thanks to the internet, there has been a lot of innovation and invention which have brought by artificial intelligence closer than it was a couple of years ago. The technological advancements that have been enabled by the internet have potential economic and social benefits. These benefits bring artificial intelligence forward for many debates. Investments in artificial intelligence socially in the economic world are increasing and governmental cross the word is trying to understand the potential benefits and risk that they are facing with increased use of artificial intelligence.

The expansion of the internet of things and the collection pod data in the process of " Big data" have created a whole new environment for the applications of artificial intelligence since its services are increasingly growing. All the application that has been made basing on the artificial intelligence technology are visible in many areas including in hospitals, in transportation, in public safety, and in target treatment. Other applications of artificial intelligence are evident in robotics, entertainment and in education but in the coming years, the applications of artificial intelligence will be great in other fields. Artificial intelligence alongside the internet has changed the way people experience the world and it has been reprieved as the new engine that will drive economic growth and prosperity in the near future. Artificial intelligence has made life very easy and a good example can be in the automatic vending machines (the US, 2015). Someone may wonder how the automatic vending machines are able to differentiate the different type of money and the value of each of the coins that are inserted in the machine. Well, the answer to such puzzling questions can only be found with an understanding of how artificial intelligence works.

Common Applications of Artificial Intelligence

Although artificial intelligence may sometimes be perceived as science fiction, there are real cases and applications of artificial intelligence some of which have become so common that they are not perceived as 21st century technologies anymore. Some of the applications of artificial intelligence include:

- *Filtering emails*: email service providers such as Google and Yahoo use artificial intelligence to filter emails. For example, the artificial intelligence systems in the emails services have been structured to reason and determine the spam messages from the important messages and filter them. Also, these systems have been designed to filter the important messages from the less important messages.
- *Personalization*: online service providers such as online stores use artificial intelligence to improve the experiences of the interface users. For example, Netflix and Amazon use artificial intelligence to understand the purchasing and shopping patterns of the interface users and use the information to improve the shopper experience. For example, the online stores can make a recommendation

on the products that the shoppers may want to be based on their previous shopping.
- *Fraud detection and prevention*: banks, credit card companies and other financial institutions use artificial intelligence to determine if there are any strange activities that have been carried out in accounts and using credit cards (the US, 2015). With the use of the different algorithms, certain activities as foreign transactions and other unexpected activities can be detected before they are completed.
- *Speech recognition*: different applications use artificial intelligence to optimize speech detection. Some of the institutions that use this technology if the Federal Bureau of Investigations when questioning suspects and the intelligence community of the United States.

The internet users understand that one of the most important things in the development and use of the internet is an understanding of the challenges and the opportunities that come with artificial intelligence. This is most important because the internet has been the key technology behind the discovery and development of many things including artificial intelligence. Moreover, it has been the main technology for the deployment of the internet.

What Is Artificial Intelligence All About?

Traditionally, artificial intelligence was about the creation of human-like systems that are able to reason and do things like the human brain. It can be further understood as narrow artificial intelligence or general artificial intelligence. Narrow artificial intelligence, which is the intelligence that human beings interact with on a daily basis, is the intelligence that has been designed to carry out specific functions that surround a particular domain, for example, the translation of a language to another. General artificial intelligence, on the other hand, is very hypothetical and doesn't work in a specific domain. This means that general artificial intelligence has the ability to work in several domains through the process of learning and performing the different task differently. Artificial intelligence works by the development of new algorithms and models that are based on the process of machine learning.

Machine Learning in Relation to Artificial Intelligence

ML, as discussed before, is the creation of algorithms that have the ability to solve a problem. These are the algorithms that have been created by computer programmers that give instruction sot a system, or rather, a computer to perform different tasks based on the information that is fed into the system as well as the commands. The computer algorithms that are used in machine learning make use of large sets of data and they organize the data into services and information basing on the instructions and the rules that have been set for the systems (the US, 2015). Machine learning is a very important concept to understand as far as artificial intelligence is concerned because machine learning which is the creation and learning of the algorithms, determine the rules that the artificial intelligence systems follow and not the computers to which the algorithms and rules are fed.

Instead of the programmers making changes and programming the computer systems at every step, machine learning allows the computers to learn from the data that has been fed without having to carry out the step by step procedures by the programmers (the US, 2015). Therefore, the computers can use a complicated and new task that cannot be programmed manually. The artificial intelligence systems and applications such as the voice and face detection applications make use of such processes.

The basic processes that are involved in machine learning involve learning different algorithms and training the data. After the algorithm has been leaned, the systems generate new rules and processed that is based on the inferences given by the particular set of data that has been sued. This is basically the essence of coming with a new algorithm which has previously been identified as the process of machine teaching (CAIA et al., 2015). By applying different sets of data for training, the same algorithms used for learning can be used to come up with different and new models. For example, single algorithms used for machine learning can be used to train a computer on how to read messages and translate a language to the other which will result in artificial intelligence.

The artificial intelligence, in this case, will come about because the computer has been trained to do just what the human brain can do. In this case, the computer will be trained on how to read, perceive, understand and relate the word to another language which it also reads, perceives and understands. The major strength of machine learning is the inferences that are given for the new instructions. The more the data is used to train the machines, the faster and better it learns. In fact, the most recent developments in artificial intelligence have been achieved because of the radical innovations that have been made on the learning algorithms that are used train machines. Moreover, the enormous information found on the internet has been another major key to the development of artificial intelligence (CAIA et al., 2015).

Machine learning and its application in artificial intelligence is onto something new, the many algorithms that have been used to make development in artificial learning are based on years of previous research and the recent developments in artificial intelligence can be linked to three major applications which are data availability, the computing power of machines and the innovation of algorithms.

- *Data availability*: at any time in like, there are about 3 billion people who are connected to the internet and there are more than 17 billion devices that are connected to the same internet. The internet of things generates a lot of data and in foraging which may be combined with data storage, decreasing data costs and therefore, it is readily available for use in artificial intelligence development (the US, 2015). Therefore, the machine learning process can make use of this information and algorithms to learn and increase its capability in handling even harder tasks
- *Computing powers*: Very powerful computers have the ability to connect different processing powers using the internet and therefore making it possible for machine learning to take place with the application of the big sets of data.
- *Algorithm innovation*: there are many and different machine learning techniques especially in structure networks which can also be referred to as deep learning. The algorithms have inspired the creation of new services. Apart from this, they have also spurred research and investments in that specific field of arterial intelligence.

Major Considerations in Artificial Intelligence

As artificial intelligence applications are increasingly being used to provide products and services. There are a lot of factors that must be put into consideration when addressing the application of the technologies. Over the recent years, artificial intelligence has been receiving a lot of attention especially because of an issue such as ethics and the impact on the general society (the US, 2015). Of most importance among the factors is an issue of the trust that internet user has for the internet. Among the factors of consideration with the use of artificial intelligence are:

- *Socioeconomic implications and impacts*: the applications, functions, and services of artificial intelligence tend to have a significant effect on the social and economic aspects of human life. The artificial intelligence machines have the ability to apply cognitive skills which human beings possess to learn, perceive, plan and to make some things possible. The artificial intelligence systems are able to perform tasks that human beings can perform and some have been observed to be more efficient and accurate than human beings. The new application of artificial intelligence means a lot of opportunities for people in such areas as healthcare. Economic prosperity and production.
- *Transparency, accountability, and bias*: The artificial intelligence systems are able to make decisions, some of which may have dire consequences on the lives of people. The artificial intelligence systems tend to discriminate some

individuals when they make decisions that may result in errors as a result of bias in the data that is used. It is quite difficult to understand how the artificial intelligence pulsations make such decisions. Therefore, achieving accountability may be difficult with the application of artificial intelligence since data manipulation is so easy.
- *Data usage*: the artificial intelligence systems through machine learning, has been proven to be efficient in data analysis and pattern identification especially when large sets of data are used. The data that is collected is used to train the machines and to increase their efficiency (Frey, 2012). With his data usage, there will always be an increasing demand of data which may increase data collection thereby raising the risk of information and data sharing as well as the associated risks, therefore, the general issue here is the privacy of the data.
- *Safety and security*: there are always new advancements in artificial intelligence and the uses of the artificial intelligence and its developments may pose challenges in security. The risks that may be brought by increased use of artificial intelligence may arise as a result of unethical behavior of the artificial intelligence agents and malicious actors learning.
- *Ethics*: artificial intelligence systems may sometimes, make decisions which may be rendered unethical. Some of the unethical decisions made by the systems may be logical with reference to the algorithms used to make the decisions. Therefore, artificial intelligence systems should be built with a lot of ethical considerations. The algorithms and the system should be developed with ethical considerations.
- *Ecosystems*: just the impact that has been brought by increase mobile networks, artificial intelligence leads to the creation of new services, applications and new ways of interacting with people and the environment. For example, the speech agents may lead to new ecosystems by creating new challenges when it comes to internet accessibility.

Challenges Faced In Artificial Intelligence Development

There are a lot of factors that may contribute to the challenges that most of the artificial intelligence developers face as they are developing the systems. Some of the challenges experienced in artificial intelligence development are contributed by factors like:

- *Interpretability and transparency especially in decision-making*: with the application of artificial intelligence in performing some of the most important tasks such as monitoring the life of a patient, driving a car or managing a financial institution, it is important that artificial intelligence developers understand how the artificial intelligence applications make the decisions (Brooks, 2017). Apart from simply understanding the decision-making process, there needs to be an assurance of transparency especially on the algorithms that are used by the applications to make the decisions. However, transparency can sometimes be limited because of such things as state or corporate secrecy. A further complication to the challenge is brought about by the machine learning process since the logic of the internal decision made by the machines are hard to understand and sometimes, they are blocked or rather, protected from other people. As much as the algorithms used to train the machines may be transparent and open, the models that are produced by the systems may not be as transparent and it may have dire consequences on the development of the learning systems. Also, still, most important is the accountable and safe development of the systems and artificial intelligence applications. Therefore, with regard to artificial intelligence, it is important to understand why they make the decisions that they do (Frey, 2012). For example, it would be important for users to understand why a self-driving car would take a turn to the left and not to the right. Moreover, it would be important to understand where the liability would fall in case the artificial intelligence applications fail. For example, if the self-driven car fails at some point and causes an accident.

- *Biases and data quality*: in artificial intelligence specifically in machine learning, the model of the algorithm that is used to train the machines highly depends on the validity of the data that is used for its development. In this system, the aspect of garbage in –garbage out may affect the quality of the learning process since the data that is used to develop the algorithm may have errors which will ultimately affect the effectiveness soft eh learning process and ultimately the functionality of the artificial intelligence (Brooks, 2017). Therefore, if the data that is used to train the machine is biased, then the whole machine will be biased. Enable to a serious risk can be in the risk assessment systems. An automated artificial intelligence system that is used to assess risk may be biased and may fail in the cases of risk assessment. Therefore, in artificial intelligence development, data reliability is very important. The challenge is that there is an increasing demand for data that is used for machine learning and increase demands mean more data collection. Therefore, in the process of data collection, little concern is given to the validity of the data which may render the whole process not credible. There is also the problem of bias minimization which is usually complicated further by the understanding of the learning process which is also very difficult especially when solving a problem involving large sets of data. As a result, it can be very difficult to realize the data that has caused a problem in the learning process and to adjust it. If the consumers of artificial intelligence have a feeling that the data used to develop the system is biased, they would have little trust and confidence in the artificial intelligence technologies (ICSITA et al., 2014).

- *Security and safety*: as the artificial intelligence applications and agents interact with the environment in which they apply, there are many challenges that they face with regard to safety and security. The security challenges that the systems may face could result from harmful behaviors and unpredictable failures. There are also chances that the artificial intelligence applications may have safety threats and challenges that may arise from the environment in which they operate. In the reinforcement of the artificial intelligence, these threats are referred to as exploration dilemmas and it only means that the artificial intelligence systems may depart from the normal success strategy that they are designed to observe and operate by exploring other options that they have in solving a problem or when they are seeking a higher and better pay off (Frey, 2012). Such errors and challenges may have devastating effects and outcomes. For example, if self-driving car experiences such as errors, it may result to a road accident since the car may make the decision for itself and rive on the wrong side of the road or make a turn where it is not supposed to which may lead to the loss of life and damage to property. Artificial intelligence systems may also have the risk of autonomous systems exploitation by actors that may be trying to manipulate the functionality of the systems. There have been several cases and incidences where artificial intelligence applications have been manipulated one example being the case of "Tay" the Tay application is a chat box that was used by Twitter to study how people interact on the platform. However, some Twitter users managed to hack the application through coordinated efforts and they manipulated it to act in a manner that suggests racial behaviors (ICITA et al., 2016). Other successful manipulations conducted on artificial intelligence applications include the attacks that are done to filter some systems and divert networks and data transfer which may lead to the exploitation of eth algorithms. The ability of the manipulation of the algorithm itself may highlight some transparency and biases issues that may result from artificial intelligence systems. The disclosure of detailed data and information about the development and functionality of an algorithm may render the artificial intelligence system vulnerable to risks. Security and safety considerations should and must be taken into consideration when talking about the many conspiracies that revolve around artificial intelligence and machine learning.
- *Accountability*: the efficiency and strength of an artificial intelligence application are based on the ability of the system to come up and generate rules with the support of elaborate instructions. However, while the technique has been proven to be effective in developing systems that may perform some of the most complex tasks such as voice and face detection, the ability should be a source of

concern especially for the users of such artificial intelligence. The moment machines, through machine learning and artificial intelligence, learn how to do things for themselves including learning and programming themselves, the developers, who are the humans, lose control of the systems and as much as the learning algorithm may show some biases, the reasoning behind the development of machine learning is that the process can be monitored and corrected. However, in reality, it is very simple to control a machine that has been trained to learn and program itself. The aspect of failure to explain why the artificial intelligence systems can make certain decisions and not the others present an accountability issue with the systems. For example, if "day" the chat box was manipulated to behave in a racist behavior, there is possibly nothing that cant be done on the artificial intelligence systems. The bigger issues come when there is a matter of accountability; most of the artificial intelligence developers are never liable for any damages that may happen as a result of the failures in the algorithms used to develop the artificial intelligence applications (IEEEWFIOT, 2014). However, the aspect of accountability is very important since there is no developer who may be willing to make changes or innovate if they are required to. However, since the internet of things is gradually growing, there are chances that the changes may be immediate if not in the near future. The flaws and malfunctions in the artificial intelligence algorithms may result in devastating outcomes and damages; there is a need for a clarification of the accountability especially on the side of the artificial intelligence developers.

- *Economic and social impacts*: Artificial intelligence applications have been predicted to bring a lot of economic changes especially in productivity. The technology will introduce new economic concepts such as the machines being able to carry out economic activities and perform new tasks cues as advanced robotics and self-driven cars. However, with the advancements in the technology, there will be a difference on how the technologies will be distributed together with the stakeholder's actions and therefore lead to a difference anthem outcomes especially in the society and in the labor markets. To the consumers of the artificial intelligence, the automation of economic activities could mean cheaper profits and higher efficiency. Artificial intelligence is also set to create a lot of jobs or it would increase the demand for the already existing jobs. However, with decades in the adoption of artificial intelligence, some of the manual jobs that are available in the present items will be automated meaning that the artificial intelligence may at the end, not caret jobs but reduce the already existing jobs. Predictions that the artificial intelligence is likely to be 40 percent more jobs compared to the current jobs and the low paying and the unlike labor will be automated (ICITA et al., 2016). However, the artificial intelligence is estimated and predicted to create a higher impact on the high skills jobs that entirely rely on the cognitive skills. However, depending on the net effects of the artificial intelligence, it could result in a more unstructured deployment in the near future. The automation of the economic world could also mean the decision of labor from the larger angle of the global scale. Economic hinges have been happening in the recent past years and production of some commodities have been hefting form the developed nations to the emerging economies. The shift has occurred largely because of the low cost of labor and the cheaper costs of the production materials. These changes in the economic set-up of the world have helped on the propulsion of some of the fastest growing economies in the world, therefore, offering more support to the global middle class. However, with the adoption of artificial intelligence, the incentives for economic growth may reduce and instead of offshoring, some companies in the world may simply automate their production systems which may lead to more local operations. The negative and the positive changes that will be brought by artificial intelligence especially in the labor market will not lack some challenges. For example, if the artificial intelligence applications will be adopted byte industries that operate in a rather concentrated industry, there could be some levels of inequality between societies (ICITA et al., 2016). The inequality that may be introduced by the systems may lead to distrust in technology especially to the internet and the artificial intelligence applications which will at the end, carry the blame for the change.

- *Governance*: the organizations, institutions, and processes that are involved in the governance of the artificial intelligence systems and applications are still very young and they do not have much experience in the systems. To a large extent, there is an overlap of the ecosystem with the related internet subjects and policies. Currently, there are efforts from the artificial intelligence stakeholders including nations, the United Nations experts and weapon governing institutions alike the legal autonomous weapons systems with the increased collection of data (ICITA et al., 2016). The bosses are concerned with such matters as how the processes are developed and how the regulations can be interpreted or adopted. One of the central focuses of the efforts of governing to artificial intelligence systems is related to the ethical operational direction of the intelligence systems as well as the implementation. Despite the complexity of artificial intelligence, the different stakeholders including industry controllers, governments and users should be given a role to play in the control and governance of the artificial intelligence systems from the beginning to the end. From the market-based regulations and approaches, all the different stakeholders should be engaged in the development and application of artificial intelligence in the years to come as they are the ones who may understand the impact that the artificial intelligence may have on their other systems. Further still, the social impacts of artificial intelligence cannot simply be mitigated by the governance of the technology and therefore, there is a need for governments and other stakeholders to have a control of the impact of the artificial intelligence and related technologies.

Recommendations and Some Guiding Principles

There are some principles that have been developed by the internet of things and they are commonly referred to as the core "abilities" of the internet of things and they are the values that are provided by the internet. As much as the development of artificial intelligence is something that is based on the internet, the current projection is that the artificial intelligence is very important for the development of the internet in the future. With that regard, there are some recommendations that have been made to guide the debate on artificial intelligence that has been ongoing for as long as the intent of things and artificial intelligence was discovered.

Ethical Considerations in the Design and Deployment of Artificial Intelligence

Principle
All the artificial intelligence builders and designers have to apply the user-centered approach when they are developing artificial intelligence applications and systems. The developers and designers have to consider the responsibility which comes collectively in the design and in the structuring of the systems as well as the use and applications. They need to create artificial intelligence technologies and systems that may not cause any harm on the internet and the users.

Recommendations
- Create and adopt ethical standards: there should be well laid ethical systems which all the developers should allow. They should all adhere to the standard and principles set by the ethical considerations in the design and manufacture of artificial intelligence. The set standards should guide al the stakeholders as well including the researchers and the users.
- Promote ethical considerations in the policies: the artificial intelligence innovation policies should all adhere to the set standards before any other activity is carried out including project funding.

Interpretability of the Systems

Principle

All the decisions that are made by artificial intelligence applications and agent should be easily understandable especially of the artificial intelligence decisions may have an impact on the safety of the public and if they may result in any sort of discrimination.

Recommendations

- Interpretability of the algorithms used: all the artificial intelligence systems must be designed in a manner that the algorithms sued should be easily understood and interpreted by the users. The minimum requirement, in this case, should be that the designers and the agents be able to account for the behavior of the artificial intelligence systems and applications (Briscoe & Caelli, 2016). The applications that may be perceived to have some implications for the safety of the public should have innovation in the event that an accident occurs as a result of a malfunction.
- User empowerment: the artificial intelligence users should be empowered in such a manner that they have a full understanding of how the system works (Briscoe & Caelli, 2016). The artificial intelligence service providers and manufacturers should be able to give the users some explanations on which the system makes some decisions.

Public Empowerment

Principle

There should be the ability of the public to understand the artificial intelligence services and their functionality. They should understand how the system works since it would be the key to understanding and trust the systems.

Recommendations

- A key skill should be the algorithmic literacy: regardless of whether it is infamies happenings on social media or other technologies such as self-driven cars, the users of the artificial intelligence have to be aware of the basic functionality of the system and applications. The users should have a basic understanding of the algorithms that were used to develop the systems and the algorithms in which the systems are functioning and the algorithms that they use to make the decisions (Briscoe & Caelli, 2016). The algorithmic skills that the users will have will also help in shaping the norms of the society around the applications of the

technology. For example, the users will be able to make decisions that may not be suitable for the artificial intelligence agents
- Public provision of information: while it may not be advisable to provide the public with full information about the functionality and processes allowed by the artificial intelligence systems and applications because of another risk, the public should have sufficient information that will allow them to question the artificial intelligence systems and the outcomes of their use.

Responsible Deployment

Principle

The capacity of the artificial intelligence agent and applications to act independently and autonomously and to adapt the behavior of the systems over time without human interference and influence calls for a safety check before the systems are deployed.

Recommendations
- Human beings and users should at all times be in control: all the artificial intelligence systems and applications should allow human beings and its users to interrupt the systems with such actions as turning them off. There is always a need to incorporate check on the processes of decision making on any system and the same should apply to the artificial intelligence systems and applications. The systems should be able to be controlled by the users to some extent and especially when there is a potential risk of physical harm to the human.
- Safety should at all items be the first priority: the development of artificial intelligence systems or any other autonomous system should vigorously be passed through tests before they are deployed. The tests are meant to ensure that the systems are safe for use by human beings. The systems should also be monitored at all times even when they are not in operation and they should be corrected as required.
- Privacy should at all items be the guiding principle: the artificial intelligence systems should be responsible for the data that they use and the data that is fed into them. The artificial intelligence systems should be designed in such a manner that they make use of the data that is needed only and delete the data immediately it becomes of no use to the systems. To help ensure the security of data, the systems should be designed in such a manner that they encrypt any data that is into transit and they should also be able to restrict entry to the data files to the authorized parties only (AAAICAI, 2016). The artificial intelligence systems should use the data in accordance with the personal data and privacy laws that regale the collection, application, and storage of the same data.

- Thinking before acting: a lot of thought should be given to the data provided to the systems as well as the instructions. The artificial intelligence systems should not be trained with biased data as the end result may be misleading the systems may not function as they are required. The concept of garbage in garbage out applied here and any information that is fed into the systems should be accurate and free from any bias to ensure that the systems perform their designated task without any bias.
- If they are connected, the artificial intelligence systems should be secured: The artificial intelligence systems work by connection and most of them work by being connected to the internet. The internet connection to the systems should at all times be secured not only for the protection of the system but also to the malware infected systems. In their development, high standard systems networks and security measures should be applied.
- Secured and responsible information disclosures: the security researchers should at all time act in good faith and they should be able to carry out security check in the most responsible manner as possible. They should be able to carry out security check without any fear of persecution. Moreover, the researchers should report any sort of vulnerability to the concerned parties. What this means is that these security experts should at all times deliver a full report to the concerned parties so that any changes, if need be, be made as soon as possible to the systems so that human lives may not be put at any risks.

Accountability

Principle

Any legal accountability should be ensured when the artificial intelligence agents replace the humanitarian agencies and the vise verse.

Recommendations
- Legal certainty: government and any interested stakeholder in the artificial intelligence should ensure legal certainties by enacting laws and making them clear the laws should govern all processes involved in artificial intelligence form development to applications. The policies and laws may also apply in the algorithmic process that the systems use to make decisions. The purpose of these laws is to ensure a clear legal environment. The government and agencies may be forced to work with other agents in this to identify any gaps in the legality of the systems. Similarly, the user and developers of the artificial intelligence should at times be in compliance with the laws and policies.

- Users first: the policymakers and the governments have to ensure that all the laws governing the development and application of artificial intelligence place the interest of the user's fist before anything else. The users, in this regard, may be allowed to make any changes and to challenges the artificial intelligence systems and applications with regard to their interests
- Up front liability: the stakeholders working with the governments should come up with a system where the liable party is easily identifiable in the vent that anything goes wrong in the system and the remedies that may be offered to the injured or affected parties.

Economic and Social Impacts

Principle

Government and interested stakeholders should create an operational environment where the artificial intelligence applications and system offer economic and social benefits to everyone equally.

Recommendations

All the stakeholders that engage in the ongoing task and debates that are aimed at determining the best strategies to seize the economic and social benefits of artificial intelligence should be educated on the potential benefits with supporting research and proof (Achuthan, Chang & Shah, 2015). However in the same manner, as the dialogues continue, they should also talk about the potential negative impacts of artificial intelligence to the social and economic set-up of the society. The debates and dialogues should address such issues as universal income, education, and social services.

Open Governance

Principle

The ability of the different artificial intelligence stakeholders, including governments, private sector players, the civil society and the academic sector to participate and inform about the governance of the artificial intelligence is very important for the safety of the systems and applications

Recommendations

Promote a multi-stakeholder system of governance: institutions, organizations and another process that are related to the governance of the artificial intelligence should be able to adopt transparent, open and inclusive approaches to the governance of these systems (Achuthan, Chang & Shah, 2015). The governance of the artificial intelligence should be based on four major principles or rather attributes which are:

- Collective responsibility
- Transparency and inclusiveness
- Collaboration
- Effective decision making

Perception of Artificial Intelligence

Certainly, human beings have become so excited about the invention of skills that are beyond the abilities of the human brain. However, some people are fearful that the artificial intelligence might be capable of more things in the future some of which may be harmful and pose a threat to the existence of humanity. A recent study was conducted by the British Science Association and according to the results; there are varied reactions and feelings towards artificial intelligence among people from different places of the world. According to the research, the most cited attributed with regard to artificial intelligence were skeptical, mistrustful and anxious. In the British study, more than

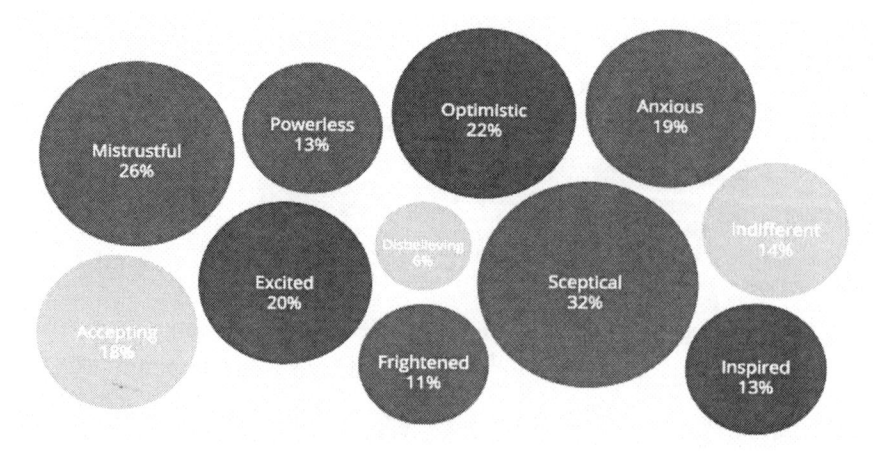

Figure 3. A survey response towards artificial intelligence among people.

200 Britons responded on what they felt about artificial intelligence and more than 36 percent of the responders said that the artificial intelligence poses serious threat and risk to human life (Lants, 2014). However, the responses that were given during the study

were highly influenced by the influence that has been created by Hollywood in the depiction of robots trying to take over the earth from human beings. The results of the study and the responses can be summarized in Figure 3.

THE FUTURE OF ARTIFICIAL INTELLIGENCE

Most times when people talk about artificial intelligence, they are referring to the robots which will in the future, compete with them for the mundane everyday tasks. While some of the perceptions might be true, a financial forecast of the benefits that the world may get from artificial intelligence speak of something else. With artificial intelligence adoption, there is an expectation of more than 8 billion increase in revenues in the United States alone (Lants, 2014). According to the forecast, artificial intelligence seems to have quoted a fruitful economic benefit in the near future.

Current Artificial Intelligence Funding

By the end of the year 2018, there will be more than 68 percent of the global organizations that will be applying artificial intelligence. At present, studies show that the most applicable form of artificial intelligence is in the companies that have a major focus on patents, innovation and the development of artificial intelligence applications.

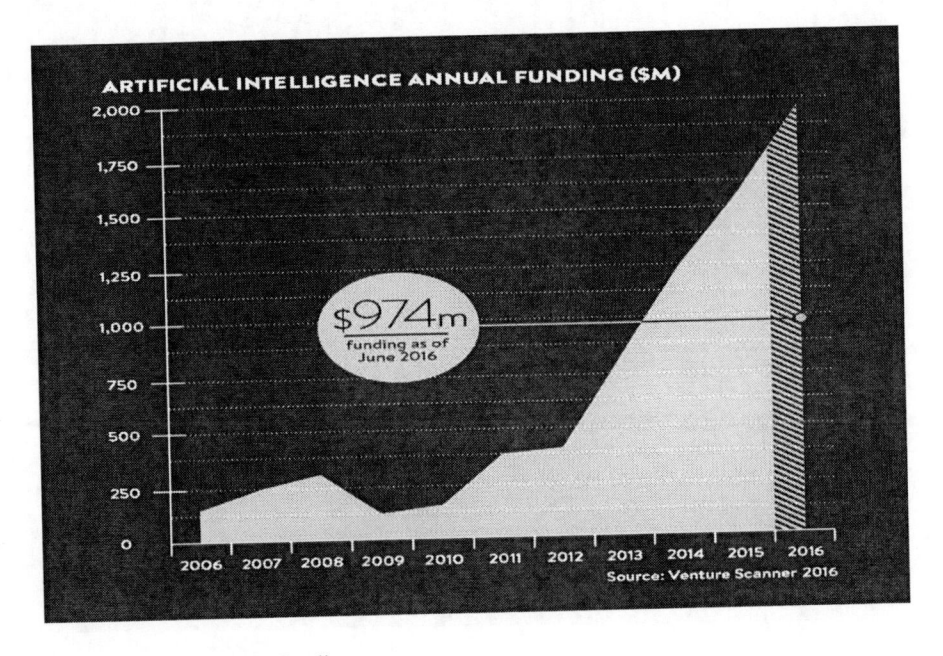

Figure 4. Artificial intelligence funding.

As at June 2016, more than 900 million had been directed towards funding artificial intelligence projects and next year's funding is expected to surpass the previous year's funding and more than 1.5 million has already been raised by companies in equity funding (CAIA et al., 2016).

Application of Artificial Intelligence

Artificial intelligence is not limited to the business sphere alone. In fact, the care bots and the robotics market could reach about 18 billion dollars by the end of the year 2020 (Lants, 2014). These are some of the best applications of artificial intelligence that have aided the increasing world populations. Among the different countries that have adopted artificial intelligence, Japan is leading with a large budget that is directed towards robots that are devoted to assisting the elderly in the nation.

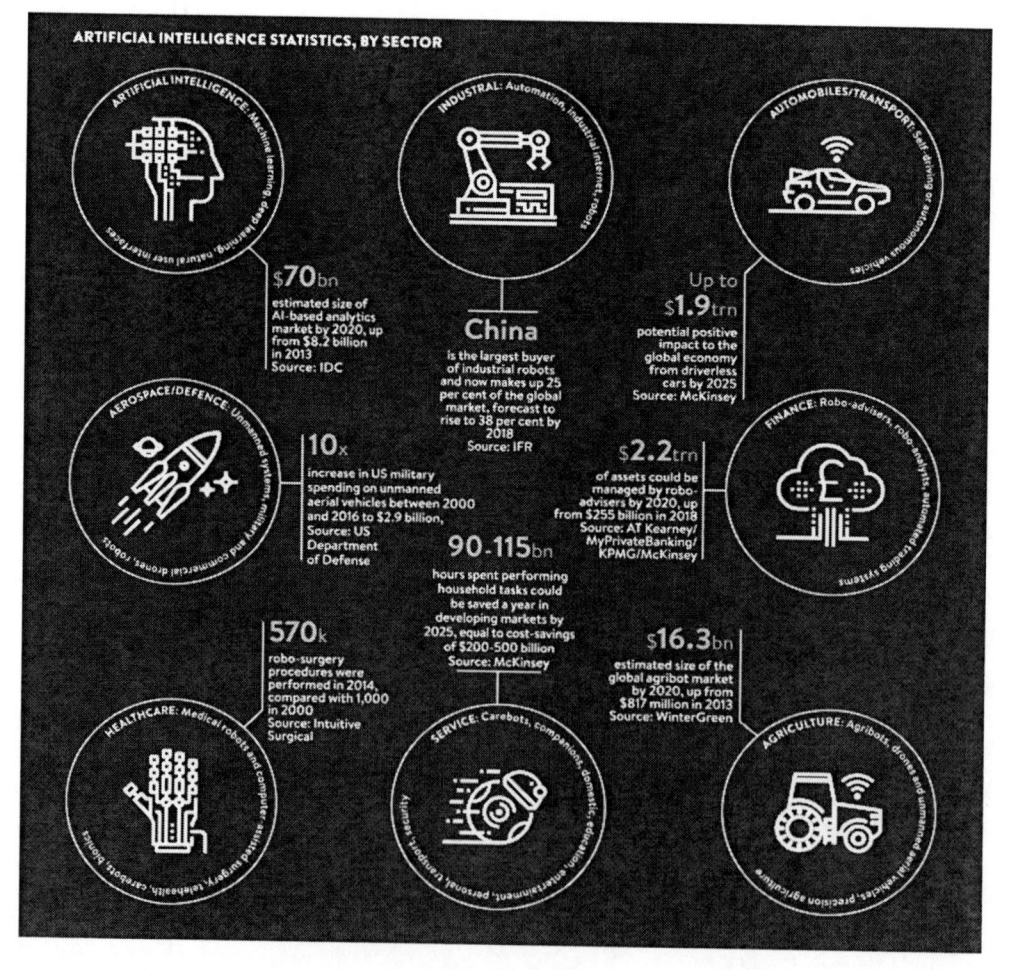

Figure 5. Application of artificial intelligence by sectors.

Top Holders of Patents

Among the companies that have already invested in artificial intelligence, Fujitsu Corporation has most of the patents in artificial intelligence and it holds the title for its invention of the human-centered Zinraui which is an application that is designed to process the feelings of human beings. The application can also process and give support in making medical decisions. The technology can also be used in mitigating air traffic. IBM follows closely with about 88 patents and their greatest creation was the artificial intelligence application that can reason, learn and process different kinds of data.

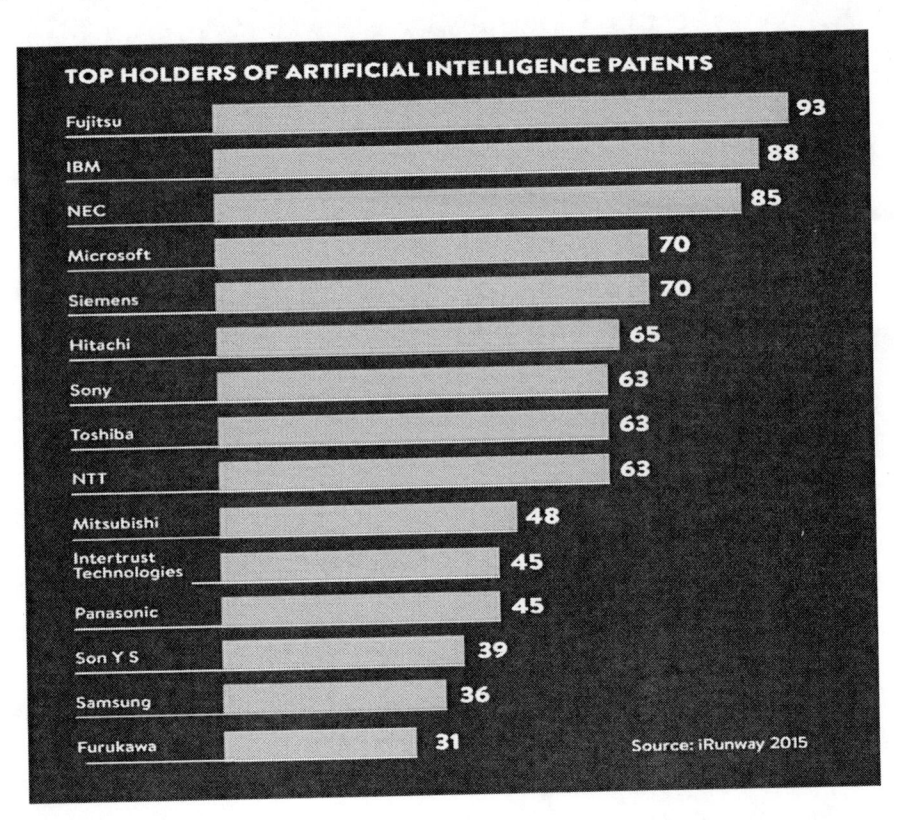

Company	Patents
Fujitsu	93
IBM	88
NEC	85
Microsoft	70
Siemens	70
Hitachi	65
Sony	63
Toshiba	63
NTT	63
Mitsubishi	48
Intertrust Technologies	45
Panasonic	45
Son Y S	39
Samsung	36
Furukawa	31

Source: iRunway 2015

Figure 6. AI investment.

Top Inventors

Different companies have realized the need to invest in artificial intelligence and Accel is the leading company among the top investors with a 500 million dollar investment in artificial intelligence (Lants, 2014). The fund was to be distributed among artificial intelligence developers. Among the ears that the company focuses, on, artificial intelligence tops the list. The second largest investor in artificial intelligence is New Enterprise Association which is a capital firm. The firm has invested a lot in healthcare.

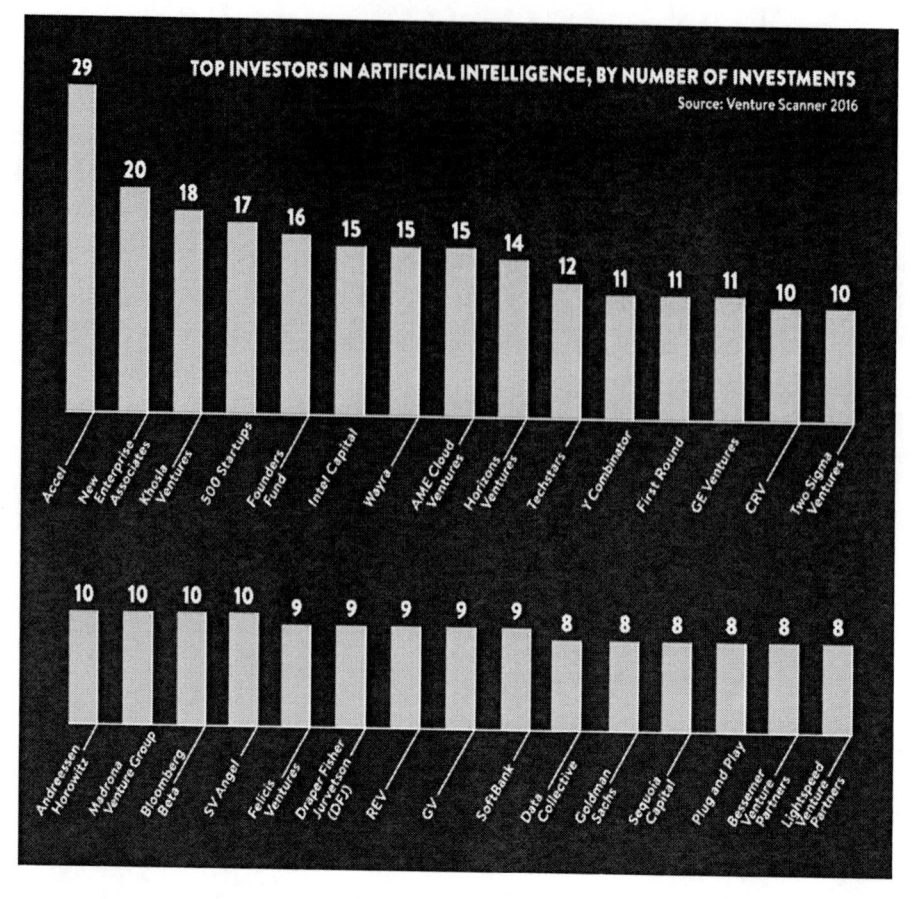

Figure 7. AI Inventor.

Venture Funding

The most funded artificial intelligence applications and sectors were in machine learning followed by language processing applications and systems. Deep learning machines followed and computer vision came fourth (ICSITA et al., 2014). From the list, it is clear that most of the artificial intelligence applications are based on machine learning since they are perceived to have more solutions that the other sectors and therefore, they receive much funding than the other sectors.

Most Applied Artificial Intelligence Applications and Solutions

Studies conducted by the narrative science in the year 2017 indicate that responses solutions and voice recognition are the most applied artificial intelligence solutions in business. Machine learning came second and virtual personal assistant systems were used by about 15 percent of the population surveyed.

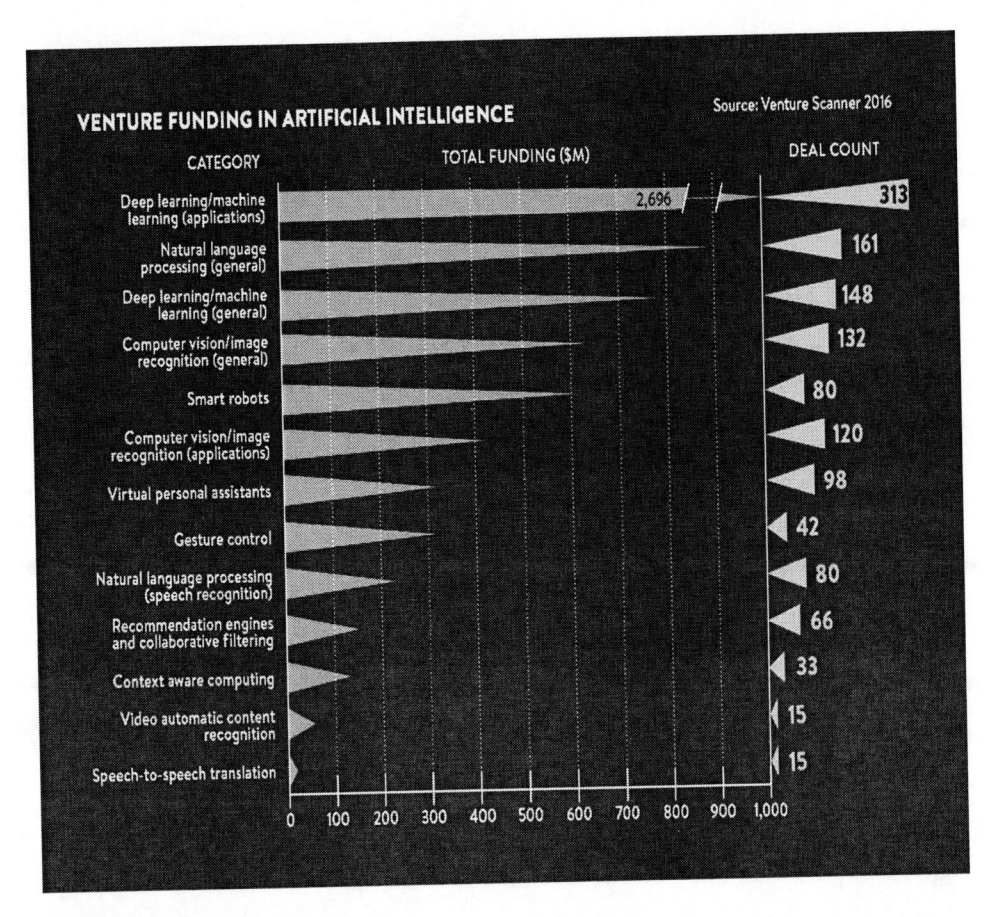

Figure 8. Venture funding.

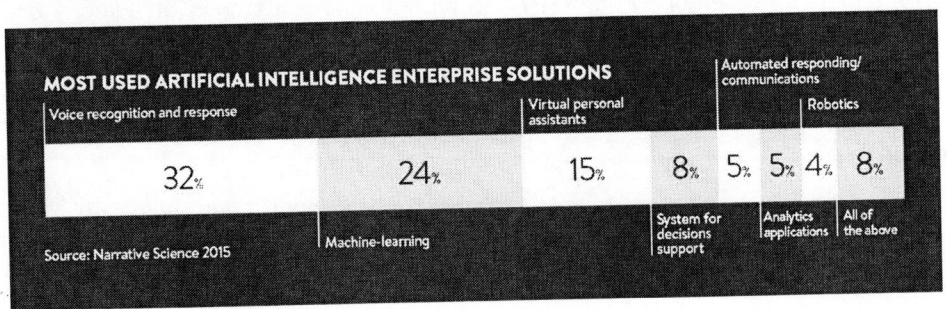

Figure 9. AI solutions.

REFERENCES

"AAAI, Innovative Applications of Artificial Intelligence Conference," *Proceedings of the Thirtieth AAAI Conference on Artificial Intelligence and the Twenty-Eighth Innovative Applications of Artificial Intelligence Conference: 12-17 February 2016, Phoenix, Arizona, USA*. Palo Alto, California: AAAI Press.

Achuthan, S., Chang, M., & Shah, A. (2015), *SPIRIT-ML: A Machine Learning Platform for Deriving Knowledge from Biomedical Datasets.*

Briscoe, G., & Caelli, T. (2016), *A compendium of machine learning*: Vol. 1. Norwood, N. J: Ablex Pub. Corp.

Brooks, T. T. (2017). Cyber-assurance for the internet of things Conference on Artificial Intelligence Applications: *IEEE Computer Society & American Association for Artificial Intelligence.* (2015). Proceedings, the fourth Conference on Artificial Intelligence Applications: Sheraton Harbor Island Hotel, San Diego, California, and March 14-18, 2015. Washington, D.C: Computer Society Press of the IEEE.

Frey, B. J. (2012). *Graphical models for machine learning and digital communication.* Cambridge, Mass: MIT Press

IEEE World Forum on Internet of Things, & Institute of Electrical and Electronics Engineers (2014): *World Forum on the Internet of Things* (WF-IoT).

International Conference on Internet of Things and Applications, Maharashtra Institute of Technology, Institute of Electrical and Electronics Engineers., & Institute of Electrical and Electronics Engineers, (2016). *2016 International Conference on Internet of Things and Applications (IOTA): 22 - 24 Jan 2016 at Maharashtra Institute of Technology,* Pune, Hotel Le Meridien, Pune.

International Conference on Software Intelligence Technologies and Applications, Institution of Engineering and Technology: Institute of Electrical and Electronics Engineers, & International Conference on Frontiers of the Internet of Things. (2014). *Software Intelligence Technologies and Applications & International Conference on Frontiers of Internet of Things 2014*, International Conference on Date 4-6 Dec. 2014.

Internet of Things: Hearing before the Subcommittee on Courts, Intellectual Property, and the Internet of the Committee on the Judiciary, House of Representatives, One Hundred Fourteenth Congress, first session, July 29, 2015.

Jalali, A., Licht, D. J., Nataraj, C., 34th *Annual International Conference of the IEEE Engineering in Medicine and Biology Society (EMBC).* (August 01, 2012). "Application of decision tree in the prediction of periventricular leukomalacia (PVL) occurrence in neonates after heart surgery," page 5931-5934.

Lantz, B. (2014). *Machine learning with R: Learn how to use R to apply powerful machine learning methods and gain an insight into real-world applications.*

Waher, P. (2015). *Learning internet of things:* Explore and learn about the internet of things with the help of engaging and enlightening tutorials designed for Raspberry Pi.

Chapter 16

THE INTERNET OF THINGS AND IT:
A PLATFORM TRANSFORMATION

INTRODUCTION

The Internet of Things (IoT) is an unknown but it is also the future of technology and there will be a time in which people make decisions on how they will join this newly accepted wave of technology. The IoT is actually not a new concept but has in use for the past 20 to 25 years. With the new addition of internet connectivity, the idea of machine-to-machine (M2M) connectivity is changing the way this communication is growing. There are already dozens of companies that are gaining an edge on the IoT market and are offering services, software, and hardware for customers. The projected market for the IoT in 2021 is $1.6 billion and there is still room for new companies to gain a lead on this technology. The IoT stack is a package of hardware, network, and software that provide data and power of the Internet in the work environment. The new IoT platforms are enabling different levels of functionality and aspects of the IoT stack. This new platform will allow for remote connections to locations, connections to things, and connections to people.

A question that is now being asked is "should we invest in an IoT platform now?" That is because the technology and ideas are still new without any lead platforms or companies that are pushing past the competition and it could potentially be a risky investment for some companies. One a company decides to invest in the particular IoT platform they may be stuck in that decision for a while because investment could be large and would take years to depreciate enough to consider a different product. In that amount of time, a front-runner platform/company could evolve the technology into something better suited to the company and the chosen platform could dissolve because of it. The trick for any company is to find the platform that most aligns with their business needs start using it.

The implications that come with the IoT integration can defining who uses the products, data, how often they are used, and how often they are paid for their use. Taking these factors into account will require companies to make a plan for the impact of the IoT on their business. These factors should include how the IoT connectivity will benefit the business in terms of cost, efficiency, and use; what problems can arise from the adoption of this technology, will upgrade address security concern that will continue to be a threat, and how the costs can be justified. Once these questions are addressed and answered then it is possible for a migration to the IoT to be successful.

Adoption of the new technology will always present new challenges to technology specialists because there will always be unforeseen events that occur in time. However it may not always require everything to be replaced when the technology becomes obsolete, but it could be helpful to integrate new stacks and platforms into the configuration as the business need grows and changes. Cost, security, and value will always influence and decision in a business especially in IT platforms.

IoT PLATFORMS: SCOPE AND FUNCTION

IoT is distinguishable from the traditional IT stack because of its connection of "things." Traditionally workstations and servers were the only connection made within a network. This was expanded upon with the introduction of industrial control. Now it is common to have Network devices connect to a variety of things that previously had no methods physically or digitally to connect. In a modern enterprise, devices may include Computers, Phones, Tablets, Printers, Physical Security (such as badge access), HVAC, Emergency (Fire Alarms/CO_2 Alarms), etc. Each of these devices connects in a different way, but they use the same or similar protocols to transmit and receive data. All IoT devices function around a central control locus. This is a core component of IoT. The centralized control allows for more devices to connect at once as long as the singular point is maintained and developed with proper allowances. IoT varies when discussing platforms, interfaces, data and how it is handled, how communications are transported, application use, and analytics. These core components can differ from device to device but are necessary for understanding and developing the scope and functionality of IoT.

The major variability of IoT will consist of three things: cost, adoption, and outcome. Cost of IoT will differ for each adopter. This will be determined by the return on investment a company can get from IoT. With little case studies around the implementation, ROI is a hard factor to sell IoT on. The adoption of IoT will also be critical for pushing the technical advancements forward. Early adopters will be able to implement their current technologies to enhance and develop better tech for others to use.

Open source will also contribute to IoT advancement allowing developers both internal and external to develop and expand on each other's ideas and conceptual solutions. The final variable for IoT will be Outcome. The outcome of the cost and adoption must be greater than the input. Without a strong outcome from IoT adoption, IoT will not expand and will inadvertently fail.

CLOUD AND THE EDGE (FOG) CONNECTIVITY

Expanding the network with the introduction of IoT means more sensors, generating more data, consisting of a wider variety of protocols, in a larger pool of networks. This creates a unique situation for network operators and engineers to plan for. Big Data is the new norm, meaning that the amount of data will be substantially more noticeable on the network that new means of network connectivity, such as cloud computing, are taken into account where before they were dismissed without thorough discussion and testing. This ever-increasing amount of data is due to the amount of sensor and software instances present throughout the network. Using small low-power devices drives consumption of IoT services, but adds complexity to the network. Advances in industrialized IoT platforms like Micro-electrical-mechanical systems and radio-frequency identification systems expand the IoT stack further while providing traditional services in a more efficient manner. Expanding IoT into the network and creating new boundaries or "edges" allow for sequential data to flow and report in real time. IoT devices can leverage these new edges in networking to build gateways, software controllers, and security controls into the network to connect with the existing technology stack. Expanding the edge focuses on data, similar to how all of IoT is focused on maintaining and reporting data. The edge also consists of existing network technologies like WAN, Zigbee, LAN, Bluetooth, etc. It important to remember that IoT is useful as it is powerful and therefore we need to ask ourselves: What data is coming from the platform? Is this something that requires real-time reporting? And Is network communication bidirectional, or directional only?

A REVIEW OF CLOUD COMPUTING SYSTEM

In simple terms, cloud computing creates an avenue of sharing vital data, storage space, software resources and applications via an internet connection. Though cloud resources are internet based on the edge user, they are provided by physical servers that are controlled by a service provider. Examples of cloud service providers are; atlantic.net,

Microsoft Azure, Apple, Amazon Web Cloud, Google Cloud, IBM Cloud, Oracle Cloud, and Samsung among many others.

In the recent few decades, cloud computing which has been a research field turned hugely into an everyday application of internet of things. And currently, information availability and accessibility has been highly successful because of cloud computing technology. Therefore, in essence, cloud computing has benefited its end users through advantages such as;

1. Real-time access to information,
2. Data backup and ease of recovery,
3. Reduced cost of information access and high levels of efficiency,
4. Automated software programming and integration
5. Quick deployment ability

Even though cloud computing is solving much of the contemporary information technology problems, it also has demerits relating to internet connectivity such as;

1. Limited flexibility and control options
2. Increased risk of external attacks by cybercriminals
3. Vendor lock-in and dependency
4. Vulnerable to malfunctioning
5. High bandwidth dependency

MODELS OF CLOUD COMPUTING AND HOW THEY WORK

For cloud computing technology to work successfully, two different protocols may adopt which include; *deployment models* and *Service models*. The purposes of these models are to ensure that the chosen cloud service providers are able to execute the needs of a particular user. For instance, an organization may need private networks due to high levels of data security they require. On the other hand, some group of companies or organizations may want to use a common database; hence, sharing of the cloud would be an economic strategy. The following are the different models.

Service Models

Software as a Service (SaaS)

Software as a service allows remote users to access the cloud and its other facilities pay for it and use it whenever they want. Accessibility may be restricted to certain capabilities of the software labeled as full or limited access options. Moreover, SaaS uses third party vendor program in which the third party controls most of the services on their side of the operator interface. Though the edge user may get full access to the software, they do not have exclusive rights to manipulate it as the encryption may not allow remote or further development. Most phone and computer applications may be downloaded from a cloud where developers have hosted them for mobile availability.

Platform as a Service (PaaS)

When users choose this option, they are allowed to access the platform remotely and be able to deploy their self-made and autonomous applications in the cloud. These software and or applications may be useful to other end users who may download or use them in the cloud. At times it may be expensive to set-up the cloud computer network due to the high cost of powerful computers needed; in this case, a developer may opt to use an available platform to allow them to showcase their products to other users using the platform as a market link.

Cloud Service Models

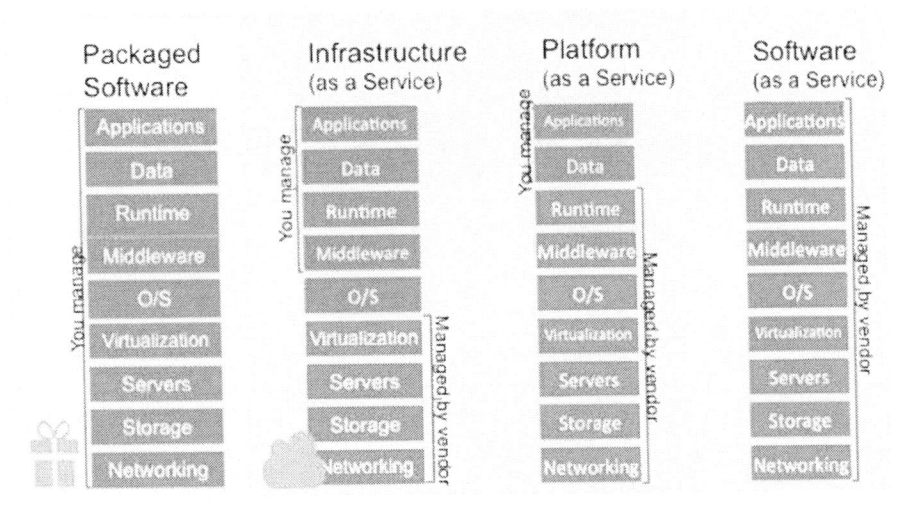

Packaged Software	Infrastructure (as a Service)	Platform (as a Service)	Software (as a Service)
Applications	Applications	Applications	Applications
Data	Data	Data	Data
Runtime	Runtime	Runtime	Runtime
Middleware	Middleware	Middleware	Middleware
O/S	O/S	O/S	O/S
Virtualization	Virtualization	Virtualization	Virtualization
Servers	Servers	Servers	Servers
Storage	Storage	Storage	Storage
Networking	Networking	Networking	Networking

Figure 1. Cloud Service Models with a summary of user identification and capability compared to service providers.

Infrastructure as a Service (IaaS)

Infrastructure as a service use provides information technology experts with the opportunity to control and manage their cloud-based systems without taking control of the cloud infrastructure. The services may include; operating systems, software and application, remote storage and network connectivity. Certain companies provide opportunities for aspiring information technology experts to remotely interact and create useful applications and make them available to others by providing them with enabling internet protocol consisting of globally interactive internet devices such as optic cables and satellite communication networks.

Figure 2. A stratosphere of service models with examples of current corporations in the global market.

Deployment Models

Cloud computing users have different specific service needs and therefore, they have been based on four significant groups of services or models. The following classification is not final but comprises of the most basic of the end user deployment needs.

Private Cloud

Private cloud works specifically to service a single organization without sharing with other users. Therefore, private clouds are secure, easy to manage and are not very vulnerable to external attacks. Moreover, in a private cloud, the user may control with ease, activities such as internet connectivity, data storage, and set levels of security in an advanced approach as compared to shared clouds. Private clouds are used by high-level security companies and organizations such as the military, banking institutions, and revenue collection organizations.

Community Cloud

When organizations have almost similar needs, they may need to use a community cloud to accommodate them and allow them to share the common database with ease. For instance, one database may be accessed by all the organizations to avoid the costs of having multiple private clouds. Examples of organizations that may use community clouds may include; government's departments of immigration, higher education loans boards, the revenue collection authorities may use a common cloud for identification of persons.

Public Cloud

A public cloud infrastructure is one that is commercially available to the public for own use. Therefore, a public cloud is managed by a single service provider and is always managed based on pay as you go basis. Public clouds are usually affordable since it can be accessed by anybody. To its demerit, a public cloud may be vulnerable to manipulation from its aggressive users and therefore not safe for private information transaction; for instance; bank or credit card details. Moreover, a public cloud is slow in connection due to a high number of simultaneous users at any particular time.

Hybrid Cloud

A hybrid cloud infrastructure combines all types of clouds under one roof and offers services according to the requirements of a particular user. Therefore, end users must first assess their needs before they choose a particular cloud to use.

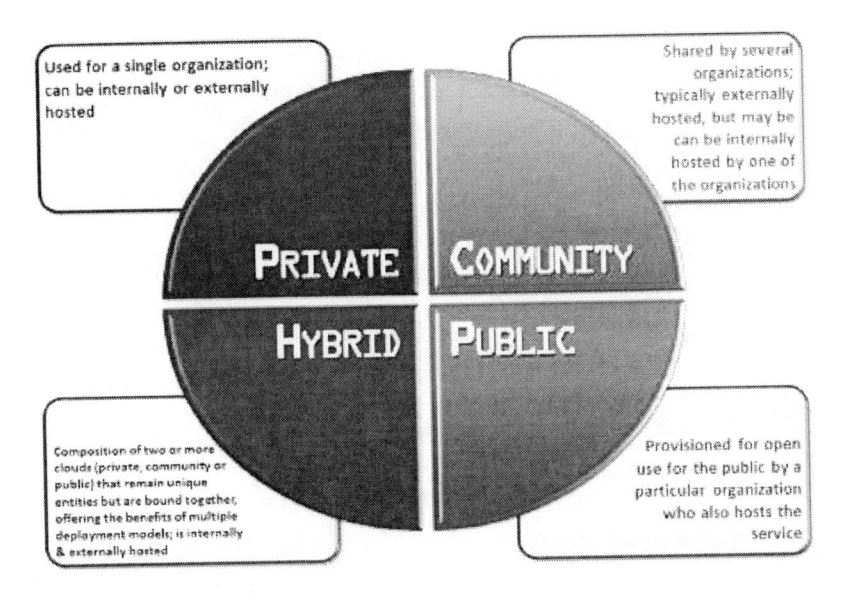

Figure 3. Cloud Deployment Models.

How to Choose the Right Cloud Model

A set of factors that inform the choice of a type of cloud to use include:

Required Levels of Security

The better the security system configured on a cloud network, the better the accessibility and internet speeds. Moreover, with high-security levels, there are low chances of unauthorized access to the network and guaranteed safety of documents. Options like firewalls, backup systems, data encryption, access authorization strengths and employee screening protocols are crucial in ensuring the safety of data. A compromised cloud system can lead to a malicious attack that may render a server identity changed or migrated to unauthorized hosting rendering the whole database exposed to cybercriminals. The best remedy against cyber insecurity is to have hardware backups and operate under multiple clouds hosting by different ISPs.

Acceptable Technicalities and Downtimes

Because cloud networks are accessed remotely, connections may be interrupted at several connection points; for instance, a power failure at the main servers, problems with service providers ISP, or even failure of a component of the server itself. Again, the network operates with several computers connected to the same network, congestion caused by many users trying to access the same data may cause jamming resulting in a downtime. An example of downtime was witnessed with Google in 2013 for only a few minutes but the slowness caused a 40% delay in global internet traffic. The 2013 glitch is reported to have cost Google approximately half-million dollars in losses.

Bandwidth and Throttling

Internet service providers assign bandwidths according to the needs of the users. For instance, high data exchange needs are charged more compared to low data download and uploads. Because the cloud infrastructures are expensive to install and require maintenance, ISP companies charge fees above certain limits of bandwidth. Therefore, if a company needs faster connections and high rates of data exchange, then it has to be assigned a large storage capacity in the cloud accompanied by a higher bandwidth capacity. For cloud storages, surfing needs, website, and email hosting, capacities amounting up to 250GB are commonly available among many service providers. ISP may throttle a user's connection when they exceed space allocations or upload copyright documents. ISP may require the user to sign up for an appropriate bundle package, acquire document licenses or totally block them from the cloud services.

Bandwidth Options and Budgeting

Cloud computing has given the opportunity to nearly everyone who needs to use software, applications, access to hardware, and internet infrastructure that they may not be able to individually afford. However, the networking efficiency is accorded to users according to the amounts they can spend on the cloud service. So, most service providers create more functionality to businesses and companies because they need an integrated operation and high bandwidths. Most cloud service providers are paid monthly, quarterly and per annum basis. More discounts are available depending on the package; for instance, silver, and gold and platinum basis.

CLOUD COMPUTING: A VALID APPROACH

Essential Features

Multi-Tenancy
Multi-tenancy is a software architecture in which a single software or application is used remotely and simultaneously by multiple end users referred to as tenants. The end users are configured on the same network in a designed virtual protocol but are allowed to access a common database. The tenants can be companies, individuals or governments whereby they are adapted to the required level of virtual services. Therefore, a given level of security is also configured on the server to provide protection of the network to the given end user. So technically, multi-tenancy feature is designed to serve as many users as possible without compromising on security, access speed, and storage spaces.

Rapid Elasticity
The elasticity of a cloud network implies the fastness and high automation commands that the system operates. At full functionality, the system may scale in and scale out depending on the usage stress on the users CPU so that buffering is optimized. Provisioning capacity offered to users is available at all levels and can be expanded as per the users' level of data exchange. Therefore, at high demand the performances accorded to a user is high and when the demand is low, the performance is lowered.

Scalability

Accessibility of cloud services has been configured to a multilateral platform to fit the querying devices. Therefore, the heterogeneity property helps the system to accommodate devices such as computer systems, mobile platforms, personal computers and other forms of Private Digital Assistants.

Reliability

Reliability of a cloud system is the ability of the component to execute commands sent to it at specified time and conditions. Reliability of cloud services can be maximized by three different approaches which include; resilience, fault tolerance, and high levels of security.

Based on Web Technologies

Web cloud service is deployed based on Internet formats, IP identifiers, and protocols; for instance; IP, URLs, HTTP and other dynamic Web architectures. Application of web-based cloud technology is evidence in Amazon's Kindle, online libraries, Gmail storages, Microsoft cloud stores, eBay's shopping and auctions.

Administration of a Cloud Computing Network

Cloud computing is primarily based on a web system in which the interface is a portal which offers system options like analytics, billings, account management, configurations, security, and many other significant control options. Optimization of performance and service request is dependent on the size of organization involved. Even though performance must always be improved at different levels of administration, change requests are not automated depending on the level of security needed; for example, functionality upgrades may be applied to improve performance through new software upgrades. So, before applying system upgrades, it is important to check compatibility options since upgrades may drop some functionality, implement functions in a different way or include undiscovered bug.

Reliability and Security of Cloud Computing

Reliability of cloud computing is the ability of the system to work with utmost steadfastness and dependency on the systems as configured. Therefore, reliability is measured in terms of the system to withstand faults, operate at optimum levels with resilience and to guarantee the security of users.

Table 1. Relations (similarity) between Fog and Cloud Computing

Fog	Cloud
Fog functions on the network edge rather than from a centralized data zone thereby consuming less processing time.	All data manipulations and operations happen in the cloud due to large capacity and transformation needs. The process consumes more time.
The use of edge servers at the fog computing nodes reduces scalability problems and response intervals.	Experience scalability challenges since designated servers are remotely located resulting in delayed response time.
Limited demand for bandwidth and data bits are transferred on designated access points as opposed to cloud channels	Clouds have a problem with bandwidth size as the data exchange are executed over cloud network channels in bits.

Table 2. Differences between cloud and Fog

	Attribute	Fog Computing	Cloud Computing
1	Security	Defined	Undefined
2	Distance between server and client	One hop	Multiple hops
3	Delay jitter	Very low	High
4	Latency	Low	High
5	Location of service	At the edge	In the internet
6	Number of server nodes	Very large number	Few
7	Real-time interactions	Supported	Supported
8	Mobility support	Supported	Limited
9	Geo-distribution	Distributed	Centralized
1	Attack on data processing	Very low probability	High probability
1	Location awareness	Yes	No
1	Last mile connectivity	Wireless	Leased line

Fault Tolerance, Resilience and Security: Fault tolerance is a system property that allows the cloud network to operate without glitches even if part of the whole system develops failure. A highly tolerant system has its total functionality active even though an interruption has stopped other parts of the system but accessibility is not lost. Resilience infers the ability to maintain an acceptable level of performance even though the cloud or some of its applications are corrupted for a moment. Resilience also means a cloud network is able to return to its optimum operating status as fast as possible post errors. Cloud security is designed in a way that server computers and network configurations are protected from harm unauthorized access, policies and licenses are not breached, and the cloud infrastructure is unavailable for manipulation. Since clouds data remain confidential, data integrity is guaranteed.

BENEFITS OF FOG COMPUTING

Organizational Benefits

The decentralization of data manipulation created in fog computing on the Internet of Things at the edge is advantageous to automated processes in companies. Fog computing has made the internet related operations easier for industries; for instance, instead of loads of data that need computation in data centers, fog computing facilitate the data analytics associated with the asset management be relayed and stored at the data centers. With regards to this application, the huge data that needed to be analyzed at the servers, no longer need transmission and in case of malfunctioning, the only data transmitted is with regards to the components that experience malfunctioning. Therefore, with fog computing on the internet of things, there is no network strain, and the time to act on data is massively reduced. This attribute of fog computing helps companies save more money that would be invested in information technology.

Resource Allocation for the Internet of Everything

Fog computing is assisting the IoT in manipulating big data under reduced strain and speed due to closeness to the edge. For instance, Cisco has applied IoT in jetliner planes with installed sensors in most parts of the plane from body, engines, winds, and wheels among other critical parts to monitor functionality. Using this approach, it is possible to single out problems in the plane faster, and easier without waiting on big data to be computed remotely in a server. Besides, companies are able to invest appropriately in network services and internet options that are more specific, agile and flexible in managing data.

End-User Advantage

End users of fog computing get there desired information faster with fog nodes than when a cloud server is used; the information analytics is also localized and does not interact with many remote servers over the internet. Hence, few parties may interact with the data, and the security of the information is heightened. This attribute of fog node helps end users of fog computing leaves the users more satisfied and secure.

CHALLENGES OF FOG COMPUTING

Security

In fog computing, service providers are diverse and not centralized as compared to cloud computing where data is controlled at the remote central servers; hence, deployment options are very important in designing the fog computing paradigm. The issue of authentication and trust with data is crucial since most users feed their information to a device and trust that the data is not accessed by anyone and that it remains safe. However, there are instances where cybercriminals may use *rogue fog nodes* where they collect information by the pretense of a legitimate party. In the end, the criminals use the information to achieve their goals which are normally financial gain.

Privacy

Fog networks may not be 100% private as its maintenance and administration are done by individuals who are assumed to have high integrity to client data. Though the system is assumed to be safe as most processes are automated and programmed, there are always information technology experts who can access and intercept the network whenever they want. So technically, even though the user may be safely stored, it may not be very private. Network security may be intercepted by criminals who are highly knowledgeable of network systems and can devise ways to externally attack it and access it through hacking.

Power Consumption

Fog computing requires many nodes at different locations to collect more precise data, to compute, and also send back to the fog. These many nodes result in high power consumption due to their numbers; therefore, they are not economical as compared to the centralized cloud systems that are few, remote, and processes loads of data in a global range. It is, therefore, imperative that software engineers improve this inefficiency by incorporating protocols like efficient filtering, CoAP, and network resource optimizations while designing networking devices so that energy may be saved.

Program Models and Network Architecture

Most IoT devices are designed in connect and leave models of stream and data manipulation; for instance, the S4 and Apache Storm. Therefore, fog computing under IoT experiences limitations in flexibility and scalability due to these fixed configurations based on the fact that for optimization and full functionality, fog computing needs a continuous resource addition to the architecture.

CONTROLLING THE DATA STAGES

Data will be the number one driving factor in IoT. Raw data can be parsed and analyzed in real time by IoT devices and protocols. This creates new workflows, new processes, and new roles in business. One such role would be the "Chief Data Officer." This role would pertain directly to the IoT implementation and engineering suite associated. This person could manage a team of individuals focused on IoT deployment and development. The CDO would ask questions like: How much data is generated? Where does the data travel? Is network communication bidirectional in these devices? What data is needed in real time? And what protocols will produce data and minimize latency? These questions will help plan for adoption and deployment of IoT in an enterprise. The CDO will be responsible for handling requests around data prioritization. The prioritized data segments will require major infrastructure expansion and development. It is also imperative to an organization to secure and maintain the integrity of the data being generated. The CDO will also be responsible for determining how to efficiently secure and store data for the data's value-life.

Controlling what is generated and how it used is the basic function of an IoT device. Businesses will need to determine what data is used for, what content type is used (photo, video, audio, binary, etc.), where it is stored, how it is managed, and why it is generated. The data current today will be irreconcilable in the foreseeable future. Today's data current and trends do not contain capacity that will be necessary for future IoT deployments. The data architecture that will exist because of IoT will redefine network engineering landscape and protocols to come. These advancements will help determine what future technologies should include and how their development affects the rest of business. The automation and complexity of a data management system can cause imbalances within an organization and require multitudes of planning and aggression towards new system plans. It is important to remember that IoT while powerful can overwhelm and underperform if not carefully planned for and implemented correctly.

END-USERS, APIS, AND APPLICATIONS:
KEEPING CONNECTIONS IN LINE WITH BUSINESS VALUE

End-User adoption is determined in the presentation layer of the IoT platform. IoT must enhance or simplify a function that was and is still required for the role. User-Adoption will face many challenges as IoT begins to emerge in modern enterprise and business function. The place where user-adoption and software integration meet is the API. API's will need to directly correlate with existing IT technology and the transition between current and emerging API tech will require proper planning and execution. Scalability and Speed are the two critical aspects an API must enhance. Data produced by IoT and connected throughout the network is expected to exponentially grow as time progresses. This shift requires platform providers to produce a manageable interface within acceptable parameters for adjustment and reconfiguration that can parallel a company's growth. Applications surrounding IoT will need a powerful but flexible platform supporting them. Employees must prepare for the difference in learning how to adapt and how to anticipate changes in the workplace surrounding IoT.

IoT focuses just as much on the software as it does the hardware. Modern apps drive consumption of data produced by IoT devices. These apps are built on the IoT API and allow for more advancements in interfaces and development within IoT applications. Because of the rapid advancements IoT and corresponding applications a public API is critical. Proprietary interfaces successfully restrict IoT, where public APIs enable more developers to work together to produce greater results and advancements within the market. The core API used to develop will remain intact, but IoT enables the API to expand and focus on scope, complexity, and interactivity. The extended API will require extensive coding for integration into legacy systems, perceivably more complex than previous integration coding requirements. As the API dynamic shifts and becomes more self-sustaining and propagated throughout the market it is important for other aspects of the business to step up and enhance the playing field, not just IT.

There are various discovery methods which are being used in order to have the provided facilitation of the communication between the IoT and the users. The resource discovery methods make use of various web-based technologies which have their respective and limitations. This includes the following methods:

Distributed and P2P Discovery Services

The peer to peer approach is used to have the adaptation of the Distributed Hash Table (DHT) techniques. It includes the multi-attribute and the given range of other queries. The Liu et al., have presented the respective architecture for the provided distributed resource discovery which aims to have the Internet of Things. The given distributed resource then provides the peer communication with the use of P2P overlay protocols. The resource peers have also handled the M2M device registration and also assist in the discovery process. For the respective resource, identification makes use of CoAP based URI which includes the resource path and the name of many other forms of the necessary endpoint. Cirani et al., have also reported the self-configuration and scalable. The IoT gateway acts as a resulted backbone for the SD architecture. The gateway then also helps to make sure for the track of things joining or even leaving the network and also maintained the updating of a list at its CoAP server. The SD is also based on the use of CoAP which is done with the use of getting a request that is being sent to and to retrieve the necessary information for the attached resources.

Centralized Architecture for Resource Discovery

Jara et al., have presented the idea of a mechanism for the overall discovery of the resources on a global basis. The infrastructure is called as "discovery" is developed which then allows the sensors to have the complete registration into the common centralized infrastructure. The mobile service is also developed when then allows the clients to discover and access the sensors. The application then also allows the advantage results in the geo-location and other context awareness which is required for the discovery phase. The application also offers for the respective avenues which are needed for the discovery. The users are also willing to have the provision of services which can register their devices and also sensors have the back-end of the architecture outcomes. The architecture, however, employees the provided Directory to the handling of different resources where each directory is attached to the respective domain and also connects with the objects of the domain over 6LowPAN, NFC and IPv6 etc.

The application, however, offers the various avenues for the discovery methods using the RFID tags. The QR codes and the NFC enable the mobile clients to the discovering. The architecture also has the implementation of the directories which then allow the respective legacy objects and the EPC based objects which are respectively to the common infrastructure. They also provide the needed integration of the real world devices into the IoT systems. At the very time, the technologies also provide ways to interact with these physical objects with the use RFID tags, QR Codes and the Bluetooth. A central registry also shows the backbone of the architecture and is also responsible for the provided indexing smart objects according to domains as they belong. The search of resources within the given domain can also be done by the simple connection to the central registry which provides the direct reference for the objects to the clients. The centralized architecture and indexing are also done using the domain. This does not consider the fact that same objects can also be shared in the various domains (W. R. Heinzelman, 2000). The communication shows that:

> "CoAP is designed to be highly modular so that resource-constrained application endpoints only need to implement the features they actually require. Around the base protocol specification, the CoRE working group is defining several extensions to provide a complete framework for RESTful IoT applications and to deal with the particular properties of constrained environments." (Things, 2015)

CoAP Based Service Discovery

CoAP includes the mechanism for the service discovery where CoAP serves as the expose the RESTful web services which can then also reply to the client requesting service discovery. The given clients also receive much information which includes the list of available resources where the attributes specifying the format of metadata of the resources etc. Although useful in several scenarios where the approach also has some shortcomings where CoAP does not specify how the thing should join the server of CoAP first time and also announce itself. There is also no specification for how the remote client can then look up into the resource directory and there is also making using RD and CoAP suffers from the major scalability issue. The user-friendly integration and other access of sensors from the provided web browsers are also used to handle these challenges. The IoT based systems also have many issues with respect to the automatic discovery sensors and to have the integration with the DNS and the system makes use of CoAP and DNS which provides the protocol translation between CoAP and DNS and provides protocol translation between CoAP and HTTP (Floris Van den Abeela, 2015). The research shows that:

> "Such a tool is particularly interesting for CoAP, which is designed for M2M communication and does not provide a standard presentation layer like HTML. Thus, we implemented an add-on for the Mozilla Firefox Web browser and thereby prototype the full Web experience for tiny IoT devices." (Things, 2015)

Semantic-Based Discovery

Ma and Zhou have also presented the ontology focused web service matching the algorithm has aimed at the IoT systems. As a respective proof-of-concept has also portrayed the ontology concept for the vehicular sensor where the algorithm calculates the respective semantic similarly relativity which combines for the work out for the maximum value of the required concepts of the web services. The matching degree is also based on the computed outcomes to find out the relevant web services. Authors Alam and Noll have also introduced the approach semantic-based framework which uses the concept of service advertisement of the smart object. They have argued that such mechanism makes the provided services registration easier which in turn facilitates the discovery. There is also semantic based service proposes the middleware which performs SD with the use of semantic web technologies on the contextual information inferred from the sensor data (Davey, 2014).

It looks at the provided discovery method from the Web of Things point of view and also makes use of discovery from the Web of Things which makes use of multiple mapping schemes. It also aims at the respective discovering the functionalities as provide by the WoT devices. The proposed DiscoWoT has also used the Microformats and the Microdata along with the major semantic web technologies over the RESTful web services. The resources are also represented semantically and implemented with the use of JSON to preserve interoperability. The major limitation of this method is used as on the idea that the resource is not connected to the web then this is not discoverable.

Search Engine for Resource Discovery

There is also a hybrid search engine SE is proposed where the author has noted that there is also very limited work on the search engine for IoT and existing ones which also does not support the multimodal search like the value-based and the keyword based criteria. The proposed SE method has moved to the limited work on the search engine for the IoT and the provided existing ones which do not mean the spatial-temporal and the valued based approach. The data which is generated by the use of these things are being stored in the storage layer. It contains the several Raw Data Storages and also each of such Storages manages the huge volume of things. The respective goal is to have the complete development of the SE to have effective multimodal query processing to obtain the data that is generated by the things in the real time.

The performance evaluation points out that with the real massive of connected sensors keyword-based searches take place based on the minimal discovering of sensor data. The performance evaluation also points out that with the huge volume of sensors where the problem of IoT-SVK which includes the lowest layers generates unstructured data and focused on the retrieving the sensor data rather than being things (Kovatsch, 2015).

Embedded Web Services via CoAP

The diverse environments where the IoT devices have the given operation to lead to the mix of the proprietary and the standard based protocols and have the respective different application models which are deployed in the Internet of Things of today. There are also numbers of standards which are being relevant to the Internet of Things. This includes the use of CoAP which was chosen for the lightweight but powerful protocol which is an ideal candidate for the integration of the constrained devices into the cloud. CoAP has also specialized web transfer protocol for the use of the constrained devices and network. In CoAP, every physical object host on the multiple resources which represent the data which is gathered from the actions and sensors that is available for the actuator.

Every resource is also accessible via the use of uniform resource identifier (URI) and also can also be interacted with the use of via PUT, POST, GET and DELETE REST methods. CoAP technology is the higher optimized version for the HTTP/1.1 for use in the low resource embedded domain. The main differences with the HTTP include the use of various connectionless UDP where support for the multicast-based group communication which includes the built-in discovery support with the use of simplified header parsing where a publish-subscribe extension is being made. The Daniel et al. presents the detailed comparison between the HTTP, CoAP, and SPDY. A typical CoAP exchange shows that RFC has specified the well-known resource as being having the entry point for the resource discovery (Guinard, 2016).

In the example, the CoAP server responds to the hosts in the light intensity and temperature resource. The server then responds to the client's temperature and responses which can then be sent to the Confirmable CON and the Nonconfirmable NON-CoAP messages. CoAP provides the mentioning of publishing subscribe extension in best effort strategy. This also then provides free from the client from having to explicit poll the resource for change. As observed for the CoAP which response with the observing of the option set as they can be sent to as CON and NON messages. In the major CoAP ecosystems, there are many other works which are relevant to our discussion (Nurminen, 2013).

CLOUD PLATFORM FOR THE SUPPORT OF COMMUNICATION MODELS AND HETEROGENEOUS DEVICES

There is a high-level approach to the presentation where the low resource IoT devices which are in the respective form of heterogeneity which are from the given bottoms. For each of the devices, the cloud-based platform hosts the virtual counterparts which are based on the available as a dedicated IPv6 endpoint. The clients then also interact only with the virtual devices and the cloud then takes care of the mapping these devices the interactions to the particular constrained devices. The clients interact only with the provided virtual devices and the cloud then takes care of mapping these interactions to the provided particular constrained devices (B. Ostermaier, 2011).

The major benefit includes the real-life sensor or the respective devices. The virtual devices are also available whereas constrained devices might be asleep or the temporarily unreachable where furthermore by deploying the platform in the cloud as it support on the demand dimensioning of the computing of the resources when loading on the platform fluctuates. This allows for the scaling efficiently as the size of the deployment for the growth and to have the avoidance of the platform computing infrastructure as outsourced to a specialized external party in the case. The CoAP also makes use of lead to the lightweight solution where the virtual devices which can be used by the conventional services as well as the low resources devices themselves. The straightforward mapping between CoAP and HTTP which has the benefits of the virtual devices and also can be easily been integrated into the existing RESTful web services.

Applications in the Industry

Within the given scope of IoT, it has also been to have wide implications in the industry domain, as well as many of the concrete applications, are now used within the context of the business, industry, consumer, and the governmental areas. Some of the major advanced scenarios include the following:

Consumer Engagement

The shopping malls and the stores are also experimenting various ways in order to blend on the digital and physical experiences. With the use of beacons, there are special kinds of message transmitters being used to push the information and messages to the smartphones of the clients on the visiting shops. They are then given the informed messages about the special offers and have the access to major exclusive context like the videos which then raise the engagement of the consumers. The beacons are also used in order to track the provided consumer along with the analysis of their particular habits and also making the use of the perfect tools for the marketers on the overall basis.

Usage-Based Insurance

The innovative players are also found in the financial industries which have provided the usage-based insurance based IoT technologies like the sensors in our cars and other smartphones applications which then automatically provide the given insurance carriers with the use of the information on the driving history of the vehicles and the performances of the drivers. They can also make use of this data which is overall generated to have the personalization and the increase in the given accuracy of the provided underwriting methods and other kinds of automobile collision policies. The Gamification strategies are also useful in order to leverage on the change and then promote the lower risk behavior on the road.

Smart-er Products

On the everyday process, the objects like coffee machines etc. are also augmented within the IoT technologies which then lead companies as adding to the connectivity and other sensors to the products thus they sell to provide not only for the additional services but also allow to get more of the insight into how these should be used. The smart object can also be capable of re-ordering supplies and also asking for the maintenance or to let on the user to interact with his or her smartphone.

SECURITY: EVERYTHING EVERYWHERE, AND FOR EVERYONE

Initially, security did not keep pace with trends in technology. The rapid advancement was creating proprietary tech and protocols and security devices and protocols were becoming outdated and insufficient unanimously. Cybersecurity is projected to be a $170 billion-dollar industry by 2020. Nothing about security enhances the functionality of a system. Security at its core impedes the ability of day to day operations by making something harder than it previously was. This is required in order maintain compliance standards and data integrity. IoT adds complexity around security because of the number of devices and data and protocols that are being added to the environment. Human beings are imperfect and create cascading consequences from security mistakes. But because of this combined with exploitable techniques in systems security will remain a hot topic and immerse itself in IoT.

As IoT progresses, like all things IT, business will need to adapt. It will be inefficient and very costly for a business to try and develop its own unique brand of security for IoT. Most likely IoT standardization and security providers will appear to assist with the shift and transition to IoT from traditional IT. Companies will begin offloading and shift work to new forms of networking like cloud computing. Security experts will work with cloud providers to provide assurance to businesses that their data is safe and not accessible from intruders. As the IoT model develops new protocols and processes around security will be put in place to provide checks and assurance for IoT implementations. These compliance checks will ensure that IoT is functioning correctly and maintaining proper security channels. This compliance will rely on the training and adoption of policies by employees and employers alike. New training and modeled implementations will be necessary for early adopters and those progressing with IoT in their environment.

Discussion and Conclusion

Interconnection of devices has been in development since the dawn of the modern enterprise. As technologies advance and emerge, adoption and integration become key aspects of driving business. As business develop their own internal landscape they must remain competitive and maintain a competitive advantage by advancing themselves in bleeding edge tech. Inefficiencies and cost will ultimately drive businesses under and it is important to remain successful and profitable. Accelerated capabilities powered by the IoT platform will create new markets and new competitive advantages. That said, companies must prepare for what is to come. IoT is the next technical revolution and real-time functionality and processes must prepare for integration and adoption with their service providers and current IT infrastructure. Business needs to dissolve the idea of singularity IT and decision makers need to shift their focus towards the future and submission to one integrated IT. The roles of consumers and producers will adapt to the new model, it is important for employees of all roles to adapt to the security constraints and development that IoT will provide.

Interconnection of devices has been in development since the dawn of the modern enterprise. As technologies advance and emerge, adoption and integration become key aspects of driving business. As business develop their own internal landscape they must remain competitive and maintain a competitive advantage by advancing themselves in bleeding edge tech. Inefficiencies and cost will ultimately drive businesses under and it is important to remain successful and profitable. Accelerated capabilities powered by the IoT platform will create new markets and new competitive advantages. That said, companies must prepare for what is to come. IoT is the next technical revolution and real-time functionality and processes must prepare for integration and adoption with their service providers and current IT infrastructure. Business needs to dissolve the idea of singularity IT and decision makers need to shift their focus towards the future and submission to one integrated IT. The roles of consumers and producers will adapt to the new model, it is important for employees of all roles to adapt to the security constraints and development that IoT will provide.

There are also some major issues and challenges which are observed while working on the Internet of Things. The application layer interoperability then provides the issues for the given usability as to have the needed improved usability into the given context of the knowledge and interest. This also includes the resource-constrained devices as well as the IoT cloud and other humans found within the loop. These pose a number of challenges for the individuals in order to have the needed connectivity among the individuals.

The given structure shows that the Internet of Things, however, deals with the highest layer of the OSI model which only handles the given services, data, and other applications. On the other hand, while working on the higher level of abstraction also provides the major possibility for the connection of data and other services from many of the given devices irrespective of the actual transport protocol which is used. On the other hand, in contrast, the Internet of Things also does not advocate on the particular application-level protocol and is also seen to be usually focusing on the provided lower layer of the given OSI stack. There is also abstraction for the complexity and other variety of the lower level protocols which are behind the given simple model of the Web which also offers the advantages. It is also done as like the Web has also become having the global integration platform which is needed for distributed applications over the provided Internet.

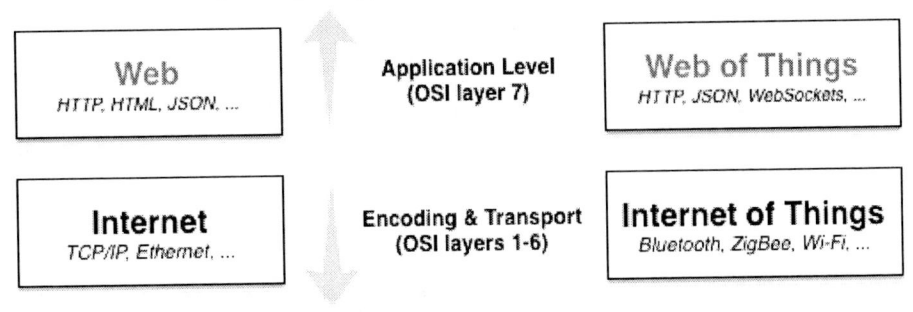

Figure 4. A comparison of IoT and OSI.

It is concluded that fog computing functions satisfactorily at the edge than cloud computing models in solving emerging information technology problems. Besides, the business world needs a high-end batch processing and involving big data exchange and storage needs that fog computing cannot guarantee. Hence, fog computing may have to be integrated with cloud computing to facilitate demanding and high batch tasks because each has its own unique advantages. Fog computing works well in helping new networking paradigms that need prompt processing with minimum delay jitters; on the other hand, cloud computing satisfactorily serves companies, organizations, and governments in processing high-end computing needs that also guarantee them maximum utility and economies of scale.

The Web of Things also gives the needed facilities for the major integration of all sorts of the devices and other applications which then interact with them. It also connects with the major hiding of the complexity and the differences which are found between several of the transport protocols as being used within the IoT. The Web of Things also allows the respective developers to make on the particular focus on the logic of their provided applications without even working to bother about how this device or the protocol will actually work overall.

REFERENCES

Aazam, Mohammad, & Eui-Nam Huh, "Fog computing and smart gateway based communication for the cloud of things:" Future Internet of Things and Cloud (FiCloud), *2014 International Conference, IEEE*, 2014.

Almorsy, Mohamed, John Grundy, & Ingo Müller: *"An analysis of the cloud computing security problem."* arXiv preprint arXiv: 1609.01107 (2016).

Arkian, Hamid Reza, Abolfazl Diyanat, & Atefe Pourkhalili, "MIST: Fog-based data analytics scheme with cost-efficient resource provisioning for IoT crowdsensing applications." *Journal of Network and Computer Applications* 82 (2017): 152-165.

B. Ostermaier, M. K. (2011). Connecting Things to the Web using Programmable Low-power WiFi Modules. *Proceedings of the 2nd International Workshop on the Web of Things*, 1-6.

Bera, Samaresh, Sudip Misra, & Joel JPC Rodrigues, "Cloud computing applications for smart grid: A survey." *IEEE Transactions on Parallel and Distributed Systems* 26.5 (2015): 1477-1494.

Bonomi, Flavio, et al., "Fog computing: A platform for the internet of things and analytics." *Big Data and Internet of Things: A Roadmap for Smart Environments*. Springer International Publishing, 2014, 169-186.

Davey, B. (2014). *Embedded Web Technologies for the Internet of Things.*

Floris Van den Abeela, J. H. (2015). Integration of Heterogeneous Devices and Communication Models via the Cloud in the Constrained Internet of Things. *SAGE Journals*.

Guinard, D. (2016, January 23). *Web of Things vs Internet of Things*: 1/2. Retrieved June 8, 2017, from Web of Things Organization: http://webofthings.org/2016/01/23/wot-vs-iot-12/.

Gupta, Harshit, et al. "*Fog Computing in 5G Networks: An Application Perspective.*" (2016).

Hong, Kirak, et al., "Mobile fog: A programming model for large-scale applications on the internet of things." *Proceedings of the second ACM SIGCOMM workshop on Mobile cloud computing*. ACM, 2013.

Jayaraman, Prem Prakash, et al., "Cardap: A scalable energy-efficient context-aware distributed mobile data analytics platform for the fog." *East European Conference on Advances in Databases and Information Systems*: Springer, Cham, 2014.

Kovatsch, F. M. (2015). *Scalable Web Technology for the Internet of Things*. Retrieved June 8, 2017, from http://www.vs.inf.ethz.ch/publ/papers/mkovatsc-2015-dissertation.pdf.

Krishnan, Y. Navaneeth, Chandan N. Bhagwat, & Aparajit P. Utpat, "Fog computing—Network based cloud computing." *Electronics and Communication Systems (ICECS)*, 2nd *International Conference: IEEE*, 2015.

Mishra, Ankur, et al., "Cloud computing security." *International Journal on Recent and Innovation Trends in Computing and Communication 1.1* (2013): 36-39.

Nurminen, P. J. (2013, July 7). *Web Technologies for the Internet of Things*. Retrieved June 8, 2017, from INTO AALTO: https://into.aalto.fi/download/attachments/12324178/Huang_Fuguo_thesis_2.pdf.

Pauli, D. I. (2011). *Californium: A CoAP Framework in Java*. Lab project thesis, Department of Computer Science.

Soumya Kanti Datta, R. P. (2017). *Resource Discovery on the Internet of Things: Current Trends and Future Standardization Aspects*. Retrieved June 8, 2017, from Mobile Communications Department, Eurecom: http://www.eurecom.fr/en/publication/4716/download/cm-public-4716.pdf.

Stantchev, Vladimir, et al., "Smart items, fog and cloud computing as enablers of servitization in healthcare." *Sensors & Transducers* 185.2 (2015): 121.

Stojmenovic, Ivan, & Sheng-Wen, "The fog computing paradigm: Scenarios and security issues." *Computer Science and Information Systems (FedCSIS); 2014 Federated Conference*: IEEE, 2014.

Things, I. I. (2015, May 13). *Towards a definition of the Internet of Things (IoT)*. Retrieved June 8, 2017, from Things, I. I. (2015, May 13). *Towards a definition of the Internet of Things (IoT)*. Retrieved June 8, 2017, from http://iot.ieee.org/images/files/pdf/IEEE_IoT_Towards_Definition_Internet_of_Things_Issue1_14MAY15.pdf.

Varghese, Blesson, et al., *"Feasibility of Fog Computing."* arXiv preprint arXiv: 1701.05451 (2017).

W. R. Heinzelman, A. C. (2000). Energy-Efficient Communication Protocol for Wireless Microsensor Networks. *Proceedings of the 33rd Annual Hawaii International Conference on System Sciences.*

Wang, Yating, Ray Chen, & Ding-Chau Wang, "A survey of mobile cloud computing applications: perspectives and challenges." *Wireless Personal Communications* 80.4 (2015): 1607-1623.

Yi, Shanhe, Cheng Li, & Qun Li. "A survey of fog computing: concepts, applications, and issues." *Proceedings of the 2015 Workshop on Mobile Big Data: ACM*, 2015.

ABOUT THE AUTHOR

Abdulrahman Yarali, PhD
Professor of Telecommunications Systems
Murray State University(MSU), Murray, KY, US
Email: ayarali@murraystate.edu

Professor Yarali received his BS, MS, and PhD in Electrical Engineering from University of Florida, George Washington University and Virginia Polytechnic Institute and State University respectively. Following his graduation, Dr. Yarali has worked chiefly in the field of wireless mobile communications technology as a technical and research advisor, engineering director, and now as a professor at Murray State University (MSU), Murray, KY teaching undergraduate and graduate courses in telecommunications systems. Dr. Yarali is the author of books, articles and research papers in advanced mobile systems. His research interests are wireless systems, IoT, and small satellites.

INDEX

#

3GPP, 22, 24
4G network, 22, 100
4G-LTE, 22
4G-LTE technology, 22
5G network, vii, 15, 22, 93, 94, 95, 96, 97, 98, 99, 100, 101, 102, 170, 173, 251, 315

A

agricultural, 217, 219
application, 1, 3, 18, 20, 24, 33, 38, 40, 45, 47, 48, 49, 50, 51, 52, 53, 54, 66, 67, 68, 71, 72, 74, 76, 80, 81, 83, 86, 94, 95, 99, 101, 105, 108, 110, 115, 118, 120, 125, 126, 127, 129, 131, 144, 147, 148, 150, 153, 163, 177, 194, 237, 238, 246, 247, 250, 255, 257, 260, 263, 268, 269, 270, 272, 273, 274, 276, 278, 281, 283, 287, 292, 294, 295, 299, 302, 306, 307, 309, 313
  architecture, 6, 7, 11, 14, 15, 16, 47, 48, 63, 94, 102, 165, 173, 199, 200, 201, 202, 203, 214, 235, 239, 240, 241, 251, 299, 304, 305, 306
  artificial intelligence (AI), vii, 28, 82, 93, 178, 181, 199, 235, 236, 237, 238, 239, 241, 242, 243, 244, 245, 247, 248, 249, 250, 251, 253, 257, 258, 268, 269, 270, 271, 272, 273, 274, 275, 276, 277, 278, 279, 280, 281, 282, 283, 284, 285, 286, 287, 288, 289
  automation, 17, 24, 95, 105, 157, 159, 161, 172, 173, 176, 180, 181, 188, 189, 190, 191, 192, 195, 196, 205, 229, 237, 247, 253, 255, 258, 277, 299, 304

B

broadband, x, 21, 55, 97, 98, 101, 102, 209, 226, 233
business, x, 1, 2, 4, 8, 9, 10, 11, 14, 20, 36, 38, 43, 48, 65, 66, 67, 69, 70, 80, 82, 83, 86, 87, 89, 91, 93, 94, 96, 97, 102, 103, 104, 107, 108, 109, 114, 115, 116, 117, 118, 119, 120, 121, 122, 123, 124, 126, 127, 133, 136, 141, 146, 147, 149, 150, 154, 157, 158, 159, 162, 164, 165, 167, 169, 171, 172, 174, 175, 177, 178, 179, 180, 187, 206, 207, 208, 212, 216, 226, 228, 231, 233, 235, 238, 241, 248, 250, 258, 259, 286, 288, 292, 304, 305, 310, 312, 314
business environment, 113, 118

C

challenges, x, xi, xii, xiii, 10, 14, 15, 16, 17, 18, 45, 50, 63, 66, 91, 92, 93, 102, 103, 104, 110, 114, 115, 120, 122, 127, 131, 132, 140, 141, 176, 187, 256, 269, 271, 274, 276, 278, 283, 292, 301, 305, 307, 313, 316
cloud, x, 8, 12, 16, 18, 20, 21, 31, 32, 36, 42, 47, 48, 49, 50, 51, 53, 54, 63, 65, 66, 67, 70, 73, 80, 81, 91, 92, 95, 97, 100, 104, 113, 125, 126, 132, 150, 152, 154, 155, 157, 160, 163, 165, 173, 175, 202, 203, 237, 241, 248, 253, 254, 293, 294, 295, 296, 297, 298, 299, 300, 301, 302, 303, 309, 310, 312, 313, 314, 315, 316
cloud computing, x, 16, 31, 42, 47, 54, 65, 95, 100, 150, 152, 293, 294, 300, 303, 312, 314, 315, 316

computing, x, xiii, 1, 17, 21, 26, 35, 36, 45, 47, 49, 63, 66, 75, 109, 151, 152, 154, 155, 157, 174, 241, 258, 264, 272, 294, 296, 299, 300, 301, 302, 303, 304, 310, 314, 315, 316
CoT, 248, 250

D

D2D, 17, 99
D2G, 18
data mining, 259, 263, 264
data processing, 162, 166, 301
defense, 12, 136, 167, 269
device management, 20, 40, 195
diversity, 22, 113, 242, 246
drones, 28, 56, 59, 102, 207

E

economic, ix, x, xi, xii, 19, 20, 90, 93, 95, 109, 132, 143, 171, 188, 211, 214, 219, 222, 256, 269, 270, 273, 277, 283, 285, 294
ecosystems, 11, 15, 26, 92, 172, 178, 180, 274, 309
education, 14, 116, 145, 217, 223, 224, 225, 226, 232, 245, 270, 283, 297
energy, xi, xii, 1, 4, 10, 11, 12, 24, 30, 31, 32, 39, 41, 49, 51, 57, 60, 61, 77, 127, 131, 168, 173, 192, 194, 217, 250, 256, 257, 260, 303, 315
energy efficiency, 12, 32
energy management, 24
Enhanced MTC (eMTC), 22
environment, ix, 3, 5, 18, 28, 31, 35, 36, 37, 38, 43, 48, 57, 58, 59, 60, 62, 63, 67, 82, 92, 102, 104, 107, 108, 118, 128, 129, 139, 151, 152, 158, 159, 160, 162, 169, 173, 202, 206, 207, 209, 210, 213, 217, 224, 227, 229, 231, 240, 241, 242, 243, 253, 254, 255, 263, 270, 274, 276, 282, 283, 291, 311, 312

F

fog, 301, 302, 303, 304, 314, 315, 316

G

gadgets, 20, 21, 37, 38, 41, 43, 44, 45, 47, 51, 54, 59, 69, 70, 71, 74, 75, 76, 77, 78, 79, 84, 85, 86, 87, 88, 91, 126, 127, 164, 239, 248, 255
Generation Partnership Project (3GPP), 22
government, xi, xii, 1, 10, 28, 42, 55, 58, 82, 108, 110, 115, 116, 132, 183, 184, 185, 186, 188, 207, 209, 211, 212, 213, 216, 217, 220, 224, 226, 227, 229, 232, 233, 259, 260, 278, 282, 283, 297, 299, 314

H

health, ix, 1, 14, 28, 36, 39, 42, 59, 87, 88, 95, 97, 111, 143, 168, 185, 186, 187, 219, 221, 222, 224, 226, 227, 228, 229, 232, 234, 250
healthcare, 14, 42, 43, 95, 129, 168, 185, 186, 205, 220, 221, 222, 223, 226, 227, 234, 259, 260, 273, 287, 315
HetNet, 95

I

industrial, 10, 11, 13, 14, 17, 24, 38, 39, 88, 95, 101, 102, 105, 126, 157, 158, 161, 162, 164, 165, 167, 169, 170, 173, 183, 184, 213, 217, 218, 219, 255, 292
Industrial Internet of Things (IIoT), vii, 9, 10, 14, 93, 157, 158, 159, 160, 161, 162, 163, 165, 166, 167, 168, 169, 170, 180
infrastructure, x, xi, xii, 9, 14, 21, 27, 28, 30, 31, 65, 93, 94, 99, 105, 106, 108, 111, 115, 116, 131, 137, 152, 160, 172, 173, 187, 200, 202, 203, 206, 211, 212, 213, 214, 215, 216, 229, 240, 241, 242, 243, 244, 257, 295, 297, 299, 301, 304, 306, 310, 312
Infrastructure as a Service (IaaS), 50, 66, 163, 248, 295
Internet of Everything (IoE), 67, 91, 234, 302
interpretability, 269
IoT and Extended Coverage GSM (EC-GSM-IoT), 22
IPv6, 30, 35, 65, 79, 306, 310

Index

L

layer, 7, 78, 80, 132, 136, 202, 203, 219, 240, 241, 305, 307, 308, 313
Long Term Evolution Machine Type Communication (LTE-MTC), 22
LoRa, 22, 24
LoRaWAN, 22, 23, 24
LPWAN, 22, 24, 34
LTE-M, 22, 24

M

machine learning, 47, 53, 65, 79, 176, 246, 250, 253, 257, 258, 259, 260, 261, 262, 263, 264, 265, 266, 267, 268, 269, 271, 272, 273, 274, 275, 276, 277, 288, 290
Machine to Machine (M2M), xii, 15, 24, 55, 85, 113, 167, 173, 174, 291, 306, 307
marketing, 4, 109, 119, 120, 147, 175, 186, 187, 262
Multiple Input-Multiple Output (MIMO), 95, 100

N

NB-LTE-M, 24
Network Function Virtualization (NFV), 199, 200, 201, 202, 203
networking, 3, 4, 25, 32, 68, 69, 82, 93, 105, 110, 155, 165, 190, 191, 199, 201, 203, 241, 250, 293, 299, 303, 312, 314

O

operational, 10, 11, 15, 43, 45, 65, 83, 101, 136, 162, 172, 278, 283

P

platform, xii, 6, 20, 21, 25, 50, 58, 63, 94, 98, 99, 100, 151, 153, 154, 162, 163, 172, 177, 178, 180, 198, 276, 291, 293, 295, 300, 305, 309, 310, 312, 313, 314, 315
Platform as a Service (PaaS), 66, 73, 163, 248, 295
privacy, xi, xii, 3, 5, 9, 10, 11, 12, 13, 14, 16, 21, 27, 28, 41, 111, 115, 128, 129, 138, 167, 177, 183, 186, 187, 188, 226, 227, 229, 230, 237, 241, 243, 251, 256, 274, 281
processing, 2, 4, 6, 7, 9, 12, 26, 31, 49, 58, 75, 77, 95, 105, 107, 110, 129, 131, 137, 146, 150, 158, 160, 162, 165, 166, 173, 203, 240, 241, 242, 243, 244, 245, 247, 259, 273, 288, 301, 308, 314

Q

Quality of Service (QoS), 6, 15, 21, 50, 51, 54

R

Radio Frequency Identification (RFID), 1, 6, 16, 21, 42, 48, 51, 55, 62, 67, 74, 75, 76, 77, 82, 84, 88, 108, 114, 174, 175, 180, 181, 241, 306
reliability, xii, 28, 94, 95, 99, 100, 101, 113, 199, 202, 257, 275, 300

S

scalability, 3, 8, 14, 20, 22, 94, 99, 152, 163, 199, 201, 202, 203, 301, 304, 307
security, x, xi, xii, xiii, 2, 3, 5, 9, 10, 11, 12, 13, 14, 16, 17, 18, 20, 21, 22, 27, 28, 32, 33, 34, 37, 43, 45, 50, 53, 70, 73, 78, 81, 83, 85, 86, 88, 89, 92, 97, 104, 108, 110, 115, 116, 122, 123, 125, 126, 127, 128, 129, 131, 132, 133, 134, 135, 136, 138, 139, 140, 141, 158, 164, 166, 167, 177, 184, 190, 191, 192, 193, 195, 200, 201, 203, 207, 226, 227, 228, 229, 232, 238, 239, 241, 248, 249, 250, 251, 254, 256, 274, 276, 281, 282, 292, 293, 294, 296, 298, 299, 300, 301, 302, 303, 311, 312, 313, 314, 315
sensor(s), x, xiii, 2, 3, 7, 8, 14, 20, 21, 25, 26, 27, 28, 31, 32, 33, 35, 36, 37, 38, 39, 40, 41, 43, 44, 46, 48, 49, 51, 52, 53, 54, 57, 58, 59, 60, 63, 66, 67, 68, 69, 70, 71, 72, 74, 75, 76, 77, 78, 79, 81, 83, 84, 85, 86, 88, 89, 90, 91, 94, 95, 96, 98, 101, 102, 105, 109, 124, 127, 158, 160, 165, 169, 171, 173, 174, 178, 180, 190, 191, 193, 195, 197, 231, 238, 239, 240, 241, 242, 243, 249, 250, 253, 254, 255, 260, 293, 302, 306, 307, 308, 309, 310, 311
SigFox, 22, 30
Smart, vii, xiii, 5, 16, 25, 26, 27, 34, 43, 44, 46, 54, 55, 59, 61, 62, 63, 71, 83, 85, 88, 89, 90, 91, 98, 99, 107, 124, 144, 159, 169, 183, 188, 189, 198, 199, 229, 230, 231, 232, 234, 237, 311, 314, 315
Smart cities, 91, 230, 232
Smart city, 5

Smart home, 5, 27, 144
society, ix, 10, 26, 37, 45, 97, 109, 119, 121, 125, 128, 132, 178, 179, 186, 189, 224, 226, 232, 233, 245, 269, 273, 277, 280, 283
socioeconomic, 96, 217, 219, 268
Software as a Service (SaaS), 50, 66, 162, 175, 248, 294, 295
Software Defined Networking (SDN), 200, 201, 202, 203

T

taxonomy, 77
technology, ix, x, xii, 1, 7, 8, 9, 14, 15, 18, 20, 24, 25, 26, 27, 28, 30, 34, 35, 38, 39, 41, 42, 43, 45, 47, 50, 56, 58, 59, 60, 61, 62, 63, 65, 66, 67, 70, 77, 82, 92, 94, 96, 101, 102, 103, 104, 105, 108, 110, 117, 118, 119, 122, 123, 128, 133, 134, 135, 137, 139, 140, 143, 144, 146, 147, 149, 152, 154, 162, 165, 173, 174, 175, 176, 177, 178, 179, 180, 181, 188, 189, 190, 191, 193, 195, 197, 199, 200, 206, 207, 208, 212, 214, 216, 223, 224, 225, 226, 231, 232, 233, 235, 237, 238, 239, 241, 243, 250, 253, 255, 258, 268, 269, 270, 271, 277, 278, 281, 287, 291, 292, 293, 294, 295, 300, 302, 303, 305, 309, 311, 314, 317
transport, 11, 29, 32, 33, 63, 75, 110, 168, 229, 313, 314
transportation, 1, 8, 10, 14, 30, 46, 55, 74, 77, 105, 137, 166, 168, 229, 241, 253, 257, 259, 261, 270

V

visualization, 17, 150

W

wearable, 5, 24, 36, 42, 43, 88, 94, 144, 250, 254, 255, 256, 260
Wireless Sensor Networks (WSNs), 20, 21, 37, 46, 50, 51, 52, 55, 61, 62, 70, 74, 77, 78, 85

Z

ZigBee, 3, 6, 17, 25, 29, 30, 32, 48, 241
Z-Wave, 6, 18, 30